B BROTHER INTERNATIONAL

# BIG BROTHER INTERNATIONAL

## *Formats, Critics and Publics*

Edited By Ernest Mathijs & Janet Jones

**WALLFLOWER PRESS**

LONDON and NEW YORK

First published in Great Britain in 2004 by

**Wallflower Press**

4th Floor, 26 Shacklewell Lane, London E8 2EZ

www.wallflowerpress.co.uk

A catalogue for this book is available from the British Library

ISBN 1-904764-18-5 (pbk)
ISBN 1-904764-19-3 (hbk)

Printed by Antony Rowe Ltd., Chippenham, Wiltshire

# CONTENTS

# ACKNOWLEDGEMENTS

Like *Big Brother*, this book has come about over several episodes. Its origin lies with the research projects of Janet Jones at the University of Wales, Aberystwyth (University Research Fund) and of Ernest Mathijs and Wouter Hessels at the Erasmus Hogeschool Brussels (RADO, project number: STI 006 RITS). The two projects met and merged in the run up to the international conference 'Big Brother': Critics and Publics', at the Vrije Universiteit Brussels (13 and 14 December 2001), organised by Erasmus Hogeschool Brussels (in cooperation with the Service of Permanent Education of the University, community centre Ten Weyngaert, and the Centre Leo Apostel). We would like to thank Wouter Hessels, Daniël Biltereyst, Cosette Castro, Annette Hill, Philippe Meers, Lothar Mikos, Maarten Reesink and Sofie Van Bauwel for their valuable contributions at that conference. We thank Peter Bazelgette for his involvement in the Aberystwyth project, and Inge Vansweevelt (Erasmus Hogeschool), Lara Verriest and Jan Willems for their commitment to the Erasmus project, and for their generous help in making it all happen. We also thank Gary Carter and Neil McCarthy for their seminar sessions at the University of Wales, Aberystwyth.

We want to direct a special thank you to Yoram Allon, Ben Walker and Del Cullen at Wallflower Press for the invaluable support during the editing of this book. Their encouragement has been of great help.

Above all, we want to express our gratitude to the contributors for their academic rigour, hard work and patience during the two years this book has been in the making. It is because of them that it meets its objectives. A very special thank you goes to John Corner for writing the foreword, and for the fascinating discussions. All remaining errors, of course, are ours.

Two of the essays in this book have appeared elsewhere. Liesbet Van Zoonen's essay appears courtesy of *The European Journal of Cultural Studies*, published by Sage Publications. Pamela Wilson's essay, from Susan Murray and Laurie Ouellette's *Reality TV: Remaking Television Culture*, has been granted permission for reprint by New York University Press. We thank both publishers for their kind permission to reprint these essays.

*This book is dedicated to Wouter Hessels*

# NOTES ON CONTRIBUTORS

Fernando Andacht is Professor of Communication at Unisinos, Brazil. His main research interests include the semiotic analysis of media representation of reality and identity. He is vice-president of the Latin American Association of Semiotic Studies. His publications have appeared in *The American Journal of Semiotics*, *Protée* and *De Signis* and in collections on interculturalism (2004) and Irving Goffman (2004). His most recent book is *El reality show: una perspectiva analítica de la televisión* (2003).

Daniël Biltereyst is Professor in Film, Television and Cultural Media Studies, since 1997 at Ghent University, Belgium. He is the promoter of several research projects funded by the National Research Council, including 'Forbidden images' (on film censorship and controversial films, 2003–06). He has been published in various European and international journals and readers. He is the programmer of the Ghent University film club, as well as a member of the board of governors of the Flemish Film Fund.

Mutlu Binark is Associate Professor in the Faculty of Communication at Gazi University, Turkey. Her MA thesis centred upon field research on the reception practices of soap operas by women audiences; her PhD thesis focused upon gendered uses of new media technologies both in Japan and Turkey. She currently teaches media sociology, intercultural communication, and new media culture. She has published widely in the areas of gender, popular culture and new media culture.

Marco Centorrino teaches Sociology of Communication at the University of Catania, Italy. He is completing his PhD at the University of Wales, Aberystwyth, UK. He has written predominantly on communication and new technologies and political communication. His most recent book is *Tomb Raider o il destino delle passioni. Per una sociologia del videogioco* (with Domenico Carzo, 2001).

Gary Carter is a media consultant working in development and related business affairs, based in Amsterdam. During the three years following the launch of *Big Brother*, he was Executive Director of Programme Affairs for Endemol International. Prior to joining Endemol, he was International Business Manager at Planet 24, the company responsible for developing *Survivor*.

Daniel Chandler is Lecturer in Media and Communication Studies in the department of Theatre, Film and Television Studies at the University of Wales, Aberystwyth, UK. His research interests include the semiotics of gender issues in visual representation (particularly in advertising) and his most recent book is *Semiotics: The Basics* (2002).

John Corner is Professor in the School of Politics and Communication Studies at the University of Liverpool, UK. An editor of the journal *Media, Culture and Society*, he has written widely on media in books and journals. Most recently he is the author of *Critical Ideas in Television Studies* (1999) and the co-editor of *Media and the Restyling of Politics* (2003). He is currently working on a history of the current affairs series *World in Action*.

Jonathan Dovey is Reader in Screen Media at the University of Bristol, UK. He is a media producer and writer, and has previously written on Reality TV in *Freakshows: First Person Media and Factual TV* (2000). He is currently co-authoring a book on computer games.

Merris Griffiths is Lecturer in Television, Media and Communication Studies in the department of Theatre, Film and Television Studies at the University of Wales, Aberystwyth, UK. Her research interests include gendered readerships of media texts, children's television and youth audiences, and the advertising industry. She serves on the editorial board of *Participations, the online Journal of Audience and Reception Studies* (www.participations.org).

Wouter Hessels is Lecturer in Film and Television Studies at the Erasmus Institute of Higher Education in Brussels. He is programmer of the cinéclub Film Forest Brussels. He was co-promotor of the research project *Big Brother Bekeken* (Erasmus Institute of Higher Education) which funded this research. He is the author of *Waarheid & Werkelijkheid* (with Ernest Mathijs, 2000), and is also a performing artist (with musician Marc Peire) and poet.

Annette Hill is Professor in Communication at the Communication and Media Research Institute, University of Westminster, UK. She is the author of *Shocking Entertainment: Viewer Response to Violent Movies* (1997) and co-author of *TV Living: Television, Audiences and Everyday Life* (with David Gauntlett 1999). She is the co-editor (with Robert C. Allen) of the *Television Studies Reader* (2003) and author of *Real TV: Audiences and Popular Factual Television* (2004). Her current research interests include television audiences and factual programming, and companion animals and the media.

Janet Jones is Lecturer at the University of Wales, Aberystwyth, UK. Her current work investigates multi-media, interactive audiences and related regulatory concerns. She was part of a research team funded by the ESRC to investigate cross-cultural audience response to the movie version of *Lord of The Rings: The Return of The King*. Other research interests include the role of journalists in mediating democracy, and the study of critical discourses on film and television. She has recently published in *New Media and Society* and the *Journal of Media Practice*.

François Jost is Professor at the Sorbonne Nouvelle Paris III University, where he is director of the Centre d'Etudes sur l'Image et le Son Médiatiques (CEISME), and teaches television analysis and semiology. He has authored numerous books and articles on cinema and television, including *L'Oeil-caméra* (1987), *Le Recit cinématographique* (with A.Gaudreault, 1990), *Un Monde à notre image* (1993), *La télévision du quotidien* (2001), *L'Empire du loft* (2002) and *Realta/finzione* (2003). He has directed short films and a feature film, and published a novel (*Les Thermes de Stabies*, 1990).

Bariş Kiliçbay works as a researcher in the Faculty of Communication at Gazi University, Turkey, and is currently completing his doctoral dissertation on reality television in Turkey, at Ankara University. He is the co-author of a book on consumer culture and Islamic veiling and his articles have appeared in the *European Journal of Communication*, *Ephemera* and the *Journal of American Studies of Turkey*. He currently serves on the editorial board of *Studies in European Cinema*.

Ernest Mathijs is Lecturer at the University of Wales, Aberystwyth, UK. His main research concerns the reception of alternative media. He has published in *Cinema Journal*, *Literature/Film Quarterly*, *Television and New Media*, and is the editor of *The Cinema of the Low Countries* (2004) and co-editor, with Xavier Mendik, of *Alternative Europe: Eurotrash and Exploitation Cinema Since 1945* (2004). He is currently working on a research project on the global reception of *Lord of the Rings*. He is chair of the editorial board of *Participations*, and is completing a book on David Cronenberg.

Philippe Meers is Assistant Professor in Communication Studies at the University of Antwerp, Belgium. His research focuses on popular media culture, film audiences, European film and international fiction flows. His publications have appeared in *Media, Culture and Society*, *Journal of Popular Film and Television* and several readers, such as *Het on(be)grijpbare publiek/The Ungraspable Audience* (2004) and *Hollywood Abroad: Audiences and Cultural Relations* (forthcoming). He is editing a reader on genre and co-editing a book series on *Film & TV Studies*, both with Daniël B.iltereyst.

Lothar Mikos is Professor of Television Studies at the Academy of Film and Television 'Konrad Wolf' in Potsdam-Babelsberg, Germany. His main research interests focus on audience studies of film and television. He recently published *Im Auge der Kamera. Das Fernsehereignis Big Brother* (2000, with P. Feise, K. Herzog, E. Prommer, V. Veihl) and *Film – und Fernsehanalyse* (2003).

Magriet Pitout is Assistant Professor in the Department of Communication Science, University of South Africa (Unisa). She teaches research methodology and media studies (including ethnography, reception research and symbolic forms of popular culture). Her doctoral thesis (1996) investigated female viewers' negotiations of messages in the multi-cultural South African soap opera *Egoli: Place of Gold*. She served as secretary of the South African Communication Association, and has contributed to several course books on media studies and research methodology, as well as refereed journals.

Jane Roscoe is Head of the Centre for Screen Studies and Research at the Australian Film, Television and Radio School, Sydney. She has taught screen studies in the UK, New Zealand and Australia, and he has published extensively in the areas of documentary, audiences and new television hybrids. She is the author of *Documentary in New Zealand: An Immigrant Nation*, and co-author (with Craig Hight, 2001) of *Faking It: Mock-Documentary and the Subversion of Factuality* (2001). She is currently completing research on documentary and performance.

Sofie Van Bauwel studied Communication Studies at Ghent University and Women Studies at the University of Antwerp. She works as a teaching and research assistant at the Department of Communication Studies of the Ghent University. She is also a member of the Working Group on Film and Television Studies of Ghent University. Her publications mostly include articles on gender, media and popular culture (in *The European Journal of Cultural Studies* and *The European Journal of Women Studies*) She is completing a PhD on gender identities in contemporary popular visual culture.

Liesbet Van Zoonen is Professor of Media and Popular Culture at the University of Amsterdam. She is the author of *Feminist Media Studies* (1994) and has published on gender and media in many international journals. Her current work examines the various articulations of politics and popular culture, published as *Entertaining the Citizen* (2004).

Pamela S. Wilson is Associate Professor of Communication at Reinhardt College in Waleska, Georgia, US. Her research interests focus primarily on nonfiction/documentary media as tools for empowerment and activism, including ethnographies of new media-based communities, and studies of regional and ethnic uses of and self-representations in media (especially Native America and the American South). Her writing has been published in *Television and New Media*, the *Quarterly Review of Film and Video*, the *Historical Journal of Film, Radio and Television*, *Camera Obscura*, *South Atlantic Quarterly* and various anthologies.

# FOREWORD

Whatever else it may represent, *Big Brother* marks a key moment internationally in the relation of television to real life and the positioning of television within popular culture. It is possible to exaggerate the originality of this moment, just as it is possible to overstate its impact, but in getting some cool, analytic distance from the more apocalyptic pronouncements made both in support and criticism of the series, the way in which it imaginatively exploits the further potential, technological and cultural, of what might seem a tired if still dominant medium has to be recognised.

The great strength of this collection, as I shall bring out a little more below, is the manner in which it follows up on this recognition through an emphasis both on international comparison and on television as a cultural industry. It thus avoids becoming trapped inside its own narrow and self-absorbed interpretative universe in the way that some academic commentary has displayed (thereby replicating features of the popular press coverage and, indeed, of the programme format itself!).

I attended a colloquium on 'Viewing Fact or Fiction' at the University of Westminster in the early summer of 2000. The event was jointly arranged by the University and the UK pressure group on broadcasting standards, the Voice of the Listener and Viewer. The most provocative speaker was Peter Bazalgette, then involved in planning the first British *Big Brother*, due to start the following month, and later to become Chairman of Endemol UK. Bazalgette started his talk by asking the audience how many of them had heard of *Big Brother*. Given the way the publicity was growing, quite a few hands went up, but by no means everyone's. Bazalgette surveyed the situation and remarked that 'If I were to ask that question again in September, everyone in the room would know about it.' However, even he could not have been aware then just how big a media event would follow, causing a good proportion of the population aged over 25 to move swiftly through knowing about the series to being sick of hearing about it. But this is perhaps to underestimate the pleasures that followed not simply from watching but from having and voicing strong opinions (indeed, a number of those over 25 seemed to regard the watching as an optional extra).

It has always struck me just how clever a title *Big Brother* is, not only and obviously by signalling the continuous surveillance underpinning the whole idea but also by slyly taking from Orwell a thrilling (rather than, as in the original, chilling) sense of threat. In seeking to achieve a stylish notoriety as part of a broad promotional bid, it would be hard to better the connotations at work here. And this is so even though, as the Danish scholar Ib Bondebjerg has wittily pointed out, the anxiety would have much stronger cause if, following more generally the lines of Orwell's dystopia, the 'problem' was not that we were watching *Big Brother* watching the contestants but that *Big Brother* was watching *us*.

There is a sense in which many of the issues surrounding *Big Brother*, often with a degree of polemical distortion, can be closed up around three terms, the 'ordinary', the 'real' and the 'honest'. The ordinary is a reference point because yet again in the short history of television we have concern being expressed at a representation involving apparently ordinary people (always, in certain dominant views, inclined towards the vulgar and the personally disappointing in ways unsuited to national visibility) being enjoyed by quite large numbers of other ordinary people. We have, in short, the problem of the 'bad ordinary', one part of the assumed badness of which is the belief that the depiction will encourage a further slide in standards of behaviour and values of living. Here, in a kind of compounding of the offence, *Big Brother*'s use of the mundane event, of casual, incidental talk and narrative duration (preparing the meal, chatting in the garden, sleeping!) carries with it for some a criminal level of the inconsequential, while for others its relaxed, expansive witnessing of a tightly contained social event is part of the core appeal.

The real is a reference point because once again it is pulled in to play its duty in indicating by contrast what television is not. Yet *Big Brother* signals its contrivance so openly and with such theatrical zest that mistaking it for a documentary would take some serious, perverse effort on the part of the viewer. Nearly all the connections with the real are heavily qualified by the general and obvious conditions of the programme's artificiality, a point not always recognised by critics eager to place it in the long tradition of television as a duper of the masses (a tradition given an unexpected and considerable revival by 'reality TV' during the 1990s).

The question of honesty comes in at several points, first of all in relation to accusations of unwarranted manipulation by the programme makers. However, more importantly for most viewers, it enters into the whole process of judging what is going on in terms of people and their interaction. How honest are their self-presentations to the viewer? For clearly we are talking about performances as well as about a measure (one always open to dispute) of observed spontaneity, of caught behaviour. How honest are they being *with each other*? Here, the terms are not only both directly cognitive (for example, lying and deception) but also emotional, in the rendering of feeling and concern. Thirdly, how honest is the broadcasting organisation being with them? It will be noted that a high degree of concern *on behalf* of the group, always potentially placed as victims as well as proto-celebrities, has featured centrally in fan responses and subsequent media pick-up. So some attention to questions of the honest and the dishonest are quite indispensable to any engagement with the series, making this term perhaps the most important of the three, regulating the way the other two are deployed. An often rather tortuous dynamics of honesty, together with the more direct dynamics of attraction and dislike, is clearly active in the much-remarked success of the series in going beyond the normal limits of viewer involvement and participation.

Thinking about *Big Brother* for a more general article about factual television I wrote three years ago, I made what I think is the necessary move of differentiating it from other kinds of 'reality TV' (always a silly term, now virtually unusable through slapdash application and a willed amnesia in most newspapers about anything in television before this season's programmes). *Big Brother* was clearly a high-concept bit of 'cooked' programming keeping a considerable distance between itself and the thrills of following ambulance teams to accidents or witnessing the hassles going on at airport check-in desks. We were dealing primarily with terms of *display* as much as *observation* and we were departing radically from the naturalistic framing that has variously accompanied documentary throughout its history. I noted that the series took us past those endless (and necessary) debates about what elements of the artificial were quietly and invisibly at work in documentary sequences (this setting, that action, those overheard exchanges). We were now presented as viewers with the contrasting task of sorting out what of the 'real' and the 'social' might be extracted from people operating in entirely fabricated circumstances, operating in a pre-prepared surveillance space which was also a narrative space (however uncertain the plot's rhythm and direction) and most importantly a game space too. Extracting 'real truths' from the elaborately staged (a place designed expressly to deliver human behaviour to the camera, people involved essentially in strategies of interpersonal competition) seems to be what is going on in a lot of viewing, even in that which cannot finally find any 'truth' at all. And here we are not making any concessions to the ludicrous view that in part *Big Brother* was a quite serious social scientific experiment designed to inform its audience and progress human knowledge as much as to entertain. It was interesting how quickly this transparently defensive strategy, along with its tame social psychologists, seemed virtually to disappear from view once the series had established itself with its target audience.

*Big Brother: 'outside and inside'*

I have suggested that the terms 'ordinary', 'real' and 'honest' carry us some way into the centre of argument about the values and pleasures of watching the series. I think the idea of outside and inside is also useful and particularly appropriate to this book. Many of the contributors go outside the framework of programmes themselves to look at their construction and their planning as successful commodities in different national television markets. This industrial process involves careful economic and production strategies, increasingly based on the use and adaptation of a proven formula. But it also involves, although some critics might deny it, a level of creative cultural engagement too. Attracting the audience, keeping them watching and encouraging them to participate more extensively than any previous series involves decisions about style, taste and values which go beyond the simply obvious. How television thinks about its audiences, how it plans to please them and how it reacts to their viewing experience are things we need to know more about and the international group of writers gathered here take us a good bit further down the road.

Outside and inside also catches at core elements of the series design. The house is, of course, the container for what is essentially a sustained exercise in interiority. Ideas about psychology lab cages, the goldfish bowl and even the prison (academics might think of Jeremy Bentham's eighteenth-century Panopticon model, remarked on by Michel Foucault) are all metaphorically active. The audience, meanwhile, are emphatically outside, a position from which they not only observe but comment and collectively make decisions which will pass across the border and help regulate and modify life inside. As the contestants are, at intervals, evicted into a cheering crowd, the cultural nature of this border is further underlined. Each such event is a little prison release drama or, in the final, intensive stages of the competition, a heroic return from space.

But, further than that, what we watch and hear going on in the house is 'outside' behaviour, the 'outside' of people (their bodies, their faces, the words they utter). And in a way that differs significantly if only by a little from the normal mode of viewing both for factual programmes and for many kinds of drama, we do this in order to infer things about the inner selves, what they are really thinking and what they are really like.

In my earlier piece, I called the process at work here essentially one of 'selving', in the sense that viewers, with a strong sense of play in their behaviour too, seek to identify the personal truths, the real core of self, character and feeling, behind the performances and the tactics of 'seeming' which each contestant is variously obliged to practice. Such disclosure may follow from sheer objective pressure (the situations or the tasks proving too much), or from a careless slip in performance, perhaps caused by the difficulty of sustaining performative coherence across a number of different contexts and developing relationships. What *Big Brother* generates, in a manner that resembles the viewing culture of soap opera but is also quite distinctive, even from later formats such as *Pop Idol*, is a realm of gossip and speculation about 'selves', caught in their competitive interaction across a wide range of mundane activities. The dynamics of attraction and dislike, to which I referred, work across the shifting alliances and bondings of the housemates as well. These bondings quite quickly become an active part of the viewing experience, further resourced by the secondary texts of newspaper commentary. So 'selving' is not only the practice of detection but also exercising the choice of who to vote off, and in having reasons for this.

*Big Brother and media theory*

Many contributors, with varying degrees of directness, raise questions about media theory in their chapters. The editors note that the series challenged many established ideas and they see a potential for broader theoretical development in the kind of scholarship that the book undertakes. Of course, media theory is by no means a coherent or very defined body of thought, it is really a convergence and conflict point for a number of ideas drawn from both the humanities and social sciences and often applied in a spirit of rather freewheeling adaptation and selectivity. Attempts to codify it into something more free-standing and 'established' almost always foreclose on the messy dynamics which make media research so attractive, and at times exasperating, a field of inquiry. However, I have noted before that one line of division running across the literature is that between broadly 'public knowledge' emphases, connecting with ideas of how the media work to produce and circulate knowledge within given conditions of political and social order, and 'popular culture' approaches, where the emphasis is on a much broader range of output, a more inclusive approach to 'meanings and values' and the use of media within everyday life. There has been a range of work that has escaped this division, and perhaps real attempts to go beyond it are becoming more frequent (certainly, this book shows its ambitions here) but recognition of it as an underlying tension still seems to me to be necessary. Broadly speaking, the public knowledge approach is strong on anxiety about the media, particularly the impact of increasing commodification on the range of what is produced and its consequences for the sustaining of critical public values. Popular Culture perspectives have placed more emphasis on the agency of audiences, the range of pleasures that the media continue to offer and the complexity of the relationship between media product and value. There has been a more widespread drawing here on postmodern ideas, a less critical approach to market frameworks as such (although some nervousness on this point is often detectable) and perhaps a broader framing of politics and the political than public knowledge researchers would usually concede. It may be worth pointing out, since I have been misunderstood on this point before, that my categorisations are simply attempts to understand the field as it is, in broad terms, rather than as it ought to be. Objections to the limitations of the perspectives themselves are therefore entirely beside the point I am making.

*Big Brother* obviously presents rather different implications for these two clusters of views, even allowing for the semi-caricature nature of my account. Within a strong version of the public knowledge perspective, its immediate identity is that of yet another, albeit rather original, piece of popular distraction, its emphasis on personality and temporary celebrity, its character as a gossip machine designed profitably to fill up spare time over summer, viewed as ideologically and culturally suspect. Within popular culture perspectives, however, there has been much more of an attempt to see it in its own terms and in the terms of those who have become fans. Just as one part of the public knowledge frame is made immediately uneasy by almost any new manifestation of the media popular (although a quiet pessimism is now seen as more prudent than open denunciation), so one part of the popular culture frame feels an instinctive need to defend popular culture from political dismissal and cultural condescension. This situation sometimes leads to an odd configuration of alliances since, on one level, commercial popular culture seems to be able to look after itself only too well, without the assistance of scholarly rescue teams. Nevertheless, as I suggested in discussing the 'ordinary' earlier, a rather dismissive view of popular pleasures is still quite widespread well beyond the academy.

It is tempting to see this kind of mutual foreclosure (of the full contours of the popular in favour of an account of the political economy of knowledge and *vice versa*) as resolvable by a bit of imagination and goodwill on both sides. But the debate about *Big Brother* illustrates yet again how superficial this kind of settlement would be and how important it is to allow the deeper differences of perception and understanding to continue to play out, even polemically. However, it could be quickly agreed that more empirical study would be useful for the argument on both sides, even allowing for predictable dispute about research design and methods. Here, once again, this volume performs a useful service for the field as a whole.

In my earlier piece on the topic, I suggested that seeing *Big Brother* within the frame of documentary probably made as much sense if not more than seeing in it relation to drama, the talk show and the game show, all of which needed to be regarded as connecting points too. My view was that the core appeal of the series, whatever the degree of staging and performance, remained close enough to the observational for documentary modes of analysis to remain suggestive. I still think this is true, although it is important not to slip from this position into the view that *Big Brother* is somehow a faulty documentary, a fraudulent documentary, a series that shows you just where documentary is going. As I indicated earlier, while certainly picking up on elements in the new mode of documentary-as-diversion, *Big Brother* works at a considerable distance from the naturalistic co-ordinates, that promise of the raw, which have caused many other kinds of reality TV to be seen to blur into established kinds of factual format (into 'documentary proper' to use a highly question-begging phrase).

In all, a quite comprehensive set of issues surrounding television has been brought into sharper focus through the impact of the series. The commentary of the newspaper stories and the national debates that they have reflected and help to sustain has also served to illuminate lines of tension and conflicts of cultural value with a useful clarity. Coming several years after the first Dutch series and with its international scope, this book will undoubtedly help consolidate a broader view of where *Big Brother* fits into the changing media pattern.

John Corner
Liverpool, October 2004

*Ernest Mathijs and Janet Jones*

# BIG BROTHER INTERNATIONAL

Think Globally, Program Locally
                                    – David Landler, *Business Week*, 1994

## What is Big Brother?

Everyone knows *Big Brother.* No longer only the all-seeing figurehead of George Orwell's dystopia, it is now an international multimedia phenomenon. The brainchild of John De Mol, it premiered on Dutch commercial channel Veronica (now Yorin) on 16 September 1999, and went on to conquer the world. *Big Brother* is now franchised to over thirty countries.

The show's inspiration was the Arizona Biosphere project of the 1990s, in which participants were confined within a dome, effectively becoming their own isolated society for two years. This coincided with the media fashion for emotive first-person television formats. *Big Brother* built on this cultural zeitgeist, and combines games, soap and documentary into one hybrid performance genre. In the *Big Brother* concept, ten ordinary people are locked up in one house for a hundred days, their everyday life is recorded around the clock by cameras and microphones. Every week the housemates must nominate two in their midst to go, leaving the public to decide the final fate of the nominees. Millions of telephone, text and Internet votes are cast, and one loser is evicted with grand ceremony each week. The winner is the last remaining resident. During their stay, all housemates are subject to strict rules governed by two principles: back to basics and no privacy. They need to complete specific tasks; often live under dire circumstances and on a strict weekly budget. They are never free from the camera's gaze or the microphone's ear. They are required to make regular 'confession interviews' with an anonymous *Big Brother* voice in a diary room.

Within weeks, *Big Brother* caused huge controversy, being accused of inhumane experimentation on people's psychological health. But it also attracted an avid following, with millions of viewers glued to their television sets, phoning in to vote and catching up with what happened in the house on the Internet. Curiously, the show became both a scandal and hit in practically every country where it aired.

## Big Brother in academia

In the few years since its inception *Big Brother* has received a remarkable amount of attention from academics. Starting with Henri Beunders' small book on the meaning of the show in a late twentieth-century public sphere, and still continuing today, it has become an exemplar of the changing face of media theory and practice, paradigmatic for some, despicable for others (Beunders 2000). The first wave of publications foregrounded its prescience. They used *Big Brother* to exemplify the future and warn against the celebration of constructed representations of everyday life on prime-time television (Meijer & Reesink 2000; Mikos *et al*. 2000; Biltereyst *et al*. 2000). Soon after, however, the show was analysed in relation to its cultural contexts. It became representative of certain evolutions in media culture (van Zoonen 2001) and media practice (Roscoe 2001), indicating that its impact was well beyond that of 'just a television show'. *Big Brother* became an academic media phenomenon, a status reinforced by the variety of ways in which it was seen as challenging media theory (see the issue of *Television and New Media* devoted to the phenonemon, 2002). As a particular point of interest, almost all studies of *Big Brother* seem to feel the need to acknowledge the importance of the ways in which the show connects to different (notions of) audiences, ranging from general conceptualisations of the public sphere, over statistic and representative audience samples, to individual audience reactions and attitudes (Tincknell & Raghuram 2002). One recurrent thread in all this audience-related research is the interest in the ways in which *Big Brother* links to theories and concepts about everyday life. As Ib Bondebjerg (2002) rightfully observes, everyday life has always been related to studying television, but never before have academics been offered the chance to see specific, concrete examples of, say, role playing, ritual behaviour, scandals, moral outrage, cultural values, and so forth at work within the scope of one format, as in the differences and similarities between life in the house and life outside it (whether it concerned participants or viewers, foes or fans).

The emphasis on audiences and the everyday life of *Big Brother* is important, because it allows the show to be put into respective cultural contexts. When one talks about audiences, one needs to be able to identify and contextualise them. And in naming the contexts of *Big Brother*, an international perspective is necessary. *Big Brother* is, first and foremost, a global phenomenon in different/similar local contexts, and needs to be approached as such.

## Big Brother International

This book tells the story of the international career of *Big Brother*. It is not only a chronicle of the many significant events that distinguished almost all national versions, but it also links them to their respective cultural contexts and audiences. A few exceptions notwithstanding, the first seasons of *Big Brother* in each territory were massive ratings successes, which then had to struggle to maintain a bond with their audiences in subsequent editions. Remarkable drops and bumps in ratings made this 'special bond' between text and context very visible. Moreover, the moral outrage around the show in many countries, from calling it an 'audiovisual Auschwitz' (Mikos 2000: 185), to the several small-scale controversies (from the sexual exploits in Italy, over near bans in Germany and Africa, and the cheating of Nasty Nick, to American attempts to sabotage) make such an approach not only desirable, but necessary. This book offers that approach.

The international focus on *Big Brother* has consequences on a textual level as well. Because of the nature of the franchise there are numerous threads that appear in many national versions. As Gary Carter (once an Endemol executive selling *Big Brother* accross the world) testifies, it is a 'genre hybrid', both adhering to and breaking boundaries of television genres (see his epilogue to this book). A Belgian producer of Endemol stressed cultural differences:

> Does the format fit every country? Yes, it does, as long as you allow a few local changes. Compare the Belgian *Big Brother* for instance with the Dutch or Spanish one. In Spain they have a swimming pool. Here, a swimming pool is considered a luxury. In Spain, with the climate they have, it isn't. But every version of *Big Brother* has chickens, because chickens are everywhere in the world. (Plas 2001: 119)

It is tempting to see the chicken reference as a metaphor for audiences. After all, they did flock to screens all over the world to witness the events in the house. But assuming a blanket format and reception is probably the biggest mistake anyone could make about *Big Brother*. To begin with, there is no uniform text; it changed from region to region (swimming pool or not). Receptions varied from country to country as well. Even within countries opinions were heavily divided. And finally, numerous changes were made between and within countries throughout the hundred days of each season, and between seasons.

Another important element that informs the content and reception of *Big Brother* is the awareness of its international public presence throughout the world. When, in the first season of *Big Brother* USA, housemates planned a walk out, they based their view on what impact it would have on their own perception of *Big Brother* in other countries. When the American producers called in a Dutch veteran producer to suppress the 'uprising', they relied on international awareness to rescue their season. When, in the fourth season of *Big Brother* UK, one houseguest was nominated to leave the house, but then subsequently sent to another *Big Brother* house (in Africa), and vice versa, the format even plays to that awareness.

Talking about 'The *Big Brother* Text' therefore becomes next to meaningless. There are so many *Big Brother* texts, made under so many specific conditions, that only through a flexible approach to each version, requiring specific tools for analysis, can the phenomenon be fully understood (if, to echo van Zoonen, ever at all).

## Multimedial interactivity and ludic representation

*Big Brother*'s international presence, and its relevance to the global-local discussion (or the discourse of glocalisation as new academic lingo has it) is the most important thread throughout the book. But there are several others, that inform the approaches, methods and conclusions of the contributions.

A crucial aspect of studying *Big Brother* is coming to grips with the ways in which the text, changing over time and space is also filtered out across multiple media. Continuing a fast-developing trend in television practice, *Big Brother* does not just rely on the television set to communicate its message to its audiences. It also relies on other 'platforms', like the Internet, live events and telephone votings. By extension, it also informs (and feeds off) tabloid narratives, public debate and spin-offs (video spoofs, music videos, pop albums, celebrity cults, and so forth). The Internet allows viewers a 24-hour peek into the participants' lives (often revealing information regular viewers have no access to); the '*Big Brother* Magazine', accompanying almost every regional version, adds to the understanding of the show by offering background information (biographies, stories of fans and relatives, explaining changes in rules, and so forth); and live events, especially around the evictions, or charity events linked to specifc 'week tasks' have, in many versions, become public events in their own rights. The link between these multiple uses of media and technological innovations is another vital element to be taken into consideration when studying *Big Brother*, especially when the grammar of its reception is in its infancy. All this calls into question the singular status of the *Big Brother* television text.

As a result, *Big Brother* also challenges ideas around television genres and categories. Spread accross the schedule, both 'prime timed' and 'niched', its genre has become so variable that it defies classic genre theory. Therefore, attempts to understand *Big Brother* also need to be aware of its status as a class of text(s), even to the point of suggesting new generic labels for this kind of multimedial reality game shows. Notions of sociology like Johan Huizinga's concept of the *Homo Ludens*, or gaming human (Huizinga 1949) and Erving Goffman's analyses of everyday experiences (Goffman 1986) are important considerations informing such suggestions.

Ludic TV or reality game show, high-tech multimedia platform or plain boring television, studying *Big Brother* requires paying attention to a multitude of perspectives. We are confident all contributions in this book offer insightful and vivid discussions of these perspectives.

The first essay is internationalist and self-reflexive in scope. Daniël Biltereyst analyses the international presence of *Big Brother* in terms of its moral (and political) reception. Starting with a discussion of the controversy surrounding *Big Brother* Africa, Biltereyst questions the use of the concept of moral panics in dealing with the ways in which *Big Brother* seems to strike sensitive chords wherever it airs. Are 'moral panics' still a tool for analysis if producers use it as a marketing auxiliary? For Biltereyst, public intellectuals need to be aware of how they can be recruited by the exact same apparatus they criticise.

All other essays in the collection concentrate on one specific territory. Liesbet van Zoonen examines the debate surrounding *Big Brother*'s very first encounter with its publics and critics, in 1999. It was in the Netherlands that the format originated, villified as an abomination, a low point in Dutch Television history. Van Zoonen looks beyond this

debate and discusses how *Big Brother* captured the 'zeitgeist' of a generation, analysing what she terms as the 'subconscious collective yearning' that propelled this series into television history's record books.

Annette Hill sets the agenda for a discussion of *Big Brother* audiences. She lays out the conclusions to a significant ESRC- and BARB-funded audience research project on television audiences of factual entertainment, in which *Big Brother* was a prominent feature. She analyses how viewers engage in a critical viewing of the attitudes and behaviours of ordinary people in the house, introducing us a theme running throughout this book: that of the debate on differences between 'the real' and 'the constructed'. Focusing on authenticity, performance and an understanding of viewers' engagements with 'the real' in reality TV, Hill discusses how specific roles and functions are picked up as clues by audiences seeking for a glimpse of the unconstructed. Daniel Chandler and Merris Griffiths build on the discussion of audiences, in providing us with an empirical piece of specialised audience research investigating some of the ways in which opinions are formed about onscreen individuals. Their research makes a distinction between a 'mirror hypothesis', suggesting that viewers will tend to relate favourably to those onscreen who are *like themselves* (the mirror) and a 'magic mirror hypothesis', representing what the viewer *would like to be like*. Their findings support the notion that differences in modes of parasocial interaction show a very strong connection to gender and sexual orientation.

Ernest Mathijs and Wouter Hessels introduce us to a reception study of *Big Brother* Belgium highlighting how different notions of 'the audience' are used by producers, commentators and in the public sphere. For them, an examination of the role of ancillary discourses provides a way for explaining attitudes (from all kinds of angles) towards the show. It shows the transition of the initial cultural concern and outrage towards more text-related concerns, dragging audiences away from the context into the text. Also dealing with *Big Brother* Belgium, Philippe Meers and Sophie Van Bauwel offer a framework for understanding the critical responses to the series. With a qualitative discourse analysis of the different voices in the press debate, the authors discuss three main theoretical frames (critical, pluralist and culturalist) and use them to stimulate the theoretical debate on perceptions of popular culture. They propose that more attention be paid to a culturalist frame which provides a clearer view on the cultural dynamics surrounding *Big Brother*.

After debating notions of the public and specific audience attitudes, the book also problematises the text. Lothar Mikos' chapter on the German *Big Brother* moves from a focus on audiences to considerations of the textual features of the series. Emphasising their mutual dependance, and drawing on theories of literary reception, Mikos agrees that the very notion of the text depends on frameworks in which reception and audiences are dominant, while also maintaining that there is no audience without the textual stimulus. Through the introduction of the notion of 'migration of genres' François Jost proposes a similar point in his article on the French version of *Big Brother*. Pushing the examination of the text into a semiotic-based investigation of genre theory, Jost argues that *Loft Story* (the French title) promises several generic interpretations for its audiences. But these promises are by no means static; they migrate dynamically between combinations of fictitious, ludic and reality modes of representation. Jost theorises how the 'fluctuating generic reception' influences the contract between the programme and the public. Also building on the question of the connection between text and audience, but linking it to an empirical reception study of *Big Brother* in two regions in Latin America, Fernando Andacht's essay combines empirical data from qualitative

research and a realist semiotic theory. In doing so, he argues that, although elusive in its portrayal of signs of the real, the *Big Brother* format nevertheless seems to offer audiences enough indexical signs to set it up as linked to reality.

With the status of both the audience and the text challenged, yet at the same time also set up as essential for understanding *Big Brother*, discussing specific cultural concerns becomes a problematic endeavour. Baris Kiliçbay and Mutlu Binark examine this problem by focusing on the relationships between fandom and contestants' cultural backgrounds in the Turkish *Big Brother*. In doing so, they pick up on the theme of personal performance, examining televisual identities adopted by contributors playing out a variety of roles that conform or challenge the precepts of a changing society. They also discuss how the one central text spawned others, observing how this quickly led to a market saturation of *Big Brother*-related products on Turkish television. Just as cultural background (even class) was a defining element in the relationship between the Turkish text and context, Marco Centorrino's discussion of *Big Brother* Italy employs textual analysis to highlight the centrality of the programme's pornographic appeal while adapting Goffman's model of interaction to critique the sexual relations in the house. Centorrino researches how this adaptation of the *Big Brother* format successfully encapsulates, in a single brush stroke, many of the defining elements of Italian television entertainment. Magriet Pitout's chapter on *Big Brother* South Africa continues the theme of a local examination of the relationship between context and text. She focuses on the particular South African reception, reflecting on the politicisation of the format with its strict adherence to a true representation of the country's diversity and newfound racial sensitivities. She analyses the role race played in the eviction of candidates, suggesting that being black in the house equated to invisibility, which ensured a degree of survival. Pitout also problematises the ongoing debate on the presumed interactivity between text and audiences, questioning the extent to which this new format actually changes the audiences' relationship with the text.

The following chapters take the element of multimedial interactivity as their main focus. This concern is not just about which black box will deliver our media in the future, it is also forcing us to re-examine the role of the audience in a contemporary television environment. As the distinction between text and audience begins to blur the viewer is promoted as an 'equal party' reworking and transforming the text at the point of consumption. Certainly *Big Brother* usefully sets the stage for a closer examination of the impact of new technology and the boundaries between notions of media consumers and media producers.

Jane Roscoe describes how central multi-platform interactivity was to the Australian version and how the new technologies that enabled media convergence were integral to its success as 'event' television. Her production study demonstrates how the function of audiences, in the role of participants transforming texts, is not just confined to areas of reception but informs the construction of the text as well, especially when 'indigenising' the format for Australian audiences (with particular emphasis on location and 'mateship'). Pamela Wilson shows how on-line narrative activism played a central role in the first season of *Big Brother* USA. This new form of media activism reflected the intersection of a counter-cultural social movement ('culture jammers') with the shifting technology of the show's dual webcasting/broadcasting premise. The convergence of technology, text and audience, at least in the short-term, noticeably upset the apple cart and jolted the corporate producers, while also having a profound effect on the behaviours and beliefs of the *Big Brother* participants, thus influencing the text itself.

Janet Jones provides empirical audience data of *Big Brother* UK and uses these to argue how the convergence of text and audience has impacted on *Big Brother* fandom over a three-year period. Jones' attempt to predict patterns of use and meaning making among interactive reality TV consumers is set amidst a view of multi-media culture as an internationally developing interplay between interactivity, media convergence and hybridity. For Jones, such developments are critical to debates of how new media theory relates to media practices.

Finally, Jon Dovey pushes media theory to a new and challenging level with an investigation of the reality TV game as an aspect of the cultural logic of an 'order of simulation'. He highlights the erosion of traditional factual television practices where empirical observation has been largely abandoned and replaced with the observation of simulated situations that *only* exist because of the intervention of the television production. Building on theories of Jean Baudrillard (on simulation) and Roger Caillois (on play), he then takes this observation to its logical implication suggesting simulation takes over from empiricism as reflected in the ludic world of Sims and gaming. He uses a finely-honed understanding of documentary history to examine how this trend may be a revival and triumph of Jean Rouch's original notion of 'cinéma vérité' in which the camera is only ever seen as a catalyst that provokes performative events, but can also be seen as evoking a 'ludic and liminoid zone of culture'.

We thought it relevant to conclude the book with a voice from media practice. In his epilogue, Gary Carter allows the reader an inside view on how the *Big Brother* format was thought up, how it was sold and how it inspired new ideas in reality TV. Building on Huizinga's concept of the *Homo Ludens*, and expanding it into a prototheory of genre hybridisation, Carter argues that *Big Brother* is symptomatic for the kind of television that fits a generation of viewers who grew up on television, who started making television about television, and who know how to negotiate performances of media identities.

There are many strands in this book, and we admit that, to some extent, its final order is arbitrary, as are all classifications. Yet we maintain that the identified threads of glocalisation, audience and receptions linked to specific textual cues, genre and the public, multimedia platforming and convergence, and ludic representations of everyday life are crucial elements for those wishing to understand *Big Brother*.

We claim nothing less than that this book offers, at the time of writing, the most complete view on the international phenomenon that is *Big Brother*. But we would be foolish to think that this is all there can be said. Much terrain remains uncharted, and we welcome all attempts to further the analysis of *Big Brother*, and the larger issues around it. We only hope this book can be of some help to those efforts.

*Bibliography*

Beunders, H. (2000) *Wat je ziet ben je zelf. Big Brother: lust, leven en lijden voor de camera*. Amsterdam: Prometheus.

Bondebjerg, I. (2002) 'The mediation of everyday life', in A. Jerslev (ed.) *Realism and 'Reality' in Film and Media*. Copenhagen: Museum Tusculanum Press, 159–93.

Goffman, E. (1986) *Frame Analysis: An Essay on the Organisation of Experience*. Boston: Northeastern University Press.

Hill, A. and G. Palmer (eds) 'Big Brother Issue', *Television and New Media*, 3, 3.

Huizinga, J. (1949) *Homo Ludens: A Study of the Play Element in Culture*. London: Routledge and Kegan Paul.

Meijer, I. C. and M. Reesink (eds) (2000) *Reality soap!: Big Brother en het multimedia concept*. Amsterdam: Boom.

Mikos, L., P. Feise, K. Herzog, E. Pommer and V. Veihl (2000) *Im Auge der Kamera. Das Fernsehereignis Big Brother*. Berlin: Vistas Verlag.

Plas, N. (2001) 'Interview with Nicole Plas (Belgian Endemol producer)', *P Magazine*, 21 November, 119.

Roscoe, J. (2001) '*Big Brother* Australia: Performing the "Real" twenty-four-seven', *International Journal of Cultural Studies*, 4, 4, 473–88.

Tincknell, E. and P. Raghuram (2002) '*Big Brother*: Reconfiguring the "active" Audience of Cultural Studies?', *European Journal of Cultural Studies*, 5, 2, 199–215.

Van Zoonen, L. (2001) 'Desire and resistance: *Big Brother* and the recognition of everyday life', *Media Culture & Society*, 23, 5, 679–88.

# CHAPTER 1

*Daniël Biltereyst*

# BIG BROTHER AND ITS MORAL GUARDIANS
## Reappraising the Role of Intellectuals in the Big Brother Panic

> People are subjected to horrible pictures which are corrupting the morals of our children.
>> – Taylor Nothale, chairman of the Malawi Parliamentary Committee on the Media (in Ntonya 2003)

## African prelude

At the moment of writing this chapter, the first pan-African version of *Big Brother* ended with the victory of a Zambian woman named Cherise Makubale. For several weeks a dozen English-speaking young men and women from twelve African countries had lived together in one big house in South Africa, under close video surveillance. In the Western part of the world, the novelty of the *Big Brother* format (and of reality TV in general) may have become commonplace and familiar, but in Africa the programme grew to be the television event of the year, and successfully captivated the continent during the summer of 2003. *Big Brother Africa* was soon the highest-rated television programme in the history of African television, bringing together millions of viewers from various ethnic and national horizons for more than a hundred days. In black Africa, where less than 5 per cent of the local population have a television set, many viewers watched the programme in bars, schools, churches and other social institutions.

Similar to what happened in Western countries, *Big Brother Africa* succeeded in triggering a wide-scale controversy. On the one hand, the programme was praised by an unexpectedly large variety of people. Former South African President Nelson Mandela, for instance, openly asked to meet the winner of the programme, while intellectuals and scholars claimed that *Big Brother Africa* successfully brought under attention issues such as AIDS, and openly questioned national stereotypes. One South African scholar, Bankole Omotoso from the Stellenbosch University, even praised the programme because it 'has done more for the political possibility of unity among Africans than politicians can ever do, for the simple reason that they've taken themselves as human beings and related across these borders' (Omotose 2003).

On the other hand, the programme was also severely criticised. In fact, only very few programmes or cultural products in Africa have been able to instigate such a cross-national public debate on cultural quality, social and moral values. In various countries, *Big Brother Africa* was attacked for its rather biased representation of crucial social and moral issues – going from vital questions on the human body, sex or health in Africa (AIDS, for instance) to differences between urban versus rural lifestyles, or between low versus high social class. More specifically, the programme was attacked for only featuring better-educated young people from an urban elite social stratum. Also, the programme's success was said to encourage poor people to buy their own television sets or to lure them into subscribing to cable television.

However, the sharpest criticism to *Big Brother Africa* was related to its supposed immoral undertone. Especially the 'shower hour', casual sex, love and nudity sequences whipped up a debate with prominent intellectuals, politicians, church leaders and other 'moral guardians' loudly raising their voices. In various African countries such as Malawi, Namibia, Nigeria and Zambia, church organisations and religious groups severely condemned *Big Brother Africa* for its 'explicit immorality'. In most countries, local and national newspapers gave daily updates upon what happened in the house, opening their opinion pages for critical comments. In various cases, public opinion makers, as well as politicians and officials from various state organisations, started to criticise the programme openly. One example is Namibia, where the debate culminated in President Sam Nujoma's public denouncement of the programme at the occasion of the launch of the official national atlas (on 28 July 2003). In his public speech, Nujoma called upon the NBC (Namibian Broadcasting Corporation) 'to stop showing this so-called *Big Brother Africa* and to start showing the history of Namibia'. The Namibian President's denouncement of *Big Brother Africa* and its plea for more decent, locally-produced content were widely taken up by the news media and public opinion.

Another case in point is Malawi where the pan-African version of *Big Brother* was severely attacked by church leaders as well as by parents and other organisations. Already in June 2003, the public controversy led to a heated debate in Parliament, where a majority of the MPs voted for an immediate ban of the programme. According to the chairman of the Parliamentary Committee on the Media, the programme was felt to be 'corrupting the morals of our children'.[1] The programme was also denounced by opposition parties, which called upon the government 'to stop that nonsense on TV' and to remove the programme immediately. However, in August 2003, Malawi's High Court decided that the national Parliament had overstepped its mandate by banning *Big Brother Africa*. In the meantime, the programme's ban and removal from the national public broadcaster led to a wider debate on the issue of free speech, information and participation, as well as on the societal role of television.

## European parallels

In reading these articles on the Internet and in Western newspapers, one can only be surprised by the parallels with the European public reception of *Big Brother*. At the least, this short African case study seems to illustrate *Big Brother*'s unique place in the history of international television: more than any other format it seems to have been able to become the object of intense social criticism and even moral anxiety on a global and cross-cultural level. In fact, one of the most intriguing facets of the *Big Brother* phenomenon has been its ability to trigger off a controversy, which one would no longer have expected in these times where no taboos are said to persist.

Ever since its first appearance in the Netherlands in 1999, the *Big Brother* format has been able to whip up a wide-scale social debate in different national contexts. Not only in Africa, but also in a wide variety of other national contexts, *Big Brother* was accompanied by forms of intense fandom and media hype, as well as encountering incomprehension, revulsion and even organised boycotts. Not only in Malawi, Nigeria or Zambia, the hysteria around the programme prompted prominent intellectuals, writers, church leaders or politicians to raise their (mostly denouncing) voices and threats to ban the programme. In some cases, such as Malawi, it effectively drove media regulators or other state institutions to act against the programme.

From a Eurocentric perspective it might be tempting to disapprove of the Malawian official denouncement of the programme. However, looking at the historical reception of the first series of *Big Brother* in Europe, one can only be struck by how the programme was able to provoke wide-scale debates, including vehement reactions of public revulsion and moral anxiety. In France, Germany, Italy, Portugal and other European countries, *Big Brother* was seen as highly troublesome in such a manner that the programme became a social phenomenon itself. In all these countries, the programme format grew into the central object of cultural, social and moral criticism, with various opinion makers and moral guardians raising their voices. In some cases, the hysteria, cult or panic around *Big Brother* drove media regulators or other state institutions to concrete actions against the programme – quite similar to Malawi.

In Germany for instance, where the programme started in March 2000, politicians, church leaders, journalists, broadcasting officials, high-rated intellectuals, writers and other opinion makers quickly entered the arena of public criticism. While in the Netherlands only few politicians ventured to publicly criticise *Big Brother*, different German political leaders openly denounced it. The Minister of Internal Affairs, Otto Schily, stated that *Big Brother* should be banned on the basis of human dignity, supported by similar claims by other elder statesmen such as Roland Koch (minister-president of Hessen) or Kurt Beck (minister-president of Rheinland-Pfalz). In the meantime church leaders, journalists and academics had opened a wider debate on the role of television, driving the *Landesmedienanstalten* (the central committee on the media) to discuss the limits of reality TV. In a historical meeting, the committee decided that the show could not be banned, but that it should at least change some basic rules. As a result, the German version of *Big Brother* had to close down its camera surveillance for at least one hour a day. However, this did not stop the audience from watching it by the millions, nor did it prevent a further denouncement by intellectual elites and moral guardians. A special feature of the German debate had been the metaphorical reference to the *Big Brother* house as a postmodern concentration camp (Broer 2000; Mikos *et al.* 2000).

Another, even more explicit, case is France where local reactions to *Loft Story* (the French version of *Big Brother*) followed a quite similar pattern. The huge ratings in the wake of the publicity over erotic scenes quickly started a wave of public protests from various sides. Religious leaders, intellectuals and politicians from different ideological orientations hackled the show from its very start in April 2001. Quality papers such as *Le Monde* made *Loft Story* into a major public event, organised several opinion polls, and opened its front and opinion pages to comments. Bands of protesters even tried to physically boycott the programme, attempting to storm through the line of riot police with the claim to liberate the hostages from the *Loft Story* studio. The police had to use tear gas to control the hundreds of protesters against 'télé-poubelle' (garbage TV). This outrage of public denouncement led to different actions taken by the national broadcasting authority (CSA). A first public intervention by the CSA occurred only one week after the start of *Loft Story*, when the authority decided in a short directive that the programme makers should take into account some basic elements of human dignity (for instance, the use of alcohol, drugs or cigarettes was forbidden). The French case is interesting not only for the wide variety of opinion makers, 'public' intellectuals and actions taken. It also shows how, again, the *Big Brother* case was able to grow into a social phenomenon itself, building up typical national/local items of cultural, political or moral sensitivities – such as a threat to quality, human dignity and French culture in the face of a globalised cultural invasion inspired by American cultural imperialism (see Biltereyst 2004).

In other European countries, a quite similar apocalyptic discourse could be observed. In fact, it is clear that *Big Brother* succeeded in quickly becoming a metaphor for a wider debate on national culture, quality and morality. In Portugal and Spain, for instance, the fuss around local *Big Brother* versions was inspired by other reality TV shows. In Spain there had been a wider public debate on controversial late shows such as *Crónicas marcianas* or *Operción Triunfo* on commercial channels even before *Gran Hermano* started. The Spanish *Big Brother* only accelerated the public debate over the immorality of programmes which seemed to exploit scandal, sexuality and the sphere of intimate private life. In Portugal, it was *O Bar da TV*, a reality show on the national commercial channel SIC in 2000, which preceded the debate on *Big Brother*. In both cases national political leaders, intellectuals, writers, bishops and other voices openly denounced the debasement of quality, obscenity, morality and privacy. And again, policy makers threatened to ban the programme, even up to inviting the national media authorities to take the appropriate measures (EBU 2001).

## The Big Brother panic

Looking back at the historical reception of the first series of *Big Brother* in these and various other European countries such as Greece or Italy, one can only be surprised by the intensity and variety of the public reactions. There have been clear national differences in responding to the metaphor *Big Brother*. In Italy for instance, *Grande Fratello* inspired many left critics, writers, intellectuals and politicians to use the programme as a conservative, even proto-Fascist programme illustrating the true populist foundations of Silvio Berlusconi's state and media power. In the Scandinavian countries, *Big Brother* successfully instigated a public debate, although the intensity of it cannot be compared to Southern European countries. In the Northern countries, including the Netherlands and Belgium (Biltereyst, Van Bauwel & Meers 2000; Mathijs 2002), it is clear that the more reserved (or less hysteric) public reception also carried signs of a significant intellectual support for the programme's progressive potentials (Bondebjerg 2002).

Notwithstanding these national differences, however, it is important to look back at this historical moment and to try to understand what happened. Some scholars and commentators tried to grab the public reception by using labels such as 'media event', 'media hype' or 'moral panic'. Especially the sociological concept of *moral panic* may be helpful here (Thompson 1998; Springhall 1998). In a classical sense, mainly from the 1970s onwards, a moral panic has been associated with a strong public denouncement of particular 'deviant' social groups (the mods, hippies, punks, drug-takers as 'folk devils') or behaviour (particular forms of sexuality, violence, drugs, juvenile delinquency). A moral panic refers to a spiralling debate and a naturalised 'consensual' feeling within society about key social and moral values being at stake. Besides the media and experts, the spiralling public denouncement is dominated by what is commonly called 'moral guardians': these include key players in the formation of public moral opinion. Through concrete action and exaggerated and moralistic discourse (in the media), representatives of major societal institutions such as the church, the state, political parties, trade unions or family organisations often tend to stigmatise nonconformist groups, ideas and behaviour. In the moral panic concept, the media are often seen as crucial in firing up the debate, not only by opening their pages to stigmatising opinions by 'moral guardians', but also by selecting experts supporting the consensual feeling. Moral panic authors indicate that in an extreme sense, the spiralling debate can give rise to a call for action and the (re)instalment of 'law and order'.

It is not difficult to link this classical idea of moral panic to the extreme reactions to *Big Brother* in many (supra)national contexts. Many of the basic constituents of a moral panic have been present in the *Big Brother* controversy, including: the role played by experts (such as psychologists, media experts, philosophers); the presence of particular moral guardians (church leaders, parents organisations); the role of the media in stirring up the debate; and the call for action and the concrete steps taken by media regulators in some countries.

However, since the 1980s, the 'moral panic' concept has been severely criticised. Authors such as Angela McRobbie (1994) have begun to question the consensual view of power in society and the role of the media in maintaining social control. A crucial point in revising the moral panic concept has been that the traditional authority of those on the moral barricades has been consistently undermined: the 'natural' and 'consensual' authority of traditional agents of social and moral control (from intellectual elites to church and a monopolistic public service broadcaster) have been opposed by a wider variety of values, tastes and norms. McRobbie indicates how, in a postmodern media environment, due to a proliferation of voices one can no longer talk about a consensual view. The concept of moral panic is somewhat outmoded because the media provide a continuous arena of struggle where various values and norms are performed, paraded and transformed by confronting them with others.

The *Big Brother* controversy might be a perfect illustration of this more complex web prohibiting a consensual view upon key values in society. In other words, it would be wrong to look at the public controversy as a spiralling debate with only denouncing voices. In most countries, these voices were often confronted with a more emphatic approach to and even praise for the programme. In Spain for instance, *Gran Hermano* received wide support by some prominent intellectuals such as the leading Marxist philosopher Gustavo Bueno who saw the show as 'attended democracy' in action (Bueno 2000). These types of interventions were more regular in Northern European countries, where some politicians even praised the programme as a school for introducing new immigrants into local customs and values (Bondebjerg 2002).

In her deconstruction of the traditional moral panic concept, McRobbie also claims that there has also been a shift in how the media exploit stories with an explicit moralistic hook. As a response to market pressures, the media seem to have upgraded the possibility of a moral panic as a sort of a working practice, using exaggerated headlines and sensational stories with a clearly moralistic angle.

So it might be true that the traditional moral panic concept is somewhat outmoded and that it might no longer be valid as a key to understand the *Big Brother* controversy – and by extension contemporary controversial media (Barker *et al.* 2001). However, we could retain some ideas, especially when we see moral panics in a more Foucaultian perspective as signs of a struggle over rivalling discourses, regulatory practices and attempts at silencing the other (Post 1998). We could (and should) try to understand and theorise the vehement reactions and wide public debate around *Big Brother* as a complex form of a late-modern *panic* in an era where no centre of moral control can any longer impose its values (for example, through censorship or even measures to promote cultural and moral elevation).

Following Kirsten Drotner (1992), the history of media panics shows how it is basically a discourse of power about who has the right to define quality standards, cultural norms and social qualifications. From this panic perspective, we could see the *Big Brother* public controversy/panic as a 'cultural seismograph', tackling central questions of social change, cultural quality and the power of those able to define it.

As intellectuals and media scholars we should be aware of this historical lesson, which goes back to the installment of film censorship, debates on the yellow press and even older media panics. However, we should also take into account how particular contemporary media formats play upon the exploitation of potential scandals and public controversy. One could even consider this programmatic tendency to explore dramatic narratives and stories with a strong moral content, as well as the urge for public debate, scandal and controversy as central features of the *Big Brother* and other reality TV genres. And in this strategy, intellectuals and public opinion makers from all sorts of origins and ideological fractions may be welcome: both public denouncement and praise create a web of attention and discursive spectacle. It is a strategy whereby societal debate ultimately becomes a key for commercial success.

*Notes*

1   See http://www.nationalmalawi.com/.

*Bibliography*

Barker, M., J. Arthurs and R. Harindranath (2001) *The Crash Controversy: Censorship Campaigns and Film Reception*. London: Wallflower Press.
Biltereyst, D., S. Van Bauwel and Ph. Meers (2000) *Realiteit en fictie: Tweemaal hetzelfde?* Brussels: King Baudouin Foundation.

Biltereyst, D. (2004) 'Reality TV, troublesome pictures and panics', in S. Holmes and D. Jermyn (eds) *Understanding Reality TV*. London: Routledge, 91–110.

Bondebjerg, I. (2002) 'The mediation of everyday life', in A. Jerslev (ed.) *Realism and 'Reality' in Film and Media*. Copenhagen: Museum Tusculanum Press, 159–93.

Broer, T. (2000) 'Echte conflicten', *Vrij Nederland*, 18 March, 58.

Bueno, G. (2000) 'Gustavo Bueno y *Gran* Hermano'. Available at: www.fggbueno.es/gbm/gb2000.

Drotner, K. (1992) 'Modernity and media panics', in M. Skovmand and K. Schroder (eds) *Media Cultures: Reappraising Transnational Media*. London: Routledge, 42–62.

EBU (2001) '*Big Brother*: an international phenomenon', *Diffusion*, *4*, 6–21.

Mathijs, E. (2002) '*Big Brother* and Critical Discourse: Shifts in the Reception of *Big Brother* Belgium', *Television and New Media*, 3, 3, 311–22.

McRobbie, A. (1994) 'The moral panic in the age of the postmodern mass media', in A. McRobbie (ed.) *Postmodernism and popular culture*. London: Routledge, 198–219.

Mikos, L., P. Feise, K. Herzog, E. Prommer and V. Veihl. (2000) *Im Auge der Kamera: Das Fernsehereignis Big Brother*. Berlin: Vistas.

Ntonya, G. (2003), 'Parliament wants no *Big Brother*'. Available at: www.nationalmalawi.com/ (Accessed 8 June 2003).

Nujoma, S. (2003) Quoted in BBC News, 'Namibians snub Big Brother ban', 30 July 2003, http://news.bbc.co.uk/go/pr/fr/-/1/hi/world/africa/3110681 (Accessed 29 July 2003).

Omotose, B. (2003) Quoted by CNN Com: www.cnn.com/2003/SHOWBIZ/TV/09/10/bigbrother.africa. (Accessed 16 September 2003).

Post, R. (1998) *Censorship and Silencing: Practices of Cultural Regulation*. Los Angeles: Getty Research Institute.

Springhall, J. (1998) *Youth, Popular Culture and Moral Panics*. London: Macmillan.

Thompson, K. (1998) *Moral Panics*. New York/London: Routledge.

# CHAPTER 2

*Liesbet van Zoonen*

# DESIRE AND RESISTANCE
## Big Brother in the Dutch Public Sphere

## Introduction

The television Internet format of *Big Brother* has made a considerable impact on international media audiences in recent years. The originally Dutch Endemol format combines television and Internet in a three-month daily surveillance of a group of people living in an ordinary house. Broadcast for the first time in the Netherlands in the Autumn of 1999, the programme was as huge a ratings hit as a source of controversy. Even before *Big Brother* could actually be watched, surprise, embarrassment and outrage dominated among the Dutch cultural, journalistic and scientific vanguard. The unseemly exhibitionism of participants, as well as the shameless voyeurism on the part of viewers, and the ruthless exploitation of ordinary people by the Endemol company were at the core of the debate. The idea of spying on people 24 hours a day with 24 cameras, and of releasing those pictures to the nation was widely seen as a low point in Dutch television history and could, according to observers, cause irreparable psychological damage to participants. After the first transmission, critics complained how tedious the programme and the participants were. However, along the way, *Big Brother* won over one sceptic after another, culminating in the programme gaining the status of being one of the most innovative shows in the history of Dutch television. Widely lauded instead of spurned like a half-year earlier, John de Mol who invented, developed and produced the programme was voted Dutch Broadcast Man of the Year 1999 by a jury of professionals.

Even before the first series ended in the Netherlands Endemol sold the format to other European countries, Germany – an Endemol stronghold – being the first to follow. After that came Australia, Argentina, Belgium, Denmark, Greece, Italy, Norway, Portugal, Poland, Spain, the United Kingdom, the United States, Switzerland and Sweden. Several of these countries have commissioned second and third runs. With the exception of the US, where *Big Brother* scored average ratings, all of these countries witnessed unprecedented viewing figures. One *Big Brother* episode in Spain, for instance, peaked at 70 per cent of the market share when one of the residents was expelled. The episode beat the concurrent semi-final of the Champions League between Real Madrid and Bayern Munich on the competing channel. The German RTL2 achieved a unique market share of 28 per cent with *Big Brother*. Swedish Kanal 5 went up from an average 8 per cent market share to an overall 25 per cent. Kanaal 2 in Belgium scored 32 per cent for consecutive episodes. In Portugal the introduction of *Big Brother* on TV1 attracted 41 per cent of the viewers. The Internet figures are even more impressive: overall the first Dutch run of *Big Brother* drew more than 52 million page views. The German *Big Brother* site received an average of 3.5 million visitors a day during the first run peaking at 5 million on some days, making it the most visited web site in Europe. The US *Big Brother* web site was America Online's best visited site (all figures from www.endemol.com/news). If one types in 'Big Brother' *and* 'house' *and* 'television' (to prevent the Orwellian meaning) into an ordinary search engine on the Internet, one receives some 200,000 sites.

Amid all the moral discussion about *Big Brother* – John de Mol has repeatedly had to explain to journalists where he 'draws the line' – the far more interesting question of why *Big Brother* was so immensely successful has less frequently been asked (for example, see Mikos et al. 2000; Weber 2000). A simple accumulation of individual and collective motives of why people watch *Big Brother* will not in this instance suffice; the impact of the show was too big, too sudden and too widespread for that. *Big Brother* did not just appeal to untold numbers of individual viewers; it somehow struck a social chord, a subconscious collective yearning, a deep-rooted invisible need. But what precisely was that yearning? On what was that need based? And will spin-offs of *Big Brother* meet that need in a similar way and to the same extent? That is the subject of this chapter.[1]

## Division

The Dutch public debate on the first season of *Big Brother* provides the first key to understanding the collective desires and needs awakened by the programme. Most arguments rest on the division between 'public life' and 'private domain', and the premise that this divide is self-evident and worth nurturing. *Big Brother* transcended this dichotomy by turning the private lives of ordinary people, with all their normal, everyday, seemingly unimportant experiences and worries, into a daily public spectacle. Something similar had already transpired in previous popular formats of Endemol Entertainment such as *All You Need is Love*, *Forgive Me*, *Soundmix Show*, *Honeymoon Quiz* and *Now or Never*, all formats originating in the Netherlands and exported to various, mainly European, countries.[2]

*Big Brother* built on the trademark of Endemol enterprises: primal experiences and emotions ('basic instincts' as it were) of ordinary people lie at the heart of hundreds of successful formats. Each of those formats has been subjected to similar criticism: one should not flaunt private emotions, nor does one relish observing these emotions.[3] A quote from a journalist commenting on *All You Need is Love* provides an example:

> Producers, when thus questioned, will always claim to be a psychotherapist or hedge-preacher, disseminating good. Yet how is it that this does not occur through impressive programmes, but rather through a seamy exploitation of emotions, both in participants and in viewers? This is all about unwanted intimacies, the screening whereof some will admit is their last resort and because they can't come up with anything better. (Verdonck 1993)

The fact that the public debate about *Big Brother* and its predecessors is so often conducted in the terms of public and private and their attendant (unwritten) codes of behaviour seems to suggest that this division is deeply rooted in our society. At the same time, however, the mass-appeal of *Big Brother* points to the fact that the moral strength of public and private codes is limited: average viewers seem wholly unaffected.

This paradox finds its origin in the history of the private sphere. The intimate domesticity that we associate with it nowadays is a relatively recent phenomenon. In pre-modern societies the private sphere did not yet exist as a separate domain. For the common people, the public realm of production and labour and the private realm of consumption and care were linked in the small social and economic units households formed at that time. The private lives of the aristocracy did not have an independent character either, but were part of a more general display of status and power. At the pre-revolutionary French court the retiring to bed (*le coucher*) and the waking up (*le lever*) of the monarch were daily public affairs to which it was a great privilege being invited as a witness (Elias 1997). A private life that distinguished itself by separation from the outside world and by specific experiences and codes of behaviour that were different from the public realm did not, then, exist: neither for the commoner, nor for the social elites. Only the emergence of the bourgeoisie, and the processes of industrialisation and urbanisation, presented 'modern' relations wherein a private domain with specific social functions and relevance came into being. The puritan ideology of the Victorian era, following earlier romantic thinkers like Rousseau, promoted the private sphere as a 'haven in a heartless world', best left to the mastery of women. Counter-claims, inspired by Marx and Engels, that the private realm was much more a capitalist invention aimed at the cheap reproduction of the labour force on the backs of womankind (Zaretsky 1977) found little support.

Private and public spheres gained momentum and imposed their own codes of conduct: rationale and restraint belonged to the public realm, then populated by men; emotions and spontaneity belonged in the private sphere, the 'natural' domain of women. This did not mean that public life had become the domain of all men; on the contrary, labourers and blacks did not qualify because of their supposed inferior powers of reason and judgement. The separation of private and public had thus also become a hierarchy by means of which the white male bourgeoisie created and mantained its own privileges: at first via countless legal mechanisms of exclusion, such as the census and male suffrage, and later in cultural prescriptions for acceptable themes, styles and behaviour in public life (see also Bourdieu 1979; Calhoun 1992; Habermas 1992).

## Resistance

Resistance against this historical division of private and public has up to now found expression mostly in the form of feminist action. The solitary confinement to the private sphere, to which women felt subjected, led to a widespread feminist movement that succeeded in putting numerous subjects which were deemed 'merely' personal on the public, political agenda (Van Zoonen 1991). The aim of the feminist and other social movements was initially not only to turn the bourgeois division between the private and the public into a political issue, but to break open those frontiers in everyday life as well. Communes thus blossomed, wherein living, working and private existence were tentatively integrated. These and similar experiments, however, never found broad appeal, and nowadays even among former initiators fatigue and disillusionment have crept in. This does not, however, mean that the bourgeois split between private and public has prevailed and is accepted. Rather, the conclusion should be that the feminist and subcultural alternative models were not met with mass acceptance. *Big Brother*'s success however proves, with wider popularity than has feminism, that the bourgeois division between the public domain, with its concomitant regulations, and the private with its own code of conduct is not widely accepted or appreciated, and has moreover lost its social functionality. The comments on *Big Brother* by the 17-year-old fan and publicist Anna Woltz very clearly point in that direction:

> If I could see what my sister is like with her girlfriends, how the maths teacher talks to his wife, how my parents behave among adults, I would not feel the need for a substitute for life. But I don't see all that. How do you learn how to read people if you only know three kinds: kids your age, teachers and parents? ... *Big Brother* is the only programme we watch and discuss every day with the whole family. At last, we have 'common' friends, about whom we can talk, think and gossip. (Woltz 1999)

Evidently the 'real' adults in Woltz's environment no longer offer such frames of reference, or not to the extent required, because they have all withdrawn into their own private surroundings. This is, after all, what is proscribed by the bourgeois codes of conduct for private and public life.

## Desire

Television in general has contributed in a great many ways to disclosing the private realm hidden by bourgeois mores. We rediscover on television what has become ever more invisible in the world around us, the private life of ordinary people: initially mostly in the enacted fantasies of sitcoms and soaps, but currently in a variety of formats in which real life is shown: talk shows, reality TV, emo-TV, docusoaps and now *Big Brother*. The obvious comment that such reality genres are just as subject to the constraints of television and are manipulated in countless ways by the makers (casting, editing, stage-management, and so on) does not undermine such an observation. The classic adage by W. H. Thomas is worth noting: 'If men define situations as real, they are real in their consequences' (in McQuail 1983). The unabashedly vociferous use of mobile phones for private conversations in public areas, the 24/7 Internet observation people with web-cams and the vast numbers of people wishing to participate in talk shows, all these are opportunities people have seized to throw off the bourgeois bodice of the private–public divide. There is obviously an enormous desire to make one's private life public; not because of a vain longing for '15 minutes of fame', as the critics invariably parrot Andy Warhol; not as a result of the supposed unscrupulous machinations by TV producers such as John de Mol; and certainly not as a consequence of a somehow underdeveloped set of standards and excessive exhibitionism. This trend suggests a nostalgic yearning for authenticity, for ties with others like oneself, for familiarity and communality, and for the social legitimisation of one's own private experiences. Such yearning is not appeased by regular 'culture' (understood as 'Art' with a capital A). After all, art does not deal with the ordinary, the everyday, but with the exceptional. Neither is it smoothened by regular culture (now understood as 'civilisation') that dictates that private life remains excluded from society and publicity.

Popular culture thus fills a vacuum left open by 'Art' and 'civilisation' (see Van Zoonen 1999). Where else than a unique co-production of the dating shows *All You Need Is Love* and *Love Letters* could a lesbian couple solemnise their marriage rituals in public before Dutch law offered that opportunity? Or, as the German newspaper *Die Zeit* wrote:

> John de Mol's programmes are time and again attempts to re-enact old rituals, to bring them closer to the public and to take up their serious substance, their cultural meaning into the mould of television entertainment and reinstating them in the process. (Minkmar 2000)

Where else other than in assorted talk shows do supposedly private, everyday experiences ranging from 'my husband beats me' to 'my wife doesn't understand me' acquire airtime? And where else than in *Big Brother* could 17-year-old Anna Woltz and the rest of Holland observe how people in their daily exchange, adjust and reposition their own stories big *and* small, their feelings, grievances and thoughts. On top of that, this was not only to be *seen* in *Big Brother*, viewers could also comment in public and get involved in the show via the official and numerous unofficial *Big Brother* websites; an activity often undertaken with enthusiasm as well as with criticism and hostility. Precisely because of this widespread yearning for collective everyday experiences no longer available in bourgeois society with its sequestered private domain, it is not surprising that participants in *Big Brother* are so incredibly average, bordering sometimes on the tedious. That seems, in fact, to be the essential core of *Big Brother*-mania.

The combination of television and Internet platforms in *Big Brother* has created a collective experience characterised by a desire for everyday communality and by a rebellion against the norms of 'civilised' public culture. That desire, not provoked by exceptional events like a skating marathon, a royal wedding, a disaster of national proportions or a soccer championship, but rooted in ordinary daily humdrum experience, forms the basis of *Big Brother*'s success. It springs from the contemporary bourgeois division between a private realm and a public realm that has isolated private life, marginalised it and made it invisible. Feminism and *Big Brother* share their resistance against that division. It is consequentially not surprising that both are popular with women.

## Spin-offs

The moment the widely shared desire for everyday recognisability became explicit through the success of *Big Brother*, spin-offs followed thick and fast, initially from the

Endemol company itself. John de Mol appointed two full-time staff solely to develop *Big Brother* varieties (Van der Heijden 2000). A Dutch executive of SBS, a channel that initially rejected *Big Brother* because it deemed the concept too extreme, ordered a spin-off even before the first series ended. John de Mol Productions churned out *The Bus* and *Chained* for SBS at breakneck speed, and *The Girls of 5* for Net5 (via 625 Productions, with whom Endemol maintains close ties). Following *Big Brother*'s conquest of Europe these formats have been exported easily and widely as well. Other producers are desperately asking around for formats that suit this demand, something that occasionally leads to hilarious capers such as the order that reached a Dutch producer to devise something positioned 'in-between *Who Wants to be a Millionaire* and *Big Brother*' (de Winter 2000).

The market for everyday recognisability created by and with *Big Brother* is now becoming specialised and diversified toward particular target groups which will pull into focus what exactly constitutes the collective desire for everyday familiarity that *Big Brother* awakened. Furthermore, the ever-greater diversity of the supply will change demand as well: everyday recognisability will one day be easily available. Demand will not diminish because of this – although John de Mol expects the *Big Brother* format itself to be exhausted four years after its inception – but rather become more varied and specific. A glimpse of this can be gleaned when we contrast *Big Brother* with its earliest spin-off, *The Bus*. This comparison will also show that the nature of the desire for collective everyday experiences and the implicit resistance against the conventions of public life are far from uniform.

## A Dutch case

*The Bus* differs in many ways from *Big Brother*. Eleven passengers take a 16-week journey through the Netherlands in a double-decker bus. Some of the passengers have to find work during the week, to earn money for food, while the rest stay in or around *The Bus*. Viewers can vote for their favourite passenger at any time of the day or night, and each week a rankings list is produced. The most popular passenger, along with a fellow passenger of his or her choice, wins four hours of freedom from *The Bus*, with 1,000 guilders to split between them. Once every two weeks, one of the three least popular passengers is required to leave *The Bus*. The decision is made by the other passengers. After four months have passed, only three passengers remain and viewers decide who will take the jackpot.

Comparing the Dutch first series of *Big Brother* and *The Bus*, one looks at a list of oppositions remarkably similar to the differences usually associated with the 'modern' and 'postmodern'. One important contrast between *Big Brother* and *The Bus* is that of the fixed location versus the travelling bus; the predictable, unchanging and impenetrable environment of the *Big Brother* house against the unpredictable and contingent issues of the bus ride. An important difference was found in the participants of the first series: *Big Brother*'s were all white and middle-class, *Bus* passengers included a second-generation immigrant and a dock-worker. *Big Brother* participants were much more subdued than *Bus* passengers, who were so outrageous in their behaviour that the broadcasting channel had at some point to hand out 'yellow cards'. These characteristics in turn led to a contrast in the 'narrative', which in *Big Brother* was harmonious, almost bland; while in *The Bus* fights and conflicts spilled from the screen, especially at the beginning. In the *Big Brother* house, mutual liaisons acquired the character of family ties, with one of the women as the presiding mother; in *The Bus* networks were ever shifting. Where treason was extraneous in *Big Brother* (participants were voted out by the audience), fellow passengers delivered the *coup de grâce* in *The Bus*.

Thinking of *Big Brother* and *The Bus* in metaphors and metonymies for 'modern' and 'postmodern' society highlights the different desires evoked by these formats. The hermetic, self-involved house can be seen as a metaphor for the modern nation-state with its clearly drawn borders and coherent group of citizens, whereas the ever-travelling bus with consistent interference from outside provides a metaphor for postmodern nomadic existence in which migration and expulsion predominate (the bus of *The Bus* was thrown out of one of the cities it visited). The white, relatively homogeneous and harmonious group of residents of the house figures as a metonymy for pre-migration modern Dutch society,[4] while the 'Bussengers', with their diverse ethnic and class backgrounds, can be seen as functioning metonymically for contemporary multicultural Dutch society. Interestingly, those differences came about rather coincidentally: the extremely temperate, 'well-behaved' casting of the first *Big Brother* series in the Netherlands was the result of all the commotion and criticism the programme generated in advance. The initial concept called for more divergent and extreme characters, but in an attempt to avoid the calamities the critics predicted would result from this experimentation with human nature, producers opted for a more stable and moderate cast. When it became clear in the course of the programme that the participants did not experience psychological damage, John de Mol effortlessly met SBS's request for *The Bus* to have more contrast and conflict built into the casting. Furthermore SBS wanted to see *The Bus* reflect their supposed average viewer. The final selection of candidates for *The Bus* was made by the audience, which had been asked in several preliminaries to vote for a candidate by telephone polling. The combination of these factors led to a company of 'Bussengers' that represented contemporary multicultural society more accurately than the *Big Brother* group. The mobility of *The Bus* came about fortuitously too. John de Mol did not want to comply with the wishes of SBS to make something that paralleled the original *Big Brother* concept as closely as possible and thus something radically different from a house emerged: a moving bus (De Mol 2000).[5]

Through a conjunction of production circumstances then, *Big Brother* and *The Bus* became the exponents of a collective desire for respectively 'modern' and 'postmodern' everyday familiarity. As a result, we can interpret the enormous popularity of the first Dutch *Big Brother* as an expression of a widely shared yearning for an organised, coherent and predictable society, not disturbed by 'Others' or by irrational conflicts and outbursts. Those who do not conform to the 'normal' order are mercilessly expelled (overly out-going women were mercilessly thrown out by the audience). Consensus and harmony rule over opposition and conflict. That is a society that no longer exists, and perhaps the *Big Brother* feeling should be primarily characterised as nostalgia. It was inevitable that *The Bus* would not become as popular as *Big Brother*: spin-offs invariably perform less well than the original format (see Gitlin 1983). Beyond that, however, the longing for collective, everyday, postmodern, multicultural, unpredictable and contradictory experience is evidently less prominent and less acute than the nostalgia for modern orderedness. Yet postmodern society is not spurned altogether, judging by the public's choice for a greater diversity of participants and by the success of *The Bus*; incomparable to that of *Big Brother* but scoring well in terms of its time-slot and its target audience.

## Conclusion

We may never be able to explain the success of *Big Brother*. Each explanation for such an expansive phenomenon can only be partial. This analysis which focuses on the resistance against the hegemony of the bourgeois public/private division and its conventions, and on the desire for recognition – in both senses of the word – of everyday modern experiences, also only covers part of the story. I have not, for instance, looked at how programming decisions may have helped to expand *Big Brother*'s popularity. In the UK, for instance, as in the US, the programme was scheduled in the slow summer season, with television offerings and news agendas at a low. Disclaimers are possible for both 'desire' and 'resistance'. The longing for everyday familiarity does not only result in pleasurable nostalgia, if one takes the line of a Dutch columnist: 'The programme is the embodiment of the Dutch nightmare ... After a mere few days you are convinced: hell is not the other, not the outside world, hell is yourself' (Heijne 1999).

Other examples of the unpleasant side of the everyday were found in great numbers on the Internet, where *Big Brother* was not only a source of intense identification for several participants, but also of deep revulsion for others. Identification and revulsion are, however, both sides of the same coin of collective recognition, and the unforeseen success of *Big Brother* shows that our ordinary, invisible private lives no longer provide enough points of reference for these. Besides, the success of *Big Brother* can be seen, as discussed earlier, as a form of rebellion against the conventions of 'civilised' bourgeois public culture, that are the result of the specific genesis and conditions of these times. It therefore comes as no surprise that parliamentary politics, the institutional advocate of the modern public sphere *par excellence*, levelled the most criticism at *Big Brother* and its spin-offs. In Germany, *Big Brother* escaped its broadcasting being prohibited by the Deutsche Medien Anstalt. It could hardly be produced in France, at least not under its own name. In the Netherlands, the Christian Democrats attempted to open a public debate about a legal ban on such programmes reacting to the upheaval caused by *Chained*. Under the guise of protecting general, universal values, traditional politicians in fact uphold a specific opinion regarding public and private which contains within itself countless exclusion mechanisms. Although cultural and social elites tend to adhere to the same framework, they fight a rear-guard battle: the Christian Democrat proposal was roundly voted down.[6] *Big Brother* and its spin-offs have taken the world by storm: the hegemony of public and private conventions as we witnessed them in the last century appears dead and buried.

*Notes*

1   With thanks to Joost de Bruin, Thomas Notermans and Maarten Reesink for their constructive and inspiring comments.
2   Endemol has exported its formats to various European countries, but aims in particular at the top five markets.
3   Inasmuch as expressions of emotion are allowed in public, they are linked to causes of general and collective import: crying at the national anthem, the grave of the Unknown Soldier or a national disaster. With thanks to Huub Wijfjes for this amendment.
4   I will leave undiscussed the fact that this homogeneity was also merely a false construct resulting from the typical compartmentalisation of Dutch society.

5 With thanks to Thomas Notermans, spokesman for Endemol, who pointed out the importance of the casting of participants and the fortuitousness of format and production choices.

6 The only spin-off that raised any social protest was *The Girls of 5*, not because of the sort of programme it was or some desire to call a halt to the blurring of social life and the private realm, however, but because local residents, ill-informed and ill-prepared by producers, feared the havoc the programme would wreak on the neighbourhood.

*Bibliography*

Bourdieu, P. (1979) *La distinction: critique sociale du jugement*. Paris: Editions Minuit.

Calhoun, G. (ed.) (1992) *Habermas and the Public Sphere*. Cambridge, MA: MIT Press.

de Mol, J. (2000) 'Big Brother', guest lecture at the University of Amsterdam, 24 May.

de Winter, H. (2000) 'Onafhankelijke producenten', guest lecture for the masterclass 'Finding the Audience' at the University of Amsterdam, 12 May.

Elias, N. (1997) *De hofsamenleving. Een sociologische studie van koningschap en hofaristocratie*. Meppel: Boom.

Gitlin, T. (1983) *Inside Prime Time*. New York: Pantheon.

Habermas, J. (1992) *The Structural Transformation of the Public Sphere*. Cambridge: Polity Press.

Heijne, B. (1999) 'Riskante afvalrace op televisie?', *NRC Handelsblad*, 24 September.

McQuail, D. (1983) *Mass Communication Theory: An Introduction*. London: Sage.

Mikos, L., P. Feise, K. Herzog, E. Prommer and V. Veihl. (2000) *Im Auge der Kamera: Das Fernsehereignis Big Brother*. Berlin: Vistas.

Minkmar, M. (2000) 'Unser grosser Bruder', *Die Zeit*, 27 January.

Van der Heijden, H. (2000) 'Programma-ontwikkeling', guest lecture for the masterclass 'Finding the Audience' at the University of Amsterdam, 8 May.

Van Zoonen, L. (1991) *Moeten strijdende vrouwen zo grof zijn? De vrouwenbeweging en de media*. Amsterdam: SUA.

_____ (1999) *Media, cultuur en burgerschap*. Amsterdam: Het Spinhuis.

Verdonck, R. (1993) 'Het tranendal', *Trouw*, 26 October.

Weber, F. (2000) *Big Brother. Inszenierte Banalit at zur Prime Time*. Münster: Hopf.

Woltz, A. (1999) 'Surrogaat voor het leven', *NRC Handelsblad*, 2 December.

Zaretsky, E. (1977) *Gezin en privé-leven in het kapitalisme*. Nijmegen: SUN.

# CHAPTER 3

*Annette Hill*

# WATCHING BIG BROTHER UK

## Introduction

In the newspaper article 'The Addicted in Search of the Evicted' fans of *Big Brother* talked about why they had travelled to London to take part in the Friday night eviction show. One fan explained: 'There are certain things that take place every decade and this is one of them, this is a phenomenon and coming here is about seeing a moment of our time in action. When it finishes, this nation is in trouble. Six million people will have to learn how to have conversations again' (Corner 2000: 7). Another fan commented: 'I've changed my routine to fit in with *Big Brother* ... when it's over I am going to cry. It'll be like losing a group of friends ... There's going to be a very big gap in my life' (ibid.).

This chapter is about the experience of watching *Big Brother* (the UK version of 2000). The way audiences watch and talk about this reality game show is significant to our understanding of the success of the series, and also its role in the development of popular factual television. Many people watched *Big Brother* because their friends and family were talking about it, and many people continued to watch *Big Brother* in order to have something to talk about with their friends and family. What people talked about is the focus here. In particular, I examine the topic of performance in relation to audience discussion of the series. Many viewers are critical of the 'performances' of ordinary people in the *Big Brother* house, and such criticism leads to debate about the truth claims of this reality game show. What follows is discussion by television viewers about the experience of watching and talking about *Big Brother*.[1]

## Research methods

Before discussing television audiences and *Big Brother* in the UK, I want to provide a brief note on the research methods used in this chapter. The audience data I refer to are taken from an audience research project on television audiences and factual entertainment. The project was funded by the Economic and Social Research Council (ESRC), the Independent Television Commission (ITC) and Channel 4. The project used a multi-method approach, combining quantitative and qualitative techniques to gather data and subsequent analysis of television audiences and popular factual programming in the UK. The main methods used were a quantitative survey, semi-structured focus groups and in-depth interviews, and the data were collected during a particular period in the development of the genre of popular factual television (2000–01).

The survey contained a series of closed questions relating to audience preferences for form, content, sub genres and use of multimedia, and audience attitudes towards issues of privacy, information and entertainment in popular factual programming. The survey was a self-completion questionnaire, and was distributed by the Broadcasters Audience Research Board (BARB) to a representative sample of 8216 adults (aged 16–65+) and 937 children (aged 4–15) during August 2000. The data collected allowed me to develop a source of information on the general public and their preferences for and attitudes to a range of factual entertainment programmes in the UK. I analysed the data from a number of perspectives, looking at programme types and content, and audience attitudes, and comparing this data with key demographic information relating to age, gender, class, education, households with/without children and ethnicity.[2]

The next stage of the audience research involved semi-structured focus groups, where the results of the survey were used to design focus group interviews with children (aged 11–14), young adults (aged 15–18) and adults (aged 18–44), who defined themselves as regular viewers of popular factual television, and were in the C1C2DE social category, that is lower middle-class and working-class social groups. The recruitment of participants involved the use of a professional qualitative recruitment agency, and quota sampling in a variety of suburban locations. I selected these participants because the results of the survey indicated that regular viewers of popular factual television were primarily in the above categories. The primary aim of these focus groups was to explore audience attraction to different types of popular factual programming, and to understand what strategies they used to watch hybrid formats within the genre. The focus groups contained a series of open questions relating to viewer responses to sub-genres within factual entertainment, the use of non-professional actors and issues relating to information and entertainment in hybrid formats. Twelve focus groups were conducted in London, each group containing 7–8 participants, and were divided according to age, gender and access to terrestrial or satellite/cable/digital television. I selected these groups because the data from the survey indicated that age and gender were key variables relating to audience attraction to factual entertainment, and it was necessary to consider a range of programming available across television platforms. Following an initial coding of the transcripts, I conducted a more discursive analysis that considered group dynamics as well as substantive judgements.

The final stage of the audience research involved in-depth interviews with ten families, with children of varying ages, over a six-month period (recruited from the focus groups). Four visits were made to the family homes during January to July 2001. Combinations of methods were used – open discussions, observation of families and participation in watching programmes – in order to understand the social context to watching factual entertainment. In addition, key issues that arose from the focus groups were explored further during the family visits. In my selection of interview subjects, the types of questions asked during the visits, and the timing of the visits, I was guided by a desire to follow new developments within the genre, and to further understand how family viewers responded to these developments in the home environment. Interviews were logged, and partially transcribed, and field notes written up during and after the period of data collection. The in-depth interviews provided a wealth of rich data and thick description, and allowed further flexibility for the project to assess the popularity of, and responses to, new hybrid formats and more familiar formats within factual entertainment.

## Watching and talking about Big Brother

Who's watching *Big Brother*? Channel 4 had the best Friday night ratings in its history, with 9 million viewers (46 per cent share) tuning in to watch the first series finale of *Big Brother*. 67 per cent of the UK population watched *Big Brother* at least once. Over seven million viewers telephoned Channel 4's hotline to vote for the winner, which broke the record for viewer participation in a UK television programme. As for the website, it received three million page impressions each day, which made it Europe's top website during the summer of 2000. The second series averaged more than four million viewers, giving Channel 4 more than a 70 per cent increase on their average broadcast share. Channel 4's digital youth channel, E4, screened *Big Brother 2* continuously during the second series, and at peak moments in the house (for example, Paul and Helen's candlelit tryst) attracted record figures, propelling the digital channel ahead of terrestrial minority channels.[3] More than 15 million viewers voted to evict contestants, either using interactive TV handsets, or phonelines. The website received a total of 159 million page impressions and 16.4 million video streams were requested.[4] The third series of *Big Brother* averaged four million viewers, with the live final attracting ten million in the summer of 2002. The fourth series of *Big Brother* underperformed from the previous year, but was still fifth place in the top ten programmes for viewers aged 16–25.[5] Table 1 illustrates the ratings for all series of *Big Brother* at the time of writing.

In terms of the survey I conducted, Table 2 profiles viewers of *Big Brother*. Out of the total sample of respondents (unweighted sample 8216), aged 16–65+, only 30 per

| Series (Channel 4) | Average (weekdays) | First Show | Final Show |
|---|---|---|---|
| BB1 | 4.6m (25%) | 3.3m (17%) | 9m (46.5%) |
| BB2 | 4.5m (25%) | 3.3m (16.5%) | 7.5m (46%) |
| BB3 | 5.9m (28%) | 5.9m (25.9%) | 10m (50.6%) |
| BB4 | 4.9 (24%) | 6.9 (29.3%) | 6.6m (34%) |

Table 1: Ratings for *Big Brother*. Source: *Broadcast*, 1 August 2003

cent of the sample had watched the programme. Of that 30 per cent, 28 per cent of men and 34 per cent of women watched *Big Brother*. 16–34-year-olds were two times more likely to have watched it than older viewers. 51 per cent of viewers with college education saw the series, compared with an average of 33 per cent of those without. Adults were twice as likely to have seen *Big Brother* if they lived in households with children. Viewers in the higher social grades were slightly more likely to watch the series than those in the lower social grades. And, viewers with Internet access were slightly more likely to watch *Big Brother* than those without. The profile overall suggests *Big Brother* attracted upwardly-mobile, educated, young adults, the target audience for Channel 4.

In relation to the television series itself, Table 3 outlines the favourite *Big Brother* experiences for viewers. Respondents were presented with a list of experiences (for example, visiting the website). The *Big Brother* experience enjoyed by the greatest

| Viewer Profile | Watching *Big Brother* (30% of adults) |
|---|---|
| Males | 28% |
| Females | 34% |
| 16–24 | 58% |
| 25–34 | 50% |
| 35–44 | 36% |
| 45–54 | 25% |
| 55–64 | 15% |
| 65+ | 9% |
| AB | 35% |
| C1 | 34% |
| C2 | 30% |
| DE | 27% |
| 15+ education | 15% |
| 16+ education | 33% |
| 17-18 education | 38% |
| 19+ education | 33% |
| Students | 51% |
| With children | 41% |
| Without children | 22% |
| With Internet access | 40% |
| Without Internet access | 33% |

Table 2: *Big Brother* viewer profile

| Big Brother Experiences | Like – (30 per cent of adult sample) |
|---|---|
| Watching the live 'eviction' programme | 59% |
| Seeing ex-contestants talk about their experience | 58% |
| Watching the nightly TV programme | 55% |
| Choosing the winner | 52% |
| Talking about the programme with friends/family | 51% |
| Choosing the losers | 48% |
| Suggesting tasks | 46% |
| Media coverage of the programme | 31% |
| Visiting the 24hour Internet site | 15% |
| Talking about the programme in chat rooms | 14% |

Table 3: *Big Brother* experiences

percentage of all respondents was watching the live 'eviction' show (59 per cent), followed by seeing ex-contestants talk about their experiences (58 per cent), watching the nightly TV programme (55 per cent) and talking about the programme with friends/family (51 per cent). Those aspects of the *Big Brother* experience that were most 'interactive', choosing winners and losers, were not as popular with viewers (52 per cent and 48 per cent), although this may have altered with subsequent versions of *Big Brother* which utilised interactive voting via the Channel 4 digital youth channel E4. Similarly, those aspects of *Big Brother* associated with the website were also not popular with viewers.[6] This was partly because during the first series of *Big Brother* the website was difficult to download to home computers. Again, this reluctance to visit the *Big Brother* website, even if viewers had access to the Internet, may have altered during subsequent series, with technical improvements and greater access to broadband in the home. Another reason why viewers were not especially interested in the website was because they wanted to watch the television show in order to join in conversations about *Big Brother* with family and friends. Media coverage of *Big Brother* also rated poorly with viewers (31 per cent). Clearly, media coverage helped to make the series a 'media event' but also saturated the market with gossip. Viewers preferred to be part of the media event through first-hand experience (watching and talking about *Big Brother*) rather than reading about it second hand.

The above statistics indicate that the experience of watching *Big Brother* is social, and involves watching and talking about the show before, during and afterwards. Paddy Scannell maintains that talk is not a minor part of the *Big Brother* experience, but arguably one of the most important features of the series:

Everyone knows that for a time in the summer of 2000 the only thing that anyone talked about was *Big Brother*. The amount of comment, discussion and evaluation that it elicited at the time, in the press, in pubs and buses and households up and down the land was enormous. This talk was not accidental but a structural feature of the show's relational totality of involvements. Involvement showed in talk so that to consider what it was that elicited such a 'discursive ferment' is to get at the heart of the programme's care structure as an event invented for television. The programme invited, indeed demanded, that not only should it be watched on a daily basis but that it should be talked about. (Scannell 2002: 277–8)

How did viewers talk about *Big Brother*? Perhaps one of the most obvious ways in which audiences engaged with the media event of *Big Brother* was to declare their involvement or lack of involvement with this reality game show. The type of common remarks made about the series illustrate an intense love/hate relationship with *Big Brother*:

> I absolutely hated *Big Brother* … I can't see the attraction to it, I don't find anything appealing about watching it. (20-year-old mother)

> It was so crap. I can't believe people watched that and I've watched it a couple of times 'cos my boy watched it, because it started appearing in the papers, on the radio, on the news even it was on. (39-year-old groundsman)

> I was totally and utterly obsessed with *Big Brother* – I sort of planned my life round when it was on and everything and the whole family loved it. (31-year-old housewife)

> I was addicted to *Big Brother*. I sort of picked it up about half-way through though, once I started hearing all this talk and I had to watch it and see what it was all about, but I did follow it all the time then. (36-year-old housewife)

Words like 'hated' and 'addicted' indicate the way these viewers situated themselves in the media event of *Big Brother*. As Scannell points out, public talk about *Big Brother* is not accidental, and the orchestrated media hype surrounding the weekly nominations and evictions created a rich space for comment and speculation about characters and events in the *Big Brother* house. The 'discursive ferment' Scannell describes as characteristic of *Big Brother* talk ensures audiences are aware of the series, even if they do not watch it. The above viewer illustrates how 'hearing all this talk' about *Big Brother* encouraged her to 'see what it was all about'. Whereas for others, public speculation about the series proved a turn off: 'all you could see on the telly, in the paper *Big Brother, Big Brother* – it does your brains in' (41-year-old carpenter).

There is a common narrative to becoming a viewer of the first series of *Big Brother*. Many viewers began watching *Big Brother* out of curiosity, or because a friend encouraged them to watch the series, or because a family member watched the series – not because they wanted to watch the series themselves. As this viewer explained:

> I remember seeing it … I turned it on and I was like 'What is this?' I turned it over. And then a couple of weeks later when there was nothing to watch I watched it. (16-year-old schoolgirl)

This gradual involvement in the series is one common to many viewers. For others, their involvement is more rapid:

I didn't like it at first, I came back ... it started when I was away, I was away for a month and I came back and like everyone was talking about it. I was like 'What on earth is it?' I didn't know what the big thing was, I put it on and I was like 'this is a joke, this is pathetic!' And then my brother kept having it on, I kept watching and I got so into it. I was addicted! I was like mad, I was like 'I love it, I love it, I love it!' So I ended up absolutely loving it and then it stopped and I was crying. I was crying at the end! [laughs] I got so into it I started crying. (17-year-old female student)

This viewer came to *Big Brother* part way through the series. Because she was out of the country, she did not witness the gradual build up of public interest in the series, and therefore entered the *Big Brother* debate when it was in full swing – 'what on earth is this?' Her initial reaction was negative, but as she was regularly exposed to the series her criticism of *Big Brother* turned into an intense attachment for the series – 'I love it, I love it, I love it!' Her emotional response to the finale is a testament to the strong impression *Big Brother* made on her life that summer.

Talk about *Big Brother* encouraged people to watch the series, and to become involved in the day-to-day lives of the housemates. As people became involved in the micro-politics of the *Big Brother* house, they talked about the series with other viewers. For Scannell, this type of snowballing was crucial to the way *Big Brother* became a media event:

Talk was necessary to formulate your own views about who should go, and for that decision to have some validity claims, it needed to be grounded in assessments of the performances of the inmates in the house. Such assessments had a cumulative weight. The more you watched the programme, the more you knew about all the inmates, their personal traits, and the ways they interacted with each other. (Scannell 2002: 278)

For audiences, *Big Brother* was something to talk about with family, friends, work colleagues and strangers:

All of my friends have been watching it. Everyone talks about it, don't they? On Saturday we went for a meal, it was a friend of mine's birthday, and we sat round the table and I suddenly went 'Can you just tell me has anyone been watching *Big Brother*?', and they went 'yeah', and then all hell let loose. 'Oh my God he's an idiot' and all that. And that was a table of twenty-five people talking about it. It was the talk of the evening. (33-year-old female care attendant)

In this example, *Big Brother* acts as social glue, bringing together a group of people who share common knowledge of the series, making it 'the talk of the evening'. Scannell's comment on the way in which talk is 'grounded in assessments of the performances' of ordinary people is significant as talk about *Big Brother* is often about how the housemates perform themselves. As the above example illustrates, it is the activities of the housemates that provide material for gossip and speculation. When a particular dramatic episode occurs many viewers want to talk about what they have seen with others – 'Oh my God he's an idiot'. This specific type of talk about the improvised performances of non-professional actors raises significant issues regarding how audiences assess a hybrid genre such as a reality game show. In the next section I examine how watching and talking about *Big Brother* can lead to healthy debate about the development of popular factual television.

## Acting up

A reality series like *Big Brother* can be understood in terms of the tensions and contradictions between the performance of non-professional actors, and their authentic behaviour in the *Big Brother* house. This is, of course, not the only way to understand *Big Brother*, and other researchers have commented on the significance of surveillance (Palmer 2002), or the concept of media events (Scannell 2002; Couldry 2002), to our understanding of the popularity and impact of reality game shows. But, in terms of television audiences, there is evidence to suggest the improvised performances of ordinary people frame discussion of this series, and indeed other reality game shows.

In an article on *Big Brother* titled 'Performing the Real', John Corner comments on the 'degree of self-consciousness' and 'display' by the various personalities in the 'predefined stage' of the *Big Brother* house (Corner 2002b: 263–4). As Corner notes, the performance of contestants gives television audiences the opportunity for 'thick judgemental and speculative discourse around participants' motives, actions and likely future behaviour' (Corner 2002a: 264). In this section I want to focus on the way audiences speculate and judge moments when the performance of non-professional actors breaks down, and they are 'true to themselves'. Corner sums up this viewing process as follows:

> One might use the term 'selving' to describe the central process whereby 'true selves' are seen to emerge (and develop) from underneath and, indeed, through, the 'performed selves' projected for us, as a consequence of the applied pressures of objective circumstance and group dynamics. A certain amount of the humdrum and the routine may be a necessary element in giving this selving process, this unwitting disclosure of personal core, a measure of plausibility, aligning it with the mundane rhythms and naturalistic portrayals of docusoap, soap opera itself, and at times, the registers of game-show participation. (Corner 2002b: 263–4)

Other researchers have also discussed this notion of 'performed selves' and 'true selves' co-existing in hybrid formats within reality programmes. Jane Roscoe and Criag Hight discuss the 'performed' nature of docusoaps, and how this type of construction of documentary footage can open up space for debate about the documentary genre (Roscoe & Hight 2001: 38). Jane Roscoe comments on how *Big Brother* is 'constructed around performance', with participants involved in different levels of performance, based on the roles of 'housemate', 'game show contestant' and 'television personality', and how audiences are invited to join in with these performances 'across the formats of the different shows' (Roscoe 2001: 482). Lothar Mikos *et al.* (2000), in their research of *Big Brother* in Germany, also suggest audiences are engaged in an assessment of performance and authenticity.

In my research, audiences frequently discuss the difference between performed selves and true selves in a hybrid format such as *Big Brother*. In the survey I conducted, 70 per cent of the adult sample believed ordinary people act up in reality programmes (see Hill 2002). This high degree of expectation about the performance of ordinary people in reality programmes means audiences spend a great deal of time speculating and assessing the behaviour of people, and comparing the motives and actions of people who choose to take part in a reality programme such as *Big Brother*. And they discuss the behaviour of ordinary people in *Big Brother* on an everyday basis. Here is a typical example of the way viewers talk about acting in *Big Brother*:

> Sometimes, I think, can you really act like your true self when there's a camera there? You know. Maybe in *Big Brother* a little bit more you can act yourself because you're going to forget after a while aren't you? But I'm a bit dubious about people acting themselves ... The way they were all acting, the way of their body movements and all that, it just looked too fake to me. (21-year-old male dairy worker)

This viewer's tentative question about being able to 'act like your true self' in front of a television camera opens the door to speculation about levels of acting in the *Big Brother* house, and individual contestants' 'true' or 'fake' behaviour.

There is a common mode of engagement when watching *Big Brother* and this is characterised by discussion that goes backwards and forwards between trust and suspicion of the behaviour of ordinary people in the house. In the following debate, a group of male and female adult viewers discuss the various 'selves' on display in the *Big Brother* house:

> Rick: With *Big Brother* you don't know if they're playing up, yeah, it's just, it's a weird scenario for them to be in, you must just think ... well, you don't know what's going on inside their head.
>
> Paul: Maybe you put yourself in that situation and, see, it's like I watch it and if, if I was on *Big Brother*, I'd want everyone to like me or ... I think of myself as an alright person but then if I was on there I'd, I'd be acting different, thinking 'I've got to do this cos people are going to like me', so maybe that's, that's why, maybe, I think they're acting up.
>
> Peter: They must have thought about everything they've done and said before they actually said or done it. Not like real life, just someone coming out with a comment, but, this could get me out this week – I better not say that, I better just say 'does anyone want a cup of tea?' Not cos I want to make it but I better ask them to look good.
>
> Pauline: Cos at the end of the day, it's a competition, isn't it? There was seventy grand on the line, wasn't there? I'd act up for it! [laughs]

Their discussion is characterised by a hesitant assessment of the abilities of *Big Brother* contestants to 'act up'. A point to remember is that the *Big Brother* contestants are strangers to themselves, and to viewers. Unlike celebrity reality game shows, such as *Celebrity Big Brother*, where we know the 'personality' of the contestants beforehand, in the case of ordinary-people shows, the participants are strangers to us. Thus, when audiences attempt to judge the difference between the contestant's performing selves and true selves in *Big Brother*, they cannot refer to past performances but must rely on their own judgement of the contestants' behaviour and 'what's going on inside their head'. Inevitably, viewers turn to their own experience, and speculate about how they might behave in a similar situation. The discussion therefore becomes one based on hypothetical situations – 'if I was on *Big Brother'* – interspersed with knowledge of the format, and the effect of the game on contestant's behaviour – 'they must have thought about everything they've done and said before they actually said or done it'.

Audience assessment of the performance of non-professional actors in *Big Brother* is often based on how well the contestants play the game, and also how well contestants remain true to themselves. In the above discussion, viewers made an oblique reference to the winner of the first series of *Big Brother* (Craig), who managed to remain popular with his fellow contestants and viewers by carefully balancing his performing self with his true self. The fact that Craig did regularly ask 'does anyone want a cup of tea?' made him appear like an ordinary person and at the same time someone who was trying to win over fellow contestants. Karen Lury suggests television audiences may be anxious about watching ordinary people perform because 'if real people convincingly "put on an act" where can sincerity, authenticity and real emotion be located with any conviction?' (Lury 1996: 126). In the case of reality game shows, any 'claims to the real' are immediately undermined by the ability of contestants to 'put on an act'. As Lury explains:

> While acting may be pleasurable when we know we are watching a performance (it is after all a 'skillful' activity) when an ordinary performer acts, we may become uncomfortably aware of how appearance and reality (the behaviour and the feelings) of the performer may be no more matched in the everyday than they are on screen. (Ibid.)

*Big Brother* has capitalised on this tension between appearance and reality by ensuring viewers have to judge for themselves which of the contestants are true to themselves. In fact, audiences enjoy debating the appearance and reality of ordinary people in *Big Brother*. There is much potential for gossip, opinion and conjecture when watching *Big Brother* because this hybrid format openly invites viewers to decide not just who wins or loses, but who is true or false in the documentary/game environment.

Lury also suggests audiences may be uncomfortable about watching ordinary people on television because they have been 'coerced into making a fool of themselves, and that their presence or image on screen has been manipulated by technicians, producers and bullying presenters' (ibid.). This type of 'uncomfortable' viewing position is applicable to certain forms of reality programming, such as crime-based reality programmes, where people may be perceived as 'victims' of ratings-driven popular factual television. However, with regard to *Big Brother*, the majority of audiences are not so much uncomfortable with the manipulation of contestants, but sceptical that anything that goes on in the *Big Brother* house can be 'unscripted' and natural. Thus, when contestants are given alcohol as a reward for completing various 'challenges', viewers are unlikely to blame the producers for the drunken behaviour of contestants, but to critically judge the housemates for making fools of themselves. Most viewers think any humiliation, or emotional trauma experienced by housemates is generated by housemates, and therefore cannot be trusted as genuine emotional experiences, experiences that in other circumstances would be viewed more sympathetically.

Most of the people involved in the making of *Big Brother* argue that ordinary people cannot act up twenty-four hours a day. For example, Dermot O'Leary, the presenter of *Big Brother's Little Brother*, which accompanies *Big Brother* on Channel 4 and E4 in the UK, claims 'no one can act for 24 hours a day, or indeed, for 24 minutes an hour, so we know that the housemates' reactions are genuine' (O'Leary 2003: 10). It is not my intention to question the insider's perception of levels of acting in reality game shows. It is my intention to question how audiences make sense of such truth claims from the makers of *Big Brother* because the behaviour of ordinary people in *Big Brother* allows audiences to assess the truth claims of the programme itself. In the following extract, a group of teenage girls discuss an infamous scene in *Big Brother 1*. In the scene, 'Nasty Nick' was accused of attempting to influence the voting behaviour of other contestants, and after denying the charge, he retreated to the bedroom, where he packed his suitcase, shed a few tears and listened to advice from fellow housemate Mel. The girls begin their discussion with a prompt from me about the possible 'crocodile' tears of 'Nasty Nick':

Interviewer: Do you think in that scene when he was crying that was really coming from him?

Sharon: Erm, it could have been, cos in a way he was kicked out and he didn't have any way of winning now and … as you saw, the public was really negative towards him …

Nicola: I don't think that's as real life as it could have been, cos they know they're going to make quite a bit of money …

Angela: [shakes her head] I felt I knew the people in there, cos after a while, although there's cameras there, in the beginning they all did act up but you can't do it all the time. You know when you're upset and crying you can't act happy, you know what I mean. And you get really close to the people, cos you like get to know them. It's really weird, cos like we're talking about them now as if we know them and it's people we've never ever met in our lives who are on TV.

Interviewer: Are there moments when you're not sure? How do you tell if someone's acting up or not?

Nicola: I think if they're just like acting out of the normal, how you wouldn't expect someone to act and you just think they're acting up whether they are or not.

Interviewer: So, it's sort of based on what you think?

Nicola: Yeah, what you think they should act like, but if they're not acting like that.

Laura: No, but some people are extroverts though, you can't say that. Some people are very forward and open-minded and they don't care what people think. But I think you can always tell when people are showing off.

Angela: Yeah, but if you genuinely like them. Say, I liked Anna and if someone said 'oh, Anna's this, oh Anna's that', I wouldn't think she's acting up, do you know what I mean. I think it depends on your attitude towards the person. Do you know what I mean? Cos people genuinely didn't like Nick cos they'd seen that he was doing these kinds of things … yeah and I hated Mel so whatever anybody said that was good about her, I was like 'oh, I don't like her, whatever she does, she's a bitch.'

Sharon: I think the only people that could tell if these people are acting up are the people that knew them. We don't know them so we couldn't really judge.

Interviewer: Do you end up judging anyway?

Sharon: Yeah, well I do!

Laura: But they have to be acting up at the end of the day cos if they want to get our votes, they can't sit there and ... say, they're a really bitchy person, they're not going to sit there and literally be a bitch about everyone cos then they're going to be kicked out. They've got to put on an act, they've got to try and make the effort and they've got to try and sweeten us up so we won't kick them out.

Angela: But none of them know, that's the thing, none of them in the house would actually really know if like one of them was acting up or not...

Laura: That's what I'm saying.

There are several points raised in this discussion that are relevant to the issue of performance. The first is that there is no clear agreement about the performing self and true self of the character of Nasty Nick. Even though he appeared to break down and reveal his true self in a moment of personal conflict, according to these viewers he needed sympathy from the public, and therefore his tears could be perceived as part of a performance. They are suspicious of Nick because they have witnessed his duplicitous behaviour prior to the housemate's intervention, and because he is a contestant in a game show. Another point is that the discussion has a backwards and forwards rhythm characteristic to talk about what is real and what is not in reality game shows. *Big Brother* is not 'as real life as it could have been' because of the game show element to the format, but contestants in the house cannot act all of the time, so parts of it are real. We 'get to know' the housemates intimately, as if they are people we have actually met in our everyday lives, but 'we don't know them' because we have never really met them. In many ways their discussion about acting highlights a philosophical conundrum – how can we really know what we are seeing is real?

The sociologist Erving Goffman, in his book *The Presentation of the Self in Everyday Life* claims we are all performing all of the time. We perform our 'selves' on various different stages, such as work or home, to various different audiences, such as our boss, or our family. For Goffman, our houses, cars, clothing and other such everyday items are 'props' and 'scenery' required for the 'work of successfully staging a character' (Goffman 1969: 203). In any social encounter, a performer will be aware of their audience and vice versa. The process of communication between the performer and audience is an 'information game', where performers will reveal and conceal their behaviour to others (Goffman 1969: 20). On the *Big Brother* stage there are two types of audience, one that is inside, and another that is outside the house. The inside audience has first hand knowledge of the performance of individuals within the group, but this knowledge is only partial, as the contestants cannot witness all the actions, or performances, of the other members of the social group. The outside audience has second-hand knowledge, but is witness to, in Goffman's terms, the 'front' and 'backstage' behaviour of the housemates via the twenty-four-hour surveillance cameras. By front and backstage, Goffman refers to moments in social interaction when an individual ceases to play a part convincingly, when we see beyond a 'personal front', to the real person inside the performer (Goffman 1969: 34). In the discussion by the teenage girls about the performance of housemates they highlighted how 'none of them in the house would actually really know if like one of them was acting up or not'. This would suggest that viewers of *Big Brother* would have a privileged position in the 'information game', and be able to anticipate future incidents or behaviour, based on prior knowledge of the front and backstage behaviour of housemates. Certainly, in the scene with Nasty Nick, confrontation by the other housemates disrupted the natural harmony of the *Big Brother* house, literally 'creating a scene' which millions of viewers tuned in to watch. The housemates' intervention provided a backstage view of one particular performer, and cast a shadow on the believability of his remaining performance in the house. Audiences were already suspicious of Nick's performance prior to the intervention, and remained suspicious at the point when he had lost everything, and was most likely to reveal his 'true self'.

Although the above discussion suggests viewers do feel they have a bird's-eye view of events in the *Big Brother* house, there is a general questioning of how viewers can really get to know these performers at all. According to Goffman, when social interaction occurs, there is a 'natural movement back and forth between cynicism and sincerity' on behalf of performers and audiences (Goffman 1969: 31). In the teenage girls' discussion of *Big Brother* there is a 'natural movement back and forth' in their talk of how viewers judge the sincerity of ordinary people in reality game shows. It is in the act of trying to judge the scene change from performing self to true self that audiences debate whether what they are watching is true or not. And, it is in the act of talking about the truth claims of *Big Brother* that audiences debate significant issues concerning the authenticity of popular factual television. The more audiences watch and talk about reality TV, the more knowledge they have about how reality TV is put together (see Hill 2004 for further discussion). As these two teenage girls explain:

Laura: The next *Big Brother* will be rubbish ... They'll be trying too hard, everyone knows what to expect now and they're all going to try so hard! They'll know now what to do and how they can win people's votes...

Angela: Yeah, but then again, we'll have just as much knowledge as they do.

## Conclusion

When audiences watch *Big Brother* they are not only watching it for entertainment, but they are also engaged in critical viewing of the attitudes and behaviour of ordinary people, and the ideas and practices of the producers of *Big Brother*. As John Ellis points out, audiences of reality programming are involved in exactly the type of debates about cultural and social values that critics note are missing from the programmes themselves: 'on the radio, in the press, in everyday conversation, people argue the toss over "are these people typical?" and "are these really our values?"' (Ellis 2003: 11).

The sites we associate with reality series such as *Big Brother* are stages where ordinary people display their personalities to fellow performers and to audiences. The fact that *Big Brother* is set up to encourage a variety of performances, as contestants, as TV personalities, ensures such programmes are viewed as 'performative' factual entertainment. The manner in which ordinary people perform in *Big Brother* is subject to intense scrutiny by audiences. Audiences gossip, speculate and judge how ordinary people perform themselves and stay true to themselves in the spectacle/performance environment of *Big Brother*. Audience discussion is characterised by a natural movement backwards and forwards between trust and suspicion of the truthfulness of ordinary people and their behaviour on TV. Whether people are true or not in the way they handle themselves in the *Big Brother* house is a matter for audiences to debate and critically examine on an everyday basis. When audiences debate the authenticity of performances in reality programming they are also debating the truth claims of such programmes, and this can only be healthy for the development of the genre as a whole.

*Acknowledgements*

I would like to thank the people who took part in the focus group discussions and in-depth interviews for their time and their insights into the viewing experience of *Big Brother*. I would also like to thank Caroline Dover for her expert assistance in this research project.

*Notes*

1. Parts of this chapter have been adapted from the book *Reality TV: Audiences and Popular Factual Television* (Hill 2004) and the article '*Big Brother*: The Real Audience' (Hill 2002).
2. With regard to ethnicity, the sample of ethnic respondents is too small in the BARB sample to allow for any useful analysis.
3. The BARB ratings for Wednesday 11 July 2001 show that 626,000 viewers tuned in to watch E4, compared to 300,000 viewers for Channel 5 and 400,000 viewers for Channel 4 at the same time, 11pm.
4. See *Broadcast*, 31 July 2001.
5. See *Broadcast*, 1 August 2003.
6. Out of the main sample, the majority of adults (83 per cent of men and 85 per cent of women) and children (74 per cent of 10–15-year-olds) had not accessed websites related to factual entertainment. The principle reason cited (by 57 per cent of adults and 40 per cent of children) was not having access to the Internet. A further 36 per cent of adults and 25 per cent of children said that they had not visited the sites because they are not interested in them. Despite the fact that 50 per cent of 16–24-year-olds have access to the Internet, 82 per cent did not access these websites.

*Bibliography*

Corner, J. (2002a) 'Documentary Values', in A. Jerslev (ed.) *Realism and 'Reality' in Film and Media*. Copenhagen: Museum Tusculanum Press, 139–58.
\_\_\_\_\_ (2002b) 'Performing the Real', *Television and New Media*, 3, 3, 255–70.
Corner, L. (2000) 'The Addicted in Search of the Evicted', *Independent*, 29 August, 7.
Couldry, N. (2002) 'Playing for Celebrity: *Big Brother* as Ritual Event', *Television and New Media*, 3, 3, 283–94.
Ellis, J. (2003) 'Big Debate is Happening Everywhere but on TV', *Broadcast*, 27 June, 11.
Goffman, E. (1969) *The Presentation of Self in Everyday Life*. London: Pelican Books.
Hill, A. (2002) '*Big Brother*: The Real Audience', *Television and New Media*, 3, 3, 323–40.
\_\_\_\_\_ (2004) *Reality TV: Television Audiences and Popular Factual Entertainment*. London: Routledge.
Lury, K. (1996) 'Television Performance: Being, Acting and "Corpsing"', *New Formations*, 27, 114–27.
Mikos, L., P. Feise, K. Herzog, E. Prommer and V. Veihl. (2000) *Im Auge der Kamera: Das Fernsehereignis Big Brother*. Berlin: Vistas.
O'Leary, D. (2003) 'Interview', *Heat*, 31 May–6 June, 10.
Palmer, G. (2002) '*Big Brother*: An Experiment in Governance', *Television and New*

*Media*, 3, 3, 295–310.

Roscoe, J. and C. Hight (2001) *Faking It: Mock-documentary and the Subversion of Factuality*. Manchester: Manchester University Press.

Roscoe, J. (2001) ʻ*Big Brother* Australia: performing the "real" twenty-four-seven', *International Journal of Cultural Studies*, 4, 1, 473–88.

Scannell, P. (2002) ʻ*Big Brother* as Television Event', *Television and New Media*, 3, 3, 271–82.

# CHAPTER 4

*Daniel Chandler and Merris Griffiths*

# WHO IS THE FAIREST OF THEM ALL?
## Gendered Readings of Big Brother UK

## Introduction

The UK version of *Big Brother* was launched in 2000 and had reached its fourth series at the time of writing. Viewers are actively encouraged to view the show 24/7 on E4, which offers a live feed to the *Big Brother* house and options to 'go interactive', with added top-ups in the form of carefully edited daily scheduled shows on Channel 4 (and S4C in Wales). It is up to us to decide which of the housemates is 'evicted' from the house on a weekly basis by phoning or texting our votes, with additional polling on-line, and our decisions are informed by the accompanying media frenzy of endless tabloid speculation. Further analysis is offered by the spin-off show *Big Brother's Little Brother* (also Channel 4), to ensure that we have plenty to talk about with friends and colleagues. Fans of the show find themselves in the company of these 'characters' for a prolonged period of time, within a virtual 'social circle', and are prompted to make judgements about them. So how do viewers relate to those onscreen?

Big Brother 2 began on 25 Friday May 2001, running for its usual ten weeks. The official *Big Brother* website posted a link to a questionnaire set up by Janet Jones and Daniel Chandler at the University of Wales Aberystwyth on 26 Saturday June (during

Week 5). We closed the questionnaire on 16 Friday July (during Week 8), having received over 8,000 responses from viewers – 2,987 male and 5,173 female (reminiscent of a ratio commonly reported for soap-opera audiences). The subset of the data that we are exploring here includes demographic data about the viewers themselves plus questions about which characters they 'liked' the most, 'disliked' the most, thought that they were 'most like', most 'wanted to be like', and had most 'sympathy for', as well as about which character was 'most similar' to someone they knew. We also asked for their reasons for making these judgements. At the time of initial posting, seven of the original ten *Big Brother* contestants still lived in the house (Bubble, Amma, Paul, Elizabeth, Dean, Helen and Brian) along with Josh, an additional housemate who had been introduced later in the series. In previous weeks, three other contestants had been 'evicted' from the house (Penny, Stuart and Narinder), while Bubble, Amma and Josh were 'evicted' during the time that we were gathering the data.

## Looking into the mirror

What might we expect in mediated relations between viewers and viewed? Social identity theory suggests that we seek out that which supports our social identity (Abrams & Hogg 1990). Lazarsfeld and Merton use the term *homophily* to describe 'a tendency for friendships to form between those who are alike in some designated respect' (Lazarsfeld & Merton 1954: 23). Successful interpersonal relationships are more often than not based on similar age, socio-economic status, religion and ethnic background (Berger & Kellner 1964; Kerckhoff 1974; Kandel 1978). The empirical evidence in relation to interpersonal relations overwhelmingly supports the proverbial wisdom that 'birds of a feather flock together' (or 'like attracts like') rather than that 'opposites attract'. While this may be true of interpersonal interaction, does it also apply to what Horton and Wohl (1956) describe as 'parasocial relations' between readers (or viewers) and texts?

From classical times it has been theorised that audiences seek some kind of reflection of themselves in textual characters. Aristotle, in his *Poetics*, argued that we must perceive the tragic hero as sufficiently like us for us to feel pity for (empathy with) his undeserved misfortune. Some theorists argue, more sociologically, that we may be drawn to textual characters similar to us in 'certain major social characteristics, such as sex, age and race' (Maccoby & Wilson 1957: 77). Perceived similarity may involve a certain amount of wishful thinking. The viewer/viewed relation between audience and textual characters is often theorised as something of a 'magic mirror' (Horton & Wohl 1956: 222). Psychoanalytically-oriented theorists have argued that we may narcissistically seek in textual characters an idealised image of what we *would like to be* (an 'ego-ideal') (Zajonc 1954).

What we may call 'the mirror hypothesis' in relation to the moving image, then, is that viewers will tend to relate favourably to those onscreen who are either *like themselves* (the mirror) or who represent what the viewer *would like to be like* (the magic mirror). Empirical evidence has been advanced to support the mirror hypothesis, particularly with regards 'reflections' of gender. For instance, Maccoby and Wilson (1957) found that, among twelve-year-olds, 90 per cent of girls and 84 per cent of boys favoured same-sex leading characters in films (both 'liking' and 'wanting to be like' them). Is the mirror hypothesis reflected in the *Big Brother 2* data? We will look at each of the key variables in turn.

## Age

| Viewers who liked... | Under-26s onscreen Brian, Bubble, Paul, Amma and Helen | | 26+ onscreen Dean, Josh, Stuart, Elizabeth, Narinder and Penny | |
|---|---|---|---|---|
| | no. | % | no. | % |
| Viewers under 26 N=4787 | 4044 | 84.5 | 726 | 15.2 |
| Viewers aged 26+ N=3389 | 2717 | 80.2 | 650 | 19.2 |
| X²=23.2 (p<0.0001) | | | | |

Table 1: *Liking, by age*

(i) When we compare the viewers who named the onscreen person they most *liked* we find that although the under-26s were overwhelmingly the most liked overall, about 4 per cent more of each group favoured those from their own age-group. This is enough to constitute an extremely significant statistical difference (see Table 1, above).

| Viewers who wanted to be like... | Under-26s onscreen Brian, Bubble, Paul, Amma and Helen | | 26+ onscreen Dean, Josh, Stuart, Elizabeth, Narinder and Penny | |
|---|---|---|---|---|
| | no. | % | no. | % |
| Viewers under 26 N=4787 | 587 | 12.3 | 1193 | 24.9 |
| Viewers aged 26+ N=3389 | 953 | 28.1 | 913 | 26.9 |
| X²=121.5 (p<0.0001) | | | | |

Table 2: *Wanting to be like, by age*

(ii) Asked whom they most *wanted to be like*, the differences became more marked. More than twice as many of the older group wanted to be like one of those popular under-26s, suggesting the influence of the magic mirror (see Table 2, above).

(iii) Viewers were much more likely to see themselves as most like one of their own age group onscreen than as like one of the other age-group. Here, the differences become very dramatic as the mirror comes into play (see Table 3, opposite).

| Viewers who *saw themselves as most like...* | Under-26s onscreen Brian, Bubble, Paul, Amma and Helen | | 26+ onscreen Dean, Josh, Stuart, Elizabeth, Narinder and Penny | |
|---|---|---|---|---|
| | no. | % | no. | % |
| Viewers under 26 N=4787 | 2096 | 43.8 | 1656 | 34.6 |
| Viewers aged 26+ N=3389 | 865 | 25.5 | 1468 | 43.3 |
| $X^2$=202.5 (p<0.0001) | | | | |

Table 3: *Most like, by age*

### Ethnicity

| Viewers who *liked...* | White onscreen | | Non-white onscreen Dean, Amma and Narinder | |
|---|---|---|---|---|
| | no. | % | no. | % |
| White Viewers N=7834 | 7036 | 89.8 | 764 | 9.8 |
| Non-white Viewers N=342 | 274 | 80.2 | 63 | 18.4 |
| $X^2$=27.1 (p<0.0001) | | | | |

Table 4: *Liking, by ethnicity*

(i) Open-ended responses referred to race only in the context of *disliking* a housemate. For instance, of Bubble, one viewer wrote: 'He's just white trash' while another described Amma as a 'moody two-faced black bitch'. The statistical comparison of white versus non-white viewers shows that while the (more numerous) housemates who happened to be white were generally markedly more popular regardless of the ethnicity of viewers, the non-white housemates were nearly twice as popular amongst the non-white viewers, who were also less likely to like the white housemates onscreen. Clearly, the mirror matters for a significant minority (see Table 4, above).

(ii) Similarly significant differences emerged when we looked at the issue of whom viewers *saw themselves as most like*. A majority of white viewers saw themselves as most like a housemate who happened to be white. While, again, more non-white viewers favoured a white rather than a non-white housemate in this respect, over 30 per cent of non-white viewers saw themselves as most like one of the non-white characters – once again, the mirror makes a difference (see Table 5, overleaf).

| Viewers who *saw themselves as most like...* | White onscreen | | Non-white onscreen Dean, Amma and Narinder | |
|---|---|---|---|---|
| | no. | % | no. | % |
| White Viewers N=7834 | 4348 | 55.5 | 1489 | 19.0 |
| Non-White Viewers N=342 | 144 | 42.1 | 104 | 30.4 |
| | X²=32.4 (p<0.0001) | | | |

Table 5: *Most like, by ethnicity*

## Social class

The only socio-cultural indicator that we had for the viewers was newspaper readership. The viewers' own open-ended responses to why they chose particular characters in response to our various questions provided scattered references to social class which referred to five of the housemates: Bubble – the only one referred to explicitly by some viewers as working-class; Dean – referred to dismissively as a *Guardian*-reader by one viewer; Paul, referred to explicitly as middle-class, and Stuart and Elizabeth, both referred to variously as middle-class and upper-class. We took the viewers' lead and examined the pattern of attitudes to these five housemates.

| Viewers who *liked...* | Bubble | | Dean | | Paul | | Stuart | | Elizabeth | |
|---|---|---|---|---|---|---|---|---|---|---|
| | no. | % | no. | % | no. | % | no. | % | no. | % |
| Tabloid[1] Readers N=249 | 653 | 15.4 | 153 | 3.6 | 213 | 5.0 | 17 | 0.4 | 110 | 2.6 |
| Broadsheet[2] Readers N=2039 | 170 | 8.3 | 184 | 9.0 | 66 | 3.2 | 19 | 0.9 | 153 | 7.5 |
| | X²=216.3 (p<0.0001) | | | | | | | | | |

Table 6: *Liking, by social marker*

[1] *Daily Mail, Daily Star, Daily Express, Mirror* and *Sun*; [2] *Financial Times, Guardian, Independent, Telegraph* and *Times*

(i) Only seven viewers referred explicitly to class as the reason for liking one of the housemates, and all of these referred to Bubble. Ten others alluded to social class as a reason for *disliking* one of the other housemates. The statistical comparison of tabloid versus broadsheet readers on the issue of *liking* produced an extremely significant difference. Clearly, tabloid readers were much more likely to like Bubble than broadsheet readers were, while broadsheet readers were much more likely to like Dean or Elizabeth. So once again the mirror comes into play for some viewers. Perceived membership of one's own social group seems to have interacted with the likeability of those onscreen for some viewers. However, the largest percentage difference (over Bubble) is only 7.1 per cent and overall these figures account for only 27 per cent of the tabloid readers and 28.9 per cent of the broadsheet readers (see Table 6, opposite).

| Viewers who wanted to be like... | Bubble | | Dean | | Paul | | Stuart | | Elizabeth | |
|---|---|---|---|---|---|---|---|---|---|---|
| | no. | % | no. | % | no. | % | no. | % | no. | % |
| Tabloid Readers N=249 | 338 | 8.0 | 284 | 6.7 | 107 | 2.5 | 54 | 1.3 | 248 | 5.8 |
| Broadsheet Readers N=2039 | 59 | 2.9 | 236 | 11.6 | 38 | 1.9 | 24 | 1.2 | 165 | 8.1 |
| X²=106.1 (p<0.0001) | | | | | | | | | | |

Table 7: *Wanting to be like, by social marker*

(ii) Echoing the pattern of liking, tabloid readers were much more likely to see Bubble as a model than broadsheet readers were while broadsheet readers were more likely to name Dean or Elizabeth as models than tabloid readers were. Here we see an intimate link between liking and wanting to be like (see Table 7, above).

| Viewers who *saw themselves as most like*... | Bubble | | Dean | | Paul | | Stuart | | Elizabeth | |
|---|---|---|---|---|---|---|---|---|---|---|
| | no. | % | no. | % | no. | % | no. | % | no. | % |
| Tabloid Readers N=249 | 394 | 9.3 | 338 | 8.0 | 276 | 6.5 | 40 | 0.9 | 579 | 13.6 |
| Broadsheet Readers N=2039 | 72 | 3.5 | 269 | 13.2 | 76 | 3.7 | 33 | 1.6 | 438 | 21.5 |
| X²=160.9 (p<0.0001) | | | | | | | | | | |

Table 8: *Most like, by social marker*

(iii) As for *seeing themselves as most like* one of the housemates, the pattern is repeated with the same pivotal housemates in this regard – Bubble once again attracting more tabloid support while Elizabeth and Dean attract more broadsheet support. Interestingly, the largest percentage point difference here (7.9) relates to Elizabeth (see Table 8, above).

### Sexual orientation

We considered the issue of sexual orientation because there were two self-identifying gay men in the programme – Brian and Josh. There were also four apparently heterosexual men in the programme but Brian was so widely popular that he became the eventual winner. There were no self-identifying lesbians in the programme this time round (although there were passing references to Amma being bisexual). We focus here on the gay male housemates and on male viewers.

| Viewers who *liked*... | Heterosexual Same-Sex Onscreen | | Non-Heterosexual Same-Sex Onscreen | |
|---|---|---|---|---|
| | no. | % | no. | % |
| Heterosexual Male Viewers N=2301 | 952 | 41.4 | 702 | 30.5 |
| Non-Heterosexual Male Viewers N=686 | 61 | 8.9 | 480 | 70.0 |
| $X^2=349.5$ (p<0.0001) | | | | |

Table 9: *Liking, by orientation*

(i) A massive majority of non-heterosexual viewers listed one of the two self-identifying gay housemates as the person onscreen whom they most liked, while of the heterosexual viewers, those who favoured heterosexual housemates clearly outnumbered those who liked one of the gay housemates. Here the principle of homophily is very strongly evident (see Table 9, above).

| Viewers *seeing self as like*... | Heterosexual Same-Sex Onscreen | | Non-Heterosexual Same-Sex Onscreen | |
|---|---|---|---|---|
| | no. | % | no. | % |
| Heterosexual Male Viewers N=2301 | 1381 | 84.9 | 246 | 15.1 |
| Non-Heterosexual Male Viewers N=686 | 122 | 25.8 | 351 | 74.2 |
| $X^2=625.9$ (p<0.0001) | | | | |

Table 10: *Most like, by orientation*

(ii) Even more dramatically, these groups showed almost opposite trends in relation to those whom they saw themselves as *being like*. In relation to same-sex screen housemates an overwhelming majority of each group of viewers saw themselves as being like someone of the same orientation on the screen (see Table 10, above).

(iii) A similar pattern (only slightly less dramatically polarised) applied to *wanting to be like* one of the onscreen housemates (see Table 11, opposite).

| Viewers *wanting to be like...* | Heterosexual Same-Sex Onscreen | | Non-Heterosexual Same-Sex Onscreen | |
|---|---|---|---|---|
| | no. | % | no. | % |
| Heterosexual Male Viewers N=2301 | 809 | 64.2 | 451 | 35.8 |
| Non-Heterosexual Male Viewers N=686 | 88 | 20.7 | 337 | 79.3 |
| X²=239.8 (p<0.0001) | | | | |

Table 11: *Wanting to be like, by orientation*

## Sex

Now we turn to the issue of whether (regardless of sexual orientation) there was any relation between the sex of the viewer and that of the onscreen character that they most favoured in terms of the various factors we were concerned with – *liking, seeing oneself as like* and *wanting to be like*.

| Viewers *liking...* | Same-sex onscreen | | Other-sex onscreen | |
|---|---|---|---|---|
| | no. | % | no. | % |
| Male Viewers N=2987 | 2195 | 73.5 | 773 | 25.9 |
| Female Viewers N=5173 | 1162 | 22.5 | 3991 | 77.2 |
| | X²= 2052.3 (p<0.0001) | | | |

Table 12: *Liking, by orientation*

(i) If we do a statistical comparison of liking same-sex versus liking other-sex the difference between male and female viewers is very dramatic indeed. At first glance we might assume that this is purely because the male housemates happened to be more likeable. If that were the case, it might be fairer to make the comparison absolute rather than relative – to males and females rather than same-sex and other-sex. Yet, an absolute comparison would still produce a Chi-Square value of 12.5 – much lower, but nevertheless a very highly significant difference (p<0.001) (see Table 12, above).

The pattern for the following factors will make clearer why a relative comparison may be justified. We might point to there being 6 male housemates compared to 5 female ones, but on the other hand female viewers were in a substantial majority (63: 37). We have already seen that *liking* is linked to the other factors. The top three in terms of overall popularity amongst our viewers were: Brian (4167), Helen (1149) and Bubble (1040). Brian was the most popular among both males (1115) and females

(3046), although this represented only 37.3 per cent of the males in comparison to 58.9 per cent of female viewers. Among male viewers, Bubble was the next most popular (18.6 per cent), while among female viewers the next most popular was Helen (14.8 per cent). Brian's extraordinary popularity certainly skewed the figures. But, as we shall see, there is more to this data than meets the eye.

| Viewers *seeing self as like...* | Same-sex onscreen | | Other-sex onscreen | |
|---|---|---|---|---|
| | no. | % | no. | % |
| Male Viewers N=2987 | 2100 | 70.3 | 226 | 7.6 |
| Female Viewers N=5173 | 3010 | 58.2 | 735 | 14.2 |
| $X^2$=105.02 (p<0.0001) | | | | |

Table 13: *Most like, by sex*

(ii) In terms of *seeing oneself as like* a housemate, in the figures overall (regardless of the sex of the viewer) the top seven were: Elizabeth (1,328), Helen (979), Brian (768), Dean (762), Narinder (612), Bubble (567) and Paul (428). Among male viewers, Dean topped this list (618), followed by Brian (440) and Bubble (415) and then Paul (385), whereas among female viewers the top four were Elizabeth (1,215), Helen (947), Narinder (560) and then Brian (326). In general, viewers were more likely to *see themselves as being like* a same-sex housemate on screen. The descriptive statistics bear out the general principle of homophily. However, a new pattern also emerges: statistical analysis demonstrates an extremely significant difference between male and female viewers in this respect. A much larger proportion of female than of male viewers (nearly *double*) saw themselves as being like an other-sex screen housemate, while 12 per cent fewer females than males saw themselves as being like a same-sex person on screen. This may lead us to see the data on *liking* in a somewhat different light (see Table 13, above).

(iii) For *wanting to be like*, the overall order was very clearly led by Brian (1488), followed by Dean (669), Helen (641), Elizabeth (515), Bubble (479), Narinder (436), Josh (377), Amma (208), Paul (186), Stuart (87) and Penny (22). For males the top five

| Viewers *wanting to be like...* | Same-Sex Onscreen | | Other-Sex Onscreen | |
|---|---|---|---|---|
| | no. | % | no. | % |
| Male Viewers N=2987 | 1685 | 56.4 | 219 | 7.3 |
| Female Viewers N=5173 | 1599 | 30.9 | 1592 | 30.8 |
| $X^2$=772.8 (p<0.0001) | | | | |

Table 14: *Wanting to be like, by sex*

were: Brian (494), Dean (394), Josh (294), Bubble (291) and Paul (144). For female viewers the top five were: Brian (992), Helen (568), Elizabeth (450), Narinder (380) and Dean (275). In relation to this issue, the statistical difference between male and female viewers was even more dramatic. Female viewers were *equally likely* to *want to be like* an other-sex housemate as a same-sex one. We can no longer downplay this apparent deviation from the primary tendency towards homophily in both interpersonal and parasocial relations in the case of sex (see Table 14, opposite).

## Reviewing the theories

This very marked pattern (both in parasocial and interpersonal relations) – which is invariably characterised as a greater relational 'flexibility' among females (rather than as a relative 'constriction' amongst males) – has been noted before in the research literature. For instance, Horton and Wohl remark that in watching films we are encouraged to 'identify' with the protagonist but that 'resistance is ... manifested when some members of an audience are asked to take the opposite-sex role – the woman's perspective is rejected more commonly by men than vice versa' (Horton & Wohl 1956: 221). The psychologist Grant Noble observes that 'researchers have long been puzzled because girls tend to "identify" with both male and female performers ... Boys, on the other hand, tend to identify only with male heroes' (Noble 1975: 53).

Building on Freudian theory, Laura Mulvey asserts that 'for women (from childhood onwards) trans-sex identification is a *habit* that very easily becomes *second Nature*' (even if it 'does not sit easily') (Mulvey 1988: 72). Indeed, Anneke Smelik suggests that 'it has become a general assumption of feminist film theory that female spectators are more fluid in their capacity to identify with the other gender' (Smelik 1999: 355). Neither film theory nor psychoanalytic theory is noted for an attention to empirical evidence, so we offer here some brief references to relevant findings.

In studies of 'modelling' in interpersonal relations, boys have been found to favour same-sex models more strongly than girls do (Bandura *et al.* 1961; Bandura, Ross & Ross 1963; Slaby & Frey 1975; Perry & Perry 1975; Bussey & Bandura 1984; Frey & Ruble 1992; Luecke-Alecksa *et al.* 1995). In one study, as early as 2 years of age, girls showed no differential emulation of female- and male-stereotyped activities whereas boys showed a stronger tendency to emulate male-stereotyped activities (Bauer 1993). Grusec and Brinker (1972) find that after 5- and 7-year-old children had watched a male and a female model simultaneously presented, the boys remembered significantly more of the actions of the male than of the female model, while the girls showed a less clear tendency to remember more of the actions of the female than of the male model.

Such findings have been echoed in studies of parasocial relations, where Reeves and Miller found that 'girls are more likely to identify with male characters than boys are to identify with females' (Reeves & Miller 1978: 83). Miller and Reeves (1976) find that 3rd–6th graders (approximately 8- to 11-years-old) overwhelmingly wanted to be like same-sex characters on television. However, while boys just named male characters, only about 70 per cent those named by girls were female. Reeves and Miller found that 'while both sexes identified more with same-sex TV characters ... females are almost equally as likely to identify with all characters on television as they are with same-sex models' (Reeves & Miller 1978: 83). Hoffner (1996) found that amongst 155 children aged 7–12 nearly all of the boys (91 per cent) chose favourite television characters of the same sex while just over half (52.6 per cent) of the girls did.

A significant developmental pattern has been noted. 'Gender constancy' – primarily a recognition of the relative stability of sexual identity – occurs about 6 years of age (Slaby & Frey 1975). Several studies have suggested that pre-school or 'pre-constant' children – boys or girls – tend to pay more attention to female than to male television characters (Anderson & Levin 1976; Alwitt *et al*. 1980; Luecke-Alecksa *et al*. 1995). Differential patterns emerge with the acquisition of gender constancy. Several studies have reported that for boys (though not for girls) gender constancy is associated with higher attention to a same-sex character on television (Slaby & Frey 1975; Luecke-Alecksa *et al*. 1995).

Many explanations have been offered for this pattern. In the Freudian tradition, identification with the same-sex parent is seen as stronger for boys than for girls because boys have to distance themselves from a primary identification with the mother. Chodorow (1978) argues that the normative pattern is for males to define themselves negatively in terms of difference from females. Certainly, sex-typing in boys has been found to be more rigid and to constrain cross-sex behaviour (Bem & Lenney 1976; Perry & Bussey 1979; Brookes-Gunn & Matthews 1979; Archer 1984; Frey & Ruble 1992). Boys tend to have a more homogeneous conception of sex roles than girls do; girls are less strongly identified with female sex roles than boys are with male sex roles (Brown 1957). Indeed, a complicating factor is that 'it is conceivable that boys would be reluctant to admit to identification with female figures even if they experienced it' (Durkin 1985: 81).

Girls may be less sex-typed because they suffer less intensive sex role pressure from adults and peers. It is more socially acceptable for females to behave in ways traditionally associated with the other sex (Huston 1983). Boys take 'sex appropriate behaviour' more seriously (Bandura 1986) and monitor their behaviour more than girls because they are more likely to be rebuked when this is seen to deviate from gender norms (Martin 1993; Fagot 1985). Parents (especially fathers) promote stronger differentiation of gendered conduct with boys than with girls (Maccoby & Jacklin 1974; Langlois & Downs 1980; Bradley & Gobbart 1989; Fagot & Hagen 1991). Bandura notes that boys tend to be criticised by teachers for engaging in activities considered inappropriate for their sex (Bandura 1986: 93). Peers also police masculinity among boys (Carter & McCloskey 1984). Negative sanctions for cross-sex behaviour are typically more severe for males than for females. The label 'sissy' is much more negative than 'tomboy' (Reeves & Miller 1978; Frey & Ruble 1992). According to social learning theory, the differential imitation of same-sex models is a key developmental phase helping to establish sex role identity. In relation to parasocial relations, the favouring of male characters onscreen by adolescent female viewers may sometimes, of course, represent heterosexual physical attraction (Fischoff *et al*. 1997; Durkin 1985: 81).

Girls realise at an early age the positive social valuation of male roles compared to female ones (Kuhn, Nash & Brucken 1978; Meyer 1980). Males have a more privileged social status. Traditionally female-related activities and characteristics are still less valued than male-related ones (Connor & Serbin 1978; Hall & Halberstadt 1980; Zalk & Katz 1978). Girls thus have an incentive to emulate other-sex models because of the perceived social power (rather than gender) of such models (Bandura, Ross & Ross 1963; Slaby & Frey 1975; Bussey & Bandura 1984) as well as notions of 'acceptance and approval' (Kohlberg 1967: 163). Sometimes, female attraction to male figures onscreen may be an attraction to stereotypically 'masculine' traits (Hoffner 1996: 399). Boys have a double incentive to favour same-sex models, because they are 'like self' and because of perceived prestige and power (Kohlberg 1967: 136).

While it would be epistemologically naïve to expect onscreen representations to 'reflect' demographic realities in the everyday world, such representations do remain symbolically important in reflecting dominant *values* in the world in which they were produced. Indeed to ignore this dimension would be to accept dominant values as 'natural' and unchallengeable. One posited reason for any tendency for more women than men to identify with other-sex characters onscreen is the overall under-representation of women onscreen (Reeves & Miller 1978: 82–3; Durkin 1985: 81; Hoffner 1996: 390; Fischoff *et al.* 1997). Luecke-Alecksa *et al.* (1995) argue that boys may need to observe adult same-sex models onscreen more than girls do partly because boys have less exposure to adult male models in everyday life. Girls, on the other hand, have less choice of same-sex screen characters to relate to. A survey published in 2002 by the Screen Actors Guild (SAG) surveyed cinema and prime-time television in the USA, declaring that 'women ... remain underrepresented in television and film'. It was reported that (although women constituted around 51 per cent of the US population), 'men received 62 per cent of the roles cast in 2001' (SAG 2002). The proportions were much the same as in previous years.

It is not simply a matter of relative proportions, however. Female characters on television and in the cinema have often been cast in minor roles or as victims while male characters onscreen have long enjoyed more exciting and interesting roles. However, some theorists argue that there may also be deeper biases. Mulvey has famously argued that (notably in its objectification of women as bodies on display) camerawork has favoured the [heterosexual] male spectator. She declares that 'regardless of the actual sex ... of any real live movie-goer ... the spectator identifies with the main male protagonist' (Mulvey 1975: 69, 12). She theorises that even female moviegoers thus identify with (and become accustomed to identifying with) what she termed the 'male gaze' (Mulvey 1975: 11). However, this purely theoretical stance has been widely criticised as overly deterministic.

Lauzen and Dozier (1999) note a correlation between the numbers of women employed behind the scenes and the extent to which women are shown on the screen. Women still constitute only a tiny minority of the writers, producers and executives in the television and film industries. Anticipated box-office returns obviously play a key role in deciding what kinds of movies are made. Many commentators refer to a widespread assumption amongst filmmakers and television producers that while genres traditionally favoured by (and primarily featuring) men (such as the western, detective story, science fiction, action-adventure) will also attract some women viewers, genres primarily associated with women (such as romance, domestic melodrama, family saga) tend to alienate the male audience (Seiter 1995: 166, 168). Fischoff *et al.* (1997) have provided evidence supporting this assumption. Men were more inflexible than women in their inclusion of films deemed as aimed at the other sex. Women were generally less dismissive of action-adventure films than men were of the romance genre. However, men in older age-groups were less gender-stereotypical in their film preferences and did include romantic films amongst their favourites. This is of course an additional disincentive against producers taking much account of female viewers. Consequently, it is hardly surprising that 'relative to films with the male point of view ... few women's films are produced' (Fischoff *et al.* 1997).

## Qualitative data

With the quantifiable patterns in mind, coupled with an outline of the research findings pertaining to gender and 'parasocial relations', we set about deciding upon a more specific focus for assessing the qualitative questionnaire responses.

Given the sheer volume of data that we collected, we decided to look in detail at the ways in which male and female respondents differentially related to the characters on-screen. We wanted to ascertain whether the gender of the respondent had a bearing on the type of *Big Brother* characters that they saw themselves as being 'most like' and the reasons that they gave for this. By extracting the key issues that became apparent when reviewing the literature, we were particularly mindful of the functioning or role of the 'mirror' phenomenon in relation to how the male and female respondents differentially related to the male and female *Big Brother* characters. That is to say, the lower likelihood of male respondents relating to an opposite-sex *Big Brother* character, and whether differential responses could be accounted for by a clearly apparent awareness of gender (by the respondent and in relation to the *Big Brother* character).

Given that the programme was primarily targeted at the 'youth' audience, we concentrated here on responses given by those under the age of 26. We likewise focused on the greatest volume of responses as per ethnic origin, extracting all responses made by 'white' viewers. We then narrowed things further by looking primarily at tabloid readerships (the so-called 'working-class majority'). As a result, we dealt with four key sub-sets of respondents:

- heterosexual white male tabloid readers under 26
- heterosexual white female tabloid readers under 26
- non-heterosexual white male tabloid readers under 26 (including those iden-tifying themselves as gay, bisexual or 'not sure')
- non-heterosexual white female tabloid readers under 26

These sub-sets could arguably be seen as the most substantial and/or important elements of the questionnaire data we collected because they formed the majority response and could be seen as broadly 'representative' of the *Big Brother 2* viewers as a whole.

It should be noted from the outset that there was a slight bias towards commenting on and responding to the *Big Brother* characters who remained in the house the longest. The first two housemates to be evicted from the house (Penny and Stuart), for example, initiated very few responses, while those who remained until the final week (Brian, Helen, Dean and Elizabeth) elicited the greatest number of responses. One might suggest that this would be expected given that prolonged acquaintance with the longer-running *Big Brother* characters afforded the audience more time to form opinions about them. While we retain an awareness of this issue, we were not overly concerned about whether it skewed the overall patterns of response, especially given the fact that there was a fairly equal gender balance amongst the housemates when the questionnaire was posted on-line.

We approached the qualitative data on a number of different, increasingly pene-trative levels. We began by asking ourselves whether there were any general patterns in the responses made by *all* the male respondents in relation to the female *Big*

*Brother* characters, and *all* the female respondents in relation to the male *Big Brother* characters. Then, we refined our focus by looking specifically at the responses given by members of the four sub-sets outlined above. The main question was whether the male and female respondents saw themselves as being most like onscreen characters for the same or for different reasons. Within the first stage of analysis (looking at responses by all the respondents), we attempted a basic categorisation of the nature of the qualitative responses – the reasons why they saw themselves as being most like a particular *Big Brother* character. This came under closer scrutiny at the second stage of response analysis (looking at specific sub-sets). It was possible to identify a number of common response patterns regarding how the respondents identified with the *Big Brother* characters. What was most interesting, however, was the fact that the respondents made few references to gender.

In general, the respondents (whether male or female and whether responding to male or female *Big Brother* characters) referred to a number of common factors – a generalised approach to determining 'likeness' – which might feasibly be accounted for in terms of the 'mirror' phenomenon. There were even many instances of viewers remarking on the mundane fact that they shared the same name as a *Big Brother* character. We were able to generate certain key fields of response pertaining to: 'positive' and 'negative' character traits, physical appearance, demographics (in the broadest sense of lifestyle and social background), the 'self' as perceived by the self (that is, considering oneself as being like a *Big Brother* character based on how one sees oneself – the 'mirror') and the 'self' as perceived by others (iconsidering oneself as being like a *Big Brother* character based on how others see you). Each of these fields of response will be considered in turn.

### Character traits

Of all the reasons given for being most like a *Big Brother* character, the dominant response type was reference to character traits (both positive and negative). On the whole, the respondents all seemed to value the same kinds of seemingly 'positive' character traits, such as someone having a good sense of humour (discussed in detail later), being laid-back and easy-going, or being honest. Likewise, the respondents picked up on and criticised similar 'negative' character traits such as aggression, loudness and being argumentative or offensive. Character traits were clearly seen by the respondents as being a powerful tool with which to 'measure' and assess which of the *Big Brother* characters they considered themselves to be most like. Indeed, of those who offered a reason as to why/how they identified with a given character, 79.6 per cent of the heterosexual males and 90 per cent of the heterosexual females referred to at least one character trait. Similarly, 84.7 per cent of the non-heterosexual males and 96 per cent of non-heterosexual females also referred to one or more character trait.

While slightly differing descriptive terms were used, the basic nature of the responses towards character traits generated a strong picture of how the audience tended to perceive (and consequently 'characterise') the *Big Brother* characters. Interestingly, these descriptive terms were essentially 'neutral' in the sense that it would be impossible to generate a list of gender-based binary oppositions pertaining to differential male and female responses towards male and female *Big Brother* characters, hence suggesting the perceived unimportance of gender.

### Physical appearance

In seeking to reveal the relative importance of physical appearance as a factor in assessing 'likeness', we considered references to the general appearance of the characters (facial features and physique), hair cut and hair colour, and clothes or fashion sense. For the most part, physical appearance was noted if respondents perceived themselves as possessing similar attributes to the *Big Brother* characters. This tendency might arguably be said to (almost literally!) reflect the classic conception of the 'mirror', in that an individual seeks out someone 'like' them. Within the entire sample of responses, those who took exception to an aspect of physical appearance – as being 'unlike' themselves in some way – contradicted the pronounced trend of seeing oneself as being 'the same' in this respect. Within the heterosexual male sub-set, for example, only Bubble and Stuart provoked mixed responses from those who wished to make distinctions. In the case of Stuart, the only respondent to refer to his physical appearance stressed that he did not have anywhere near the same kind of 'muscles', while one respondent claimed to be 'not as ugly' as Bubble was, and two others drew the line at his wearing stupid hats!

Similarly, in the context of the heterosexual female sub-set, responses were fairly consistent and straightforward for all the *Big Brother* characters, except for Helen. The main issue to arise from the data was Helen's blond hair colour. It is arguable that this was one of Helen's most distinguishing features, but it is also something that has endless socio-cultural connotations. Indeed, the issue is fraught with complexity in the context of this data because it was often unclear whether the respondents were simply referring to 'blond hair' as a point of fact, or whether they referred to 'blond' in relation to apparent levels of intelligence, as a code word connoting someone who is stupid, thick, dizzy and/or dumb. There were numerous comments to the effect of: 'I'm like Helen, but I'm not as blond as she is.' This is an intriguing point to note, in that physical appearance can often act as a precursor for judgements about character and even metamorphose into a kind of character trait in its own right.

### Demographics

When making judgements about 'likeness', some of the respondents did refer to age, gender, sexual orientation, nationality, class/social background, ethnicity or profession. These demographic factors might be interpreted as having varying degrees of impact and significance both to the respondents and to the wider society – an effective dem-onstration of the 'mirror' being tilted at different angles.

One notable pattern that emerged was the divide between those respondents who saw themselves as being most like a *Big Brother* character as a direct result of 'demography', and those who saw themselves as being most like a *Big Brother* character except for a particular demographic detail that did not 'match' with their own. The responses to Brian and Josh were interesting within the context of the heterosexual white male sub-set, for example, given that both characters were openly gay. While many of the respondents saw themselves as being most like Brian, sexual orientation was an issue for 13 of the 78 who gave a reason because they took great pains to stress that they themselves were 'not gay'. Likewise, 4 of the 7 individuals who saw themselves as being most like Josh distanced themselves from the 'gay thing'. Similar patterns were evident in the heterosexual female sub-set. This trend seemed indicative of the fact that 'demography' could act as a form of distinction, as much as a point of relation – a kind of 'anti-mirror' as much as a 'mirror'.

Characters such as Bubble and Paul, on the other hand, prompted more definite 'like-drawn-to-like' reasons based on demographic factors such as class/social background, in that they were frequently seen as representing 'London geezers', 'lads' or 'normal blokes down the pub'. Similarly, Dean drew positive responses for being a Brummie and a bit older than the other contestants, Brian drew parallels for being Irish and Helen for being Welsh. These qualitative responses clearly tie in with the quantitative data outlined earlier, and support the 'mirror' idea in its most fundamental sense.

Gender prompted distinctions from all audience sub-sets, with frequent reference to being most like a *Big Brother* character *apart from sex*. In the context of the non-heterosexual male and female respondents, for example, two men saw themselves as being most like Elizabeth and Narinder respectively, even though they stressed that they were 'not female', while two women saw themselves as being most like Bubble and Josh respectively, even though they were 'not male'. Here, at least, the respondents were clearly aware of gender as a differential factor, although one could argue that because the greatest proportion of qualitative responses made no reference to gender it was largely 'invisible'. Again, the nature of the distinctions made in the context of demographics might point at contradictions and tensions between the 'mirror' and the acknowledgement of 'difference'.

### Intelligence

An interesting branch of demography, tied in with the factors of social class and background, which became apparent as a distinct reason for acknowledging 'likeness' was the apparent intelligence of certain *Big Brother* characters. We looked at issues relating to: intellect, levels of education, apparently high and/or low intelligence. Interestingly, all references to 'intelligence' pertained to the apparently high levels of intellect exhibited by the *Big Brother* characters, except in the context of Helen where respondents consistently referred to her apparent stupidity. In these instances, respondents either admitted to being as 'thick' as Helen was, or marginally less stupid.

In the case of Helen, the heterosexual female respondents were divided in their reference to her 'intelligence'. While 57 of the 434 respondents followed the general trend of admitting that they were as thick as she was, 12 of the 434 respondents went to lengths to stress that they were not nearly as stupid. One particularly amusing response might, however, lead us to suspect that levels of 'stupidity' were fairly consistent amongst those who saw themselves as being like Helen as one respondent professed: '(I) do pride myself with a little more interlectual [sic] skills'!

One interesting and more general point to note was that there was often a positive correlation between apparent intellect and perceived social class. Dean and Elizabeth emerged as the two characters most frequently perceived as intelligent, and were additionally referred to as being 'middle-class' or 'well educated', supporting the emergent patterns from the quantitative data in relation to newspaper readership.

### Concepts of the 'self'

There was a greater tendency for respondents to assess *Big Brother* characters in terms of the 'self' as perceived by the self, rather than in terms of the 'self' as perceived by others. However, one might reasonably account for this given that many more individuals possess a stronger concept of how they see themselves compared with how they are seen by others, so ensuring a clearer basis for comparison.

Two further interesting phenomena emerged from an initial 'sweep' of the qualitative responses, with implications for perception of the 'self' in relation to the 'mirror' phenomenon. Firstly, many respondents often interpreted 'liking' and 'being most like' a *Big Brother* character as being one and the same thing (something already apparent in patterns that emerged from the quantitative data). In other words, if they liked a particular character for whatever reason, they were also likely to see themselves as being most like that character. This might well be a case of 'like choosing like' in the sense of the 'mirror' – seeking out a similar individual and forming a bond with them. Alternatively, one might seek out individuals perceived to be 'like' oneself as a form of ego-boost, whereby a recognisable and 'likeable' trait in one person can be transferred to the self as being equally 'likeable' (particularly in the eyes of others), illustrating the concept of the 'magic mirror'.

Secondly, a number of respondents talked about themselves as being most like not just one but a composite of more than one *Big Brother* character. That is to say, the respondents tended to pick and choose a selection of different character traits and behaviours, as exhibited by more than one character, seeking to build a picture of how they saw themselves. A (heterosexual) male respondent, for example, when giving a reason as to why he saw himself as being most like Paul, commented: 'I'm more like a cross between Brian and Paul. Like Brian, I can be funny, serious and caring. While like Paul, I can handle pressure without letting it get me down and I never let my head get too big when being complimented.' Similarly, a (heterosexual) female respondent commenting on Elizabeth noted: 'I am torn between Elizabeth – because although I stick to my beliefs I can also be a very calming influence, Amma – because I find it hard to talk about my true feelings and although loud I'm quiet around louder people, and Paul – because I'm vain.' This tendency to 'identify' with more than one *Big Brother* character points at the fact that seeing oneself as being most like someone is highly complex and very much down to how individuals perceive others (often in the context of or in relation to themselves).

## Humour

An interesting factor came into play in relation to the 'self' or more specifically the 'social self', across all viewer sub-sets, which was consistent and universal reference to the importance of humour. We found repeated patterns of response while looking at the abundance of references to: sense of humour; being humorous; being fun/ny; being a joker, prankster, trickster, entertainer or comedian; being witty or 'a laugh', or being comical and amusing, which also feeds back into the importance placed on positive character traits (see Cann & Calhoun 2001). Probing deeper into established research in relation to humour, we began to realise that it intersected the key factors addressed in this chapter – gender, sexual orientation, popularity and power – in direct relation to the 'mirror' phenomenon.

Humour is an essentially positive feature of social interaction; it is something that we are drawn to, where being able to laugh with someone is affiliative. A shared sense of humour demonstrates a common point of view and outlook on life, becoming an integral part of what is termed 'in-grouping', creating micro-boundaries and marking as 'other' anyone outside that group. Indeed, humour is central to the formation of interpersonal relations (Cann, Calhoun & Banks 1997). Within the broader research on humour and its various social functions, the classic gender pattern is seen to emerge (see, for example, Lundell 1993). In the context of a mixed-sex social group, men are more likely than women are to prompt laughter from both men *and* women within that group (Provine 2000). This can feasibly be explained in terms of an unspoken power relation amongst genders, where men are granted the 'licence to be funny' based on their perceived social status (a trend echoed in research on humour in the workplace, where the all-powerful boss is guaranteed to prompt more laughter to jokes than a mere worker would – see Coser, cited in Provine 2000: 29). With this theory in mind, one might reasonably argue that the male *Big Brother* characters would prompt more laughter from or be perceived as more humorous by the ('masculinised') audience simply because they were male and not necessarily because they were more entertaining than their female counterparts.

The situation for women is complex, in that more laughter will be apparent in single-sex groups, where women interact with one another in the 'feminine' context, than would be socially 'allowed' in a mixed-gender group with its established male-biased power dynamics. Female humour, as found cross-culturally and in studies of female stand-ups (Provine 2000), falls into two categories – political and self-deprecating – where the latter is arguably more apparent in the domesticated context of *Big Brother* and arguably more acceptable to both genders because it is less intimidating and outwardly challenging. In light of this, Helen was the clearest demonstration of self-deprecating humour during comical declarations about her own stupidity.

The most illuminating issue relating to the apparent importance of humour, however, might help to cast light on the seemingly universal appeal of Brian as alluded to in our earlier review of the quantitative data (cf. Cann and Calhoun 2001). Essentially, Brian epitomised the gay stereotype as an 'unthreatening honorary woman', offering a view of the male world in a non-male way. He clearly played up to his role – as cast by the other *Big Brother* characters and stressed by the respondents who spoke of his exuberant 'campness' – and performed the essentially 'feminine' humour role of non-political self-deprecation. This is where an explanation for his universal popularity is likely to lie, in that Brian's humour was satisfying for both males *and* females (in and out of the house), in that he proved non-threatening to the men and on a par with the women, ensuring that it would be difficult for anyone to actively object to or pull against his presence.

## Conclusion

We began by outlining the 'mirror hypothesis' – that viewers will tend to relate favourably to those onscreen who are either *like themselves* (the mirror) or who represent what the viewer *would like to be like* (the magic mirror). Our statistical analysis showed that the attraction of onscreen characters for *Big Brother 2* viewers did seem to be related at least partly to the extent to which these characters reflected some key demographic features of the viewers themselves (age, ethnicity, social class and sexual orientation). However, there was a marked departure from this pattern in relation to sex: while the underlying pattern was sustained (usually most viewers were drawn to onscreen characters of the same sex), significantly more female viewers were prepared to relate to an other-sex character onscreen than male viewers were (a pattern which had been noted before in the research literature).

Our qualitative data supported the mirror phenomenon, with viewers being drawn to those who were in some ways like themselves. However, viewers themselves rarely referred to demographic factors and focused primarily on the assessment of (positive and negative) character traits. Given the high levels of statistical significance in the quantitative data, what appeared to be happening was that most viewers were not aware of the importance that (a significant number of) viewers attach to the demographic reflectivity of the mirror – in this sense, viewers seem to think in terms of looking through a window rather than into a mirror. Of course, we are seldom conscious of the extent to which our attitudes or behaviour conform to social trends, and we routinely think of ourselves as largely autonomous individuals.

As for those female viewers who favoured male characters onscreen, the reasons they offered did not reveal any distinctively different traits that they admired in these males. If female viewers are indeed 'more flexible' in favouring other-sex characters onscreen, then they do not seem to be conscious of this. There is, of course, often a gap between what people say (as a conscious process of articulation) and what they do (in relation to how they routinely behave). Perhaps, as Mulvey suggests, 'trans-sex iden-tification is a *habit* that very easily becomes *second Nature*' (Mulvey 1988: 72). While our data strongly supports the phenomenon outlined in the literature – that females are more likely to relate to an opposite-sex onscreen character – it does not go very far in explaining it. However, it can be seen as part of the 'magic mirror' phenomenon: a desire to 'be like' may, as some of the theorists suggest, represent a desire for some of the power accorded to males in patriarchal societies – most obviously, in this case, the desire for the power of popularity. Both 'the mirror' and 'the magic mirror' relations between the viewer and the viewed seem to be a largely invisible phenomenon but this invisibility may increase rather than reduce its significance (Chandler & Griffiths 2000). We all live in a highly-gendered social world where the 'masculine' is the unspoken 'norm' for both males and females.

*Liking* is evidently related to *seeing oneself as most like* and *wanting to be like* (we cannot, of course, establish the direction or strength of causality from survey data). In the extreme example of the eventual winner, 72.8 per cent of those who *wanted to be like* Brian (1084/1488) also *liked* him and 72.7 per cent of those who *saw themselves as like* him (558/768) also *liked* him. We have referred only in passing to the problematic concept of 'identification', which in our own usage has been no more than convenient shorthand for 'seeing oneself as most like'. However, we should note that the three inter-related factors we have discussed have frequently been treated by researchers as indirect measures of a process of viewer identification with onscreen characters (typically in filmic narrative). Whether or not viewers 'identify' with those onscreen, it seems that they may at least sometimes be seeking those onscreen who are in some sense a reflection of themselves. While the 'mirror' may be largely invisible, for some viewers at least, their relations with those onscreen are intimately involved with their own sense of identity.

*Acknowledgement*

The authors would like to thank Jason Rutter, Research Fellow at the ESRC Centre for Research on Innovation and Competition, University of Manchester (UK) for his specialist advice on issues of 'humour'.

# Bibliography

Abrams, D. and M. A. Hogg (1990) *Social Identity Theory: Constructive and Critical Advances*. Hemel Hempstead: Harvester Wheatsheaf.

Alwitt, L. F., D. R. Anderson, E. P. Lorch and S. R. Levin (1980) 'Preschool Children's Visual Attention to Attributes of Television', *Human Communication Research*, 7, 52–67.

Anderson, D. R. and S. R. Levin (1976) 'Young Children's Attention to *Sesame Street*', *Child Development*, 47, 806–11.

Archer, J. (1984) 'Gender Roles as Developmental Pathways', *British Journal of Social Psychology*, 23, 245–56.

Bandura, A. (1986) *Social Foundations of Thought and Action*. Englewood Cliffs, NJ: Prentice-Hall.

Bandura, A., D. Ross and S. A. Ross (1961) 'Imitation of Film-Mediated Aggressive Models', *Journal of Abnormal and Social Psychology*, 66, 3–11.

_____ (1963) 'Vicarious Reinforcement and Imitative Learning', *Journal of Abnormal and Social Psychology*, 67, 601–67.

Bauer, P. J. (1993) 'Memory for Gender-Consistent and Gender-Inconsistent Event-Sequences by Twenty-Five-Month-Old Children', *Child Development*, 64, 285–97.

Bem, S. and E. Lenney (1976) 'Sex Typing and the Avoidance of Cross-Sex Behavior', *Journal of Personality and Social Psychology*, 33, 48–54.

Berger, P. L. and H. Kellner (1964) 'Marriage and the Construction of Reality', *Diogenes*, 45, 1–25.

Bradley, B. S. and S. K. Gobart (1989) 'Determinants of Gender-Typed Play in Toddlers', *Journal of Genetic Epistemology*, 150, 453–5.

Brookes-Gunn, J. and W. S. Matthews (1979) *He and She: How Children Develop Their Sex-Role Identity*. Englewood Cliffs, NJ: Prentice-Hall.

Brown, D. G. (1957) 'Masculinity-Femininity Development in Children', *Journal of Consulting Psychology*, 21, 197–202.

Bussey, K. and A. Bandura (1984) 'Influence of Gender Constancy and Social Power on Sex-Linked Modeling', *Journal of Personality and Social Psychology*, 47, 6, 1292–302.

_____ (1992) 'Self-Regulatory Mechanisms Governing Gender Development', *Child Development*, *63*, 1236–50.

Cann, A. and L. G. Calhoun (2001) 'Perceived Personality Associations With Differences in Sense of Humor: Stereotypes of Hypothetical Others with High or Low Senses of Humor', *Humor*, 14, 2, 117–30.

Cann, A., L. G. Calhoun and J. S. Banks (1997) 'On The Role of Humor Appreciation in Interpersonal Attraction: It's No Laughing Matter', *Humor*, 10, 1, 77–89.

Carter, D. B. and L. A. McCloskey (1984) 'Peers and Maintenance of Sex-Typed Behavior: The Development of Children's Concepts of Cross-Gender Behavior in Their Peers', *Social Cognition*, 2, 294–314.

Chandler, D. and M. Griffiths (2000) 'Gender-Differentiated Production Features in Toy Commercials', *Journal of Broadcasting and Electronic Media*, 44, 3, 503–20.

Chodorow, N. (1978) *The Reproduction of Mothering: Psychoanalysis and the Sociology of Gender*. Berkeley: University of California Press.

Connor, J. M. and L. A. Serbin (1978) 'Children's responses to stories with male and female characters', *Sex Roles*, 4, 637–45.

Durkin, K. (1985) *Television, Sex Roles and Children: A Developmental Social Psychological Account*. Milton Keynes: Open University Press.

Fagot, B. I. (1985) 'Changes in Thinking About Early Sex Role Development', *Developmental Review*, 5, 83–98.

Fagot, B. I. and R. Hagen (1991) 'Observations of Parent Reactions to Sex-Stereotyped Behaviors: Age and Sex Effects', *Child Development*, 62, 617–28.

Fischoff, S., J. Antonio and D. Lewis (1997) 'Favorite Films and Film Genres as a Function of Race, Age and Gender'. Available at: www.calstatela.edu/faculty/sfischo/media3.html

Frey, K. S. and D. N. Ruble (1992) 'Gender Constancy and the "Cost" of Sex-Typed Behavior: A Test of the Conflict Hypothesis', *Developmental Psychology*, 28, 714–21.

Grusec, J. E. and D. B. Brinker (1972) 'Reinforcement for Imitation as a Social Learning Determinant with Implications for Sex Role development', *Journal of Personality and Social Psychology*, 21, 2, 149–58.

Hall, J. A. and A. G. Halberstadt (1980) 'Masculinity and Femininity in Children: Development of the Children's Personal Attributes Questionnaire', *Developmental Psychology*, 16, 270–80.

Hoffner, C. (1996) 'Children's Wishful Identification and Parasocial Interaction with Favorite Television Characters', *Journal of Broadcasting and Electronic Media*, 40, 389–402.

Horton, D. and R. R. Wohl (1956) 'Mass Communication and Para-social Interaction: Observations on Intimacy at a Distance', *Psychiatry*, 19, 215–29.

Huston, A. C. (1983) 'Sex Typing', in E. M. Hetherington (ed.) *Handbook of Child Psychology* (Vol. 4) New York: Wiley, 387–468.

Kandel, D. (1978) 'Similarity in Real-Life Adolescent Friendship Pairs', *Journal of Personality and Social Psychology*, 36, 306–12.

Kerckhoff, A. C. (1974) 'The Social Context of Interpersonal Attraction', in T. Huston (ed.) *Foundations of Interpersonal Attraction*. New York: Academic Press, 102–43.

Kohlberg, L. (1967) 'A Cognitive-Developmental Analysis of Children's Sex-Role Concepts and Attitudes', in E. E. Maccoby (ed.) *The Development of Sex Differences*. London: Tavistock, 81–173.

Kuhn, D., S. C. Nash and L. Brucken (1978) 'Sex-Role Concepts of Two- and Three-Year-Olds', *Child Development*, 49, 445–51.

Langlois, J. H. and A. C. Downs (1980) 'Mothers, Fathers and Peers as Socialization Agents of Sex-Typed Play Behaviors in Young Children', *Child Development*, 51, 1237–47.

Lauzen, M. M. and D. M. Dozier (1999) 'The Role Of Women On Screen and Behind the Scenes in the Television and Film Industries: Review of a Program Of Research', *Journal of Communication Inquiry*, 23, 4, 355.

Lazarsfeld, P. F. and R. K. Merton (1954) 'Friendship as Social Process: A Substantive and Methodological Analysis', in M. Berger, T. Abel and C. H. Page (eds) *Freedom and Control in Modern Society*. New York: Van Nostrand, 18–66.

Luecke-Alecksa, D., D. R. Anderson, P. A. Collins and K. L. Schmitt (1995). 'Gender Constancy and Television Viewing', *Developmental Psychology*, 31, 5, 773–80.

Lundell, T. (1993) 'An Experiential Exploration of Why Men and Women Laugh', *Humor*, 6, 3, 299–317.

Maccoby, E. E. and C. N. Jacklin (1974) *The Psychology of Sex Differences*. Stanford,

CA: Stanford University Press.

Maccoby, E. E. and W. C. Wilson (1957) 'Identification and Observational Learning from Films', *Journal of Abnormal and Social Psychology*, 55, 76–87.

Martin, C. L. (1993) 'New Directions for Investigating Children's Gender Knowledge', *Developmental Review*, 13, 184–204.

Meyer, B. (1980) 'The Development of Girls' Sex-Role Attitudes', *Child Development*, 51, 508–14.

Miller, M. M. and B. Reeves (1976) 'Dramatic TV Content and Children's Sex Role Stereotypes', *Journal of Broadcasting*, 20, 35–50.

Mulvey, L. (1975) 'Visual Pleasure and Narrative Cinema', *Screen*, 16, 3, 6–18.

_____ (1981) 'Afterthoughts on "Visual Pleasure and Narrative Cinema" Inspired by *Duel in the Sun*', *Framework* 6, 12–15; reprinted in C. Penley (ed.) (1988) *Feminism and Film Theory*. New York: Routledge, 69–79.

Noble, G. (1975). *Children in Front of the Small Screen*. London: Constable.

Perry, D. G. and L. C. Perry (1975) 'Observational Learning in Children: Effects of Sex of Model and Subjects Sex Role Behavior', *Journal of Personality and Social Psychology*, 31, 6, 1083–8.

Perry, D. G. and K. Bussey (1979) 'The Social Learning Theory of Sex Differences: Imitation is Alive and Well', *Journal of Personality and Social Psychology*, 37, 1699–1712.

Provine, R. R. (2000) *Laughter – A Scientific Investigation*. London: Faber and Faber.

Reeves, B. and M. M. Miller (1978) 'A Multidimensional Measure of Children's Identificiation with Television Characters', *Journal of Broadcasting*, 22, 1, 71–86.

Screen Actors Guild (1999) Press Release (3 May). Available at: www.sag.org/diversity/press_releases/pr-la990503.html

_____ (2002) Press Release (1 July). Available at: www.sag.org/pr/pressreleases/pr-la020701.html

Seiter, E. (1995) 'Toy-based Video for Girls: *My Little Pony*', in C. Bazalgette and D. Buckingham (eds) *Not In Front of the Children: Screen Entertainment and Young Audiences*. London: British Film Institute, 166–87.

Slaby, R. G. and K. S. Frey (1975) 'Development of Gender Constancy and Selective Attention to Same-Sex Models', *Child Development*, 46, 849–56.

Smelik, A. (1999) 'Feminist Film Theory', in P. Cook and M. Bernink (eds) *The Cinema Book* (2nd edition). London: British Film Institute, 353–65.

Zajonc, R. B. (1954) 'Some Effects of the "Space" Serials', *Public Opinion Quarterly*, 18, 4, 367–74.

Zalk, S. R. and P. A. Katz (1978) 'Gender Attitudes in Children', *Sex Roles*, 4, 349–57.

# CHAPTER 5

*Ernest Mathijs and Wouter Hessels*

# WHAT VIEWER?
Notions of 'the Audience' in the Reception of Big Brother
Belgium

## Introduction: media and notions of the audience

One of the most polemic debates in the study of contemporary culture concerns the
interaction between media and its audiences. This chapter aims to contribute to that
debate by analysing how one specific media format, *Big Brother* Belgium, works with,
and brings along, different notions of 'the audience', depending on what perspective is
taken towards the viewer.[1] Generally, our goal is to bring some clarity to the complex
ways in which notions of 'audiences' play a role in how media texts are produced,
received and negotiated. Specifically, it is our intention to analyse to what extent media
texts and viewers themselves work with implicit (not necessarily less or more 'real')
notions of the audience, and how media studies should be aware of these notions in
order to choose its approach towards researching audiences.

*Big Brother* has become a worldwide phenomenon since its first broadcast in
1999, and much has already been written on the show (for writings dealing with *Big
Brother* Belgium see Biltereyst *et al*. 2000; De Meyer 2001; Mathijs 2002a; Mathijs *et
al*. 2003). Many of these writings address the relationship between media texts and
their audiences (see Mathijs 2002a for an overview of first season commentaries), and

several attempt to study the *Big Brother* audience (Hill 2002; Willems 2002). But what seems to be missing from many is a clear view of the different notions of audiences operating in the *Big Brother* discourse. Not only do authors using the word 'audience' mean different things with it, they also tend to ignore changes in the constellation and activity of actual and implied audiences throughout time. Instead they seem to treat an audience as a given set of data, habits and opinions, something which can be identified as 'the *Big Brother* audience', for now and forever.

A brief example of differences in the reception of the first and second season of *Big Brother* Belgium shows how much difference there can be in what 'the *Big Brother* audience' is. Press comments described viewers' engagement with the first season of *Big Brother* in terms of voyeurism, moral decline, peepshow-ism and, eventually, a tasteless desire for the new and exciting. Comments on the second season hardly used these terms at all. Instead, newspapers and magazines reported on the anticipated success of the show (the audience ratings) on expectations (especially of fans) and hardly ever addressed moral concerns any more (Mathijs 2001). It was as if, in a few months, the definition of 'the *Big Brother* audience' had shifted dramatically. *Big Brother* viewers had suddenly been equipped with an entire different set of needs, desires and habits. Instead of tasteless voyeurs, they were now depicted as curious thrill seekers.

The problem here is not so much the actual viewers; it may well be that different people watched the second season differently from the first. More remarkable is that these viewers should all of a sudden have taken on a completely different set of viewing habits. Previous attempts to study such changes have only led to vague descriptions like 'audience fatigue' and 'renewed audiences' (Mikos 2000).[2] A more detailed study is justified, however, and this not only calls for qualitative research, it also points to the necessity of naming the notions of audiences which operate in the *Big Brother* discourse.

This chapter, then, tries to investigate 'the *Big Brother* audience' by analysing the discursive environment of the second season of *Big Brother* Belgium. It asks in which ways producers and press handle specific expectations and impressions of the audience. It also asks how viewers view themselves. As such, this research investigates the bond between perceived audiences and real audiences. First, we will focus on how notions of the audience inform the production processes of *Big Brother 2*. We will specifically address the *audience awareness* of the format, the way in which producers try to anticipate and respond to perceived viewing experiences of *Big Brother*. Next we will investigate the press and public reception of the show. Controversies and aspects of morality in the 'politically correct discourse' around *Big Brother* play an important role here. Finally we will comment on the so-called 'real audience' of *Big Brother*, asking real viewers for their experiences.

## In search of 'the Big Brother audience': an overview of the literature

Before moving onto the research itself, it is worth looking at what kinds of audience notions already appear in other studies of *Big Brother*, what these seem to be missing and how this effects methods of searching for 'the *Big Brother* audience'. Even though the show itself has only been running since 1999 there is already quite a tradition of dealing with its audience.

The very first book to appear on *Big Brother*, by Henri Beunders, uses two notions of the audience. Beunders distinguishes between a 'public sphere' (in a Habermassian sense) that is being challenged by the coarseness of the format, and a 'real audience' (the actual viewers and fans) who exemplify the failure of that public sphere, celebrating its demise (Beunders 2000). Similar divisions are to be found in other early publications by Lothar Mikos (2000), Irena Costera Meijer and Maarten Reesink (2001) and Gust De Meyer (2001), as well as in countless commentary pieces on *Big Brother*, from *The Sun* to the *The New York Times* to *Cahiers du Cinéma* and *Le Monde Diplomatique*. With the exeception of Mikos, who uses materials from the RTL channel and focus group interviews, none of these contain actual analyses of audiences. And even Mikos places his analysis firmly within the two-tier distinction between public sphere and actual audience.

Daniël Biltereyst *et al.* (2000) make a first effort in tackling the diversity of the *Big Brother* audience. Building on work by Reesink, Biltereyst links *Big Brother* to two different viewing attitudes (both psychoanalytically inspired): a distanced attitude, associated with 'voyeurism', and an engaged attitude, associated with the concept of 'identification' (Biltereyst *et al.* 2000: 46). Further on, he adds two more psychologically motivated viewing attitudes to that: *Big Brother* may lead viewers to 'reflect' on '(inter)personal and emotional relations' and suggests 'participation and power during successive episodes of the show' (Biltereyst *et al.* 2000: 49). This quadruple distinction is much more sophisticated than previous ones, and allows for a range of theoretical considerations of viewing attitudes and roles. Yet, like Beunders, there is no elaboration as to *how* these attitudes and roles are actually embodied.

Attempts to link such attitudes to actual viewers can be found in several large-scale analyses of the 'real audience' of *Big Brother* (Hill 2002; Jones 2003). Annette Hill's investigation of the viewing habits of 8,000 viewers of reality TV[3] concludes that *Big Brother* viewers are not that different from whoever watches other reality TV programmes, with the notable exception that the show seems to attract a younger audience, and that adults with children made up a larger proportion of the audience than usual (Hill 2002: 331). Hill also concludes that viewers take on a range of complex viewing attitudes of attraction, approval and distinction in how they watch *Big Brother*. The most important reason to watch was to see how 'real people cope in a manufactured situation', how group conflicts evolve, and how participants deal with confessions – this of course refers to the 'engagement' and 'distancing' mentioned by Biltereyst (Hill 2002: 333). Hill also notes the tendency of viewers to use information from the show in discussing 'issues such as ethics or privacy'. In general, she states, '*Big Brother* spurs viewers to separate truth from fiction' while the 'general attraction to the management and/or transformation of the self' is the most important motive for how the show is being watched (Hill 2002: 336). Janet Jones' (2003) research largely confirms these conclusions, adding to it a tendency of viewers to stress the interactive elements of the show.

Although these studies allow for a quite accurate sketch of the *Big Brother* viewer, they are also limited. By focusing on what they call 'the real audience', through methods that allow the investigation of 'normal viewers' relation to the programme (questionnaires, interviews, focus groups), they only cover part of the spectrum identified by Beunders, ignoring the ways in which these audiences are being prepared, stimulated or hindered in taking on specific attitudes and roles in viewing *Big Brother*. For one, they do not succeed in explaining which actual attitudes fit which actual viewers, and where exactly the changes take place. Some studies have tried to cover this, by pointing out that viewing attitudes towards *Big Brother* have changed over time. For instance, an analysis of press and critics in Belgium shows that there has been an evolution from resistance to the format, to condoning it, to even support of it. And as Pamela Wilson's chapter on media-activism and *Big Brother* in this collection shows, diverse attitudes towards the show can give way to actual, physical attempts to intervene in it (Wilson 2004). And in her study of self-confessed fans of *Big Brother,* Jones points to the relevance of the ever-returning discussion on the activeness/passiveness of that audience. Her results also seem to indicate that the *Big Brother* format exactly defines itself through the multiple, diverse ways with which audience interaction is sought, established and broken up. In other words, *Big Brother* questions the ways *in which* publics are active/passive, and *to what extent (and when)* there is high or low audience investment (Jones 2000, 2003).

## Ancillary discourses and chronology in studying the Big Brother audience

These, and related, issues point to the necessity of re-addressing differences in how audiences are described (as implied or real), as well as in how comments on these audiences are embedded in larger discourses (on 'the public sphere' for instance). For lack of space, we will not go into that debate now. Suffice to say, at this point, that discussions about 'the end of the audience' (McQuail 1997: 138), 'the fragmented audience' (Gauntlett & Hill 1999: 288) and the importance of 'public roles' (Barker 1998: 184–91; Barker & Brooks 1998a: 218–32; 1998b) are among the most important concepts that need to be empirically addressed when talking about *Big Brother* audiences.

Adding to that, we would like to single out the significance of 'ancillary materials' (Barker 2004), a concept trying to point to the discursive importance of materials accompanying the media text.[4] As virtually every discussion of *Big Brother* emphasises, knowledge of what goes on around *Big Brother* (as opposed to what happens in the house) is of crucial importance for an informed understanding of the multimedia format, including the live exit shows, Internet coverage (24/7 live streams), press (*The Big Brother Magazine*), flow overs (reports on *Big Brother* in other shows – even in news bulletins) and spin-offs (*Celebrity Big Brother*). In his article on *Big Brother* as a ritual event, Nick Couldry calls these multimedia characteristics crucial for its interpretation (Couldry 2002: 286–90). This multimediality should hence also be taken into account when analysing *Big Brother*'s audiences.[5]

An essential part of studying ancillary discourses involves temporality or, better, topicality. All too often, audience research is a snapshot of a situation, offering interpretations between *such* snapshots as if they were evolutions of changes *in* audience attitudes. Hill recognises this problem when she stipulates that her corpus might in some way be affected by school holidays (Hill 2002: 331–2). Tellingly, Paddy Scannell refers to *Big Brother* as a *temporal event*, with which he means not so much its temporal aspect as its topicality (Scannell 2002: 272). Topicality, or the temporal co-occurence of arguments/discourses on the media text with arguments/discourses that are considered to be culturally relevant at the time (mostly of philosophical, sociological, political or moral nature) make media formats 'hot', turning them into a legitimate part of culture, whether it be hype, craze, trend or controversy. Taking topicality into account when dealing with *Big Brother* thus allows the cultural agenda of the time (and to some extent cultural history) to play a role in studying audiences' interaction with media.[6]

Both ancillary discourses and topicality have informed our methododology while studying *Big Brother* Belgium audiences. In the first instance we analysed how the producers of *Big Brother* have tried to use timing and topicality in anticipating, illiciting and reacting to controversies surrounding their format. This part of the research is based on interviews with production managers, directors, editors and crew, utilising published interviews and field work within the production company. On the basis of this data we can see how producers work with notions of the audience. We specifically concentrate on *Big Brother 2*, and refer to previous analyses for comparison (Mathijs 2002). Among the notions we specifically address are textuality and controversy. The second stage of this research, addressing the public discourse on *Big Brother*, also involves a comparison over time, between seasons one and two. We have analysed all *Big Brother*-related articles in the Flemish-speaking Belgian press, from prior to the show's first episode to a month after its final.[7] Third, we conducted a small-scale research into the so-called 'real audience' (the material viewer rather than the conceptualised viewer), asking fourteen viewers between 19 and 70 years old to keep diaries of their viewings of *Big Brother 2*. The diaries contained a semi-structured questionnaire (asking respondents to fill these in before the first diary entry and after the last) as well as a series of open questions set to illicit a free and personal report on their viewing attitudes and experiences.[8]

## The presumed audience and the Big Brother Belgium producers

The notion of the audience producers work with is of capital importance in researching the reception of *Big Brother*. A big problem with these anticipated and/or presumed audiences is the reliability of data about them. Making abstraction of pre-broadcast preference measurements, all there is to go with is the opinions of the makers them-selves, whether officially recorded (either in interviews or internal documents), or *off the record*.

Unsurprisingly, there is little data available and producers are not keen on sharing the few bits that are. Nevertheless, judging from interviews, it becomes clear that, for the first season, producers where predominantly concerned with the relationship of the audience to the commercial aspect of *Big Brother*. Given the fact the show was designed to be as profitable as possible (Verriest 2001: 108–12), all information on audiences was directed towards measuring that. Undisclosed documents do indeed show that audiences were primarily thought of in terms of 'how many *Big Brother* hamburgers they bought'. Apart from that, producers remained vague in their conceptualisation of *Big Brother* audiences. When pressed on the issue, they revert to psychological terminology. In interviews with producer Herman Bral (producer for the broadcaster *Kanaal 2*) this psychological discourse was a substantial frame of reference for talking about audiences (Verriest 2001: 160, appendix 8). And when network director Eric Claeys comments on the often repeated claim that *Big Brother* is 'non-television' (degraded television) he not only mentions the number of viewers, but also their psychological motivations:

> If *Big Brother* was non-television, we wouldn't have 1.7 million people watching the final episode? Admittedly, the programme appeals to voyeurism and viewers' curiosity, but those are exactly the same motiviations that make people read an interview with Gerrit De Cock [co-host for the second season]. Let us be honest, in this branch of work that's what we're all after. (*HUMO*, 2 October 2001: 32)

The use of psychological terminology is also recurrent in comments on *Big Brother 2*. Next to voyeurism, identification plays an important role:

> In any case, the people need individuals whom they can look up to, and with whom they can identify themselves. Television has a great power in that respect, even if there are downsides to that. (*Big Brother Magazine*, 28 November 2001: 50)[9]

These psychological frames of reference are extremely similar to the ones identified by Biltereyst *et al.* They polarise audience attitudes from passive (identification, addiction) to active (involvement), and they use generic keys (live show, soap) to differentiate between them (more activity with live shows, more passivity with soaps).

Many of the producers and hosts also hasten to stress the appeal *Big Brother* Belgium had among the higher socio-demographic categories. For host Walter Grootaers this needs to be linked to the textual qualities of *Big Brother*.

> You cannot really object to *Big Brother* if you possess some kind of intellectual capacity. Moreover, it has been shown that *Big Brother* can boast a faithful following among the so-called intellectual viewer of Canvas (Public Broadcaster's Second Channel). (*Big Brother Magazine*, 19 September 2001: 50)

What this particular quote shows is that connecting audience attitudes with the *Big Brother* text allows its producers to make claims about the quality of their product: apart from suggesting that they assume at least some kind of reciprocality between text and audiences ('people watch because the show is good'), it also enables them to reinforce their position against aesthetic attacks (of which there were many during the first season). As Claeys puts it: '[*Big Brother* is] fine, delicious television of superb quality and made with respect' (*HUMO*, 2 October 2001:32). The flipside of this is of course that it raises questions as to the agenda and 'quality' of the producer's own audience research.

Claeys also uses the connection between text and presumed audience (and its sensitivities) as a means of addressing the controversial reputation of the show. He even attempts to stress the constructedness of the show in trying to defuse some criticism:

> Above all, *Big Brother* is stripped of all sensationalism. If only you knew how much explicit nudity we have thrown out of the series. Cheap television producers would instead have included as much breasts and bottoms as possible. We never showed masturbation scenes either, except for the fiddling of Betty under her sheets. If any twelve-year-olds had been watching, they must have thought she was scratching her toes. Honestly, I don't understand all these criticisms. After all, *Big Brother* is only broadcast for one half-hour a day. Is that not allowed? Next to the hundreds of other programmes we can watch every week, *Big Brother* is actually an enrichment of the television landscape. (*HUMO*, 2 October 2001: 32)

But at the same time Claeys recognises the importance of broadcasting contestant Betty's 'fiddling', which presumes some kind of predetermination in the relationship between audience sensitivities and the text from the maker's point of view.

Actually, controversy is a recurring thread in discussions of *Big Brother* Belgium, both in its first and its second season. The producers are able to use 'controversy' to their advantage in two distinct and oppositional ways. On the one hand the producers have been forced, especially during the first season (see Mathijs 2002a), to defend themselves against accusations of indecency and sensationalism (Claeys' quote above echoes this). On the other hand they have, especially during the second season, tried to employ the notion of controversy as a means of ensuring continuous attention for the show (exactly the kind of thing they were accused of doing during the first season). This complicated double use becomes very visible in the run-up to the second season, as a stage in between the 'defending' and 'exploiting' as it were. The following quote dates from the first couple of weeks of the second season of *Big Brother*, but still refers to the first season controversy:

> Critics can't help being hypocritical. There are those who cannot say anything good about *Big Brother*, yet they are always watching it. But what I find much worse is the comments of those who never watch but do have strong opinions about it. (*Big Brother Magazine*, 19 September 2001: 50)

With remarks such as these, the producers seem to be forcing the issue of controversy back on the agenda. It means they ackknowledge its importance for the show's success, and are willing to exploit it. Yet they are not willing to take on the responsibility. So, when the actual controversy in the second season does erupt (as a result of a 'sex orgy' between the contestants), the producers stress textuality again, emphasising that what happens is part of the 'staging'; part of 'the game', suggesting that censoring this would prevent viewers from being able to make up their minds about the contestants. When Bral (producer) addresses the issue, he makes the link between controversy and textuality very clear, but he also shows his willingness to exploit the situation.

> Yes, we were surprised, but we were of course also very glad with what happened. It would be hypocritical to say we weren't happy with what happened ... Everybody knows the rules. Last year, we broadcast everything as well. Only then the sexual activities were spread over several weeks. (*Het Nieuwsblad*, 6 October 2001)

Note that the connection between controversy and textuality (as well as the willingness to exploit) is related to chronology, to what happened in the first season. Knowing that during the first season there was a huge amount of criticism that eventually led to nothing (and even transferred into a kind of admiration, see Mathijs 2001; 2002a), the producers employ this knowledge to make the assertion that it is not the show that is controversial (the text is still the same), but it is the viewers' attitudes, especially those of the critics, that are changing, something they refer to as *hypocrisy*.

The controversies around *Big Brother* Belgium demonstrate to what extent the makers use notions of the audience to market, defend and promote their product. It also demonstrates the producers' beliefs that the attitudes of the audiences they presume to be theirs can, in their opinion, be influenced, both by contextual elements (forcing controversy on the agenda), and by textual elements (the rules of the game). Psychological explanations as 'identification', 'addiction' and 'voyeurism' are employed to explain those attitudes. Contrary to what many producers and editors think, this does not necessarily mean that their presumed audiences actually behave the way they think they do. So, ironically, while producers and editors think they may be influencing audiences, it may actually be the case that it is the perceived behaviour of the presumed audiences instead that influences the production practices and, hence, the text.

## Textuality and controversy in the public reception

If the connection between textuality and controversy is of key significance for the producers, it is also of dominant importance to the public reception of *Big Brother*. According to most observations, the public debate on *Big Brother* is open to a wide range of participants, including critics, journalists, public intellectuals, politicians, opinion leaders and, of course, the producers themselves (Beunders 2000; Meers and Van Bauwel 2001; Mathijs 2002a). Given the active participation of the producers in the public debate (see above), it is worth investigating how this has fostered tensions.

For starters, it is necessary to point to the status of the debate. As mentioned earlier, the two seasons of *Big Brother* worldwide have resulted in quite distinct receptions. It has forefronted the importance of ancillary discourse (what fuelled the debates?) and chronology (how did the debates evolve?) in relation to notions of audiences in the discourses around the show. In the specific case of *Big Brother* Belgium, the awareness of the serial character of the show seems to have played a key role. At the end of the first season, there was a general feeling that any second season would have to deal with comparisons to (the success of) the first. This makes the period *between* the two seasons, and at the *beginning* of the second season, extremely important in setting the tone for its public debate and reception.

Generally, a strong emphasis is laid on textuality. During the first season a shift in attention occurred, from the contexts of the show to its textual features and this is continued between the two seasons and at the beginning of the second season. There is a general tendency to emphasise happenings related to the game (attention for small changes in the rules and for differences in the house's interior, wide coverage of the selection of candidates). The aim, especially in the newspaper press (which near the end of the first season undoubtedly benefited from coverage of the show), is to establish a direct link of recognition with the first season, while at the same time pointing to differences with it. Those differences are also related to the textuality of the show, and often stated in positive terms, expressing the expectation that the second season will be 'more thrilling', 'more intense'. It is remarkable that both the supporting press (often linked to the network VTM) and the more sceptical press (*De Standaard*, *De Morgen*, *HUMO*) hardly differ from each other in these predictions (Mathijs 2002b). This general consensus of agenda-setting should not be underestimated, as it helps to create the framework for the public reception and for how actual viewers will come to deal with the second season.

Does this mean that controversy disappears from the public agenda in the run-up to the second season? It does not, because, as has been stipulated above, the producers made sure that controversy was frequently addressed in interviews (if only in getting back at critics). It does mean that there was no 'natural' inclination to address controversy. Given the fact that controversies have played major roles in publicising *Big Brother* around the world, there has always been an implicit assumption that these controversies were provoked by the producers and editors, and, given the statements from Bral and others, it can safely be assumed that much effort has gone into ensuring that there would be controversy surrounding the second season (Mathijs 2001; 2002b).

A good example of this is the attempt to focus on sex. The above-mentioned 'sex orgy' in late September inevitably received much press attention and was widely debated (it was front-page news, and the newspaper *Het Nieuwsblad* even devoted an entire page to it a week after it happened). The post-show antics of runaway contestant Liesl, as a porn star, received equal attention (*P. Magazine*, 17 October 2001; *Big Brother Magazine*, 17 October 2001), but every single shot of nudity, and every request for contestants to pose naked for *Playboy* was widely reported (*Het Nieuwsblad*, 29 November 2001; 5 December 2001). It resulted in numerous debates and comments (letters to the editor, lead comments, see *Knack*, 10 October 2001; *HUMO*, 16 October 2001). In each case, the producers and editors were accused of illiciting and provoking such controversies. But the willingness to continue the debate can also be seen as an attempt by critics and commentators to return to arguments they themselves feel comfortable with. Arguments on morality, decency, aesthetics and sensationalism do allow for a much safer condemnation of *Big Brother*, evoking the tolerance for the text. The major difference is that by the time the second season controversies erupt, these comments are no longer grounded in actual viewers' concerns.

A perfect example of how notions of audiences inform the balance between textuality and controversy in both the producers' views and the public reception is the way the second season deals with the 11 September attacks on the World Trade Center in New York and the Pentagon in Washington. In the first instance, and true to the text, the inhabitants of the house were not informed of what happened. The fact that there was hardly any public outcry over this (not even in the show-business pages of newspapers), demonstrated the then dominance of *Big Brother* as a text in the public discourse. However, this dominance was threatened when the contestants reacted with utter disappointment to the fact that their weekly assignment had failed (they had glamour nude pictures made which were supposed to be published in major magazines – a clear attempt to stir some controversy). Their disappointment may be justified, but given the context it suddenly became inappropriate. It is not so much the fact that textuality is being overshadowed by elements from the outside world that is remarkable here, it is the fact that 9/11 is an ancillary discourse which no one in the public debate had control over. As a result, and in reaction to growing pressure from public opinion, the producers decided to inform the contestants. The official excuse for doing so was that a distant family member of one of the contestants had died in the attack. The network's official spokesperson visited the house and explained the situation (accompanied by images of the attack on a television screen!). This led to emotional reactions from the contestants, in turn leading to wide coverage of their genuine empathy. In a way, the informing of the contestants restored the balance between textuality and controversy and reinstated them as humans again when they were in danger of becoming mere characters (*Het Nieuwsblad*, 19 September 2001). A few weeks later, it becomes clear the balance was definitively restored when, accompanied by captions such as 'BB Wins The War' (*Het Nieuwsblad*, 9 October 2001) the public discourse accepts that 'the show must go on'. As Edwin Van Overveld writes in *P. Magazine*:

> Although only a few weeks ago friend and foe were shouting that the world has changed forever, once again today more people are watching *Big Brother* than the news. And that is a good thing. (*P. Magazine*, 17 October 2001: 3)

The 9/11 case study shows that ancillary discourses *can* cause the fragile balance between text and context in public debates to tilt. It also shows that such imbalances can be restored by recuperating contexts into the text. It points both to the importance of ancillary discourses and to the fact that by working dynamically with notions of audiences any imbalance can quickly be restored. At several points during the 9/11 case participants in the public debate have worked with different notions of the audience, shifting from 'uninterested in *Big Brother* because of the importance of 9/11', to 'concerned then outraged over the contestants lack of empathy', to 'a condolance for the contestants' shock', and 'back to the order of the day'. At no point in those few weeks have these notions actually been checked, and at no point has there been any doubting the fact that the participants in the public debate *knew* how people felt. It has always been assumed they did.

Put cynically, 9/11 shows that the name of the so-called public can and will be used to employ (and exploit) mechanisms to restore any shifts in the careful balance between text and context caused by unforeseen ancillary discourses. More objectively, the analysis of the public debate on *Big Brother* Belgium suggests that theoretical notions of audiences play an important role in debating its presence, limiting and setting frames of reference.

## The 'real audience': the diary as truth

By now, it should be clear that whoever the 'real audience' of *Big Brother* Belgium is, it comes freighted with assumptions, contradictions and actions. It is accused of doing things it may never have done (condoning, peeping, identifying, outrage). Its frames of reference seem to be bordered, with no escape possible. This makes the 'real audience' as much a theoretical notion as the 'presumed audience' or the 'public.' It is interesting, then, to see to what extent the 'real audience' effectively complies with these assumptions, if it uses the frames of reference, obeys them, and sees itself as a factor in determining both production practices and public opinion.

The results of our diary research show, in the first instance, a united view on what kind of viewers our respondents thought the show was meant for. The questions we included that asked them think to about what kinds of viewers they thought the makers had in mind when developing the show almost invariably led to an identification of 'a youth or young adult audience with loads of free time' as the prime target, with 'heavy television viewers' and 'sensation seekers' as notable exceptions. Tellingly, these are always referred to as 'they'.

When queried on their own viewing, our respondents demonstrated a broad range of comments and attitudes. Every single respondent had an outspoken opinion on *Big Brother*. They varied from extremely negative ('total aversion'; 'of no use to viewers'; 'lack of inspiration'; 'boring'; 'very bad television'), to nuanced ('in fact it's ridiculous but I like watching it'; 'rubbish, but I like watching it'), to extremely positive ('I love to see how people with different characters have to put up with each other for some time'; 'there is someone from Bruges and that makes it more fun to see'; 'quite thrilling', 'fascinating and relevant for society'.). No one seemed unopinionated about the show. Overall, there are more negative than positive remarks, and it is predominantly women who seem to be using positive terms.

Remarkably enough, hardly any respondents make comparisons between the first and second seasons (this was also noted in the research by Willems 2002). Those who do make comparisons do not tend to prefer the first season over the second, although, given the overall ratings for and public discourse on the second season, this was something that could be expected. The only time there is a real preference for the first season is when specific aspects of the show are discussed ('the winner of last year has more of an influence on things'; 'in my opinion the inhabitants of *Big Brother* One were more creative in collecting money'). Apparently, simularities and differences over time are not perceived as crucial to our 'real audience'. They also seem to resist thinking about the context of the show.

Looking at the viewing attitudes more closely, we found that most respondents concentrated on the textual element of *Big Brother*. At the foreground of the text are the contestants. Every respondent had a specific opinion on the contestants, often focusing on their relationship to cultural stereotypes in terms of personality, attitude and actions ('Thierry is always the simple, good-natured soul'; 'I am getting more and more sick of Dominique's face'; 'The show is Kurt's! Braggish attitude, even rude'; 'Aurore is very positive, full of life and spirit'; 'The way in which Kurt left the house was stupid. Very full of himself'). Apparently, *Big Brother*'s contestants invite extreme opinions, something that can be linked to how they are usually polarised in the public discourse (Mathijs 2002a; 2002b), but which contrasts with the producers view on that particular textual element. Claeys (Network Director VTM) suggested that: 'What is more beautiful than a group of nice, ordinary Belgians who control the script of their programme themselves?' (*HUMO*, 2 October 2001: 32).

Our diarists who did not like the contestants tended to be dismissive of the format as a whole. On the other hand, those respondents who said they liked the format tended to reflect more on the rules of the game, and how it is played. As a result, opinions on contestants are frequently connected to narrative components ('I hope Aurore gets the free card'; 'I would rather see Thierry leave'; 'In my view Thierry had deserved more, considering his efforts during the whole period'; 'The attitude of Kurt was appalling, he cannot deal with his nomination'). Bringing in the game rules to explain their personal opinions about the contestants allowed our respondents to view them as 'participants' rather than 'persons as such'. It means that, regardless of the focus on textuality, a thin distinction between people and characters remains, and it is exactly these small differences that are emphasised. In stressing the textual elements, our 'real audience' also reverted to some of the psychological terminology dominating the public discourse and also reinforced by the show's producers. Almost every diary claims that voyeuristic tendencies and a general curiosity are the most dominant reasons for watching *Big Brother*. Identification or the need for entertainment only feature in three diaries, but they are often alluded to. In contrast, an urge to follow sensationalism or the need to keep up with the hype is mentioned only once.

Next to textuality, controversy is also mentioned by respondents. Even though our small sample does not really allow for socio-demographic generalisations, a clear 'age' demarcation arises here, one that is not addressed by either the makers or in the public debate. All respondents older than forty, questioned the moral values displayed in *Big Brother*. The following comments were made about one specific episode where the contestants got drunk, leading to a 'sex orgy':

> I never drink alcohol but I can understand people who appreciate it. But it was again too much. Alcohol destroys so much, in every way, and the influence on the inhabitants!! And on some viewers?

*Big Brother* has no cultural value. Everything comes down to sex, arguing, and intrigues ... Everything resolves around alcohol and parties. Is this TV? ... Everything resolves around amusement, taking a sauna and teasing each other. The two ladies in the house don't do any work, just amusement. Is this life? Is this reality? ... It is the least I ever saw on TV. A waste of time.

Given the fierceness with which such moral judgments are made it is extraordinary that our diarists only sporadically accused the producers of provoking controversy ('A perverse attempt to sex up *Big Brother*'; 'Everything resolves around money and profit ... Everything is over-the-top. Sensationalised. They only show the images they [the television makers] want to broadcast. Everything is about stirring emotions'). Whereas similar remarks in the public debate and by the producers seemed to indicate some sort of connection between textuality and controversy, our 'real audience' seemed to prefer to make connections between controversy and contextual elements. In other words, the reasons for finding *Big Brother* controversial were often linked to ancillary discourses, rather than the text itself. The following quotes put this in perspective: 'I never drink alcohol but I can assume that ... it was too much again', and 'I wasn't looking forward to it because I absolutely don't like Casinos' (one assignment involved Casino games). Both quotes refer above all to the respondents' own attitudes and experiences, and how they use these to give meaning to the textual elements. The value they ascribe to that text is hence more a result of the negotiation of their own attitudes (a discourse to which neither makers nor public debate can relate since it belongs to the audience's private sphere)[10] than a pure deliberation on textual cues. This does not necessarily mean that such negotiations automatically infer a negative valuation of the show, as the following quote demonstrates:

The goal of *Big Brother* is probably only to entertain. Yet I expect that such programmes contain some 'messages' as well (smoking/drinking is bad, BOB campaigns [a Belgian 'if you drink don't drive' campaign], safe sex). In a pleasant way, but still ... I followed everything, I empathised with the inhabitants.

The context is recognised via the reference to 'messages', which are immediately connected to the frame of reference of televisional education. The positive connotation, encapsulated in the psychologically tinted 'empathised' does not block that recognition, nor does it prevent an implicit negative judgement on the contestants' behaviour (it is assumed here that they smoke, drink, drive when drunk, and have unsafe sex).

In sum, many of the features identified by the producers and in the public discourse are also present in the 'real audience'. There is an explicit emphasis on textual elements, connected with psychological terminology for how the viewing experience relates to them. There also is a tendency to stress controversial elements, but instead of linking them to the text they are rather linked to the ancillary discourse of the viewer's own attitudes and experiences, thus informing their opinion about the contestants.

## Conclusion

Notions of audience used by producers, in the public discourse and by 'real viewers', although very different in origin and goal, do seem to have some features in common. They use psychological terminology to explain viewers' (or their own) attitudes (with differences between 'active' and 'passive' positions); they stress the importance of reconising and dealing with the text (the rules, the plot); and when those textual elements collide with ancillary discourses, that is where controversy is evident.

At the same time there are differences, which often relate to agendas. For the participants in the public discourse a traditional balance between text and context (a heritage of modernism) remains predominant. Their tirades against 'postmodern hedonism', 'moral decay', 'the creation of a television event' and 'peeping tomism' all stem from that frame of reference. The producers and editors use a different framework: they try to reduce everything to the text, putting it forward as a 'great piece of work', and using it as a shield against any ancillary discourses that penetrate the storyworld (using the rules as a shield). Whenever intervention is inevitable it is seen as 'taking responsibility' (actually saving the text). For the 'real audience' ancillary discourses are less threatening. Instead, they are employed as crucial aspects of the meaning-making process, and they corroborate what 'real audiences' find controversial.

The most important conclusion needs to be that, taken together, all these similarities and differences allow for the identification of two general viewing attitudes with the *Big Brother* audience: a 'real one' (lacking another term), and a perceived one. The 'real attitude' is the one which directs and structures the mechanisms of making meaning (it differentiates textual elements and identifies controversies). The perceived attitude is not so much linked to actual viewers, but is rather the result of agendas of public concern (guarded by gatekeepers to the public discourse) and production strategies (guarded by the media industry). In both types of attitudes ancillary discourses play an essential role.

*Notes*

1 This chapter is part of a research project set up in 2000 by the RITS department of the Erasmus Institute for Higher Education Brussels, in collaboration with the Department of Communication Studies of the Free University of Brussels. It was financed by the Research Board of the Erasmus Institute for Higher Education Brussels (RADO, project number: STI 006 RITS). The project has since included a collaboration with the Department of Theatre, Film and Television Studies of the University of Wales Aberystwyth. We would like to thank Inge Vansweevelt (Erasmus Institute) and Janet Jones (UWA Aberystwyth) for their support to and comments on this project.

2 These observations were first presented at the international conference 'Big Brother: Critics and Publics', Free University of Brussels, 13 and 14 December 2001, organised by the research project (in cooperation with the Service of Permanent Education of the University, community centre Ten Weyngaert and the Centre Leo Apostel). We would like to thank Lothar Mikos, Maarten Reesink, Philippe Meers, Sofie Van Bauwel, Annette Hill, Janet Jones, Cosette Castro and Daniël Biltereyst for their contributions.

3 Hill's study dealt not exclusively with *Big Brother*, but 28 per cent of the 8,000 viewers of her sample did mention *Big Brother* (from the ESRC Press Release).

4 The concept of ancillary materials is not all new. It builds on what Thomas Austin (2000) has called 'dispersible texts'.

5 In what follows we will expand Barker's original term 'ancillary materials' to non-material information, and refer to it as 'ancillary discourses'.

6   For a non-*Big Brother*-related example of emphasising chronology in reception studies, see Mathijs 2003.

7   Initial results of this part of the research were first presented at the Society for Cinema Studies conference in Denver in 2002, in the panel 'Redefining the Factual: Factual Television from a Global Perspective'. We thank Annette Hill (University of Westminster), Robert C. Allen (University of North Carolina), David Crane (University of Califormia, Santa Cruz) and François Jost (Université de Sorbonne) for their comments. The first steps of the research were presented at the Society for Cinema Studies Conference in Washington in 2001.

8   There was no possibility of comparing with the first season in this case, but we have been able to use (but not quote) research carried out by the network broadcasting *Big Brother*. Additional data has been collected through recent research executed by Jan Willems, who has investigated the relationships between the forst two seasons of *Big Brother* Belgium with students (Willems 2002). We thank Jan Willems for giving us access to his data and for his collaboration on the research project.

9   This is just one of many similar remarks. Others can be found in *Big Brother Magazine*, 7 November 2001: 50 and 14 November 2001: 50.

10  Additional information on the respondents, which we cannot disclose for reasons of privacy, reinforces this impression.

*Bibliography*

Austin, T. (2000) *Hollywood, Hype and Audiences*. Manchester: Manchester University Press.

Barker, M. and K. Brooks (1998a) *Knowing Audiences: Judge Dredd, its Friends, Fans and Foes*. Luton: University of Luton Press.

_____ (1998b) 'On Looking into Bourdieu's Black Box', in R. Dickinson, R. Harindranath and O. Linne (eds) *Approaches to Audiences: A Reader*. London: Arnold, 218–32.

Barker, M. (1998) 'Critique: Audiences 'R' us', in R. Dickinson, R. Harindranath and O. Linne (eds) *Approaches to Audiences; a Reader*. London: Arnold, 184–91.

_____ (2004) 'News, Reviews, Clues, Interviews and Other Ancillary Materials – a Critique and Research Proposal', in *Scope*, available at http://nottingham.ac.uk/film/journal/articles/news-reviews.htm.

Beunders, H. (2000) *Wat je ziet ben je zelf. Big Brother: lust, leven en lijden voor de camera*. Amsterdam: Prometheus.

Biltereyst, D., Ph. Meers and S. Van Bauwel (2000) *Realiteit en fictie: Tweemaal hefzelfde?* Brussels: Koning Boudewijnstichting.

Couldry, N. (2002) 'Playing with Celebrity: *Big Brother* as Ritual Event', *Television and New Media*, 3, 3, 283–93.

Dahlgren, P. (1998) 'Critique: Elusive Audiences', in R. Dickinson, R. Harindranath and O. Linne (eds) *Approaches to Audiences: A Reader*. London: Arnold, 298–310.

De Ceulaer, J. (2000) 'Een spelletje mens-erger-je-niet: *Big Brother*', *Knack* (30 August), 26–31.

Dejonghe, H. (2000) '*BB* rijdt met de bus', *Film and Televisie*, 506, 36–7.

De Meyer, G. (ed.) (2001) *Big Brother; een Controversiële Real Live Soap*. Leuven-Apeldoorn: Garant.

Hessels, W. (2000) 'Kijk: het gewone wordt buitengewoon ... belachelijk', *De Morgen* (21 September), 2.

Gautlett, D. and A. Hill (1999) *TV Living; Television, Culture and Everyday Life*. London: Routledge.

Hill, A. (2001) 'Real TV: Audience Responses to Factual Entertainment', working paper, presented at SCS Conference, Washington.

_____ (2002) '*Big Brother*: The Real Audience', *Television and New Media*, 3, 3, 323–40.

Jones, J. (2000) 'The Post Modern Guessing Game', *Journal of Media Practice*, 1, 2, 75–84.

_____ (2003) 'Show your real face! A Fan Study of the UK *Big Brother* Transmission 2000, 2001, 2002', *New Media and Society*, 5, 3, 400–21.

Mathijs, E. (2001) 'Receptie *Big Brother* Verschuift', *De Standaard*, 1 September, 4.

_____ (2002a) '*Big Brother* and Critical Discourse; the Reception of *Big Brother* Belgium', *Television and New Media*, 3, 3, 311–22.

_____ (2002b) 'After the Shock: Topicality and Controversy in the Reception of *Big Brother*'s Second Season'; working paper, presented at SCS Conference, Denver.

_____ (2003) 'AIDS References in the Critical Reception of David Cronenberg: It May Not Be Such a Bad Disease after All', *Cinema Journal*, 42, 4, 29–45.

McQuail, D. (1997) *Audience Analysis*. London: Sage.

Meers, P. and S. Van Bauwel (2001) '*Big Brother* is You, Watching; A Qualitative Analysis of the Debate on *Big Brother* in the Belgian Quality Press'; working paper, presented at SCS Conference, Washington.

Meijer, I. C. and M. Reesink (eds) (2000) *Reality soap! Big Brother en het multimedia concept*. Amsterdam: Boom.

Mikos, L, P. Feise, K. Herzog, E. Pommer and V. Veihl (2000) *Im Auge der Kamera. Das Fernsehereignis Big Brother*. Berlin: Vistas Verlag.

Scannell, P. (2002) '*Big Brother* as Television Event', *Television and New Media*, 3, 3, 271–82.

Verriest, L. (2001) *Regisseren of registreren?; een inzicht in de productiestructuren van een nieuw televisiegenre: de reality-soap (case: Big Brother)*. Brussel: VUB Licentiaatsverhandeling.

Willems, J. (2002) *Reality-tv en Big Brother door de ogen van studenten; een perceptie-onderzoek*. Brussel: VUB Licentiaatsverhandeling.

Wilson, P. (2004) 'Jamming *Big Brother*: Webcasting, Audience Intervention, and Narrative Activism', in E. Mathijs and J. Jones (eds) *Big Brother International: Formats, Critics and Publics*. London: Wallflower Press, 196–211.

# CHAPTER 6

*Philippe Meers and Sofie Van Bauwel*

# DEBATING BIG BROTHER BELGIUM
Framing Popular Media Culture

## Introduction: Big Brother and studying popular culture

The *Big Brother* reality soap format, in all its national versions, conquered audiences throughout Europe and the USA within a period of just one year since its first release in the Netherlands. As a controversial product of popular media culture, it has provoked public and academic debates on the blurring of the boundaries between fiction and reality, private and public sphere, and the violation of privacy. In Belgium, where *Big Brother* was first broadcasted on commercial television channel 'Kanaal 2' in the autumn of 2000, it was the media event of the year. During the broadcasting a lively debate developed in the quality press (see also Mathijs 2002). Several opinion makers from various backgrounds expressed fairly extreme views on this programme. It is remarkable how a fairly simple entertainment format such as *Big Brother* could generate such commotion and outrage.[1]

This chapter does not focus on textual or formal characteristics of the programme itself, but on the public debate on popular culture, using popular culture theories to discover that there are remarkable parallels between the larger academic debate on the study of popular media culture and the specific debate on *Big Brother*. Even more so, the popular media culture product *Big Brother* functions as an interesting starting point for a much wider discussion on popular culture theories. In the first and most elaborate part of the paper, we focus on different frames on popular culture, using (albeit artificial) categories of three main theoretical frames (critical, pluralist and culturalist). Critical, pluralist and culturalist scholars vary firmly in their analysis of popular culture phenomena, on several levels such as the status of the audience, the role of the economy, and aesthetics. With regard to *Big Brother*, these views on popular media culture products provide a background that allows for the framing of a specific and prominent artefact of contemporary commercial media culture. In fact, there are remarkable parallels between the established (positive and negative) frames on mass culture and popular culture, and such well-known academic discourses are revived in the public debate on a specific commercial media product such as *Big Brother*.

In a smaller, second part we focus on a case study of the Belgian version of the *Big Brother* format and, more precisely, on the vivid public debate in the quality press that developed during the broadcasting of the programme. We analyse how traditional theoretical positions on popular media culture (ranging from very critical/pessimist to extremely positive) are to be found surprisingly alive in the discursive field of the *Big Brother* debate. Through a qualitative discourse analysis of the different voices in the press debate, we find remarkable resemblances with arguments on popular culture on various levels such as audiences, participants, the media landscape, society, and so on. Here, *Big Brother* is often considered to be symptomatic for something else: either developments in the (commercial) media landscape or larger trends in society. In the final discussion, we will highlight the parallels of our research results with the general frames and arguments on popular media culture and reflect on possible reasons for these striking similarities.

## Framing the popular

Popular culture is hard to define. Tony Bennett argues that the concept of popular culture is 'virtually useless, a melting pot of confused and contradictory meanings capable of misdirecting inquiry up any number of theoretical blind alleys' (1980: 18). There are difficulties posed by the concept itself which partly stem from the implied otherness which is constructed when using the term 'popular'. It is always defined in contrast to other conceptual categories and it is in effect an empty conceptual category, yet the need for distinctions seems to be necessary when the concept of popular culture is articulated. Using aesthetics and taste, a normative discourse is connected with the notion of popular culture. In this discourse the cultural distinctions are used to support broader class distinctions and taste becomes an ideological category. As Pierre Bourdieu argues, the consumption of culture is: 'predisposed, consciously and deliberately or not, to fulfill a social function of legitimating social differences' (Bourdieu 1984: 5). There are a number of ways in which the term 'popular culture' has been used. Mostly linked or even equated with the term 'mass culture' it refers to cultural processes at work amongst the general public (Downing *et al.* 1990: 33). Popular culture can also be described as widespread and common public texts (Barker 2000: 388). Defined in a quantitative way, this approach is often linked to qualitative aspects. From this perspective it is yet another variant of the high/low cultural frontier, one which mostly reproduces the 'inferiority' of the popular. Because of its associations with the assumed cultural preferences of the 'uncultivated' or non-discriminating (McQuail 1994: 39) popular culture generally has a pejorative connotation. As a term it is frequently used 'either to identify a form of culture that is opposed to another form, or as a synonym or complement to that other form' (Edgar & Sedgwick 1999: 285). Popular culture therefore is a term whose definition is dependant upon the position or the frame from which one looks at 'it'. The precise meaning giving to popular culture will therefore alter.

One core element is that popular culture is primarily seen as (a) commercial product(ion). A second core element is the assumption that popular culture is defined by the popularity of certain cultural products. In this second core element we see an ambiguity in both the academic and the public debate on popular media culture. These discourses can be described lapidary, much like debates about whether products are good or bad because they are popular or popular because they are good or bad. As O'Sullivan *et al.* suggested, this ambiguity is not simply a matter of the personal prejudices of critics: 'it is implicit in the position of those people and products that can be described as popular' (O'Sullivan *et al.* 1994: 232). We can distinguish two different aspects in this ambiguity. The first aspect can be described as the extent (or the ambiguity of this extent) to which popular culture is imposed on audiences, or derived from their own tastes and experiences. The second ambiguity concerns the extent to which popular culture is an expression of a subordinated class position or a potentially liberating source, which resists the dominant culture.

Within the field of cultural studies a simple definition of the term popular culture, as the culture that appeals to the general public, conceals a number of complexities and nuances. According to Edgar and Sedgwick (1999) the concept is often used to identify a form of culture that is opposed to another or as a synonym or complement to that other form. The precise meaning of popular culture is therefore variable as it is related to folk culture, mass culture or high culture. Although the concepts of mass culture, folk art and popular culture can be differentiated from one another, we see that these terms are often used as synonyms (Gramsci 1971).

Based on the elitarism-populism continuum we use three major categories to differentiate the positions in the debate on popular culture. Despite the fact that the continuum polarises the perspectives on popular culture, it is a useful way to have a overview on the three major positions in the debate. We will discuss the critical frame, the pluralist frame and the culturalist frame and consider these frames as the three major positions on the continuum.

### The critical frame
*Top-down, the passive audience.* Building on the classical sociological difference between *Gemeinschaft* and *Gesellschaft*, mass culture is seen as an outcome of mass society, which is equivalent for urbanisation, technology, industrialisation, bureaucratisation and alienation. Initially, mass culture is synonymous with reduction to the lowest common denominator, leveling down of the social and the loss of personality. Theories of mass culture dominant in American and European sociology in the 1930s and 1940s situated popular culture in relation to industrial production. They focused on those forms of popular culture that were subject to industrial means of production and distribution. Popular culture was therefore seen as being imposed on the people (Edgar & Sedgwick 1999: 285). In this frame of thinking, audiences where assumed to be passive con-sumers *manipulated through mass media.*

In the inter-war period there was a broad consensus on the idea that mass media exercised a persuasive influence. Curran, Gurevitch and Woollacott (1982:

11–12) pointed out that underlying this consensus was the establishment, through the application of new technology to mass production of communication, of mass audiences on a scale that was unprecedented. Second, and underlying this consensus, urbanisation and industrialisation are considered as creators of a volatile, unstable and alienated society, easy to manipulate. Many scholars saw how the mass media were used during World War One and how the public was brainwashed by powerful propaganda. The media propelled 'world bullets' that penetrated deep into its inert and passive victims (Curran *et al*. 1982: 12).

Although we can distinguish between elitarian mass culture theories and left critical theories on popular culture, these perspectives use similar discourses to criticise mass and popular culture.

*Economics rule*. In a broad perspective, many critical authors assume that popular culture is an instrument of social control and ideological reproduction. The popular-isation of the media only serves political-economic interests and does not question the existing order. This point of view is prominent in the concept of the 'culture industry' of the Frankfurt School. This contradictory term attempts to grasp something of the fate of culture in late capitalist society. The account of the culture industry is seen as economic and as integral part of the reinterpretation of dialectical materialism. The culture industry serves to transform use-value into something that is produced by the capitalist system. Adorno and Horkheimer coined the term 'culture industry' to suggest that culture interlocked with political economy and production of culture by capitalist corporations (Barker 2000: 44). In this frame popular culture is seen as mass deception which secures the stability and the continuity of the capitalist dominant hegemony.

Applied to reality TV this would mean, according to Bill Nichols (1994: 56), that it does nothing else than reproduce the existing order. Techniques of personalisation and dramatisation have to draw the attention of the audience. The so-called 'new television', with its focus on authenticity and spectacle, wants to attract broad audiences in order to attract advertisers. Reality TV, and first-person media, also show us how the contemporary media sector tries to exploit each part of people's personal life. The exploitation of the broad social themes and ethical questions points the view of the audience on the personal while – in this way – it conceals the real background of it. Infotainment and tabloidisation only contribute to stereotypical representations and limited knowledge of the 'big' issues (Sparks & Tulloch 2000).

*Low taste and narcotics*. Next to the political economic arguments we can also recognise aesthetic judgments based on the dichotomy of high and low culture. Mass culture and popular culture are often contrasted with more traditional forms of culture or high culture.

Opposite to high culture, mass culture and often popular culture refer to cultural products, which are made solely for the mass market and are associated with homogenisation, standardisation and commercialisation. This conception of the mass and mass consumption is linked to the notion of quality or, better, the loss of it. Popular culture is opium for the masses and like mass culture it is a culture which lacks intellectual challenge and stimulation, preferring escapism instead. In this context, the old-fashioned hypodermic-needle model of communication reappears. This class-based value system maintained the superiority of the 'high' elite culture against popular mass culture. On the other end of the continuum we can define the pluralist frame which can be positioned opposite of the culturalist perspective.

## The pluralist frame

*Bottom-up, the active audience.* John Fiske (1987, 1989) is the main author who vindicated popular culture. Often labeled as a radical revisionist, Fiske's arguments are similar to those of liberal effect researchers, in celebrating the self-willed independence of people (Curran 1982: 136). According to Storey (1997: 206) this position can be understood in political terms as 'an uncritical echo of liberal claims about the sovereignty of the consumer' and at worst it is 'uncritically complicit with prevailing "free market" ideology'. For Fiske (1987), the primary virtue of popular culture is precisely that it is popular – both literally 'of the people' and dependent on 'people power'.

In this framework the notion of mass culture refers positively to the cultures of the masses, taking its values from the idea of the mass of ordinary people as the main agent of progressive social change. The notion of mass culture no longer carries a pejorative connotation and is conceptualised as a hybrid product for expression in a contemporary idiom aimed at reaching people. In this pluralist frame the audience is seen as an active audience. Popular audiences create their own meaning with popular texts and bring to bear their own cultural competencies and discursive resources. Here, popular media texts are defined as the outcome of their reading and enjoyment by an audience. Emphasising that there are multiple readings of a popular text opens a way for escape from potential social control.

This optimist view on the empowerment of the audiences is based on the notion of resistance. Stuart Hall (1996: 287) defines resistance as a changing metaphor for cultural change, allowing us to think about cultural transformations. According to Barker (2000: 347) resistance has to be in pursuit of named values. Especially in the politics of the field of cultural studies resistance is a normative concept. So television and popular culture are the dominant cultural artefacts of our contemporary modernity and have enormous inventiveness and power to change. By resistance through pleasure, the audience has semiotic power and the competence to resist the dominant hegemony.

*Minimising the market forces.* Popular culture is regarded as the meanings and practices produced by popular audiences at the moment of consumption. This means that the study of popular culture centres on the uses to which it is put. These arguments represent a reversal of the commodities that serve its interests in favour of exploring how people turn the products of industry into their popular culture serving their interest (Barker 2000: 47). While in this frame it is also clear that popular culture is largely produced by capitalist corporations, Fiske finds 'popular vitality and creativity' leading to 'the possibility of social change and the motivation to drive it'. The culture industries have to make big efforts to get the public to consume popular culture. According to Edgar and Sedgwick (1999: 287) Fiske distinguishes between the financial and the cultural economies within which cultural artefacts circulate. While the former is concerned with 'the generation of exchange-value, and thus with the accumulation of wealth and the incorporation of the consumer into the dominant economic order', the latter is concerned with 'the production of meanings and pleasures by, and for, the audience'. Precisely because the production of meanings within the cultural economy is not as readily controlled as the production of wealth, the audience, as producer of meanings, is credited with considerable power to resist the financial forces or incorporation. In this frame popular culture is considered a key site of resistance to capitalism. The power of the corporations and the determining role of economic forces are minimised.

*Taste and pleasure*. Rejecting the argument that lines of division of cultural capital follow the lines of division of economic capital (cf. Bourdieu), this frame assumes that there are two economies, with relative cultural and social autonomies. Even if most people in a class society are subordinated, they have a degree of 'semiotic power' in the former economy, that is the power to shape meanings to their own desires (McQuail 1994: 103–4). Popular culture is a tool for resistance and power, and it is a democratic media. Boundaries are left behind and the dichotomy between low and high culture and the class differentiation in values and tastes are blurred. In this pluralist perspective it follows that for popular culture anything can be turned into a joke, reference or quotation in its eclectic play of styles, simulations and surfaces. Strinati argues that if popular cultural signs and media images are taking over our sense of reality – this means style takes over content – then it becomes difficult to maintain a meaningful distinction between art and popular culture (Strinati 1995: 225). This was exactly the fear of mass culture critics: the take over and the subversion of high culture. These arguments seem to be similar to the discourse of the mass culture critics but in this frame the blurred boundaries of high and low culture are read as positive.

### The culturalist frame

In the debate on popular culture it is clear that a number of authors try not to adhere to polarised positions. The fixed positions of the critical frame do not leave much space for alternatives. On the other hand they do raise fundamental questions on the concept of popular culture. They question the ideal, democratic patterns of the media claimed by the pluralist framework. The culturalist framework is not simply a third way between the pluralist and the critical perspectives. As James Curran points out there is a necessary reappraisal that responds to the weaknesses of the liberal and the radical paradigms:

> The radical conception of the media as top-down agency of control and its antithesis, that of the media as a bottom-up agency of empowerment, need to be revised in favour of the view that the media are more often institutions which are exposed to cross-pressures both from above and below. (Curran 1982: 154)

Curran assumes that there is little possibility of distinguishing an elite from a mass taste because everyone is attracted to some of the elements of popular culture. Tastes will always differ and varying criteria of assessment can be applied. But in this culturalist perspective there is an acceptance that media culture is an accomplished fact and it has to be treated on its own terms (McQuail 1994: 103). The culturalist frame was developed as a critical voice into cultural studies. Questioning the notion of the active audiences and popular culture produced by 'the people', the concept of consumption was revisited. McGuigan (1992), for instance, criticised Fiske's abandonment of any form of political economy, which leads to the acceptance of the free market and consumer capitalism (Barker 2000: 364).

The contemporary transformation of the media is placed in a framework of consumer culture, but assuming that culture is indeed an economic product. Similar to the pejorative conception of popular culture in left, right and centrist versions, culture is seen as commodified. But in this culturalist framework the concepts of passive consumption and media manipulation of popular taste are left behind. Cultural products and consumption can be useful and can give meaning to activities.

In this framework we can see a transformation of the notions of mass culture and popular culture. Together with their normative discourses they are left behind for the notion of media culture. In an attempt to abandon the negative view on specific cultural artifacts on the one hand, the notion of mass culture used in the critical frame is not articulated as often. On the other hand, the very optimistic concept of popular culture of the pluralist frame is abandoned and replaced by the notion of media culture. This culturalist notion which tries to gain a place in between the two poles on the elitism-populism continuum can be understood as normative in the way it focuses on the centrality of media in the articulations of cultures. Media are considered as democratic and other cultural artefacts are left behind in the analysis of democratic possibilities.

In the contemporary consumer culture experiences, emotions, pain and joy often represented in reality TV are commodified. Private and everyday life experiences are offered for consumption by media. But this does not mean that they are of no value or use. The recent evolution of new factual formats has to be seen as profit maximalisation. But at the same time they are considered as an integral part of the consumer culture. But, as Ib Bondebjerg states, and with him many other authors (see Biltereyst *et al.* 2000; Corner 2000; Dahlgren 1995; Dovey 2000; Langer 1998; Livingstone & Lunt 1992), there are possibilities created for a certain democratisation of the old 'public service' notion. Commercialisation and consumption do not rule out a broadening of the public debate and knowledge. And in this commodified world, civil society functions of the media such as participation, accessibility and forum do retain their potential. A culturalist perspective claims that the commercial forms of reality TV and first-person media cannot simply be seen as the end of the ideals on media and society. Especially in Europe we see a 'creation of a new mixed public sphere, where common knowledge and everyday experience play a much larger role' (Bondebjerg 1996). In this framework the contemporary consumer culture is considered a fact. It is a frame where, besides political and economic arguments, democratic possibilities are not expelled. With Bondebjerg, we stress the need for critical perspectives: 'dramatising

| CRITICAL PERSPECTIVE | CULTURALIST PERSPECTIVE | PLURALIST PERSPECTIVE |
|---|---|---|
| 'mass culture' | 'media culture' | 'popular culture' |
| top down | consumer culture | bottom up |
| passive audience | democratic possibilities | active audiences |
| high/low culture | culture and tastes | multiple decodings |
| inferiority of the popular | civil society functions | semiotic power |
| homogenisation | | agents of progressive social change |
| standardisation | | resistance and pleasure |
| escapism | | subcultures |
| hegemonic capitalist system | | democratic media |
| pessimistic | | optimistic |
| production centered | | audience centered |

Table 1: *Critical, culturalist and pluralist perspectives on the elitarism-populism continuum*

crime, personal problems and social issues in fascinating forms does not necessarily create the basis for public knowledge' (Bondebjerg 1996: 37). There is still a question of balance, relevance and putting things into appropriate perspectives and context. This means that a celebration of the new formats has to be avoided without denying the new possibilities for public knowledge, participation and debate.

## Big Brother in the Belgian quality press

*Discourse and method*
We turned to the public debate on *Big Brother*, a typical product of commercial popular culture, to examine if, and how, critical, pluralist and culturalist frames on popular culture are active. We focused on the articulation of *Big Brother* and the particular discourses on *Big Brother* in the Belgian quality press. There are no real tabloids, nor is there a strict hierarchy between newspapers in Belgium; yet there is a clear division between so-called quality newspapers and more popular papers. We chose the quality newspapers because the 'exercise in distinction' (Biltereyst 1999) they display is most clearly visible in these media. The different publication formats are opinion articles, columns, interviews and other articles. The focus is mainly on the Flemish press during and after the broadcasting of *Big Brother 1*.[2]

Through a close reading of the texts we qualitatively analysed the different positions and voices in the quality newspapers on *Big Brother*. Five items which were articulated in relation to *Big Brother* were clustered: content, form and participants; audience consumption; *Big Brother* and the media landscape; elite/high vs. mass/low culture; and *Big Brother* and society. Various kinds of opinion makers can be distinguished: journalists (media journalists, chief editors), academics from various backgrounds (social psychology, media research, ethics, philosophy, history, astronomy), TV professionals (commercial and public service television, production and managerial level), marketing professionals, politicians and writers.

*Content, form and participants*
With regards to form and content, opinions on *Big Brother* are very outspoken. The form of *Big Brother* is often described as 'boring' and 'ugly', although for the supporters these features make it 'all the more fascinating' to watch. It is also seen as highly dramatised, and, according to film lecturer Wouter Hessels, 'more pathetic than the most cheesy Hollywood film' (Hessels 2000). A central feature of the content of *Big Brother* is its so-called 'claim on reality'. Opinions differ strongly on this. While writer Erwin Mortier considers it 'as fake as possible' (Mortier 2000), others do reserve some room for considerations of its 'realness'.

This discourse on 'the real' is closely connected to opinions on the participants of *Big Brother*. In this respect, the claim on reality can be divided in two: the programme's reality, and the authenticity of the participants' behaviour. Authenticity and reality are juxtaposed to fakeness. Critics agree that people in such extreme situations can hardly show real emotions. In extreme circumstances, 'conflict is driven to a paroxysm, and no comparison is possible with everyday life', 'They lose their authenticity' (Raes 2000). *Big Brother* then becomes 'a game show in being yourself' (Van Weelden 1999). This comes as no surprise to these authors, since the selection of characters is made to serve the sensational narration. Others, more enthusiastic, disagree and believe that their emotions are real, pure and not faked. Opinions regarding stereotyping differ as well.

Whereas negative voices stress the fact that *Big Brother* demands 'simple characters whose experiences can be summarised in a spicy or a sentimental story' (Van Weelden 1999), more optimistic discourses focus on the possible role of *Big Brother* in changing stereotypes, and the fact that social taboos such as homosexuality, gender roles and sexuality are brought into the open.

Discourses on the status of the participants differ widely. The participants are often depicted as exploited victims, with a central thesis being that their human dignity is violated, that it is an attack on their freedom and that they lose control over their acts. Taking this one step further, authors reflect on the dangers of such a programme. Extreme reactions are forecast by some psychologists, on the basis that it is not possible to foresee what behaviour will develop because of the extreme situations. However, opposite views stress the self-determination of the participants as consenting adults, fully aware of the concept, and choosing to participate. The view 'that they are exploited by media tycoons shows a lack of respect for the common man and is pure paternalism' for political editor Yves Desmet (2000). It plays a role in their identity formation. Even public service professionals stress that the discussion about the need to protect the participants is very old.

Reflections on stardom occur frequently, especially in terms of devaluation of stardom. It is no longer necessary to have certain abilities to become a star. *Big Brother* participants are 'an elite out of nothing, national heroes without any exceptional skills or qualities whatsoever' (Hessels 2000), invoking obvious references to David Bowie ('We can be heros, just for one day') and Andy Warhol ('15 minutes of fame'). But for enthusiasts, such as popular culture professor Gust De Meyer, this does not entail a devaluation: 'Stardom is humanised, this is not decay, it is perfect democracy, why gaze at an ideal image when we can recognise ourselves in ordinary people?' (De Meyer 2000).

*Audience consumption*

Generally speaking, discourses on the *Big Brother* audience can be situated within two frames, both adhering to classical views on audiences. Negative voices stress the passivity and stupidity of the audience of *Big Brother*. Metaphors on animals and fast-food are frequent, as are references to lowest common denominators: 'the viewing cattle swallows whatever it is offered, like chickens who eat garbage' (Bodifée 2000); it is an 'insult for anyone with a minimum of brains and sense of good taste' (Mortier 2000). The audience is described as not being rational, but merely 'looking for the kick of voyeurism and sensations' (Hessels 2000). As participants, viewers equally are victims, because they are being misled. Programme producers are subsequently labeled as 'despots of audience rates', launching 'a mind-numbing promotion campaign' (Bodifée 2000). The old-fashioned hypodermic-needle model even reappears: 'Probably the perverse effect of *Big Brother* will be that camera control becomes something normal after this programme' (Raes 2000). As in soap opera research, the substitution argument is mentioned, with *Big Brother* 'a surrogate for human encounter and expression of emotions, people care more about soap characters than about their real neighbours' (Raes 2000).

Optimist voices stress the activity of the *Big Brother* audience, claiming *Big Brother* is an interesting programme from which audiences can learn and derive pleasure. *Big Brother* is then considered as instructive training: 'a school for life and human relations' (Beunders 2000). It shows audiences 'how everyone wears a mask to hide behind, and that in daily life everybody plays a role too' (De Meyer 2000). For marketing professionals and trend watchers, the advantage of *Big Brother* is that it 'shows people with their defects because audiences are sick of the perfect appearance, the ideal image of people in full control of their lives' (Moens 2001).

### Big Brother and the media landscape

In most articles, *Big Brother* is seen as a symptom, example or illustration of the contemporary media landscape, and that of television in particular. Interpretations of the actual situation of the media are reflected in the analysis of *Big Brother*. As Desmond Morris notes, there is hardly anyone who chooses a middle way, it is either 'brilliant innovative television' or it is 'the worst example of trash television' (Morris 2000).

On the negative side of the discursive field, *Big Brother* is described through metaphors of death, disease, dirt and drugs: 'We collectively drove a dagger in the rattling body, decency is dead' (Mortier 2000); 'the audience is addicted to this kind of visual heroin, the population is intoxicated and brainwashed' (Bodifée 2000). For another opinion maker, it is an example of a 'media virus' (Van Weelden 1999). Yet other discourses refer to disaster: 'the floodgates are open for a flood of mind-killing rubbish' (Bodifée 2000). The same writer also stresses the 'downward evolution' of media and television, with *Big Brother* as the perfect example of deterioration: 'it is the low point of an evolution'. The image is that of the crossing of limits: 'How far can you go?' (Raes 2000); 'is it acceptable to do this as entertainment?' (Hoorens 2000); 'it is one step further in the direction of perversion' (Lenaerts & Depauw 2001). On the other side of the discursive field, positive voices consider this evolution to be more upward, and regard *Big Brother* as a new form of television: '*Big Brother* is a unique form of innovative television', 'the culminating point in an evolution: it fits the spirit of the times' (De Meyer 2000). It becomes 'a new chapter in television history' (Poppe, in De Ceulaer 2000) and produces 'revolutionary television' (Desmet 2000).

*Big Brother* is also represented as symptomatic of the general trend of focusing on subjective reality and giving the voice to the man in the street. This trend is evaluated in different ways as well. Whereas for enthusiasts the man in the street finally gets to speak for himself instead of someone else speaking for him, for critics this 'banality is made so extraordinary that it becomes ridiculous' (Hessels 2000).

### Elite/high vs mass/low culture

Most of the critical discourses on *Big Brother* can be framed within a debate on high and low culture. A central concept is quality, understood as complexity, subtlety and distance: 'There is something missing on television: complex programmes … we need a call for better television' (Asselberghs & Carels 2000); '*Big Brother* is a slap in the face of television professionals who seek quality' (Mortier 2000). Within the Belgian media landscape, this divide is traditionally associated with the contrast between commercial and public service television, something which is also reflected in the debate on *Big Brother*. Commercialisation is part of the mentioned downward evolution: 'diversity has diminished since commercial television arrived, the ideology of the free market does not work in the sector of news and culture: quality and diversity diminish proportionally with rates and profits' (Bodifée 2000); and public service television distinguishes itself as more respectful of people: 'public television respects the audience more, doesn't cross certain borders, and has more added value'. Elaborating on this, public television manager Christina von Wackerbath puts her definition of quality in contrast with *Big*

*Brother*: 'the task of public television is respect for the citizen, tolerance, democracy, social cohesion. *Big Brother* is voyeurism, without respect for the individual and with little added value' (Von Wackerbath 2000). Other television professionals for public service television also distinguish their approach from *Big Brother*: 'it is a programme you don't even want to show your naked bottom. They start from the argument that it is not necessary to make a decent programme' (Eelen & Van Dijck 2001). The host of another reality TV format *The Mole* (on VRT, the public channel) says: 'this is a kind of programme which I am associated with regularly, more than I want, because it is a kind of television I want to keep a distance from' (Devlieger 2000). On the other side of the spectrum, professionals from commercial television consider this to be a hypocritical attitude. They point to the importance of the context: 'If it would be aired on public service television, accompanied by experts, it would have a highbrow image, now there is something sordid about it' (Alloo, in De Ceulaer 2000).

A broader discussion deals with the extremes of elitarism and populism. For defenders of popular culture, such as Yves Desmet, *Big Brother* is at the centre of the contemporary television debate: 'It shows the frustration of an intellectual elite that has monopolised the medium during decades and sees its place taken over by the actual target group of the medium: the mass audience. It demonstrates the struggle for power over the medium, with aesthetic and ethical arguments' (Desmet 2000). What is at stake is the position of intellectuals in the media landscape. The debate can be analysed as an exercise in mediatic distinction – critique on *Big Brother* functions to strengthen one's own quality label (Bildereyst 1999).[3] This implies for the optimists that the paternalism has ended and that the viewer is finally taken seriously. As an exercise in distinction, it is remarkable that if intellectuals 'admit' that they watch, it is 'for mere entertainment' with their 'brains on zero, to watch and enjoy, just like soaps' (Los 2000).

*Big Brother and society*
*Big Brother* is not only articulated as symptomatic for media developments, the comparison is taken one step further: *Big Brother* becomes an illustration of contemporary society. Classical theories of the mirror function of the media are present, as well as issues such as democracy, ideology and politics. The most pessimist voices see *Big Brother* as one step closer to the beginning of a totalitarian regime: 'the audience as voters: a mass that succumbs in stupidity and wallows in totalitarian ideology' (Bodifée 2000). *Big Brother* then means 'a danger for the political system: a democracy buried under rubbish' (Mortier 2000). Mass media are surrogates for real life: 'we live in a neurotic society, feelings of loneliness are soothed by television as drug, opium for the people' (Raes 2000). More nuanced voices consider *Big Brother* as symptomatic of our society, but they articulate this argument differently. In their view, we 'already live in a *Big Brother* house' with all the information technology, surveillance cameras and so forth (Beunders 2000).

## Discussion

In this brief analysis of the different discourses on *Big Brother* in the press, it has become clear that traditional arguments of the debate on popular culture reappear. It is extraordinary how a single television programme format can address almost every discourse in the larger debate on popular media culture. The discourses blend almost perfectly with the theoretical frames we elaborated on above. Overall, it seems hard to find a nuanced view on *Big Brother*. Voices seem to be polarised, either in favour or totally against it. The question remains if this is a merely a feature of a mediatised debate, or if it is related to the nature of the programme itself.

What does this tell us about the media (in Belgium) and the way intellectuals reflect upon it in the public space? A certain hegemonic intellectual public opinion – extremely negative in its discourse – was countered by an opposing populist discourse, that was as extremely positive in its articulation of *Big Brother*. And, as if the achievements of more than three decades of research on popular television and popular media are simply neglected, *Big Brother* audiences are seen as either passive and/or stupid victims of commercial exploitation or self-conscious active pleasure seekers; *Big Brother* participants are either exploited puppets in a media game or stardom-aspiring individuals with complete self-determination; *Big Brother* is the low point in the downward evolution of the commercial pulp entertainment television or revolutionary television of the twenty-first century, giving a voice to the common man; a symbol for a nearby mass totalitarianism or a splendid metaphor for our contemporary anxieties.

The link with well established academic critical and pluralist frames are crystal clear (see Table 1, above). More critical voices take their inspiration from the critical perspective, where inferior mass culture is seen as intoxicating a passive audience seeking escape. Product homogenisation and standardisation are the negative results of a hegemonic capitalist system. On the other end of the continuum, more positive voices in the debate on *Big Brother* connect with the pluralist frame where the positive notion of popular culture entails a bottom-up approach with active audiences using their semiotic power for multiple decodings. Resistance and pleasure of the audience are central. In combination with the representation of average people this can add to a more democratic media landscape.

The question remains why *Big Brother* triggers such a polarised debate? In the first place the format itself addresses central issues regarding our contemporary society: privacy in the age of surveillance cameras and Internet marketing, mediatic presence as part of our identity formation, blurring boundaries between fact and fiction, private and public, and so forth. This is combined with a well-orchestrated media plan for creating controversy and moral panic. This debate was deliberately fuelled by the producers of *Big Brother*, controversy then becoming the perfect trailer.[4] *Big Brother* is a television format that needs a huge marketing campaign for its launch to be successful. Producers keenly decided to focus on the 'extreme' features of the format by fully exploiting its controversial potential (violation of privacy, sexuality, and so forth). The mechanisms of a moral panic reaction in public opinion were put in place. Using mostly negative or condemning statements on *Big Brother* made by public figures as material for the publicity campaign, and in the pilot episode, producers managed to set the agenda for the debate on the programme.[5]

The creation of a media hype has been extremely successful, as in other countries. But there is more to this controversy than mere marketing strategy. As in other countries, several opinion makers entered the debate on the 'perverse, amoral and dangerous character' of *Big Brother*. In Germany and in the Netherlands, a vigorous debate developed. Negative reactions came from politicians (in Germany),[6] judicial instances (Germany), academics (psychologists, doctors in the Netherlands, sociologists in the UK),[7] religious organisations (Germany) and consumer organisations (UK, Portugal, France)[8] or media institutions (Turkey, France).[9] The fact that so much was written about *Big Brother* not surprisingly fitted perfectly in the 'highly successful' image spread by the marketeers. Opinions on *Big Brother* were in this sense included and commodified into a marketing strategy beyond its own limits.

Experiences and emotions represented in reality TV are equally commodified. Private and everyday life experiences are offered for consumption by media. But commercialisation and consumption do not rule out a broadening of the public debate and knowledge. We plead for a culturalist view that not only offers the most productive frame to analyse popular culture products such as *Big Brother*: at this point culturalist perspectives can equally offer new insights in the public debate on *Big Brother*. It supplies a viable and balanced way to put polarised – theoretical and public opinion – positions, as reflected in the press debate, in perspective. A celebration of the new formats is avoided just as is the denial of new possibilities for public knowledge, participation and debate. On the one hand avoiding negative claims, on the other hand refraining from populist speculations, this point of view acknowledges the media landscape as a context of institutions exposed to cross-pressures both from above and below.

In the case of the Belgian debate however, culturalist voices were seldom heard. In a polarised media environment, balanced voices often get lost. As illustrated in our case study, the culturalist perspective remained a rather marginal voice in the public debate on *Big Brother*. The fierce reaction from intellectuals in the press makes one reflect further on the nature of the media debate and the apparent necessity to be either totally in favour of or totally opposed to *Big Brother* and other popular media culture products.[10]

The *Big Brother* debate in the Belgian quality press was indeed a perfect alibi for a discourse of distinction by the 'well thinking' intellectuals in Belgian society and professionals of public service television. We noticed that the traditional intellectual stand against popular culture is still strongly present in intellectual public opinion. Scholars have to engage in this public debate to refine this discussion with research-based arguments. The position of academics dealing with these issues is a fragile one, balancing on the borderline between cultural elitist pessimism and populism. The elitist pessimism, a discourse thought long gone in academic discussion, still has large acceptance in broader intellectual public opinion, as was illustrated in our case study.

*Notes*

1   The authors wish to thank Daniël Biltereyst for his useful suggestions and critical comments on a previous version of this paper, presented at the SCS 2001 Conference in Washington DC. Parts of this article are based on Biltereyst, Van Bauwel & Meers 2000.

2   The corpus consists of 25 articles in quality news papers and magazines: three columns, six opinion articles, 14 interviews and two other articles, from *De Morgen* (considered as a 'progressive' left newspaper), *De Standaard* (considered as a 'conservative' centre-right newspaper) and the *Financieel-Ekonomische Tijd* (a financial newspaper that evolved into a general newspaper). A conservative Catholic and Royalist French-speaking newspaper *La Libre Belgique* was included in the analysis because of one opinion article by a Flemish psychologist. The only 'quality' weekly in our corpus is *Knack Magazine*.

3   Since *Big Brother* is not a worthy cultural product, it is certainly not accepted as an object for academic attention and research. Academics who deal with the subject

are compared with 'small businessmen and shopkeepers who also want a piece of the *Big Brother*-pie' (Asselberghs & Carels 2000). For public service television professionals, positive opinions of academics on *Big Brother* are 'nonsense, a painful example of how bad the situation of academics is in Flanders'; it proves, in their view, 'that you don't necessarily learn something at university' (Lenaerts & Depauw 2001).

4  'Critique is essential, if everybody thinks you're good, there is no excitement, it is better to have people who support you and others who despise you. This stimulates the discussion' (Paul Römer, producer *Big Brother* Netherlands and USA).

5  The following statements were used to feed the controversy pipeline: 'They are adults who do it to themselves' (Dirk Sterkx, liberal VLD politician); 'It is an inappropriate attack on privacy' (Etienne Vermeersch, ethicist); '*Big Brother* corresponds precisely to what the human being is: a voyeur' (Hugo Camps, journalist); 'We will follow meticulously the events in *Big Brother*' (Stefaan De Clerck, then chairman of the Flemish Christian Democrat Party).

6  In Germany, the Landesanstalt of Hessen threathened a ban on *Big Brother*.

7  David Miller of the Media Research Institute (Stirling University) filed a complaint against the two psychology professors who commented on *Big Brother* for professional misbehaviour.

8  A French consumers organisation called upon the public to dump their garbage in front of the building of channel M6.

9  The French Conseil Superieur de l'Audiovisuel summoned the producers of M6 not to violate the respect for human dignity.

10  Near the end of the first season Daniël Biltereyst and the authors expressed in the press a culturalist perspective on *Big Brother* and reality TV. This was met by a fierce reaction from several intellectuals. In a sense then, this study is the reflection of a lived experience as media scholars who took a stand in the public debate on *Big Brother*. Though this might have complicated the necessary distance from the research subject, it urged us to reconsider our position as media scholars researching popular culture in the public space.

*Bibliography*

Asselberghs, H. and E. Carels (2000) 'Taartstudie', *Financieel-Economische Tijd* (10 December).

Barker, C. (2000) *Cultural Studies. Theory and Practice*. London: Sage.

Bennett, T. (1980) 'Popular Culture: A Teaching Object', *Screen*, 34, 15–27.

Beunders, H. (2000) *Wat je ziet ben je zelf. Big Brother: lust, leven en lijden voor de camera*. Amsterdam: Prometheus.

Beunders, H. (2000) 'De bastaarden van de avant-garde', *De Morgen* (8 September).

Biltereyst, D. (1999) '*Big Brother* als metafoor', *Samenleving en Politiek*, 6, 8, 44–6.

Biltereyst, D., S. Van Bauwel and Ph. Meers (2000) *Realiteit en fictie: tweemaal hetzelfde?* Brussel: Koning Boudewijnstichting.

Bodifée, G. (2000) 'Big Brother wacht al lang', *Knack*, 49, 174.

Bondebjerg, I. (1996) 'Public Discourse/Private Fascination: Hybridisation in True-life-story Genres', *Media, Culture & Society*, 18, 27–45.

Bourdieu, P. (1984) *Distinction: A Social Critique of the Judgement of Taste*. Cambridge: Harvard University Press.

Chambers, I. (1986) *Popular Culture: The Metropolitan Experience*. London: Methuen.

Corner, J. (2000) Documentary in a Post-Documentary Culture? A Note on Forms and their Functions. *Working Paper in Public Communication nr.1*, University of Liverpool.

Curran, J. (1982) 'Rethinking Mass Communications', in M. Gurevitch, T. Bennett, J. Curran and J. Woollacott (eds) *Culture, Society and the Media*. London: Methuen.

Dahlgren, P. (1995) *Television and the Public Sphere*. London: Routledge.

Dauncey, H. (1996) 'French reality television', *European Journal of Communication*, 11, 1, 83–106.

De Ceulaer, J. (2000) 'Een spelletje mens-erger-je-niet: *Big Brother*', *Knack* (30 August).

De Meyer, G. (2000) 'Kunst par excellence', *De Standaard* (16 December).

Desmet, Y. (2000) 'De meerwaardezoeker loert graag door het sleutelgat', *De Morgen* (16 September).

Devlieger, M. (2000) 'De Bus rijdt te ver. Michiel Devlieger vindt Nederlands reality-programma "waanzin"', *De Standaard* (27 January).

Dovey, J. (2000) *Freakshow: First Person Media and Factual Television*. London: Pluto Press.

Downing, J., A. Mohammadi and A. Sreberny-Mohammadi (eds) (1990) *Questioning the Media*. London: Sage.

Edgar, A. and P. Sedgwick (eds) (1999) *Key Concepts in Cultural Theory. London*: Routledge.

Eelen, J. and T. Van Dijk (2001) 'Perverse "reporters" spelen met de tijdgeest', *De Standaard* (22 February).

Fiske, J. (1987) *Television Culture*. London: Methuen.

_____ (1989) *Reading the Popular*. Boston: Unwin and Hyman.

Gramsci, A. (1971) *Selections from the Prison Notebooks*, in Q. Hoare and G. Nowell-Smith (eds) London: Lawrence & Wishart, 376–7.

Gurevitch, M., T. Bennett, J. Curran and J. Woollacott (eds) (1982) *Culture, Society and the Media.* London: Methuen.

Hall, S. (1996) 'For Allen White: Metaphors of Transformation', in D. Morley and D. K. Chen (eds) *Stuart Hall: Critical Dialogues in Cultural Studies.* London: Routledge, 287–307.

_____ (1996) 'On Postmodernism and Articulation: An interview with Stuart Hall', in D. Morley and D. K. Chen (eds) *Stuart Hall: Critical Dialogues in Cultural Studies*. London: Routledge, 131–50.

Hessels, W. (2000) 'Kijk: het gewone wordt buitengewoon … belachelijk', *De Morgen* (21 September).

Hoorens, V. (2000) 'Een pervers spel voor ramptoeristen', *De Morgen* (18 September).

Howarth, D. (2000) *Discourse*. Buckingham: Open University Press.

Laclau, E. and C. Mouffe (1985) *Hegemony and Socialist Strategy*. London: Verso.

Langer, J. (1998) *Tabloid Television: Popular journalism and the 'Other News'*. London: Routledge.

Lenaerts, T. and B. Depauw (2000) 'Mannen onder elkaar', *De Standaard* (20 January).

Los, R. (2000) 'Af en toe zet ik mijn verstand op nul', *De Morgen* (15 September).

Livingstone, S. and P. Lunt (1994) *Talk on Television: Audience Participation and Public Debate*. London: Routledge.

Mathijs, E. (2002) '*Big Brother* and Critical Discourse: The Reception of *Big Brother*

Belgium', *Television and New Media*, 3, 3, 311–22.

McGuigan, J. (1992) *Cultural Populism*. London: Routledge.

McQuail, D. (1994) *Mass Communication Theory: An Introduction* (3rd edn.). London: Sage.

Mehl, D. (1994) La télévision compassionnelle', *Réseaux*, 63, 117.

Moens, J. (2000) '*Big Brother* was maar een begin: het wordt nog banaler', *De Morgen* (15 February).

Morris, D. (2000) 'Is *Big Brother* voyeuristisch?', *De Standaard* (19 September).

Mortier, E. (2000) 'Iedereen was mooi', *De Morgen* (16 December).

Nichols, B. (1994) *Blurred Boundaries. Questions and Meaning in Contemporary Culture*. Bloomington: Indiana University Press.

O'Sullivan, T., J. Hartley, D. Saunders, M. Montgomery and J. Fiske (1994) *Key Concepts in Communication and Cultural Studies* (2nd edn.). London: Routledge.

Raes, K. (2000) 'They shoot horses, don't they', *De Morgen* (14 October).

Reesink, M. and I. Costa Meyer (2000) *Reality-soap! Big Brother en de opkomst van het multimediaconcept*. Amsterdam: Boom.

Sparks, C. and J. Tulloch (eds) (2000) *Tabloid Tales*. London: Littlefield.

Storey, J. (1997) *An Introduction to Cultural Theory and Popular Culture* (2nd edn.) London: Prentice Hall/Harvester Wheatsheaf.

Strinati, D. (1995) *An Introduction to Theories of Popular Culture*. London: Routledge.

Van Weelden, D. (1999) 'De soap van de toekomst. *Big Brother* en de tien kleine Nederlandertjes', *De Morgen* (11 November).

Von Wackerbath, C. (2000) 'Ik ben geen cultuurpessimist', *Knack* (25 October).

# CHAPTER 7

*Lothar Mikos*

# BIG BROTHER AS TELEVISION TEXT
## Frames of Interpretation and Reception in Germany

At the dawn of the twenty-first century an international format entered the global television market: *Big Brother*. The show was invented by the Dutch enterprise Endemol. After a very successful run at the Dutch channel Veronica (up to 6 million viewers watched the show) it was sold to other countries, firstly European countries like Belgium, Denmark, Germany, Great Britain, Italy, Poland, Portugal, Spain, Sweden and Switzerland and then to other countries like the United States, Australia, Argentina, Brasil, Mexico, Russia, South Africa among others (Hill 2002; Mikos *et al.* 2001). In short, *Big Brother* was one of the most successful television shows all over the world.

By the summer of 2001 there had been three seasons of *Big Brother* in Germany. The first ran from March to June 2000, the second from September to December 2000, and the third from January to May 2001. The first and the second seasons were very successful; the third suffered from some lack of interest by the audience. Therefore the commercial television channel RTL 2 pulled the show from their schedules. In 2003 it was relaunched as *Big Brother – The Battle* and ran from March to July with some success and a respectable market share for the channel.

Regardless of these fluctuations, the fascinating character of the show and the main attraction for the audience is the specific structure of *Big Brother* as a television text. Most viewers in every country where *Big Brother* was the media event of the year have had access to it via the television set. Even if the television show was aided by several other forms of access to the format like the Internet, mobile phones, the tabloid press, tabloid television and talk shows, the television shows remained the central focus of audience attention. In this chapter I would like to argue that the textual structure of the television text and its textuality (Fiske 1987: 96) is central for the fascinating character of the show in audience responses. Furthermore it provides different readings and meanings of *Big Brother*. That is shown by the results of a reception study in Germany. Before I analyse the textual structure of *Big Brother* Germany I will give a brief introduction of the theoretical and methodological background of our research (Mikos *et al.* 2000). In addition to the analysis of the television text I will also give a short description of *Big Brother* as media event, as a multi-media platform with different levels of participation. Finally, the comparison of the reception of the first and third seasons of *Big Brother* in Germany shows how the change of the textual structure leads to differences in success. Generally the success of the show must be seen in the context of social change at the beginning of the twenty-first century and the development of television entertainment in a global media market.

## A multi-perspective approach of studying media phenomena

In analysing *Big Brother*, we have to consider a deep mediation of everyday life (Bondebjerg 2002). Different media are important for people in how they organise their life. Television is a special case because it is accessible at any time for nearly every household. It is part of everyday life and it has an increasing influence on people's world views. Yet analyses of texts and audiences seem to be unaware of each other. If we look at analyses of television texts we are confronted with, in most cases, a lack of knowledge about their relationships to audiences. At best, there are only assumptions of ideological effects; crude thoughts about how ideological elements are realised through the systems of representation. On the other hand, if we look at audience studies we are forced to consider, in most cases, an unawareness of media texts. There may be acknowledgement of the fact that audiences of specific media texts, like soap operas, are constructed, but the specific textual structures are ignored. The main focus of audience research is with the processes of making meaning and not the textual structures that prefigured this processes. If we want to understand the fascination of media texts for audiences we have to bring textual analysis and audience research into contact with each other. Maybe then it will be possible to understand how media texts position both the individual viewer and specific audiences.

Therefore it is necessary to consider on the one hand that a media text has to be performed by a viewer and on the other hand that people only become viewers or audiences under specific conditions in everyday life. As John Storey has noted on the reception of literary texts by readers: 'In other words, a text only becomes a text when read, just as a reader only becomes a reader in the act of reading; neither can exist outside this relationship' (Storey 1999: 73). Neither media texts nor viewers exist as ontological entities. Rather, they come into existence by being realised in time at a given place. Media texts are symbolic materials that are used by authors/producers and readers/audiences to make meaning for the social construction of reality. Media texts become part of the social circulation of meaning in societal discourse structures.

In this context it is important to refer to the concept of reception aesthetics that goes back to the German literary theorist Wolfgang Iser. In his work on novels he insisted that the reader is important for the performance of a text, and the text can be seen as an instruction manual for the reader: 'Reading is an activity that is guided by the text; this must be processed by the reader, who is then, in turn, affected by what he has processed' (Iser 1978: 163). This guidance is possible because of an implied reader in the text. The textual structures offer the reader a possibility of active reading and of its performance. Therefore meaning of a text is the result of a dynamic interaction between text and reader. Reception activities are thus established in the text itself, as structuring characteristics of the text. The viewer, so to speak, is present as a structure in the text. Because the text intends to interact with a viewer, the structure of the viewer in the text has the nature of an incitement. The text itself becomes an instruction to the viewer to act. The specific textual structures as instructions to viewers and the implied viewer or the implied audience becomes the subject of textual analysis (Mikos 2003a).

A reception aesthetics of media combines the analysis of film and television texts with the analysis of reception activities, focusing on the text/viewer interaction in the reception situation, but without neglecting its grounding in social, cultural, societal and everyday life contexts – specially in view of the fact that both text and viewer themselves refer to their contexts. The dynamic interaction of text and reader/viewer takes place in a specific time and space. Therefore it is necessary to be aware of the social, societal, cultural and historical contexts. As Ien Ang has noted, 'contexts are not mutually exclusive but interlocking and interacting, superimposed upon one another as well as indefinitely proliferating in time and space' (Ang 1996: 253). The processing of film and television texts by different audiences in different times and spaces takes place in different reading formations (Bennett & Woollacott 1987: 64). Text and context are inseparable: 'Text and context are always part of the same process, the same moment – they are inseparable: one cannot have a text without a context, or context without a text' (Storey 1999: 73). Therefore it is indispensable for the analysis of media texts to keep in mind the dynamic interaction of text and viewer and the contexts of this process (Mikos 2003a). With reference to *Big Brother* as a television text we have to consider different audiences that perform the text in different ways in different contexts. Therefore the duties of the analysis consists of a textual analysis of the implied viewer or implied audience, an audience research, a discourse analysis and an analysis of the different contexts.

Following the traditions of triangulation in qualitative research the study of *Big Brother* in Germany uses multiple methods, theories and objects. According to the so-called Babelsberg model of media research (Mikos 2003b) the search design consists of four main parts: a textual analysis, an audience study, a discourse analysis and a contextualisation of the first and the third season of *Big Brother* in Germany. The multiplicity of methods, or triangulation, 'reflects an attempt to secure an in-depth understanding of the phenomenon in question' (Denzin & Lincoln 1998: 4). At the centre of the textual analysis were the daily summaries and the live eviction shows. The audience research consisted of focus group interviews, a representative survey of 1,002 people during the first season and a representative survey of 1,012 people during the third season. The discourse analysis focuses on the discussion of *Big Brother* in the main newspapers and journals in Germany. The media event was seen in the contexts of the history of television entertainment in Germany, of the global programme market and of the social change at the beginning of the twenty-first century. In the following sections of this chapter I will focus on the textual analysis and the results of the audience study concerning the interaction with the *Big Brother* text.

## Big Brother as television text: frames of interpretation

Looking at television guides or newspaper articles, several genre names of *Big Brother* appear. Some call it just 'TV show' or 'game show', journalists favour 'psycho-show' or 'reality-show', some call it 'container-docu' or 'docusoap', most TV-guides prefer 'reality-soap'. This variety of names shows that *Big Brother* must be a hybrid genre, dealing with some sort of reality and authenticity. It 'can be classified as created for TV factual entertainment, or real people programmes' (Hill 2002: 330). *Big Brother* combines elements from different genres like docu-soaps and game shows, talk shows and television tabloids that Jon Dovey (2000) called 'first person media', webcams and soap operas. Therefore it is not really new because it combines well-known elements from other genres.

First, *Big Brother* combines elements from behavioural and personality-oriented game shows. By the nominations and possibility for the audience to vote for contestants to leave the house, the show has also the character of a tournament. These kinds of shows are well known and the rules remind of sport events. The editing of the taped material from the 28 cameras that tape 24 hours down to a 30-minute show follows the strategy of soap operas and docu-soaps. As a direct pre-format we can consider MTV's *The Real World*. The first *Big Brother* episode, showing the contestants moving into the house, and the weekly talk-shows, where the nominations and house exits were shown, combine traditional talk shows with journalistic television tabloids. Short portrait films of the contestants, visits with their families and with friends were a major element of the first episode. In the studio they have experts like a psychologist or an astrologist to commentate on the contestants future. *Big Brother* uses well-known formats of television entertainment. A new element combined in a television show is a narrative use of the Internet, although the concept of webcams is not altogether new in the Internet universe. A unknown number of webcams show beaches, coffee machines, bars or people on streets around the world 24 hours a day, or they show the everyday life of people, mostly of the so-called camgirls.

The *Big Brother* format is a hybrid of elements from game shows, drama series, behaviourally oriented games and forms of documentary, it 'contains several sub-programmes within itself' (Bondebjerg 2002: 183). The format can therefore be defined as follows: *Big Brother* is a behavioural and personality-oriented game show staged according to the narrative devices and dramaturgical structures of soap operas, but based within the real-time stage of the *Big Brother* game (see Mikos *et al.* 2000: 28). In this sense, it is not a docu-soap or a real-life soap, but a carefully produced drama of authenticity – a format referring to the everyday world of the viewers and candidates, which can be defined as performative reality TV. Central to the television text *Big Brother* is the staging of real people in a situation created for screening. It is constructed around performance; on the one hand performance of the participants as housemates and as contestants of a game show, and on the other hand performance of the producers by staging an edited version of the footage from the house. The participants have to manage 'their images within the house, the housemates also have to perform for the audience who can, potentially see everything they do' (Roscoe 2001: 482). Central to the performance of the producers is the editing of the daily summary by the rules of docu-soaps and soap operas.

There are three types of docu-soaps:

1  with a narrative focus on a specific location like an airport or a hospital;

2  with a narrative focus on specific persons or characters like policemen or cheer-leaders;
3  with a narrative focus on specific themes like having a baby or building a house.

*Big Brother* includes elements of all three types: there is a specific location, the *Big Brother* house; there are specific characters, the participants or contestants; and there is a main theme, 'back to basics', the slogan of the show. The editing rules of the daily summaries are those of soap operas with the following main characteristics: There is a parallelism of the narrative time structure to the everyday life of the audience. If there is a new daily summary that summarises the life of the participants during one day at the *Big Brother* house, there is also a new day in the everyday life of the audience members. Soaps have an ongoing narrative that seem endless. The *Big Brother* narrative must come to an end because of the tournament structure of the game. One of the main dramaturgical characteristics of soaps is the intertwining of several plot lines. For the daily summaries of *Big Brother* the producers also create several plotlines that show different relations of the housemates or different topics they focus. The aesthetic focus of soaps lies on the dialogue of the characters with a frequent use of close-ups and medium close-ups. More than fifty per cent of all actions in the *Big Brother* house shown on television are dialogues, mainly on the topic of interpersonal relations. The relations are narrated from the subjective viewpoint of the characters. During the screening of *Big Brother* the games and topics of discussions in the house are all from the point of view of different housemates. And essential for soaps is the cliffhanger at the end of an episode, the interruption of the narration at a highly dramatic plot point. The *Big Brother* episodes work with the voice-over narration that dramatises the events and actions in the house in a specific way at the end of a daily summary (Ang 1985; Geraghty 1991).

   *Big Brother* is a hybrid television text on three levels: on the level of genre as discussed above, on the level of discourse because there are 'very different forms of discourse in and the same genre' (Bondebjerg 2002: 184), and on the level of aesthetic staging referring to 'the fact that *Big Brother* is a staged reality, which the participants, the producers and the audience are all very aware of' (ibid.). There are also different levels of narration that lead to different frames of interpretation. The notion frame is not used in the sense of Erving Goffman (1986) who distinguishes primary and secondary frames for the interpretation of reality. The interpretive frames of *Big Brother* are more like the modulations of secondary frames in the sense of Goffman. There are seven levels of narration in *Big Brother*:

1  It is a *game*, where a number of contestants have to live in a house for a hundred days that is observed by cameras and where they have to perform as housemates;
2  This game is created for television and addressed to an audience, therefore it is a *game show* where contestants try to win the game and the prize and where they have to perform for a television audience;
3  Part of the game and the game show are *other games* like sport games, gambling or performing as talk show guests or popstars;
4  The daily summaries of the events in the house are edited and narrated by the conventional rules of *soap operas*;
5  There is the level of *social reality* in *Big Brother* in two ways: on the one hand the life of the participants in the house is their social reality during their stay, on the

other hand the participation in the show has consequences for the social reality of the contestants, for example when they become famous;

6　*Big Brother* is a format that shows *self-reflexivity* in relation to the five other levels, for example in some situations of conflict between the housemates one of the contestants try to calm down the others with the sentence: 'It's only a game', or when the participants address the cameras directly;

7　There is a level of self-referentiality in *Big Brother* because the participants quote other television programmes and a whole range of different media texts out of the universe of popular culture.

Every level of narration has the status of a frame of interpretation. So it is up to the viewers, whether they consider a moment of the programme as a game, a game show, a soap, a game in the game, social reality, or whether they are aware of the self-reflexivity or the self-referentiality. Of importance is their own knowledge of television referents as well as their own cultural and social orientation. The public debate demonstrated that politicians and most critics defined *Big Brother* as social reality, while the contestants saw it as a game, while the producers defined it as a show. During the public debate, each side tried to set their own definition as the dominant and only true one. It is important to see that each definition as well as each format element blends into each other. *Big Brother* is everything at the same time – show, game, soap and social reality – and there is a constant shift between all seven levels. The interpretative frames from which the audience can choose are an important moment of the fascination.

The textual analysis shows that the arrangement of the hundred-day game basically follows a soap dramaturgy. It is structured by plot lines that run across several episodes. The show invents and makes use of cliffhangers and teasers. The documentary, footage material is thus constructed into a developing, forward-looking plot that in the style of a soap always asks: what comes next? The soap characteristics are very strong in the construction of the television text.

The narrative flow of the soap is interrupted on Sundays with a live studio talk format that offers another angle on the participants. Functionally, the Sunday talk episode is integrated into the continuing soap narrative, as it presents a stage for generating new conflict potentials and changes of constellation among the participants. The reigning principle of montage strives to decode the residents' actions from a variety of perspectives. This technique is derived from fictional feature film and television series formats. Each resident is defined clearly as a character with narrative functions within the overall story, and they can thus function as fictional figures. The serial episodic character and numerous narrative techniques employed in the *Big Brother* story are thus drawn from the soap opera genre. However, a moment of unpredictability is injected into that genre by the conditions of the game show, affecting both the narration and the aesthetics of the programme, and functioning as a generator of tension and marker of authenticity: 'No matter how constructed the event, or how closely it conforms to the structure and narrative of soap opera, there is always a potential element of unpredictability in the show' (Roscoe 2001: 481). The documentary tendencies in the choice of narrative techniques serve to support that aspect.

In both editing and in the drawing of characters, the show moves between the two poles of fictionalisation and documentarisation. At one extreme, the visual techniques make constant use of the surveillance situation, i.e. it is signaled to the viewers that the participants are under observation. At the other extreme, the surveillance situation is often concealed via a conventionalised 'invisible' montage, which puts the viewer right in the middle of the events. Among the show's characters/contestants, we see a vital tension between the stigmatising and fixed definition of characters through the narration, and the residents' opportunity to 'break out' of their assigned stereotypes in the course of the weekly tasks assigned by the show producers, a possibility granted by the lack of a predefined script. Beyond this, the documentary element is injected through the residents' individual confessions to the camera in the 'confession room' which is kept confidential from the other contestants. The confession room simulates face-to-face communication with the viewer and borrows from the classic interview form. Whereas the episodes broadcast during the week consist of edited summaries of each day, the live portions during the Sunday talk show can indeed be considered documentary, allowing participation in a situation with little dramaturgic preparation. In contrast to classic documentary, however, this does not record a pre-existing social reality, but a situation initiated by the game itself.

The causal combination of techniques adopted from the two genres of documentary and fiction is constitutive to the text and characterises the peculiarity of the format on the level of text analysis. The promise of authenticity raised by the moment of 'reality' is unusual for a conventional soap. The additional narrative framework of the game show further allows the format to go beyond previous docu-soaps. The tension of the programme is generated through consciousness of the predefined plot points – the nominations of candidates for expulsion by residents, and the subsequent expulsions based on the viewer phone-in vote – in combination with the dimension of unpredict-ability. Therein, too, lies a moment of interaction for the audience. But only through the use of fictionalising techniques can the events of the real 'competition' be told as the story of a hundred-day residential project, thus facilitating the recipients' emotional participation. Every expelled candidate appears directly at the host's interview table – as a multifaceted figure with a *Big Brother* biography, as a representative of social values and behavioural forms in a community. The fictionalisation and authentication strategies invite the audience to perceive the various frames of the format within this context of tension. The combination of different genre elements and the different levels of hybridisation and narration make it possible to address 'a wide and potentially diverse television audience' (Tincknell & Raghuram 2002: 205). That is central to the characterisation of the show as 'television event' (Scannell 2002).

*Big Brother* as television text works on several levels. Each of the levels correlates to a specific frame of interpretation as a modulation of secondary frames in the sense of Goffman that serves the social construction of reality. Therefore *Big Brother* can be seen as an open text that has to be produced by the participants/contestants and the audience within their framework of life-world knowledge and the social und cultural circulation of meaning. It is the participants and the different audiences which produce *Big Brother*, in talking about the conditions of the format and the intermingling of fictionality and authenticity.

But *Big Brother* as media event is more than a multi-level and multi-hybrid television text. It works as a multi-media platform that contains a weekly printed *Big Brother*-journal, an official website, several fan-pages, a computer game, portrayals of the show in various radio and television formats and tabloid newspapers and journals, hit singles by former participants. These various parts of the media event construct two different forms of relation between *Big Brother* and the audience. On the one hand there is a strong element of active participation, not only by voting via mail, phone or SMS but also by the several activities offered by the websites including chats, live observation of the participants via visual webcam access, commentaries on the participants and a game. On the other hand there is a strong intertextual dimension of *Big Brother*. The portrayals of the participants in the press are very important for the audience's judgement of them because they show different perspectives than the television show (Jerslev 2003). The 'different texts contributed to the wider text that was *Big Brother*, while helping to develop different and contesting meanings about it' (Tincknell & Raghuram 2002: 208). The participating role of the audience is also central to the success of the format. But as the audience study in Germany shows only 12 per cent of the *Big Brother* viewers (more than one time a week) called in to give their vote and only 22 per cent of the voters have had access to the website. Even if *Big Brother* can be seen as a multi-media event the cause of the very success was the television text with its various levels of hybridisation and narration.

## The reception of Big Brother Germany

The audience study of *Big Brother* was conducted by using a representative survey and focus group discussions held with a group of 15-year-old female pupils and a group of university students. The results establish the underlying motives and modalities of audience reception, and reveal the mechanisms that generated the fascination of *Big Brother* on television. The survey showed that only very few *Big Brother* fans called in to give their votes. They also visited the *Big Brother* website only very rarely. The extreme success of the site in due of numbers of visits, therefore, must be generated by a specific Internet community. These results confirmed the path to analyse the television-material since that is what most people see. The survey confirmed that young people seem to enjoy the show. In the age group of the 14- to 29-year-olds almost a quarter (23 per cent) followed *Big Brother* several times a week. Nineteen per cent watched the programme once or twice a week, only 4 per cent of this age group had never heard of *Big Brother.* In comparison, in the age group of the over-50-year-olds only 2 per cent can be considered as *Big Brother* viewers. Since the *Big Brother* fans are young people it is logical that most of them are still in school or university. It is also interesting that *Big Brother* fans are better educated than general German residents. This might be explained by the fact that younger Germans are higher educated than older Germans. These results from Germany are comparable to the results from the UK (Hill 2002: 331). Different from daily soaps, where the main public are young females, *Big Brother* is followed by men and women almost equally, with a slight majority of women.

After finding that young people between 14 and 29 years old are the frequent *Big Brother* watchers, we held one focus discussion group with high-school students (15 years old) and one with university students (27 to 31 years old). One of the main findings was that *Big Brother* fascinated them because of the various frames through which it can be observed. It is the tensions between the reception as a game show, as the Saturday live show, as a soap opera, and the cumulative effects of real-life, which made the format interesting. The viewers themselves are aware of changes in the interpreting frames during their reception. For them, the excitement is often generated by their speculations on the 'right' reception. When are the candidates being authentic? When is it staged? What part of it is just the game? How does it affect real life in the house, and in the candidates' lives after *Big Brother*?

Going along with the change of interpreting frames is one substantial motive underlying the reception of *Big Brother*: 'talking about it'. A psychological analysis of the candidates, why they behave in what way, is very much a primary element in the process of making meaning of the show. Members of both discussion groups mentioned that immediately after the show they would call their friends to recapitulate what had happened in the last episode. They analyse the emotions, feelings, wishes and social interactions of the housemates. The motive of psychologising about the participants is very strongly influenced by the question of authenticity. In the analysis after the broadcast, viewers often attempt not only to explain the behaviour of the candidates psychologically, but also with regard to the question of whether their behaviour is authentic – and whether their actual behaviour was even shown on screen. To the question whether the actual behaviour was shown, or edited, there were interesting differences between teenagers and older students. While the schoolgirls especially found little interest in the residents' daily activities like eating, showering, getting up, and so on, and were therefore even pleased that the producers generated tension through the editing. The group of students were more fascinated by the everyday real life and the lack of a script. They were also more critical towards the possibility of the television station to edit and cut out certain parts. A lot of their speculations cumulated around the question as to what they were missing out on and what happened in reality. The students believed that the television station influences the behaviour of the housemates, not by giving them a script, but by the games and jobs they had to do during the day. Especially by deciding what kind of person would be sent into the *Big Brother* house to substitute for a candidate that voluntarily left the house early, the station can influence the social interaction. It was also the students who were amazed by the professionality of the marketing accompanying the show. They talked in depth about the *Big Brother* contestant Zlatko, who became an instant media star, and who was interviewed in several shows.

This is demonstrative of the tensions that exist during the reception of the show. On the one hand the audience is dealing with 'real' and normal people. It starts to feel with them, like or dislike them. On the other hand the audience wonders how authentic they are. The feeling of watching a soap opera is dominant during the reception phase, but the viewers' emphasis on the authenticity of the candidates or of their behaviour limits that feeling. One of the schoolgirls in the discussion group described *Big Brother* as a soap opera with an unknown beginning and end. Therein lies the fascination. *Big Brother* follows the soap convention, but at the same time it is not predictable, since there is no script, and since there are aspects of real life in which no one can intervene. The framing of following a soap opera is so dominant that the reception as a game show is overwhelmed. The elements of competition and game seem to vanish in the memory of the audience. Our results show that for the regular and frequent viewer of *Big Brother* the most important motivation is derived from the dramaturgical structures of the soap opera, in combination with the appeal of the unpredictability of a game with 'real' people. This leads to a perception of difference between fiction and authenticity, explaining the very success of the first (and second) season of *Big Brother* in Germany.

But the third season of *Big Brother* in Germany failed. The representative survey shows that 39.9 per cent of the viewers of the first season characterised the third season as boring and 32.2 per cent declared the participants as uninteresting. The textual analysis of the third season shows a shift in the editing of the daily summaries and in the staging of the game show. While the first and the second seasons of *Big*

Brother were very 'soapish' the third season was only little 'soapish'. There was no focus on the personal relations of the participants, but rather on individual characters as social stereotypes. While in the first and second seasons a major focus was the everyday life of the housemates, the producers tried to create events in the third season with visits from celebrities, or a dinner with various sorts of insects, or putting the candidates under hypnosis. During the first and the second season the housemates always discussed the conditions of the life inside the house, in the third season they always talked about the life outside the house. They insisted on a difference between the life in the house and outside, thus bringing about a sense of role-distance. In contrast, the participants of the first and second seasons performed a role-play as housemates and candidates of a game show. The role-distance of the participants is one of the reasons for the characterisation of the third season as boring by the audience. The difference between their life inside and outside leads to a lack of uncertainty. So there is no reason for the members of the audience to discuss whether the behaviour of a participant is 'real' and authentic or not. The editing principles and the staging of the game show in the third season led to a perception of real people playing the role of real people in a television setting. There was no reason to talk and wonder about it.

## The historical and social context of the success of Big Brother

According to a long-running complaint, television has lost its 'original event' character. *Big Brother*, however, may certainly be called a major television event (Scannell 2002). The media – especially the guiding medium of television – have developed specific modalities for portraying reality. In these we see not only the structural conditions that make up each medium, but also the structural conditions of societal change. As a 'cultural forum' (Newcomb & Hirsch 1984) television makes the diverse life-worlds within society into issues. It does not offer a self-enclosed worldview, but (re)presents the variety of life-forms and life-styles within an elaborated, pluralised society. The *Big Brother* format therefore must be located within the development of entertainment formats in television, and related to social developments at the beginning of the twenty-first century. The format is an expression of the increasing life-worldly orientation of television programmes resulting from the competition between public and commercial broadcasting – which in the entertainment sector has culminated with performative reality TV (Keppler 1994). The hybrid *Big Brother* format, a mixture of various entertainment formats and a combination of various genres, is an expression of this general development.

*Big Brother* is also an expression of the social developments that can be described as reflexive modernity (Beck *et al.* 1994; Giddens 1991). These may be characterised as an ever more complex elaboration of society into pluralised lifestyles and life-forms. However, so-called individualisation tendencies lead to new forms of social creation and adoption of communality. Within the pluralised society, traditional institutions can no longer provide generally valid values and standards or patterns of meaning, so that people are increasingly forced to bring meaning into their own lives themselves. This increased subjective effort is accompanied by a simultaneous lack of orientation. In this situation, stability and dependability are offered by the medium of television, which is constantly available and presents a broad variety of life-views. As a cultural forum, television can still communicate across the lines of the partly disparate life realms of people. Therefore it plays an increasingly important role in providing social orientation.

The flexible person demanded by the pluralised society must present himself on the identity market so as to remain connected to the society. The reflexive modernity is accompanied by a more flexible identity-building that 'creates room to "play" with roles and identities' (Bondebjerg 2002: 161). Here television assumes a dual function. First, it serves up a menu of fictional and 'authentic' personalities to the viewers. These offer new identity patterns that viewers can adopt in their own everyday lives, as they seek to prevail on the identity market of social reality by themselves offering new symbolic commodities. Second, in its performative formats television opens to people the possibility of portraying themselves on the identity market of television, and by doing so to raise their identity market-value within social reality. In *Big Brother*, the participants are allowed to present themselves in the medium itself. For the viewers, the programme is a source of fresh symbolic commodity for potential use on the real-life identity market. Until now, these social changes and related demands on people have been clearest among youth and young people up to thirty years of age. Thus it is no wonder that the *Big Brother* format is especially popular among the younger target groups.

In certain ways, the *Big Brother* participants represent the new flexible people, and can thus become heroes in a time of insecurity. This operates quite apart from the way in which young people apparently no longer have any problems with making public appearances on the everyday medium of television. In this way *Big Brother* is part of the transformation of the public sphere: 'The reflexive modernity and the new awareness of the self in public and private life, as well as of the mediation of the self in a network society moving from a nation state to global frames which also interact with local levels, is the fuel of the new reality genres' (Bondebjerg 2002: 162). Therefore *Big Brother* is not the cause but the symptom of a general change in society and the global and local television markets. The reasons for its success as television text is its hybridisation and its several levels of narration as interpretive frames connected to the life-world and everyday life of audiences in a multiple, reflexive network society.

*Bibliography*

Ang, I. (1985) *Watching Dallas: Soap Opera and the Melodramatic Imagination*. London: Methuen.

Ang, I. (1996) 'Ethnography and Radical Contextualism in Audience Studies', in J. Hay, L. Grossberg and E. Wartella (eds) *The Audience and its Landscape*. Boulder, Colorado: Westview Press, 247–62.

Barker, M. (2000) *From Antz to Titanic. Reinventing Film Analysis*. London: Pluto Press.

Beck, U., A. Giddens and S. Lash (1994) *Reflexive Modernisation*. London: Polity Press.

Bennett, T. and J. Woollacott (1987) *Bond and Beyond: The Political Carrier of a Popular Hero*. London: Macmillan.

Bondebjerg, I. (2002) 'The Mediation of Everyday Life: Genre, Discourse, and Spectacle in Reality TV', in A. Jerslev (ed.) *Realism and 'Reality' in Film and Media. Northern Lights. Film and Media Studies Yearbook 2002*. Copenhagen: Museum Tusculanum Press, 159–92.

Denzin, N. K. and Y. S. Lincoln (1998) 'Introduction: Entering the Field of Qualitative Research', in N. K. Denzin and Y. S. Lincoln (eds) *The Landscape of Qualitative Research. Theories and Issues*. Thousand Oaks: Sage, 1–34.

Dovey, J. (2000) *Freakshow: First Person Media and Factual Entertainment*. London: Pluto Press.

Fiske, J. (1987) *Television Culture*. London: Methuen.

Geraghty, C. (1991) *Women and Soap Opera. A Study of Prime Time Soaps*. Cambridge: Polity Press.

Giddens, A. (1991) *The Consequences of Modernity*. Cambridge: Polity Press.

Goffman, E. (1986) *Frame Analysis*. Boston, MA: Northeastern University Press.

Hill, A. (2002) '*Big Brother*: The Real Audience', *Television & New Media*, 3, 3, 323–40.

Iser, W. (1978) *The Act of Reading: A Theory of Aesthetic Response*. London: Routledge & Kegan Paul.

Jerslev, A. (2003) *The Reality Game Show and Celebrity Culture*. Paper presented at the Colloquium 'Staging Reality' at the University of Stirling, January 2003.

Keppler, A. (1994) *Wirklicher als die Wirklichkeit? Das neue Realitätsprinzip der Fernsehunterhaltung*. Frankfurt: Fischer.

Mikos, L. (2003a) *Film – und Fernsehanalyse*. Konstanz: UVK/UTB.

___ (2003b) *Framing of Reality and Aesthetic Staging of TV Reality Shows*. Paper presented at the Colloquium 'Staging Reality' at the University of Stirling, January 2003.

Mikos, L., P. Feise, K. Herzog, E. Prommer and V. Veihl (2000) *Im Auge der Kamera. Das Fernsehereignis Big Brother*. Berlin: Vistas.

Mikos, L., E. Haible, C. Töppler and L. Verspohl (2001) '*Big Brother* als Globales Fernsehformat. Ein Vergleich länderspezifischer Inszenierungen', *Medien Praktisch Texte*, 4, 57–64.

Mikos, L. and E. Prommer (2002) 'Das Fernsehereignis *Big Brother*. Analyse und Vergleich der drei Staffeln in Deutschland', in A. Baum & S. J. Schmidt (eds) *Fakten und Fiktionen. Über den Umgang mit Medienwirklichkeiten*. Konstanz: UVK, 325–37.

Newcomb, H. and P. Hirsch (1984) 'Television as a Cultural Forum: Implications for Research', in W. Rowland and B. Watkins (eds) *Interpreting Television: Current Research Perspectives*. Beverly Hills: Sage, 58–73.

Roscoe, J. (2001) '*Big Brother* Australia. Performing the "Real" twenty-four-seven', *International Journal of Cultural Studies*, 4, 4, 473–88.

Scannell, P. (2002) '*Big Brother* as a Television Event', *Television & New Media*, 3, 3, 271–82.

Storey, J. (1999) *Cultural Consumption and Everyday Life*. London: Arnold.

Tincknell, E. and P. Raghuram (2002) '*Big Brother*: Reconfiguring the "active" Audience of Cultural Studies?', *European Journal of Cultural Studies*, 5, 2, 199–215.

# CHAPTER 8

*François Jost*

# LOFT STORY
## Big Brother France and the Migration of Genres

'Reality TV arouses French passions', was the headline of *USA Today* on 19 June 2001. Actually, for some weeks, intellectuals, politicians and journalists were in confrontation on an unusual field: television criticism. At the heart of this confrontation was the broadcasting of *Loft Story*, the French version of *Big Brother*, launched by Endemol. Why had this programme so much success and caused so much debate? The contention of this chapter is that the real novelty of *Loft Story* was to put the spectator in a crisis, by mobile communication strategies as well as by making a product from multiple traditions, so that, instead of stemming from an already known genre, it migrated from one television genre to another, according to several discourses and interpretations, meeting during that process very different publics.

Speaking of 'genre migration' implies a number of presuppositions. Indeed, in order for this expression to acquire meaning, it is necessary to admit that genres are not stable and static objects without any history, and that their structure is not established once and for all, like a map one could follow. Building on Schaeffer's contention that 'texts are complex semiotic acts' (Schaeffer 1989: 131) we believe that the allocation of labels to text is a much more arbitrary operation than it would seem at first sight.

Depending on the kind of communication one wishes to make, genre classifications change. They change because of the multiplicity of the semiotic material in use (language, images, sound, music, and so forth), and because they are the battle ground for social actors with diverging interests: producers, who must endow their products with a generic identity in the interest of mass-production and mass-circulation; television channels, who need to name their objects in order to make them desirable; mediators, such as the press, who agree or not to circulate these categories to the public; and lastly the spectator, for whom categorisation is a regulating concept necessary for his/her interpretation.

If each of these presuppositions is frequently admitted, it is less frequently that the epistemological consequences follow, notably concerning the construction of a communicational model suitable for explaining the relation between the media and the receiver. Thus, Jean-Marie Schaeffer asserts that fiction is based on the acceptance of a shared 'feint' (Schaeffer 1999).[1] If the reception of a text of fiction, as fiction, for instance, does not depend on the ontological features of the text, if it requires pragmatic criteria, we must push the logic to its end and consider that texts do not show themselves necessarily for what they are (or for what their authors think they are), and that the interpretation does not necessarily coincide with the instructions of the paratext. According to Umberto Eco, the text fixes limits to its interpretation, beyond which there is only place for its use (Eco 1992). One would gladly follow him if the system in which the cultural goods circulate today was concerned with the 'veracity of the text'. But things are quite different: it is high time to abandon the model of author and reader sharing a common interest, at least in the current situation of the publishing market and the globalisation of formats.

## Television and the genre contract

From this point of view, television offers a privileged ground of study. The idea of migration invites to question the intangibility of the interpretative frame, which the 'contract' between text and viewer supposes. When Philippe Lejeune introduced the autobiographical pact, it was a question of breaking with the paradigm of textual immanence: the constitution of the autobiographical contract adopts the point of view of a reader who will detect the peritextual indications of a contract that he must accept for a good interpretation of what he reads (Lejeune 1975). Other uses of the concept have been made since, almost always assuming common attitudes between reader and text. The most frequent relates to the concept of 'suspension of disbelief', without ever asking whether this attitude is universal. By seizing the concept, speech analysts have emptied it of any paratextual dimension: the contract is a priori put as the obliged mode of media communication (Charaudeau 1997).

Although it claims to avoid the Jakobsonian paradigm of communication, the contract eventually thinks the Other under the epistemological angle of understanding, and conceives reading as a symmetric process where the reader understands what the author means. The associated concept is then that of competence, textual, narrative or fictitious. To understand the text in the right way, the receiver should mobilise rules, even encyclopaedia, which actualise this 'lazy' text. The place given to the Other is that of an understanding subject, endowed with a textual willingness, which makes him interpret the text – within certain limits – more than to use it (Eco 1992; 1996).

This symmetry, although it offers the reader or the spectator the apparent freedom of being a potential author, sometimes reduces the receiver to nothing, but to agree with the aims of the sender. So, Patrick Charaudeau defines the double 'informative contract' in the following way:

the purpose of the contract of media communication defines itself as a dual aim, each corresponding to a particular symbolic aim: the aim of 'making known', the aim to inform so to speak, which tends to produce an object of knowledge, according to a civic logic: to inform the citizen; and the aim 'to make feel', the aim to gain attention, which tends to produce an object of consumption according to a commercial logic: to attract the largest possible audience in order to survive competition, as well as ethical: to seduce in order to educate. (Charaudeau 1997: 73)

Far from agreeing, the informative contract is defined with a single purpose: 'to make the other share its own intentionality' (ibid.). The asymmetry of this contract, drafted and dictated by the sender, is moreover registered at the heart of the linguist's formulation: 'to be as credible as possible while attracting the largest possible number of receivers' (ibid.). Under the appearance of an agreement, Charaudeau is only confirming the aims of the sender, as proves the fact that it is a question of being credible. If this consideration may well inhabit the minds of journalists, one wonders how it could govern its reception. The receiver of the written, radio or television media, does not ask for credibility of information, but rather for truthful or proved information, that is to say for an information whose truthfulness is judged, under certain conditions, as with a common assertion. Credibility belongs to the sophist, which the journalist sometimes is.

This shift of position of the Other – from a free subject endowed with reason to that of consumer of a media information governed by the requirements of profitability – operates a surreptitious change of paradigm: from the explanation of a cognitive model to the legitimisation of the trade logic at the centre of the media by the addressee himself. Thus, the contract loses its value as a heuristic tool to become a general notion, contradictory in its terms, a *petitio principii*. Understanding a text would only be to accept the strategies of the one who wrote it, to work them out. Following the idea of co-construction of meaning, this model can hardly account for the different and divergent interests that attract the spectator to programmes. But above all, the contract can be criticised in so far as it does not supply an efficient model for analysis. While it is claimed that fiction presupposes a contract of fiction based on the suspension of disbelief, that games require a contract of entertainment, and that reality shows require a contract of assistance, we are not more advanced than the doctors of Molière when they brandish the soporific virtue of the opium for explaining that this drug causes sleep.

## Genre as a promise

The strategy of imposing the meaning of documents is precisely what characterises television communication in the era of the advertisement. Far from circulating alone, any television document is accompanied by a multitude of interviews of the actors, with press releases, and so forth. In effect, all these peritexts, paratexts, and epitexts are so many promises relating to the symbolic pleasure that the spectator will enjoy.

I would like to replace the contract by the model of the promise, whose heuristic virtue seems superior to me (Jost 1997). This is based on three propositions:

1   Genre is the token which regulates the circulation of texts or broadcasting pro-
    grammes in the media world;
2   The text or the programme is a complex semiotic object (I leave aside the fact of

knowing if one can really consider a programme as a text);

3   From the previous points follows that genre is a construction by exemplification of some samples of properties which the text possesses among others. A serial can be perceived as a fiction, but also as a document in order to trigger debate, thus a document on reality.

In the context of television, the channel is the *onomaturge* authority, if one may say so, which decides or proposes – the nuance is of importance – the generic nature of the document. As promissive act, this quasi-baptism (it is indeed a question of baptising every programme) looks like an unilateral act, as far as Paul Ricœur defines it in the following terms: 'it is an assertion neither true nor false, but that can fail or come to a sudden end, or be empty, or be invalidated; on the other hand, it is a assertion which does what it tells: to say "I promise", it is to promise' (Ricœur n.d.). In fact, the promissive act carried out by the genre is dual.

Firstly, a promise constitutive of the genre, which forges the horizon of expectation inherent to a genre. It is necessary to clarify that this promise, which engenders beliefs, deals also with shared knowledge. How could we otherwise explain Eco's observation:

> Having myself experienced writing two novels that touched millions of readers, I realised an extraordinary phenomenon. Up to ten thousand copies (variable estimation according the country), one generally finds a public familiar with the fiction contract. After that, and especially beyond one million copies, one enters a no man's land where it is no longer sure whether readers know about this contract. (Eco 1996: 102)

What then is the value, even metaphoric, of the contract? Instead of considering the readers as ignorant of the fiction pact, is it not better to say that part of the audience does not know what fiction means or refuses to make a fictional use of fiction, preferring not to suspend its disbelief? As for television, a lot of people believe they know what live broadcasting is about, while associating it a with a vague idea of indexicality present in any technique of photo-chemical or electronic reproduction. The promise is not thus in the genre, but is the object of a learning.

Secondly, A pragmatic promise. To know what fiction or live broadcasting means does not save from errors of interpretation or from gaps with regard to the sender's instructions. If certain texts or programmes are at once recognisable – as 'novel', 'fiction film' or 'game' – numerous current media objects play on the ambiguity. A perfect example are reality shows, the label of which plays skilfully between reality and spectacle, as well as 'télé-réalité' or 'real tv', and others. If the media are eager for ill-defined products, it is because they play with the spectator's interpretation better than other products through categorisation. This act of allocating a name to a thing carries out a second promise, a pragmatic one based on two commitments: as regards the interest and feelings the programme will beget; as regards the guarantee of finding in the programme the qualities exemplified by the trailers, promotion spotlights or the communication in the other media.

In so far as the publicity can play on the interpretation of the programme by the audience, inciting them to classify it in a given category, it follows that analysing a television programme implies examining all the elements which participate in its communication: reviews published by channels to inform professionals, press releases, interviews with directors, writers or actors, the titles of the programmes, the trailers, and so forth. All these sources contribute to formulate a promise to the audience, which will then be confronted with the act that the programme represents by itself and with the greater or lesser credulity of the public. Let us note in passing, that if this promise more or less reveals the explicit aim of the channel, it should not be confused with its strategies: a channel, as any speaker, can say something with a purpose and carry it out for other unconfessed reasons. As viewers, we only know the admitted aims; it is the task of the analysis to lay bare the strategies.

What comes across as a unilateral act at first sight, this promise is obviously a commitment with regard to the other: 'the one who promises obliges himself only as far as he is committed towards the Other' (Jacques 1999). Contrary to the media contract which imposes the enunciator's law to the receiver (that of the largest number, of audience in particular), the promise confers to the Other 'the correlative right to require'. This relation of complementary reciprocity solves the theoretical difficulties raised by a model of a strongly asymmetric communication, where the only freedom of the one who listens or who sees, is to espouse the aims of the enunciator. There is another consequence: the promise is only efficient through mutual confidence: 'It is a statement which establishes and supposes a certain rapport among the speaker and another person in the context of an adjusted behaviour' (Jacques 1999: 240), which very logically implies, that the lie is destructive for the reciprocity of the persons.

One of the errors of the media contract partisans is to claim to clear up the cognitive dimension (that is, how does one understand a text?), while establishing a relation among the actors of communication, which belongs to a moral reflection. One obliges the Other to enter its intention, and this law of the strongest is masked by the lure of mutual agreement. Now, if one wants to understand media communication, the first gesture must be to separate the question of 'narrative competence' from the nature of the relation uniting the actors.

Having determined the transcendental conditions of the migration of the genres, it remains to be seen on which territories the generic movements occur. My second thesis is that the territory on which emitter and receiver meet, or are in confrontation, can be delimited *a priori* and that only the movements are indefinite.

## The territory of television genres

Any television programme is interpreted according to one of the following worlds:

*The real world*. Facing television, the first question is to know if the signs refer to existing objects in our world or if they refer to chimeras or fictitious entities. Certain programmes or certain films claim to refer to our world and to bring us information in order to improve our knowledge. This relation, in the final analysis, is a matter for an exercise of proof. Information shows, documentaries and live television give us the feeling of directly accessing events, as 'witnesses' of the world. Live broadcasting gives a feeling of authenticity, which we prefer above all, even when the information is not clear enough or when the spectacle is of a lesser quality. The promise of speaking about the world does not belong only to live broadcasting, it is common to all films and to all programmes that promise a discourse of truth which we interpret on the grounds of truth or falsehood.

*The world of the fiction*. Although the world of the fiction looks more or less like ours, it owes nothing to it. Authors are free to invent and we recognise this freedom. It is for them to decide if a human being becomes shorter after having undergone atomic radiation or that they grow or become invisible. All we ask of them is not to change the rules every minute! If they are consistent, we agree to believe in all that they will tell us. Fiction has nothing to do with lies. Moreover, deception regulates our reception. Objects, actions, all the signs of fiction refer to an imaginary and mental universe and what we require from fiction is that it respects the rule of coherence of the universe created, with postulates and properties which support it. Beyond that, errors of screenplay are at stake...

*The ludic world.* Umberto Eco, who was one of the first to show the role of the opposition between information and fiction in the categorisation of television programmes, noticed that one type of programme remained difficult to place on this map of beliefs – the game: 'Does it tell the truth or stage a fiction?' (Eco 1985: 203). The answer is not obvious: games often appeal to a sharing between truth and errors: there are right answers and wrong answers, the presenter himself often appearing as the guarantee of truth (sometimes helped by a jury or by a referee). However, the same presenter can obviously lie, for example, by telling a story to test the sagacity of the candidate; he can play roles, disguise or 'make fun'. But is it necessary to end, with Eco, with a mixed reality – fiction?

If I refer to my definition of genre as the promise of a relation to a world, it is necessary to go further. We recognised 'two manners to make worlds': or to refer to our world – which we call reality-, or make reference to a mental world. In both cases, the signs aim at a certain transparency, especially involving images and sounds: they are less important than they appear. But it can occur that the sign refers to itself, in a reflexive way, while referring to an object. This posting of the sign as such, which depends on what is called the audio-visual enunciation, joins one of the definition features of the game – and it is moreover what some people blame it for. Indeed, according to the Larousse encyclopaedia, the game is 'a free physical or intellectual activity in which one engages for pleasure'. Certainly, this 'wantonness' knows degrees, since the activities aim above all at pleasure or entertainment, bringing the player a selfish physical pleasure, which Roger Caillois (1967) classified under the term of ilinx, a Greek word literally meaning 'whirlwind of water': games based on the search for dizziness, for acrobatics, falls, skids, and so forth. On the contrary, games where the player dissimulates or acts as a person without the intention of deceiving the spectator are near to fiction without creating a fictitious world. They belong to what Caillois (1967) names mimicry, which points as much to the child playing police and thieves as for the actor interpreting a role. To the 'for real' of information, which points to the world as referent, and the 'for forgery' of fiction, which aims at a mental universe, it is necessary to add a 'for fun', in which the mediation takes itself for object, as it is a question of playing with language (enunciation), of playing with the game for its own sake. I thus propose to qualify this third logical possibility as a ludic (playful) world. In short, these three worlds – the real, the fictitious and the ludic – can be schematised thus:

# The worlds of television

The criteria of a programme's valuation thus differ according to the reference worlds, but television communication is a dynamic and uncertain process: no programme is ever classified for certain. The channel makes propositions by the act of naming, while the televiewer, taking it into account or not, appropriates it more or less. It is the reason for which, rather than to place a genre once and for all on this triangle, I prefer to leave it blank for the moment. Each particular analysis of such programmes and the programming should fill it out. Certainly, it would seem natural to place games on the ludic, television news on real and series on fictitious. Nevertheless, in fact, it happens that fictions are presented as reality or reality as a show. The specificity of a programme like *Loft Story* or *Big Brother* is indeed to be situated at an equal distance from these three poles, and able to migrate from one region to another, according to the point of view from which the programme is considered: the first migration comes from a communication strategy of the channels, the second is the production of the show by its designers and producers, and the third from its reception.

When a brand of mass consumption launches a product, it has reserved spaces to give it meaning and to promote it: advertisement – in France, at least – is absolutely separated from other programmes and, except in some spaces, brands have at best to speak about themselves, as in some magazines, where a presenter, under cover of news, comes to praise a product. In order to 'sell' a programme, channels have at first to get their own channels to broadcast a lot of teasers for the televiewers, but they also get all the media to do so ... with the exception of rival television channels. All the speeches of communication, which should have belonged to the field of advertisement, have moved, without any trouble – and free of charge – into the news. So, to understand the link with the televiewer, it is necessary to take into account all that comes around and before the programme, in short, its context.

In this respect, the communication campaign of M6, the channel broadcasting *Loft Story* in France, deserves to be studied to better understand the essential role that the invention of the word 'télé-réalité' had in the process of imposing a meaning on the televiewer. Three words characterised *Loft Story* according to the press releases: 'interactive real fiction'. These three words summarise the three possible ways of looking at television: observing the reality (putting the programme in the real world), following it as an invented story (fictitious world) or participating in the programme thanks to an attributed role (ludic world). The skill of the promoters of *Loft Story* was to call on this range of possibilities in order to 'sell' the programme, which allowed them to adopt a mobile communication strategy: when a battle seemed lost on one of those three fronts, it was enough to abandon it brutally for the benefit of another one, leaving the interlocutor in front of his own contradictions.

To launch the first season of the programme, the first strategy adopted was the authenticating strategy. *Loft Story* promised to be in touch with reality better than any programme before. Each time when, in France at least, a channel wants to tighten the link with its televiewers, it appeals to the argument of reality: whether it was at the start of the second channel, which inaugurated its programmes with *Jeux de société* (1963), a programme 'without comedians', which claimed to be about 'télé-réalité' or when TF1, after its privatisation, promised its viewer to transform him/her into an 'actor of his(her) history' (1991).

Some days after the launch of *Loft Story*, Alexis de Gemini, who was responsible for the programme on M6, talked on the radio by launching the topic: the young people of the loft would be representative of a generation or, even, of French society.[2] Obviously, this hypothesis presupposes that the inhabitants of the loft forget the conditions in which they are, a point de Gemini did not forget to point out: 'The participants forget the cameras and we look at a life which each one of us can recognise.' During the first broadcast, the presenter went as far as to encourage the belief that cameras could broadcast anything: 'Nothing escapes the twenty-six cameras … We will miss nothing of the quiet or agitated nights. Even at night, they are going to be filmed with infrared cameras.' The essential promise of live broadcasting, which carries in itself a sort of guarantee of authenticity, of an accordance to the represented world, even if it does not exclude editing, plays a determining role in the authentication of the programme. The apparatus of 26 cameras and 50 microphones would be totally transparent and the inhabitants of the loft would have forgotten, from the beginning, why they were there and the presence of cameras fixed to the wall. This process of cancellation of the sign would allow to reach two objects.

The first one is the afilmic world (the real world), which can be defined by opposition to the profilmic world of the film; that is, this world as arranged for the camera. The broadcast would be characterised by the following features: (a) it is not narrative, as it is based on selection and the power to explain; (b) it is in 'spectatorial focalisation' (Jost 1987) because, while nothing escapes us, it is not the case for the persons in the loft who can only see what they are living; (c) the programme is judged on the axis of truthfulness. The second object is the human being, or, if one prefers, every actor of the loft. Man is the measure of everything. While for Plato appearance was less real than the Being represented by the Idea, for the media what is most real is appearance and truest among appearances are those belonging to everyday life. The idea is not new on television and it exaggerates the privilege granted to testimony: the concrete individual would be defined less by his social position, his ideas, or his realisations than by his life on a day-to-day basis, even though this daily life would be cut off from any social anchoring. For such a reduction to be possible, it is necessary to assume that the *in vitro* experiment does not differ from the *in vivo* experiment, which no scientist would confirm. To what extent do people who have neither a job, nor any concern for getting one, nor any contact with the outside world, live an everyday life close to ours? *Big Brother*'s mirrors replaced the test tubes of the biology labs.

One understands where this strategy of authentication leads to. If these images are to be taken literally, they may give rise to criticisms of playing with the life of the candidates, who are victims of harmful psychological experiments. Rather than to argue against these criticisms, the marketing television benefits from the big lability of television genre and avoids the ground on which it is attacked (the real world), and begins a first migration. Presenting the programme from the ludic angle is going to allow to dedramatise the debate and to make the programme less objectionable. The president of M6's board of directors, Thomas Valentin, was in charge of this delicate mission after Gemini's disappearance from the media scene. He claimed:

It is a game. It is not reality. That is why we tried to invent this word of real fiction (*fiction réelle*). Fiction because there is a *scénarisation*, there are rules of the game. And reality, because it is about real people and not actors. (Valentin, on *Le téléphone sonne*, France-Inter, 4 May 2001)

The 'marketing' positioning of the programme changed along the way, something which would have been completely impossible for a basic consumer programme. The emphasis on reality aroused too many criticisms connected to *Big Brother*'s concentration-camp apparatus, so that it was quickly abandoned. For the fears caused by the 'for real' (*pour de vrai*), came the lightness of the 'for fun'. This change of point of view has the inconvenience of reviving the suspicions on the small interventions with the 'reality' of the loft. On this point, the comments of the vice-president of M6's board are rather embarrassing, to say the least. On one hand, he will grant that there is '*scénarisation*, when one asks them to do a few things'. On the other, he will oppose the absolved freedom of the loft inhabitants, during the 'rest of the time'. For attracting and keeping the desire of the televiewer, the daily programme should transform the abounding material of the live broadcasting – full of injury times and troubles – in fast summaries, which give life to the look of fiction. But, as it would have been bad politics to put forward the inevitable 'arrangements' of the fictitious story, Valentin argued instead for the impossible exhaustiveness and for a selection guaranteed by the brand M6: one cannot show everything for material reasons; as the daily programme lasts only a few dozen minutes, 'one is obliged to choose'; and one must not show everything, for ethical reasons. The channel guarantees a certain morality and it cannot allow anything to be broadcast.

And finally, it was necessary to 'sell' this prime-time programme, which is most important in the development of the product, as the programme brings the main part of the advertising resources back. In this case it reduced the 'live' of the loft to a small portion (hardly 10 per cent), leaving much more space for the animation set. To attract the largest share of the audience, a third argument was necessary, that of 'interactivity' and it was up to the presenter himself to introduce it: 'It is you who will write the story, it is you who will change the script', the audience is told. From a rhetoric point of view, this new promise has multiple advantages. On the one hand, it finished the operation of communication started by Thomas Valentin himself, which intended to break down the idea that everything had been prepared beforehand. On the other, it strengthened the authentication of the programme: the reality would not be told by *Loft Story* – as the daily programme could make the spectator believe – it would give itself to us.

While fiction supposes a narrator who controls the events and who knows their series, in this case the public itself would be this powerful (omnipotent) narrator on the future of the real persons. This promise has two symbolic advantages: the first one, purely demagogic, is to give a power of decision to the televiewer; the second to hasten the forgetting of the apparatus and to make it transparent.

Speaking of 'télé-réalité', of 'real fiction' or of 'interactive game' is not equivalent: these three positions corresponded in fact to a very skillful campaign for launching the programme. At first, it was a matter of implanting the live on TPS (*television par satellite*), of provoking massive subscriptions: it was thus necessary to sell the programme under the angle of 'télé-réalité'. This objective was reached by the sudden increase of subscriptions and the consulted Internet pages. Second, it was necessary to bring televiewers to the prime-time programme – and make them accept the *scénarisation*. This aim was carefully reached. Initially programmed at 18.30, the summary only moved towards the strongly competitive schedule of 19.20 as its success became apparent. Third, the interactivity, which should boost the sale of new products, was a success. During the broadcasting of *Loft Story* there were 20 million calls a week

in order to eliminate the candidates, which, after sharing with France Telecom, brought in a reported 5.6 million euros.

## Genres that will all end up in Loft Story

Programme formulae make up a sort of gigantic network, difficult to disentangle, without any real origin nor end, where every programme is built by keeping track of the previous ones, in the form of reviews or rewritings. It is absurd to believe that a programme radically innovates or that it represents the last stage of an evolution (the 'télé-réalité' as the end the television history). It is better to admit once and for all that television is the recording studio of the aspiration of society and that it evolves more or less with the same rhythm.

A little short-term history is necessary for isolating the ingredients that produced the success of *Loft Story*. Reconstructing the genealogy of these programmes, we will understand better why the current receipts satisfy a certain public. Let us follow again the three fold partition of the television worlds. *Loft Story* is at the point of convergence of three ways: the authenticating way, opened by reality shows and by talk shows, the fictitious model of the sitcoms, and the reuse of different entertainment arrangements.

The real break between intimacy programmes and the film heritage occurred with *Psyshow* (1983), when couple psychology became a spectacle of its own, as the title indicates, by the simple fact that interpersonal relations were staged in the space of a set, in front of a presenter and a psychoanalyst – the reknowned Serge Leclaire – among a public of friends and family. To present their problems, films told the life of both man and woman, played by comedians. Such a representation tends to transfigure the anonymous person into a one-day star. He/she becomes the focus of attention. Ten years later, reality shows will go even further, asking couples to play their own lives for cameras. This time, the anonymous person is filmed at home, then summoned to play the scenes of intimacy on the set. Each feigns to be natural and pretends to forget that he/she is under the limelight. It is the realm of what I called the '*feintise*' (Jost 2001). The couple feigns the scenes of intimacy, as if there was no camera. At the request of the psychoanalyst, it replays, for example, in a reserved space of the set, a recurring quarrel. These 'psychodramas', subjected to the expert's eye, in spite of their visible simulation, nevertheless deliver the truth of man and woman, truth that will be revealed to the public.

Previously, documentaries had been interested in private life, but they did it through the interview, based on confidence and understanding, in such a way that the public confession of the secrets was in a sense indirect, of secondary consequence, of which the interviewee was not completely aware at the time of the recording. In reality shows, the anonymous persons collaborate with television, they agree to give themselves in spectacle, either by replaying their life, or by exposing themselves in the studio in front of the public.

In the era of the webcam, which transforms the private space in a television studio, and which offers each one the possibility of giving himself in spectacle, it was necessary to invent a formula which associates this desire of exhibitionism/voyeurism with the penetration of a lived intimacy – and not only feigned or replayed. Hence the double contribution of *Loft Story*. First, the set of the loft naturalises the set. Although everything is mastered, it looks like a private space, to the point that the decorator of the programme can assert: 'the notion of decor loses its value because everything is true' (*Le Monde*, 16 June 2001). This assertion neglects two or three details as the fact that the architecture of the loft leaves no hidden space in order to make visible all the comings and goings, that the ceiling is replete with lighting systems, and that microphones hang from the ceiling!

The space of the always reaffirmed mastery of production which organises the game, the set of *Loft Story*, is also built on tested receipts of authentication. At its basis we find the necessary passage through the studio for connecting to live broadcasting. All big live shows, from the events in Romania to the funeral of Mitterrand, to the first Gulf War, owe their suspense only to the fragmentation of time which masks the 'injury time', while at the same time producing expectation (Jost 1999). Several sequences contribute to this fragmentation, all necessary for the dramatisation of the event: the report, the opinion of the invited expert, the comments of the journalists. Reality shows were very quickly inspired by this apparatus to distract from the boredom by developing different modes: the report-portrait on the candidate, testimonies by close relations, and interpretation of the facts by a shrink. *Loft Story* combines them all.

Let us start with the portrait. As soon as a candidate carried out a 'remarkable' action, as soon as one of them risked elimination or was eliminated, the presenter announced a report which recollected his/her personality. The portrait, as the flashback in cinema, supplies the spectator with the standards which are going to allow him/her to judge the candidate either by confirmation of the announced image, or by the construction of differences. It will be said repeatedly, for example, during *Loft Story*, that X or Y is not in accordance with the image that the report gave us on the first day.

The second device imported from the reality show is the presence of relatives and friends on the set. Contrary to what is said, the fact that children live their television experience under the glance of relatives is not new. Reality shows of the 1990s already promoted relatives to the position reserved to them in *Loft Story*. In *L'Amour en danger*, as in its ludic version *Pour une nuit ou pour la vie* (French version of *Blind Date*), where one saw protagonists for marriage put to the test by a whole series of games, the relatives on the set were very much in demand. A female friend came to testify to the good character of a man whose own wife accused him of rash temper. A mother praised her daughter in front of her future son-in-law, and so forth. In such programmes, close relations were already moral guarantees, ready to support the cause of their friend. At the time of *Perdu de vue*, some relatives were seen testifying that their daughter, who disappeared in mysterious conditions, lived an irreproachable life without any problems. On one hand, the relatives clarify the present by their knowledge of the past, which allows them to moderate certain more or less shocking attitudes in the eyes of the audience; on the other, they are interviewed by the presenter as if they were the parents of a star and, by the narrative of their own sudden and unexpected fame, they accredit that of the locked 'lofteurs'.

The third inheritance of reality shows is in the 'shrink's' presence. In *Psyshow*, as in *L'Amour en danger*, the psychoanalyst had a dominant role, since he/she had to solve the problems which troubled the couple; the plan was simple – it was a matter of going back to early childhood to reveal the origin of the trauma and then to send the reconciled couple back home. The shrinks of *Loft Story* do not have such a well-defined task. They only accompany the present and slightly complicate the first level reading which the viewer gets: the shrink knows that there is a hidden sense, his role is to reveal it and, especially, to reassure us concerning the absence of after-effects incurred by the 'lofteurs'.

## Reality in the image of realism

In the 1990s, many parents could not help judging the '*séries collège*' (in France, *Hélène et les garçons*) as an unreal space, where boys and girls lived in separate dormitory rooms, reducing the world to a world 'behind closed doors, where only friendly and loving relations are enacted, as if the heroes were removed from the world to experience their initiation into feelings' (Pasquier 1998: 217). Today, there are some parents who agree to watch their offspring evolve in such a setting without being shocked by its artificial appearance or the events that take place therein.

For their part, the children, now adults, do not seem surprised to see this reality built on the model of the fiction they watched with passion not so along ago. The space of the loft would be very improbable in reality. In fact, it is directly inspired by the construction of the socialisation places of television fiction: at first, the sofa is, as in a number of sitcoms (such as *Friends*), the place of rediscovered community, where the 'lofteurs' find themselves when the presenter communicates with them, during the live broadcast. More surprising still, the bathroom is the place of little secrets. Once again the model followed by *Loft Story* is not so much inspired by French reality than by series like *Ally McBeal*, where the large unisex toilet is a place for conversations. Obviously, the decoration of the loft targets young televiewers who eventually identify other people's reality – the older who live beautiful adventures – with that represented by sitcoms. This is maybe one of the keys of the success of the programme with teenage audiences.

In fact, the 'lofters' have another way of filling their time: they dress up, have a karaoke, mime an award ceremony, do a quiz, and so forth. All these activities proposed by the 'owner' transform the living room into a small set reminiscent of the ones that are built in television studios. The lofter's games re-enact the big successes of television games of the past years: the karaoke of *La Fièvre du Samedi soir* (TF1), the long self-congratulatory ceremonies of the media industry (*Sept d'Or*, *Césars* – French Oscar ceremony), the games of questions and answers based on indiscretions. The leisure activities of the inhabitants of the loft are filled with imitations of television entertainment that previously occupied their evenings. Playing at television becomes the ultimate reality.

## A fluctuating generic reception

What 'contract' should we invent to describe the relation that channels establish with their televiewers? The fluctuating communication strategy of channels and the hybridisation of programmes testifies to the malleability of programmes towards the generic classifications and to the ceaseless movements of the tectonics of genres.

Let us imagine a model viewer, full of good will, who would try to follow the instructions of the channel broadcasting the programme: should he/she see the programme as a documentary – and pity the hard living conditions of the lofteurs – or consider it as role play? Can he/she do both? It is difficult, in so far as we agree with Roger Caillois' analyses about mimicry, based on the fact that the player 'by playing at believing, makes himself and others believe that he is another' (Caillois 1967: 61). It is an activity based on the absolute separation from these two worlds: contrary to the impostor who passes himself off as another for dishonest purposes, the player, whether a professional actor or a child dressing up, does not aim at deceiving the spectator. In this context,

> the corruption of mimicry occurs when the enactment is not taken as such any more, when the one who is dressing up believes in the reality of the role. He does not play this other any more. Persuaded that he is the other one, he behaves accordingly and forgets who he is. The loss of his deep identity represents the punishment for the one who does not know when to stop at this game as he enjoys borrowing another personality. (Caillois 1967: 167)

Some candidates of *Loft Story* were in this intermediate situation, not knowing any more if they should be themselves or act a character.

Autobiographical pact or ludic contract, it is necessary to choose one or the other; candidates as well as viewers. For the model-televiewer who enters the logic of the promise, the stake is not the same. The sender does not impose upon him an attitude which would be the transcendental condition of its reception, he proposes him a sense that he may always refuse. The presenter told us the first evening: 'The candidates are cut off from the world, they have neither press nor television nor computer.' From the second week, two new candidates replaced two other candidates excluded in mysterious conditions, bringing with them a multitude of outside information (about the programme and its reception, and so forth); some days later, it is someone else's turn to be allowed out for the burial of his grandfather and to reintegrate into the loft afterwards. Then, it was the turn of the expelled lofteurs to visit those who were still in the loft. Then we learned that every week, the candidates could use a computer to correspond. The spectators were allowed to send them picture postcards, and newspapers were introduced massively, allegedly to prepare their reintegration in the 'real' world, and so forth. What was left then, after all, of the seclusion from the world which motivated the experiment? What was left in the end of this so-called break from the world which justified the show? Very little as it turned out.

As for the other rules announced on the first evening to the televiewer, they were all forgotten afterward. Whether it concerned the obligation of looking after the vegetable garden, of doing the housework, or of taking one's shower at a set time, promising the viewers a scheduled display of nudity. None of these rules-commands were respected, neither by the candidates nor by the producers.

Curiously enough, not abiding by the promise does not have the same effect on the media as it does on persons. While, in case of the interpersonal communication the consequences are the loss of confidence of his author, there did not necessarily follow any penalties from the audience. Although none of the promises of the first day were held, the televiewers remained as numerous on the last day, even more than on the first. Does it not mean that, in spite of all their efforts, the media never succeed in looking like this Other that we are? The channel, a symbolic being we endow with anthropomorphic qualities, will never be a being of flesh and blood endowed with intelligence, the way we are, which explains perhaps that we permit it a lot of behaviours that we would not accept coming from a human being.

So we are led to this paradox: on one hand, the promise is constituent of the personification of the media, particularly television. Assuming this anthropoid feature they come forward as a partner in our minds. On the other, the accomplished promises result all the more easily in the lie as the Other does not go to the end of his 'right to require'.

Is it not strange that few people were shocked because M6 did not respect the rules of the game, even when, every day, citizens complain about politicians that do not res-

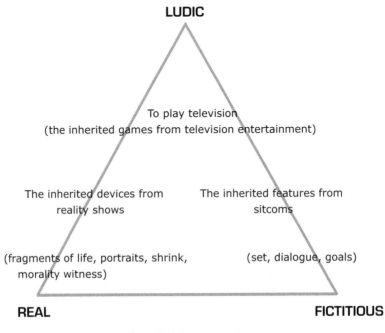

LUDIC

To play television
(the inherited games from television entertainment)

The inherited devices from
reality shows

The inherited features from
sitcoms

(fragments of life, portraits, shrink,
morality witness)

(set, dialogue, goals)

REAL

FICTITIOUS

*The television apparatus*

**Big Brother International**

pect their promises? How is it that a channel, watched and known by everyone, can change as it thinks best the rules that it has settled? Such is the exaggerated power of channels: they define what is reality, invent worlds and laugh at promises which they made to the televiewers. Yet their promises work so well that, some months later, some analysts are still persuaded 'that the participants were cut off from the world, without television and without mail' (Tisseron 2001: 33).

The most gullible ones, those who believe in words more than in these television acts that programmes represent, have mentally erased the programme apparatus – its set, its presenter, its interviews – only to remember the images of the loft (statistically very scarce during prime-time). Reducing heterogeneous genres just to one of these dimensions, they made the whole programme slide towards the 'real', forgetting all that could push it away from this pole. Some people concluded therefore that it was the most true 'documentary' that one had ever seen on the French youth; others saw a new era of intimacy therein, and a third category, according to Serge Tisseron, saw a period when each would play with his own image and would play with the surveillance systems of all kinds, to the extent that he asserts: 'intimacy is where I am and when I want it' (Tisseron 2001: 76).

Young people watched *Loft Story* as they had watched *Hélène* some years before: the realism inherited from the sitcom naturalised the lofteurs' life and gave it the look of 'real' life. Thanks to skilful casting, each came to occupy a role in the economy of the daily chronicle. *Loft Story* is in some respects the authenticating remake of *Hélène*. That the events are lived by the candidates did not change fundamentally the processes of attraction or aversion to the actors. Is there not an amazing resemblance between the character of Johanna, in *Hélène*, valued by the teenagers for her fragility and her misfortunes with Christian, and that of Loanna, defined more or less in the same terms by her supporters, who became popular when a boy treated her badly? While the narrative mechanisms that move the spectators are the same in both cases, there is another feature that brings the sitcom and the loft close together, namely the two-way exchanges between life on the screen and life outside the screen. The characters of *Hélène* were strongly linked by their biography to the actors: same first names, same past. The plots were constructed, according to the production, from the observation of the life of the group outside the set. Last but not least, Hélène, the eponymous character of the sitcom, was not only a young woman of fiction who dreamed of becoming a singer, but also a 'true' singer performing everywhere in France. Fiction was thus the stepladder to her real success. Thus, on one hand, some fictions ensure the promotion of real careers; on the other, these authenticating games give life to a pastiche of fiction, the success of which will be the passage in the reality of the showbiz.

Finally, another part of the public backed both horses: while making the hypothesis that they were manipulated by rules promulgated by the channel, some televiewers entered the world proposed to them by means of votes. One could find intellectuals boasting to having phoned to eliminate so-and-so ... an attitude of distinction that sets the taste for the commonplace as a supreme value.

In short, the logic of the sender, the structure of the programme and its reception give genres a polymorphic shape. For the needs of communication, the same programme can migrate from one genre to another. If such a strategy of mobility is possible, it is naturally because television actually is an intermediate and temporary product resulting from devices stemming from multiple genres, so that every programme is a kind of unstable mixture of all which preceded it. But in the end, it is not sure whether it is a characteristic typical of television: did not the success of *The Blair Witch Project* come from this oscillation between the authenticating shape of the report and the construction of a world borrowed from fairytales?

Whatever distances between strategies and receptions, the triangle of the worlds delimits the theoretical field of the migration of genres. But the position of the programmes as well as the deformations of the figure would allow tracking down important modifications in the history of the forms. If the distribution of the communication strategies on each of the angles reveals the care with which marketing television tries to touch the public by all possible means, the study on the French television of the 1970s shows on the contrary, that many programmes are situated, by their producer at equal distance of the real, fictitious and ludic, at the intersection of the medians.

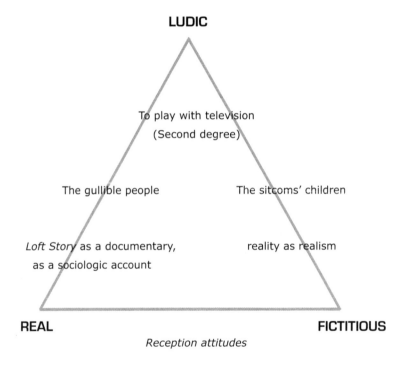

*Reception attitudes*

## Conclusion

Placed under the sign of mixture of reality and fiction, the 1970s flirted with borders to the extent of turning it into a game. Nevertheless, this fusion of worlds is not a confusion. Indeed, this marriage of opposites does not aim at strengthening the illusion of a possible transcription of reality but rather at developing the televiewer's reflection on representation. To what extent is the image and those who build it an invention of reality? What is the borderline between fake and fiction? These questions are asked by the films of Robbe-Grillet or Godard, the paintings of the movement Support/surface, or by television programmes.

Today it looks as though the LF (ludic/fictitious) side is getting closer and closer to the opposite angle (real). The phenomenon does not only concern the territory of 'télé-réalité', which bases its main selling argument on the invisibility of the semiotic cut. The debates that enthralled televiewers on the set today populate the conversations of our thrillers. Thriller series sometimes come to occupy the time slots of the previous reality shows and they are the logical result of a movement begun for a long time and which claims to relieve fiction of its fictitious character. Policemen are no longer heroes above us, but common people, shaken between the routine of their district police station and the problems of their private life. Games as well, rather than drawing the televiewers away from their world, bring them back to their daily condition: whether it is a question of getting rid of the 'weakest link', which means getting rid of the one who hinders the group by his/her bad answers or to evaluate one's own capacities by the intervention of a massive IQ. All programmes claim to speak in the name of reality.

The theoretical model of the contract has missed out these gaps, sometimes going as far as to postulate that any text aligns the reader with its semiotic functioning. The hypothesis of the complexity of texts make us see things otherwise: a text of fiction, because it speaks about the reality from a certain point of view, can be presented as authenticating, while an almost live broadcast can provide pleasures close to those of a fiction, if the casting is well done. Thus, we see in our times of mass media communication a lot of uses which are worth certain authorised interpretations (like *Loft Story*).

Nevertheless, these migrations of receivers inside the genres do not know other fields than those of the strategies of communication or of the products themselves. The actors of communication, as the texts themselves, migrate within the same space confined by the three worlds described in this article, in such a way that, in order to observe their movements, suffice it to stack the three triangles which schematise their position and to look at them by transparency, as Tintin in *The Secret of the Unicorn*, who discovered the place of the treasure, thanks to a kind of virtual palimpsest.

*Translation by Luc Shankland*

*Notes*

1   The French word is 'feintise', an old word which translates from 'Fingiersein' and which means more or less 'simulation'.
2   *C'est-à-dire*, RTL, 2 May 2001.

*Bibliography*

Caillois, R. (1967) *Les Jeux et les homes*. Paris: Folio Essais.
Charaudeau, P. (1990) *Le discours d'information médiatique*. Paris: Nathan-INA, coll. Médias-Recherches.
Eco, U. (1985) 'TV: la transparence perdue', in *La Guerre du faux*, Paris: Livre du poche, 1996–220.
_____ (1992) *Les Limites de l'interprétation*. Paris: Grasset.
_____ (1996) *Six promenades dans les bois du roman*. Paris: Grasset.
Jacques, F. (1999) 'Remarques sur la promesse et le pardon. La théorie du langage à l'épreuve de l'éthique', *Transversalités*, 71 (July–September).
Jost, F. (1997) *L'œil-caméra. Entre film et roman*. Lyon: Presses universitaires de Lyon.
_____ (1997/98) 'The promise of genres', *Réseaux, The French Journal of Communication*, 6, 1, 99–121.

_____ (1999) *Introduction à l'analyse de la television*. Paris: Ellipses.

_____ (2003) *La Télévision du quotidien. Entre réalité et fiction* (second edition). Bruxelles: De Boeck-INA/Collections Médias-Recherche.

Lejeune, Ph. (1975) *Le Pacte autobiographique*. Paris: Seuil/Collection Poétique.

Pasquier, D. (1998) 'Lecture des personnages des séries', in J. Bourdon and F. Jost (eds) *Penser la television*. Nathan: Paris, 216–33.

Ricœur, P. (n.d.) 'Volonté', in *Encyclopédia universalis*. Paris: Club Français du livre-Encyclopedia britannica.

Robbe-Grillet, A. (1978) 'Fragment d'une autobiographie imaginaire', *Minuit*, 31. Reprinted in *Le Miroir qui revient*. Paris: Minuit.

Schaeffer, J. M. (1989) Qu'est-ce qu'un genre littéraire? Paris: Seuil/Collection Poétique.

_____ (1999) *Pourquoi la fiction?* Paris: Seuil/Collection Poétique.

Tisseron, S. (2001) *L'intimité surexposée*. Paris: Hachette/Pluriel.

# CHAPTER 9

*Fernando Andacht*

# FIGHT, LOVE AND TEARS
## An Anaysis of the Reception of Big Brother in Latin America

### How real is real?: the meaning of Big Brother for the Latin American audience

The title of this introduction alludes to Paul Watwlawick's (1997) popular discussion of a constructivist approach to reality. It seems somehow appropriate to invoke it at the beginning of an analysis of the meaning that a TV format which manifestly aims at representing the real, a reality show, has for its public. To fulfill this analytical goal, we must deal first with what semiotician C. S. Peirce described as 'blocks in the road of inquiry' (Peirce 1.135),[1] namely, false assumptions which jeopardise the scientific method in any field of research. I attempt to do so by a double analytical effort, one which conjoins empirical data from a qualitative research – focus groups and individual interviews – and a realist semiotic theory that subjects the data to a pragmatic analysis of the very notion of reality show, more specifically, of the *Big Brother* format such as it was produced in two Latin American areas, the River Plate area (2001) and Brazil (2004).[2]

Peirce's semiotic tool for elucidating the meaning of 'an intellectual con-ception', the pragmatic maxim, holds that:

> In order to ascertain the meaning of an intellectual conception, one should consider what practical consequences might conceivably result by necessity from

the truth of that conception; and the sum of these consequences will constitute the entire meaning of the conception. (Peirce 5.9)

In this reception study, each elicited opinion on *Big Brother* will be construed as a practical consequence of the format. In Peircean terms, each opinion is an *interpretant* of it, that is, a more developed sign of this reality show. The notion of interpretant refers to the objective content of an act of understanding, to the *meaning of a sign*, which leaves out of the analysis the person who does the interpreting. The purport of every kind of sign is to produce an interpretant; therein consists the process of sign action. From this analytical perspective, any possible meaning of the *Big Brother* format originates in the process of generation of sense created by the programmeme as a sign in interaction with its local audiences. These are construed as the social, historical location of the interpreting activity. A sign may have the size of a single programmeme or the complexity of an entire edition of the format, for example *Big Brother Brasil 4*, but its meaning must be always sought after in another sign, such as in the actual utterances in the interviews with audience members.

Such empirical and interpretive procedure contrasts with much of what has been written on the Endemol format, a flourishing critical tradition which deserves to be described as 'speculations on the negative' (Hill 2002). Although the phrase refers to the European context, it is also a common practice in Latin America (see Andacht 2002; 2003a). Before discussing in some detail its meaning effects, a few preliminary remarks on the *Big Brother* format itself – the structure of the sign – are in order. This format is a hybrid, the innovative result of the mixture of two traditional TV genres, namely non-fiction (news, talk show) and fiction (the sitcom, the soap opera). Elsewhere (Andacht 2002a), I proposed the term 'melochronicle of the interaction order' to account for the basic ingredients whose upshot is the *Big Brother* format. Emotional conflicts such as those amplified in melodrama, together with the type of humour produced by transformed interactional situations typical of sitcoms are blended with a detailed record of everyday interaction of (more or less) ordinary people who go about their unscripted though overtly patterned everyday affairs, in an enclosed and electronically scrutinised abode. These familiar TV components bring about a partly different media product.

In opposition to the mostly morally-based critical accounts of *Big Brother* which have steadily appeared in Latin American critical and academic milieus, I argue that:

(i) the regular audience of the show tends to view it as an *indexical genre*, that is, as a TV format which owes its specificity to the generation of signs of existence, especially those which are in connection with the bodies and with the doings of the participants (rather than with their words), as well as with the interaction order wherein such recorded events occur.

(ii) since the beginning, *Big Brother* has been surrounded by a clinging negative aura of incensed discussions about its authenticity, or rather its want of it. Whether to manifestly believe in the real status of what the reality show depicts, or to express scepticism about its actuality, there is little doubt that the public's response revolves around this semantic axis. And this is also the situation of the critics and scholars who have been writing about it.

(iii) the most noticeable tendency in the opinions generated by the show in the audience of the two Latin American regions researched is a fair split, even an oscillation between a firm belief in the genuineness of the format's *index appeal*, and the strong suspicion that its most memorable moments are carefully staged by the participants of *Big Brother* in complicity with the producers.

I will attempt to show that there is little evidence in the data of the interpretants generated by the audience to support a number of critical and scholarly accounts of the Endemol glocal reality show. This is by no means to say that *Big Brother* is good or has a positive influence on society. It does mean that many of the assertions from media critics and from academia do not deal adequately with what is specific of it, with its actual meaning effects in the audience. The main unsupported claims may be summed up thus:

(i) *Big Brother* dissolves the traditional fact/fiction border thus creating mild havoc in the audience's consciousness. In fact, it is often said that what the format represents leans towards fiction rather than towards any form of documented reality, which runs counter to the viewers' actual experience.[3]

(ii) *Big Brother* is a morally and aesthetically meaner kind of soap opera. This claim presupposes the complete fabrication of all that is represented, as well as an utter lack of specificity of this TV format.

(iii) *Big Brother* exploits as its main attraction psychological perversions, for example the audience's voyeurism and sadism, as well as its relish for banality. The empowerment to watch other people's intimacy and to expel them from the game by voting would therefore justify the darkest prophecies of Frankfurt's Critical Theory.

As such, this chapter complements my previous inquiry on the *Big Brother* format (Andacht 2002a; 2003a; 2003b; 2003c; 2004a; 2004b; 2004c), which was based on the observation and semiotic analysis of this reality show. That research focused on the programmeme's *immediate interpretant*, that is, its range of interpretability, which is a logical outcome of the sign's structure, its plausible meaning.[4] A reception study like the present one deals with the *dynamical interpretants* of a programmeme, or 'the actually occurring interpretants' (Ransdell 1986) – what the public in fact understood about it. To avoid the kind of unscientific, impressionistic position of outright denunciation or of apology to which a new-fangled TV entertainment such as *Big Brother* gives rise, I present some of the findings of an ongoing qualitative research with the Latin American public of *Big Brother*. One positive outcome of it is the possibility of openly positing research questions concerning the type of interest that the public has in the kind of real(ity) catered by this format. While constructivism describes reality as 'the mental construction of those who believe they have discovered and investigated it' (Turrisi 2002: 126), my pragmatic approach takes meaning to be an autonomous phenomenon, and thus it does not depend on the public's or the critic's *willful construction* of it. Meaning, here, is the upshot of the interaction between the format as sign structure with the public's interpretive competence. Incidentally, this analytical move implicitly points out what is wrong with many unwarranted academic and critical discussions of the *Big Brother* format.

## Previous findings on the lure of Big Brother: the index appeal

Elsewhere (Andacht 2002a), I proposed the *index appeal* as the main meaning effect of the *Big Brother* format. This notion is the historical result of the convergent evolution of media technology and of the 'expressive turn' (Taylor 1989) of eighteenth-century Romanticism. A consequence of this sociocultural tendency is the growing fascination of the television audience with their fellow human beings' *sign transpiration* or *sign exhalation*. Rather than the sex appeal of the attractive faces and bodies which are exhibited in various degrees of nudity in the house of *Big Brother*, the main attraction of the format, and a likely explanation of its remarkable worldwide audience success lies in its index appeal. It is the possibility of watching expressive bodies which must dwell in a backstage region (Goffman 1959) without the benefit of a façade or front as a refuge, and who cannot but scatter a large amount of *iconic indexes*, that is, qualitative expressions or symptoms of the self. The key issue concerning the audience's response is to discover whether the public is interested in the kind of full contact experience that can be afforded only by indexical signs, described semiotically as a 'real physiological force' on the interpreter: 'like a pointing finger, (the index) exercises a real physiological force over the attention, like the power of a mesmeriser, and directs it to a particular object of sense' (Peirce 8.41).

Granting that no television programme, film or play is wholly original, it can be argued that the specific meaning effect of *Big Brother* is based on its predominantly indexical nature. The mesmerising indexical power of the format is able to survive even the overt manipulative strategies of the local TV producers, wherever this television formula is made.[5] In contrast with the apparent sexual lure – the *sex appeal* – of the format, I posit its index appeal as the basic semiotic mechanism of attraction: the compulsive beckoning or tangible call of the index, which is used as a more or less reliable connection with the soul or true self of the participants of *Big Brother*, and as a plausible way to reflect on the self in modern society, in a more ample fashion.

As further *Big Brother* editions are produced, the audience gradually loses its initial innocence regarding its mechanism, and people become wary of its blatant marketing of every spontaneous aspect represented in it. Nevertheless, it is still the index appeal in *Big Brother* which enjoins and summons its old and new fans to literally follow the tracks of the dwellers of the house where not much happens, symbolically-wise, i.e., in terms of verbal language, but where these denizens of the back region transformed into a fully-lit front region cannot but keep on producing more 'interaction order' (Goffman 1983) raw material. Based on these matters of the body-recorded, the audience may (and does) reflect on their own footprints left behind, in their non-filmed everyday world.

What does the audience look for when they watch a reality show such as *Big Brother*? I want to argue that any answer ought to include the unrepeatable index experience, which, at every instant, unexpectedly manifests itself in the domain of filmed human interaction, when such behaviour is not previously scripted. Whether a script be masterfully or clumsily written, what is relevant here is that such a guide not only stipulates each word to be said, but also includes the director's guidance and thus fixes in advance each facial or body gesture with which the preordained dialogue is to be enacted. To a large extent, the opinions presented below consist of a lively discussion about the presence or absence of such a symbolic guide. The audience's conclusions rely on the observation of indices, the signs whose sole function is to point stubbornly to an object which exists. Based on such evidence, the audience judges the degree of authenticity of the voluntarily locked-up human beings.

## Findings of the qualitative research of the Latin American audience of Big Brother

In this section, I discuss some findings of a qualitative study with members of the Uruguayan and of the Brazilian audience of two editions of *Big Brother*. The 2001 Argentinian version (*Gran Hermano1*) was produced by the powerful Telefé network and was broadcast simultaneously to Uruguay, where three focus groups were made (Hillel & Martorano 2002). The 2004 Brazilian version (*Big Brother Brazil 4*) was produced by the Rede Globo network, the world's fourth largest. A dozen personal interviews and a focus group with high-school students who regularly viewed the reality show were undertaken in Brazil.[6]

The aim of this study is to compare the regional audiences' opinions to find out whether there is any similarity in the interpretants generated, and to use this outcome as empirical evidence of the meaning of the format. The similarities found were remarkable, especially given the significant differences between the two research settings, the largest being that the Brazilian audience had already been exposed to three previous productions of *Big Brother*, and thus they may be considered as self-styled experts in the workings of it. For the Uruguayan audience, the only previous experience had been the non-direct broadcast of the Spanish edition, *Gran Hermano*, in 2000. Not only was the outcome known long before it was shown in Uruguay, but the time slot allotted to the programme was not even prime-time, 11.30pm. The disparity, however, does not jeopardise this inquiry, whose aim it is to elucidate what kind of format *Big Brother* is, once we apply the pragmatic maxim to the responses of its regular public. Rather than a fully-fledged comparison of the two Latin American audiences, my aim is to find out what these regional viewers actually consider most characteristic of *Big Brother*. I also search for evidence concerning their judgement on the issue of *Big Brother*'s authenticity. It is evident that there is no mind-boggling confusion of fact and fiction created by viewing *Big Brother*; audiences do manage to discern the show proper – what the production team and the more histrionic participants try to do – from the facts which, like a semiotic transpiration, simply take place there, in the observed house.

The gathered opinions have been divided in six classes, and are represented in Diagram 1, overleaf. It shows the basic elements that the analysis of the elicited opinions discovered: three *semiotic objects* and three *interpretants* thereof. The semiotic object is the logical element which determines meaning by soliciting some fitting medium, here it is the interviewees' verbal language and gestures (for example laughter, pauses), which, in turn, generates a further, more developed sign of that same object – its interpretant, the meaning of the recalled episodes of *Big Brother* (the sign's object). As illustration, I present two quotations concerning the central issue involved in the reception of *Big Brother*, namely, the steady elucidation of the true nature of what the *Big Brother* participants are up to in the house: whether they are being themselves, or whether they are just skilful amateur performers who try to peddle a shabby dramaturgical act for the real thing:

> You stay three months inside that house, I guess you sometimes forget you're being recorded, even if it's fighting, even when you start kicking the hell out of things (*chutando o pau da barraca*)! (32-year-old woman, elementary teacher, *Big Brother Brazil 4*)

> I do not believe that any person can be performing for 18 hours a day during such a long time. You perform in some things, obviously you must be much more flexible, but you can't be flexible all of the time! (male university student, *Gran Hermano1*)

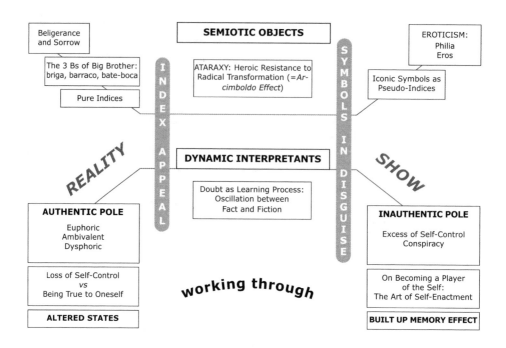

Diagram 1: In its upper area, there are the three semiotic objects or topics that the interviewees chose as most representative of *Big Brother Brazil 4*. In the lower part, we find the three meaning effects or interpretants of those objects. They range from a strong conviction in the fabrication or falsehood of what they watch or in its total authenticity – to an oscillation between opposite beliefs. The discussion revolves around the axis of Authenticity (pure indices) and Inauthenticity (symbolic fabrication).

The two opinions summarise many of the audience's recurrent concerns. If we had to place these statements within Diagram 1, they would be on its left margin, the *Authenticity* pole. Although none of these results have any statistical significance, it is worth noting that this kind of common-sense reasoning is shared by most of the people in the sample of *Big Brother Brazil 4*'s public, and, to a lesser extent, by the Uruguayan public of *Gran Hermano1*. The first opinion pits incredulity in acting natural, in such an unnatural setting, against the considerable length of time this ordeal lasts. The interviewee leans towards belief in the naturalness of it all, rather than towards skepticism, due to the inordinate effort it would take these rather ordinary people to put up a convincing show for such a length of time. However, there is a noticeable note of caution in one utterer: what was translated as the hedge 'I guess' (in Portuguese: *acho*), qualifies the assertive force, just as the adverb 'sometimes' does – at other times, the authentic behavior could be less, or maybe none. Another key evidence to argue for the index appeal as the defining element of *Big Brother* is the fierce belligerence of the participants. This is the kind of behavior I describe as the three (other) B's in *Big Brother Brazil 4*: *briga, barraco, bate-boca*,[7] the most prominent indices present in the Brazilian data. These words are used very often in the interviews to evoke, judge, celebrate or lament the frequent quarrels, fierce disputes and bitter arguments which remained in the audience's memory as the basic ingredient of the fourth Globo-Endemol production, in 2004. The indexical counterpart, according to the Uruguayan audience, is provided by the abundant tears, sobs and anguish displayed by the participants of *Gran Hermano1*, in 2001.

## Three main kinds of discussed event in the interaction order of Big Brother

The most memorable sequences of *Big Brother Brazil 4*, according to the audience, can be analysed as semiotic objects. The evoked items of the format's furnishings generate more developed signs or interpretants, and they do so by means of signs which refer to them, that is, the language used to recall them. Belligerence, eroticism – sexual or friend-like – and ataraxy are the three foremost semiotic objects around which the audience discussion evolves.

*Belligerence and Sorrow: the three B's of Big Brother Brazil 4 and the agitated, humid signs of Gran Hermano1*

On the left hand side of Diagram 1, we find the two most typical expressions of altered states in the two Latin American editions of the reality show. It is the outbreak of violence in the interaction order which, for the Brazilian audience, reveals the indexical nature of *Big Brother Brother 4*: whenever a quarrel erupts in the house, all comments point to the actuality of what is being represented in the programme. This triggers the three B's – *briga, barraco, bate-boca*. The same goes for the emotional outpourings of sadness that characterised *Gran Hermano1*. In them, the audience found reliable signs of the format's specificity (the representation of the real), even if what was shown was negative or disturbing from, for example, an ethical point of view. The importance of the indexes of intense sorrow in *Gran Hermano1* was directly related to the greater prominence of the confession room in it, in comparison with its lesser prominence in *Big Brother Brazil 4*. The confession room even had its own voiceover, which addressed participants with therapeutic-like serenity, at the crucial moment of nominations.[8] Sad and angry tokens of index appeal had the following features:

(i) Violent attitudes in the house afford 'time-out instances' (Jensen 1995), opportunities for the public's intense 'working through' (Ellis 1996) interpretive activity. Outright aggressiveness is evaluated ambivalently: it is fun to watch but morally low, even despicable, in the audience's ethical universe (a demeaning Portuguese term '*baixaria*' is used to decry it). Scenes of intense sorrow in *Gran Hermano1* arouse sympathy, and the conviction that this *is* real life. Both rage and grief are seen as a low point in self-control.

(ii) The indexicality embodied by the aggressive or woeful display, their index appeal, is not questioned by the public. It has status of a symptom of the real anger or grief of the person involved in the emotional outbreak, and not that of a performance staged to manipulate the audience.

The following quotations illustrate these features:

The insults of Marcela against Solange I find the most real aspect of *Big Brother Brazil 4*, the rest is just cheap sentimentality, 'yeah, we're all such good friends'. But when she yelled 'you dumb, arrogant...' during that part my heart was beating so fast, at home! (22-year-old high-school teacher, *Big Brother Brazil 4*)

I mean they were all serious, and if someone said something, they cried. It is as if their senses are over-aroused. So anything may make you even more sensitive. (Male, university student, *Gran Hermano1*)

Euphoric, dysphoric or ambivalent as to their ethical status, belligerent or sorrowful behaviour tends to be taken at face value, it is a key ingredient of the format's *reality* component. To quote a Brazilian teacher who confessed to being a *Big Brother Brazil 4* fan: 'the reactions are real, they are unpredictable, aren't they?' The *show* or performative component is most clearly generated when the production distorts these indexical signs, by sheer repetition, special effects, soundtrack, and other tricks which turn a documentary-like instance into a grotesque videoclip of the expression of human emotions, such is the purport of the 'Arcimboldo effect' (Andacht 2004a).

*Eroticism in Big Brother, the weakest link in the belief process*

In the two previous Brazilian editions, couples formed during the programmeme obtained some popularity, the winner of the penultimate one being a case in point. However, love affairs and friendship ties are judged negatively. What in *Big Brother Brazil 2* (2003) was interpreted as the tenacious and, to some extent, convincing attitude of a young man who tirelessly strove to conquer the object of his unrequited love has now become implausible.[9] Any overt attempt to form a couple is now interpreted as a symbol in disguise (right side of Diagram 1), that is, the participant's stratagem to persuade the audience that what is a calculated gesture to win be taken as a passionate attraction for someone in the house. Roughly the same is valid for any manifest friendship token: it is either interpreted as a thinly disguised conspiracy or, as a would-be betrayal, a failed attempt of impression-management to improve the participant's image.

> I even root for some of them. But I didn't like Juliana and Marcelo's relationship. I found it was so disgusting to see them engaged in some heavy necking (*se agarrando*) in front of the TV cameras. The other ones, in the other editions, at least tried to hide themselves, but not these ones. (32-year-old woman, maid, *Big BrotherB4*)

> And even the friendship relationships, I don't know to what extent there can be something sincere or if it's just to avoid a possible vote. (20-year-old man, student, *Big Brother Brazil 4*)

Sarcastically, the next opinion expresses approval of a recently evicted part-icipant by pitting a cynical account of her attitude against the implausibility of making friends in *Big Brother*:

> I think that she (Marcela) was the one who was playing best, but she fell out of luck and was thrown out. But she was playing well, making partnerships, conspiring, thinking. It's a game, there ain't any friend-making over there, they're all in it to get to reach the goal and to win the money (33-year-old male, technology student, *Big Brother Brazil 4*)

*Ataraxy: a most admirable and tedious kind of index appeal*

The only kind of performance in the interaction order which is positively evaluated by both the audience of the fourth Brazilian edition (*Big Brother Brazil 4*) and that of the first River Plate edition (*Gran Hermano1*) is the anti- or non-performance described here as *ataraxy*, a way of keeping to oneself which is represented with the hard to translate Portuguese phrase '*ficar na dele/dela*'. The expression denotes the social virtue of not meddling or conspiring with some participant against others, and the ethical virtue of remaining true to one's old, normal self. The idealised identity, previous to the full immersion in *Big Brother*'s house, is that of a truly common, ordinary person, with no special talent. An ataraxic behaviour such as it is exemplarly embodied by *Big Brother Brazil 4*'s winner, the first woman ever to win in Brazil, is taken as a convincing evidence of a mildly heroic resistance to the ambivalent lure of the 'Arcimboldo effect', namely, all the devices used by *Big Brother*'s production to transform ordinary life into mass entertainment. Instead of trying to make an art out of self-enactment (Goffman 1971), an ataraxic attitude involves the almost total suppression of self-consciousness and the minimal expression of self-enactment, therefore it enables the difficult feat of carrying on normal behaviour in the most abnormal circumstances. Cida, in *Big Brother Brazil 4*, and Marcelo, the winner of *Gran Hermano1*, appear as paradigms of this restrained manner of acting, in the uncanny house of Endemol:

> But for instance, Marcelo played without bothering anyone, and without gossiping around! (Female university student, *Gran Hermano1*)

The quote is revealing in that it paradoxically employs a condemnatory term to describe a participant – *playing* entails turning into a full-time performer of the self – together with words of praise for his ataraxic attitude: the latter is powerful enough to cancel the former. The next quote is also from *Gran Hermano1* and does something similar by joining 'showed' with 'natural way', as if in *Big Brother* the participant could have her/his naturalness and show it too:

> It's all fine with Marcelo, because the guy showed that he is firm! (Female university student, *Gran Hermano1*)

The next comments provide an equivalent of the above interpretants:

> It's not like Tiago, who abided (*ficou na dele*). I really liked what he told Ju the other day. It was natural, he said he hadn't enjoyed her comments, that he was on his limit. He showed he was bothered, but in a natural way, without falseness. (33-year-old male technician, *Big Brother Brazil 4*)

> Their behavior is one of the worst ones from all editions. They were fre-quently fighting, they swore all the time, and tried to call the audience's attention at every second, I mean, at least some of them, because Cida abided (*ficou na dela*), and you saw what the result was. (29-year-old woman, nursery attendant, *Big Brother Brazil 4*)

Cida, *Big Brother Brazil 4*'s winner, and Tiago, the penultimate to leave the house, got into the programmeme not through the conventional casting procedure, but by buying *Big Brother Brazil 4*'s fanzine, and sending a cut-out coupon for participating. An upshot of their unusual entrance in the house was to make the carefully selected participants seem artists, or the artistes who, in fact, some were.[10] Against all odds, both lower-class youths gradually began to display a winsome simplicity which at first was hidden behind an inhibited mutism, their initial low profile. Comments in both Latin American audiences agreed in pointing out that this kind of quiet, plain behavior was the very opposite of the erotic displays, and so they took it as an expression of utmost authenticity.

> She [Cida] was the caricature of an absent-minded Brazilian, without much education, without many chances in life. I thought she would be eliminated straight away, because she was the weakest of the lot, the ugly duckling. (32-year-old woman, elementary teacher, *Big Brother Brazil 4*)

## Three main interpretations or kinds of belief in the main events of the interaction order

The basic interpretants of what are taken to be the most remarkable elements of *Big Brother* are wholehearted belief in the actuality of what is represented, total scepticism, and an oscillation of belief between both extremes.

*Belief in the authenticity of Big Brother*

An interesting difference in the interpretants of the format from the two regional productions is the greater importance of the confession room in *Gran Hermano1*, which elsewhere I describe as *Big Brother*'s 'deep backstage' (Andacht 2003a, based on Meyrowitz 1989). Correspondingly, a significant part of the revelation of the participants' true self took place in that tiny, sealed-off place. This was the case with Tamara, an attractive, exotic-looking young woman who, whenever she had to go there to name two housemates, wept, sobbed uncontrollably until her face became red, swollen, disfigured by her grief. This was perceived as a clear instance of the format's index appeal. The audience found it hard to believe that what they watched was only a performative stunt to win popularity or the public's sympathy:

> But in the very end, I felt sorry for her. I said, well, if Marcelo doesn't win, I want Tamara to win! (Female university student, *Gran Hermano1*)

> But that chick [Tamara] was like ... really sensitive, she looked like ... a chick ... who really cared. She lived in a state of a ... kind of ... constant sensitivity. At every instant, she started to cry. (Male university student, *Gran Hermano1*)

> Oh yeah! She was crying all the time, did you see her eyes what they looked like? (Female university student, *Gran Hermano1*)

The next quote exemplifies the audience's ethical ambivalence: while there is no doubt that savage belligerence is as good an index appeal as you can get in this format, there is also the negative impression that it creates of those who are directly involved in violent behaviour:

> Concerning the fights, I guess it's something the audience in general doesn't like watching ... this is a negative point the participant is going to have, so, in general, at least in my opinion, the fights are more sincere, more real, because if they

are fighting, they're losing some points, which is not good for them. (20-year-old male student, *Big Brother Brazil 4*)

An expression of belief in the authenticity of this kind of TV representation often comes up in debates on the supposedly fabricated character of the format. Somebody in a focus group offered an instance of *Gran Hermano1*'s index appeal as hard evidence. After someone asserted that everything was planned in the programmeme through the casting, which involved even Marcelo, the most believable and plainlooking participant of *Gran Hermano1*, there came a sharp ironic retort which made much of an unexpected fact that completely changed the group dynamics in the house, and the outcome of that first edition:

And what would have happened if Gustavo had not left the house, what could we have done then? (Male university student, *Gran Hermano1*)

This ironic remark alludes to a participant who, of his own accord, left the house after less than a month. It is implausible to think of such a move as a sly strategy, especially if one bears in mind that it was the first edition. To leave the game by one's own choice is a most spectacular index, since it cancels all further symptoms by this absolute and final one: the gesture of withdrawing one's own body as a reaction to the pressures of the house.

Here is a typical interpretant of the presence and deeds of Marcelo, once he comes into the house, after Gustavo left it:

I wanted Marcelo to win because he seemed the more normal, with more principles. He was more like me! (Male university student, *Gran Hermano1*)

This opinion echoes some of those given above in connection with *Big Brother Brazil 4*'s odd couple. Together they express a central point in the viewing experience of this audience: the show is compensated by the indexical element that the public infers from the ataraxic attitude: the Portuguese '*ficar na dele/dela*', to abide, to keep on being what you really are (what you were out there in the world) corresponds exactly to the Spanish '*mostró que el loco es firme*' ('the guy showed that he is firm').

The index appeal not only creates a belief in the authenticity of what is shown in *Big Brother*, it also produces appreciation – a euphoric attitude – and its very opposite – a dysphoric one. The former describes the sympathy with what is seen as the participant's spontaneous, honest attitude. The latter is rare but reveals the format's deep ethical ambivalence: who is deemed to be the best player is often judged to be the worst person. Such is the case with the comments on Gastón, the 'villain' of the River Plate's first edition. Here is a part of a lively discussion on Gastón's coming out of the closet, his confessing his bisexuality early on in the programmeme. Some think that this was staged, others that this was just the way he was:

The production only shows us summaries. They choose what to show us. The guy who edits it may make him (Gastón) seem much more gay than what he in fact is. And there is also the issue that bisexuals do not show off so much as this guy did. A bisexual does not show himself to be bisexual, he doesn't proclaim loudly, with pride: 'Hey, I'm bi and I love men and women!' (Male university student, *Gran Hermano1*)

If we take into account the strong taboos in matters of sexuality in Latin America, it seems unlikely to the audience that someone would say this were it not true. There is also the widespread suspicion that attributes pertaining to the participants, to their identity, are regularly blown up by this format, they are distorted until they are ready for easy TV mass consumption, a kind of accelerated videoclip made with fragments of the person's real profile. Therein consists the Arcimboldo effect which is characteristic of the *Big Brother* format.

In sum, belief in the existence of pure indexes, of sheer, unadulterated reactions to what goes on in the house, points either to the heroic resistance against the Arcimboldo effect favoured by the production team, or to the perverse playing by the rules – the willingness to perform according to this aesthetic code – which has been assimilated as the participant's duties, and not as a formidable obstacle to be somehow overcome.

*Disbelief in authenticity: when the participants become players*

In the interpretation of her quantitative study, Annette Hill (2002) concludes that both the management and the transformation of the self of the participants of *Big Brother* are the main attraction for the viewers of the British format. The findings of the qualitative analysis of the Brazilian and Uruguayan data indicate that it is the former but not the latter which constitutes the basic interest for this audience. Rather than any transformation, it is the resistance to be changed by the bizarre situation in which they find themselves that seems to hold the viewers' attention and to elicit their enthusiasm and support for a participant. Two typical ways in which the performative, inauthentic attitude manifests itself are friendship ties and erotic attraction: the former is seen as a covert manipulation to avoid being expelled; the latter as cold, manipulative image control.

> Marcela was Zulu's friend and she voted against him to save her neck. (15-year-old high-school student, *Big Brother Brazil 4*)

> Another one who was a fake was Rogério. When he became the leader, he used to say, 'Dourado, it's wonderful that you became part of my life.' (14-year-old high-school student, *Big Brother Brazil 4*)

> Géris was also a fake, she told Dudu, 'I didn't vote against you.' Then, he went out of the house and saw she had actually done it. (14-year-old high-school student, *Big Brother Brazil 4*)

Interestingly enough, the greatest scepticism not only coincides with a current critical position, but also borrows its expression: *Big Brother* is considered to be just another soap opera:

> People don't want to listen, it's just like with soap operas. Thanks to the soap opera you don't see the rubbish you must eat everyday, I mean you see what you wish you had, what folks'd like to be. That's why I find it so terrible, it isn't life itself! To me it's just fiction, a controlled fiction, right? (Male university student, *Gran Hermano1*)

In contrast with this incredulity, there is one display of friendship which is interpreted as an undeniable appeal. The *Big Brother Brazil 4* winner, Cida, is rem-embered as the only participant who offered to sacrifice her own permanence in the programmeme as a token of friendship:

> When Juliana became the leader, Cida told her she would rather be voted so that her friend (Tiago) wouldn't be. (32-year-old woman, maid, *Big Brother Brazil 4*)

*Doubt: oscillation between two beliefs on the representation of the real*

A peculiarity of an index appeal-based TV format is that its attraction cannot last long, precisely on account of the predominance of that semiotic element. To use a technical analogy, we may say that *Big Brother builds up memory*: what has an intense flavour of actuality in one edition cannot but appear as a rehashed piece of stale performance in a later one. Semiotically, this involves the natural evolution of a pure index, a fact that comes into being as a reaction which points to its object compulsorily,[11] into a symbol, a conventional rule of interpretation which can be expressed as ritualised behavior (for example necking, yelling, and so on), or as words. This is a specific flaw caused by *Big Brother*'s format specificity:

> Of all the love affairs none of them seemed real to me, only that of the French guy, Serginho and Vanessa (in *Big BrotherB1*), right? It was innocent, naïve, it was more real! (22 year-old-woman, high school teacher, *Big Brother Brazil 4*)

While the audience finds it hard not to believe that participants sometimes act natural or make some real friends due to the forced intimacy and the stress, this public thinks that the obsession to win the money prize rules out that possibility, and turns what could be a living reality into a TV show:

> Everything's carefully planned. They may even become friends, sort of ... in a locked-up house you just have to live with others and then you make friendships. But whenever the money gets into the picture, if you can, you help your friend out, but if you can't, too bad for him! (33-year-old male student of technical school, *Big Brother Brazil 4*)

> It isn't like real life concerning the activities [in the house], it is real life concern-ing the relationships with persons. (Female university student, *Gran Hermano1*)

> Because from the very instant that there are cameras, I don't know if it's life itself. Besides as they're all locked up there ... like it all becomes more... (Male university student, *Gran Hermano1*)

Common-sense reasoning serves as a powerful ally for the Authenticity pole in this belief oscillation process, while the 'building up of memory' drives belief in the opposite direction, that of Inauthenticity. Among the middle-class interviewees, there is widespread mistrust of such a powerful media enterprise as Rede Globo. However, the index appeal embodied by the two outsiders of *Big Brother Brazil 4*, who are both lower class and entered the game through the *Big Brother Brazil 4* fanzine, serves as a powerful antidote:

The fights I used to watch, it's like, you know … that can also happen to you with your friends, if you quarrel with them, and then you make up again. (Male university student, *Gran Hermano1*)

Sorry but those are feelings! They are not all friends, but after four months, how can you not have any feelings? (Male university student, *Gran Hermano1*)
It can all be manipulated, but not all the time, eventually they will have to show what really goes on, and that's that. (26-year-old male technician, *Big Brother Brazil 4*)

Even the friendships … I don't know whether they are sincere, or if it's all just to avoid a possible vote. (20-year-old male student, *Big Brother Brazil 4*)

There was a selection which was maybe manipulated, we don't know how they act at Globo. But there were people chosen from the audience, then I think that in contrast with previous editions the basic difference is that, [before] people were all chosen by Globo … they say that two or three different people were chosen, that even Cida and Tiago went there through the fanzine and that Solange got in by popular vote. (32-year-old female librarian, *Big Brother Brazil 4*)

All three kinds of dynamic interpretants revolve around whether the audience believes or not in what it watches. Credulity, incredulity and considerable doubt concerning the actuality of what is represented in the TV format constitutes its main attraction. What all these opinions share is 'working through' (Ellis 1996), a lively reflection on the tension that exists between television as a place of total control and manipulation in modernity, and the sign exudation of observed bodies in a bizarre setting in which their owners must self-consciously compete to be themselves. Their task of Sisyphus is to show themselves in a natural way, when every move is an overt self-enactment, and thus an impossible task. In such an dilemma lies the central concern for the *Big Brother* audience of the two studied regions.

## Conclusion: mass perversion or a real attraction for the real self?

To sum up, I will present a critique of the three most common, empirically unfounded claims concerning the meaning of *Big Brother* in this part of the world. Our reception analysis of the audience response to the *Big Brother* format in Brazil and Uruguay shows that:

(i) Far from dissolving the frontier between factual information and invented fiction, a central strategy for watching this TV programme consists in focusing on the evidence or *index appeal* that is perceived in it. It enables the public to separate what is understood to be authentic – a revelation of the participant's true self – from what is thought to be fabricated for the spectacularisation of the interaction order. The latter involves a media-induced transformation of the real person into a skilful, cynical player of the self. The terms involved in this metamorphosis are elaborate forms of self-enactment (Goffman 1971), and the endless struggle of self-knowledge celebrated by the public as fierce resistance to the format's implacable machinery.

(ii) For this audience, not even the noticeable manipulations which they believe are constantly done by the production of *Big Brother* can alter the documentary nature or 'indexing' (Carroll 1997) of the format. Despite the melodramatic elements which are overtly played up through the editing of the recorded material, and the visible use of special effects – in the daily and weekly summaries – all this does not turn its indexical nature into a new-fangled, amateurish soap opera. This evaluation in no way diminishes the ethical objections raised against *Big Brother*'s distorted representation of everyday life.

(iii) The main counterargument against the current critical and academic view of *Big Brother* is the motivation which can be inferred from the positive and negative opinions of the studied audience about the meaning of *Big Brother*. Theirs is not sex-driven, voyeuristic behaviour. What comes out as decisive for Latin American audiences is the steady observation of the ordeals of the self, when submitted to the uncanny temptations and hazards of the filmed house. Not the sex appeal of the good-looking participants, but their ethical stamina and disposition to resist the distorted represen-tation of their all-too-real bodyprints in the interaction order – the *index appeal* in its inevitable manifestation – is what drives this audience, according to the present recep-tion analysis.

When in a recent Brazilian reception study (Girardello and Orofi 2002), a 7-year-old girl is asked what she has found most interesting in her TV watching experience, her reply brings in her professional vocation:

> When I grow up, I want to be a soap opera actress … because it is an arranged life (*uma vida combinada*). You rehearse and you know already what you'll do. In our life, people don't arrange anything. You don't know what will happen.

The child's witty answer brings to mind the quoted comment of the Brazilian high-school teacher on the specificity of the *Big Brother* format: 'the reactions are real, they are unpredictable, aren't they?' It is hard to beat the simplicity and accuracy of this account of the lure of *Big Brother*'s index appeal. While they are discussing different media issues, the child and the woman drive their point home: this is what is most touching about the *Big Brother* reception experience – touching in a literal, indexical sense, and in an emotional one, too. Instead of a dizzying mix of the popular soap opera and the high-brow documentary, in this public's interpretation *Big Brother* is a short-lived alternative to the fixed narrative format, whose enjoyment lies in the incantatory repetition performed with state-of-the-art technical perfection. That is why we all rely on most TV fiction being a format in which all has been wholly arranged ('*combinado*'), as the girl rightly said. *Big Brother* functions also as an alternative to the artistic representation of the real (almost) as it can be found out there, usually in the margins of society. The documentary includes behaviours which have not been rehearsed or directed.

Neither an emotion-laden fiction, nor a politically-engaged audiovisual feat which aims at wrestling out of the world the truths few want to face, the reality show is interpreted as a format which affords its audience a chance to look for, contemplate and evaluate some glimpses of the self. Through them the public gleans for what of truth and of falsehood real, everyday life may offer them. Since 'you don't know what will happen', as the child said, in spite of the gross commercialism, of the controversial exploitation of private life that the Endemol format carries out, it still contains enough indexical features to set off a pursuit of the authentic amidst a thick forest of deceit and of make-believe. It may not be a bad idea to observe these meaning effects or dynamical interpretants as they are embodied in the audience response of these two

Latin American regions, in order to account for the novelty as well as for the traditional aspects of a new television format such as *Big Brother*.

*Notes*

1   Peirce will be quoted with the conventional notation: 'CP [x.xxx]', which refers to volume and paragraph in *The Collected papers of Charles S. Peirce* (1936–58).
2   The River Plate area is the region around the delta of the river with the same name. It is used to refer to both countries, Uruguay and Argentina.
3   For a similar discussion on the documentary film genre being maintained, even if it is found to contain falsehoods (for example, in propaganda), see Carroll (1996: 224). Obviously, this affects the reliability of the film as a source of *bona fide* evidence, but does not affect the genre as such (it is a poor documentary, but not a fiction film).
4   Ransdell (1986) defines it thus: 'The *immediate interpretant* is the range – always vaguely circumscribed – of the interpretant-generating power of the sign at a given time.' In the particular case of *Big Brother*, time is especially relevant given its relying on indexical elements, which are defined by their singularity, their here-and-nowness, which makes repetitions vulnerable to suspicion.
5   Jost (2001; 2002) argues against the notion of the novelty of the *Big Brother* French format (*Loft Story*). However, a case can be made for what is different in it, which, I think, is due to the high indexical content of the format. This structural feature accounts for the relevance of 'the interaction order' (Goffman 1983) in it. The situational meanings which emerge when people are face to face afford the viewers the opportunity for becoming real tourists of this microsociological realm, one which it is pleasing to observe from afar, since normally we are so deeply engrossed in it, that we cannot gaze at it with detachment.
6   The gathering of the Brazilian data was done in Porto Alegre, and in the nearby cities São Leopoldo and Canoas. The field study was done with the collaboration of research assistants Caroline Comunello and Liú Batistiani dos Santos, with the support of the Graduate Communication Programme of Unisinos, and with Research Grants awarded by UNISINOS and FAPERGS.
7   The three Portuguese terms may be translated as 'fight, riot, quarrel', respectively.
8   To 'nominate' a participant is the ironic term used to denote the process whereby two candidates for expulsion are voted every fortnight by the participants, so the audience may have a chance to choose one.
9   That occasion was a notorious instance of the *Arcimboldo effect*: a Mexican style soap-opera called *Algemas da Paixão* (*Handcuffs of Passion*) was literally grafted onto *Big BrotherB2* sequences to ridicule the frustrated attempts of Tyrso to win the love of Manuela. This may have contributed to gaining the public's sympathy for the young man's ordeal.
10  The group included an attractive model and stripper, a female boxer, two professional wrestlers, one of whom was also a personal trainer. None of them quite fits into the strictly ordinary people category, although none of them were famous. But for Cida, and, to a lesser extent, her fanzine mate Tiago, the rest were remarkably telegenic, twelve beautifully-built and cared-for bodies.
11  An example of pure indexes is the heartbeat-measuring gadget that is wired to the body of the candidates who are up for expulsion on the 'execution wall' day (*o paredão*): the audience gets to read their worried soul on the TV screen live.

# Bibliography

Andacht, F. (2002) 'Big brother te está mirando. La irresistible atracción de un reality show global', in R. Paiva (ed.) *Ética, cidadania e imprensa*. Rio de Janeiro: Mauad, 63–100.

_____ (2003a) *El reality show. Un abordaje analítico de la televisión*. Buenos Aires: Norma.

_____ (2003b) 'Uma aproximação analítica do formato televisual do reality show *Big Brother*', Galáxia. *Revista transdisciplinar de Comunicação*, 6, 245–64.

_____ (2003c) 'El signo indicial en la representación televisiva de lo real'. *XXVI Congresso Brasileiro de Ciências da Comunicação*. Available on CD-Rom.

_____ (2004a) 'Formas documentárias da representação do real na fotografia, no filme documentário e no *reality show* televisivo atuais', *Lusocom VI*, Available on CD-Rom.

_____ (2004b) 'Duas variantes da representação do real na cultura midiática: o exorbitante *Big Brother Brasil* e o circunspeto *Edifício Master*'. Paper presented at the *XIII Compós*, Universidade Metodista. Available on CD-Rom.

_____ (2004c) 'De l'irresistible 'indice-appeal' d'une attraction mondiale: *Big Brother* vous touche', in *Les Temps Télévisuels. Big Brother*. Paris: L' Harmattan, 43–91.

Carrol, N. (1996) 'From reel to real', in *Theorising the Moving Image*. Cambridge: Cambridge University Press, 224–40.

Ellis, J. (1996) 'Television as working through', in J. Gripsrud (ed.) *Media and Knowledge: The Role of Television*. Bergen, University of Bergen Working Papers No.2, 55–70.

Girardello, G. and M. I. Orofi (2002) 'A Pesquisa de Recepção com Crianças: Mídia, Cultura e Cotidiano'. Paper presented at the *XII Compós*, Rio de Janeiro, UFRJ. Available on CD-Rom.

Goffman, E. (1959) *The Presentation of Self in Everyday Life*. New York: Anchor Books.

_____ (1971) *Relations in Public*. New York: Harper Torchbooks.

_____ (1983) 'The interaction order', *American Sociological Review*, 48, 1, 1–17.

Hill, A. (2002) '*Big Brother*: the real audience', *Television and New Media*, 3, 3, 323–40.

Horton, D. and R. Wohl (1956) 'Mass communication and para-social interaction. Observations on intimacy at a distance', *Psychiatry*, 19, 3, 215–29.

Jensen, K. B. (1995) *The Social Semiotics of Mass Communication*. London: Sage.

Jost, F. (2001) *La télévision du quotidien. Entre réalité et fiction*. Paris: De Boeck.

_____ (2003) *L'empire du Loft*. Paris: La Dispute.

Meyrowitz, J. (1989) *No Sense of Place: The Impact of Electronic Media on Social Behavior*. New York: Oxford University Press.

Peirce, C. S. (1931–58) *Collected Papers of C. S. Peirce*. C. Hartshorne, P. Weiss, A. Burks (eds.). Cambridge, MA: Harvard University Press.

Ransdell, J. (1986) 'Charles Sanders Peirce (1839–1914)', in *Encyclopedic Dictionary of Semiotics*. The Hague: Mouton de Gruyter, 673–95.

Taylor, C. (1989) *Sources of the self: The Making of Modern Identity*. Cambridge: Harvard University Press.

Turrisi, P. (2002) 'The role of Peirce's pragmatism in education', *Cognitio*, 3, 122–35.

Watzlawick, P. (1977). *How Real is Real?: Confusion, Disinformation, Comm-unication*. New York: Vintage Books.

# CHAPTER 10

*Baŗis Kiliçbay and Mutlu Binark*

## MEDIA MONKEYS
Intertextuality, Fandom and Big Brother Turkey

### Introduction: a brief history of reality TV in Turkey

Reality programming in general was not new to the Turkish television audience before the *Big Brother* format was imported. During the 1990s, an important decade for Turkish television because of the boom in private television networks, a plethora of new genres and formats invaded most of the private channels. Talk shows, call-in shows, docu-dramas, paparazzi shows and a variety of reality programmes referred to as 'reality shows' as a whole that gained remarkable success are the most significant examples of these new programmes.[1]

Although some features of these shows were copied from foreign examples, they nevertheless managed to establish a unique style combining already existing techniques and themes with narratives addressing the sentimentality of the Turkish audience. The majority of these programmes revolve around individual stories of ordinary people, almost always represented as victims, crime spectacles organised around such strong discourses as authority, justice and security, or other narratives using reality techniques to 'reveal' the reality long-concealed by the State television under the mask official (televisual) discourses. Another significant aspect of the 'reality shows' was the appearance of famous media personalities (anchorpersons, soap opera stars, singers and journalists) as narrators. The programmes used, for the first time in Turkish television, authentic footage from live camera records, footage from surveillance videos, amateur recordings of the event, interviews with eye-witnesses, repetition and slow-motion presentation of the events, close-ups and voiceover narration. The narrator was located among the people either involved in the events portrayed or used as a part of the fictive audience, and this position let her/him guide various interpretative strategies, which make the presenter not only a narrator but also a mediator. The narrator depends on the 'power of camera' to capture 'every single moment' of the event (Ferveit 1999: 793).

Considering the uses of narrative strategies, we propose to classify reality shows under two sub-formats. The first one we call 'social control texts' where accidents, homicide, personal and social catastrophes are narrated, and the show is built upon the search of the 'criminal', the responsible or the 'deviant'. For example, *Polis Imdat*, *Sıcagı Sıcagına* and *Teksoy Görevde* are the best representatives of this sub-format. In the second sub-format, in contrast, the show seeks for a social solution both for those excluded from society and lower-class 'victims'. Victimisation of marginal groups and individuals is mostly based on stereotyping and social labelling. We call this second tendency 'populist texts'. *Söz Fato'da* and *Yetis Emmioglu* are examples of this sub-format. The former is presented by a movie star while the latter has a popular singer as the host. The popularity of and record ratings achieved by these shows could be partially explained by the audience's desire to watch ordinary and 'real' people's supposedly unedited stories at home and also by the innovative character of the programmes bringing together a variety of narratives and genres. Even television news and other 'serious' programmes have transformed elements of their content to emulate this newly discovered format and its narrative strategies such as dramatisation and sensationalisation, by including stories of the same kind presented as 'news'. This said, it is easier to claim that the reality shows of the 1990s in Turkey were the first hybrid television format. This hybridity was also the result of mixing Western ideas with 'local' discourses, stories and mediations. However, this hybridity is not only an intrinsic character of reality TV but also a result of the rapid commercialisation of the television industry, and in the case of Turkey, the discovery that large profits could be earned through the manipulation of a thirsty audience parched by State television for decades. The hybridity of new television texts is due, according to Norman Fairclough, to the mixed use of information, fact, dramatisation and fiction; the mixture of official, public and everyday languages and experiences; and finally, the mixing of factual and personal narratives (see Bondebjerg 1996).

Between the early reality shows and the so-called reality TV represented by the emergence of an adaptation of the international *Big Brother* show, Turkish television audiences have been introduced recently to some other 'quasi reality TV' shows. These are for the most, 'local' productions, developed in Turkey and promoting some so-called Turkish values. The best example of this constructed, hybrid format is a game show called *120 Milyon* (*120 Millions*), launched by Show TV in 2001, where two persons (or in the later seasons, two families) have to spend one month in separate houses and work in jobs arranged for them by the production company, earning only the minimum wage set by the Turkish government. The one who had spent the least amount of money during the month is the winner. The contestants were filmed in their (prepared) daily routine, while working, shopping, paying bills and spending time in their temporary home. The values encouraged in this format are a moral and financial endurance since the two participants are supposed to survive while trying to spend as little money as possible. This endurance that is generally attributed to lower-class families, particularly to a number of workers who get the minimum wage, is the embodiment of a discourse on poverty and all the positive attributes 'naturally' associated with it. Thus, the participants symbolise the ordinary and humble Turkish citizen forced to live with the minimum. This constructed programme successfully blends a poverty discourse with the powerful televisual discourse, resulting with the emergence of new celebrities who are simply filmed in their daily lives while trying to survive. The audience generally ignored the very fact that this was nothing but a game, and not only empathised with the participants but also supported them in their 'rough path'. Furthermore, the show also represented the 'reality' of Turkish people faced with the economic and financial crisis.

*120 Milyon* is one of the examples in Turkey of an innovative television format that obtained unexpected ratings everywhere it has been introduced. Camera surveillance, showing the participants as if they were caught in their daily lives, is common to both *120 Milyon* and international formats like *Big Brother* or *Biri Bizi Gözetliyor* (*Someone Is Watching Us*), its Turkish counterpart.

## Big Brother Turkey: someone is watching us

The difference between reality show, as a specific format unique to Turkey, and globalised reality TV has been evident with the emergence of a totally new television show introduced to the Turkish audience in 2001. *Biri Bizi Gözetliyor* is an adaptation of *Taxi Orange*, a format adapted from *Big Brother*, its more famous sibling. The differences between *Big Brother* and *Taxi Orange* are limited to some regulations concerning the voting and the compulsory job that the participants exercise in *Taxi Orange*, namely taxi driving. The basic features and notions of this new format remain the same in both programmes. Jane Roscoe claims that the Australian *Big Brother*, is 'a national thing' though it is an international format regardless of geographical location (Roscoe 2001: 475). Similarly, Ib Bondebjerg maintains that reality TV 'combines a global format with a very "glocalised" perspective' (Bondebjerg 2002: 159). We argue, in the same line, that *Biri Bizi Gözetliyor* includes many national characteristics and that a part of its popularity amongst the audience could be related to the embodiment and performance of several national values and characteristics, which altogether put *Biri Bizi Gözetliyor* quite apart from its international examples or precedents. These differences are not only limited to national features but also to some other technical and production-related details. The producers of the original format, Dutch Endemol, were not sympathetic to enhanced interactivity, that is, the possibility for web users to view the show online. The American counterpart of Endemol, on the contrary, sought to change the format in order to expand the visibility of the show (Andrejevic 1996: 106).

Now, many national examples of *Big Brother* have official websites that allow online viewers to watch the show 24 hours a day. While this was the case in many *Big Brother* adaptations, the Turkish production company of *Biri Bizi Gözetliyor*, Senkron, introduced the show, live for 24 hours a day, on a pay-per-view digital channel on Digiturk, also belonging to the bigger corporation, while at the same time it was still possible, like in other international examples, to view the show online.[2] Since Digiturk is not a widely viewed channel, because of the existence of many other free national channels, the un-edited *Biri Bizi Gözetliyor* show (broadcast around the clock) did not reach a majority audience. Instead, most audiences preferred (or were obliged) to watch the edited version of the show on the free national channel, Show TV. These were edited highlights broadcast in prime-time and on Saturday for the weekly finales. The popularity of *Biri Bizi Gözetliyor* grew quickly in the first few weeks of transmission, and the format was established for the next series with the new season of *Biri Bizi Gözetliyor*, starting in March 2002. This time, however, the production was based at another nationwide, transnational channel, Star, and the un-edited live show was carried by its sister channel Kanal 6, which was also broadcast nationally. This change was the beginning of a new era in the short history of *Biri Bizi Gözetliyor* in Turkey. Now the majority had access to the live round-the-clock coverage and appeared to greatly enjoy watching their new stars on TV 24 hours a day. As a result, *Biri Bizi Gözetliyor* embraced new meanings, and became an overall stronger phenomenon than it had been in the past. During the first seasons, the audience had to rely on the production company's conscious manipulation of characters, events and debates among the *Biri Bizi Gözetliyor* housemates. Given the chance to watch the whole show un-edited, the audience developed new viewing strategies and yet new fandom aspects appeared and become more visible during the third season of *Biri Bizi Gözetliyor*.

To date there have been five seasons of *Biri Bizi Gözetliyor* and four of the follow-up show *Orada Neler Oluyor* (*What's Going on Over There?*). This show adopts the basic features of the original *Big Brother* format and is essentially another competition bringing together all the participants for a second time (including those from previous seasons). The gaming rules function in a similar way with the popular 'voting off' system. The first seasons of *Biri Bizi Gözetliyor* and *Orada Neler Oluyor* could be watched on the pay-per-view channel and on the official website. Edited parts of the show were broadcast each night, dubbed with voiceover narration and sub-titles and presented by the hostess. This daily show called *Görmedikleriniz Duymadiklariniz* (*What You Haven't Heard and Seen*), built a character for each of the participants every night and shaped the audience's perception. Plots were constructed by the production company, by manipulating the so-called reality and then by the fan groups either on the official online forums or on the daily television updates. The voting system for *Biri Bizi Gözetliyor* was based on the regional separation of phone calls or cell-messages. In the first run of *Biri Bizi Gözetliyor* an opposition between the Western regions and Eastern regions developed. As a result, the dominant moral codes and dominant gender roles began to be discussed by both the contestants and the audience. In the second season, new topics such as homosexuality and intimate 'affairs' among the contestants were to be discussed. Particularly, the issue of 'being a man like a man' (*erkek gibi erkek olmak*), as opposed to the supposedly gay contestant, Volkan, came to the fore. (The 'manly' contestant later won the contest.) Also in the second season, a multicultural group was created. Edi, the winner of the prize in *Biri Bizi Gözetliyor 2* was Armenian and a devout Christian; Ali, who finished in third place, was a black Muslim; Hacer, who finished in second place came from a small town in Anatolia and promoted her rural origins. There was even a middle-aged single mother, who liked to act like a mother-figure to all the contestants in the house. After the second season ended, Hacer released an album (a trend established in previous series). In the second season of *Orada Neler Oluyor*, there was a special gathering bringing together all first- and second-season contestants in a winter resort house to compete for a car. This show was well covered in the larger media because of internal wrangling and a 'scandalous' love affair between a 35-year-old woman, Hülya, and a 19-year-old man, Melih, which quickly became big news for sensational magazines and various paparazzi shows. Even a 'serious' television discussion programme held a special night to discuss this affair thoroughly. The affair continued through the winter and reached its culminating point when the parents of Melih organised a press conference to declare that their son had no relation whatsoever with Hülya and claimed that she used him to get all the attention. The fact that the older woman was a single parent raised strong moral opposition amongst a large segment of the population, whereas several women participating in discussions supported her. Hülya later published a book, *Herseye Ragmen* (*Despite Everything*), discussing the affair and all the controversies it raised and Melih released an album, as this was somewhat becoming the rule.

As mentioned earlier, the third season heralded a major change as the programme was broadcast live 24/7 reaching a far greater audience. This strategy drastically changed the overall perception of the show and many viewers started adopting new watching practices like spending their time in front of the television set and in the case of house wives, doing all the chores in the room where the television set is switched on. Fan communities spread all over the country and played a major role in interpreting and negotiating the meaning of the show and its reality. In the third season, the discourse of 'being a man like a man' kept its importance while 'being a woman like a man' was coined by one of the female contestants. Among the inmates, an aggressive former television presenter, a tourist guide later lauded for representing the ideal Turkish youth, a lower-class bus driver, a retired white-collar officer who was happy to receive respect from his younger rivals, an aspiring singer (who was not lucky enough to release his album after his 'release' from the show), a teacher candidate who is also an aspiring poet and a male contestant without a professional identity who claimed to be a humble 'Eastern', were the most visible. The audience of the third season also witnessed the growing of a new ethics concerning honesty, sincerity, humility and political correctness, although the former television presenter, Gaye, was clearly opposed to the ethics espoused by the majority of the housemates and as a result became a very popular contestant. The opposition between the political correctness of Kaan, the male winner, and the incorrect masculinity of Gaye, the female, was constantly being highlighted by the production team either in the captions on the official website or in the audience discussion programmes directed by the hostess of the show.

The fourth season brought together a macho who refused to do any chores using instead the female housemates almost as 'servants'; a fake-psychologist who later confessed that he did not even have a university degree; a school teacher in her 50s; a butcher; a lower-class male teacher candidate who won the grand prize and a lower-class 'hunk' who had recently completed his military service. In the previous season several fan communities expressed their wish to see the lower-class bus driver as the winner but were disappointed.[3] However, the winner of the fourth season was a poor man, the son of a housewife and a factory worker. Tension, this time, did not arise from political correctness and vulgarity but constant debates around the educated and the uneducated, and the social status of housemates. According to Pierre Bourdieu, 'taste, the propensity and capacity to appropriate (materially and symbolically) a given class of classified, classifying objects or practices, is the generative formula of lifestyle, a unitary set of distinctive preferences' (Bourdieu 1984: 173). Based on Bourdieu, Chad Dell indicates the relation between taste and social distinction: 'taste is a marker of social differences' (Dell 1998: 91). Following these comments, we argue that the fan communities supporting each contestant represented different and various social tastes whereby the contestants' 'meanings' and identities were formed and reproduced.

The lack of tension in season five came from the fact that the production team chose to cast housemates who were all educated, middle-class and mature. Strong differences reflecting class, social taste and education were no longer a feature of the narrative, and the fifth season show became known as 'five-star *Biri Bizi Gözetliyor*'.[4]

The most significant change in this last season was made in the voting system. The winner of the week set by the public vote would name another contestant who, in turn, would be voted off by the majority of the participants. Until this season, the winner was the only one authorised to vote off another contestant. The winner was again a male and an Armenian, while in the follow-up show *Orada Neler Oluyor*, a woman won the grand prize. The hostess of the show said while greeting her: 'Welcome to the world of stars', and handed her a certificate designating her as a star.

## Social responses and press comments

The huge success of the first season of *Biri Bizi Gözetliyor* reverberated in various ways throughout Turkish society. While some groups were only interested in the 'game', that is, the televisual identities of the participants and the televisual reality, a so-called 'social movement' was getting underway through Internet forums devoted to discussions about the show. A group of university students published a 'call for transparency' in June 2001, which was partly supported and adopted on Internet forums. This text called upon the production company, Senkron TV, to reveal all the secret strategies such as 'manipulating' the results of the weekly votes and the 'reality' of the show, and requested that both the production and the telephone company make the details of the voting public.[5] Some individuals, including members of conservative political parties, participating in audience discussion programmes predictably expressed their disquiet, arguing that this show was against Turkish culture and its moral codes. And recently, in June 2002, a columnist of a daily newspaper launched a petition against *Biri Bizi Gözetliyor*.

Another restriction imposed upon the show was the government's regulatory control. The Radio and Television High Council (RTÜK) sanctioned Show TV by taking it off the air for one day because the programme contravened 'general moral codes, peace of the society and Turkish family make-up'. Some writers and columnists supported this sanction. A columnist wrote that the programme did not represent the 'Turkish youth' and the High Council itself declared that it caused 'negative effects' on young people because it revealed 'immoral intimacies' between 35-year-old single mother Hülya and 19-year-old Melih. Show TV maintained that this show was broadcast in 17 countries in the world and they were never accused of 'being immoral'. The High Council, on the other hand, claimed that they received reproaches from 2,817 people throughout the country and even a petition in which the channel was requested to broadcast the show later at night, with other 'erotic' programmes. Elsewhere, the verdict of the High Council was severely criticised. In a communications congress held in Istanbul, for instance, the 'return of the censorship' was denounced. The third season of *Biri Bizi Gözetliyor* was once again sanctioned by the High Council in April 2002, on the same grounds, but this time added these words to its verdict: 'The contestants in this show are shown living communally. The show creates a pseudo-life in which young people think that everything is legitimate in order to obtain money and fame.'

The *Biri Bizi Gözetliyor* phenomenon has also been widely discussed in national newspapers and magazines. Some of the columnists were particularly interested in the show and have published articles discussing this new phenomenon in Turkey. The general attitude of these columnists was a negative one. They argued that *Biri Bizi Gözetliyor* was the embodiment of the neo-liberal values integrated into everyday life and they criticised the visibility of ordinary people who did not do anything but gossip or dance and one columnist referred to this new culture as a 'voluntary torture society' (*Milliyet*, 17 March 2002). This new culture, they claimed, is evident in the way of life of the youth, with a tendency to consume rather then to read or to produce; accentuate obscenity, and highlight their visual appearance rather than their intellect (*Radikal*, 25 March 2001). One columnist quoted a housemate saying, 'I've done many things up to now: dance, aerobics, step, music, modelling', and concluded her article by stating that these activities could only be called 'doing nothing' (*Radikal*, 19 May 2001). Another columnist argued that Turkey has been 'post-modernised before it became modern' referring to this phenomenon, rather pejoratively, as 'the awakening of a Nation' (*Milliyet*, 19 October 2001). Other critiques referred to the nature of the programme and argued that it promotes voyeurism, instant celebrities and 'empty' conversations. The daily television reviewer of *Milliyet* compared two young women coming from a rural background: the first one lives in a small village and will be the first Turkish woman ever to participate to the Winter Olympics and the second one is Hacer, a participant to the second season, again from a rural background but who chooses to become a celebrity by participating to a game show (*Milliyet*, 1 January 2002). To some, *Biri Bizi Gözetliyor* represents the 'false ideals' embraced by society's youth and to others the programme itself contributes to the banality of culture, especially television culture.

This debate is older than *Biri Bizi Gözetliyor* but has been rejuvenated with this phenomenon. It addresses two 'levels' of discursive dialogue surrounding the series: an 'official' level in which discussing *Biri Bizi Gözetliyor* is denied because 'there are far more important problems in Turkey' and a 'civic' level in which the audience, in its daily life, discuss and gossip about the new celebrities of *Biri Bizi Gözetliyor* (*Milliyet*, 19 October 2001).

## They are watching us: Biri Bizi Gözetliyor and fandom

In Turkey fandom has been most notably associated with such things as being a follower of a sports team or a devotee of a particular music performer. After the emergence of *Biri Bizi Gözetliyor*, a new fan culture and fan communities appeared. This reality TV format was naturally predisposed towards creating fan communities through its multi-platform access and hybridity, enabling audiences to participate in several ways and to construct multiple meanings. Some of the *Biri Bizi Gözetliyor* audience devoted both their leisure time and work time to watching the show as often as possible. They also participated in ongoing discussions about the events and the relations among the contestants through both official online discussion forums and audience discussion programmes such as *Görmedikleriniz Duymadiklariniz* and *Ates Hatti*.[6] *Görmedikleriniz Duymadiklariniz* became an important realm where fan communities achieved visibility. This audience discussion programme is specifically devoted to *Biri Bizi Gözetliyor* and produced by the same team. Each week *Görmedikleriniz Duymadiklariniz* features the eliminated contestant talking about her/his life in the house and the relationship with other housemates. In the third season the format evolved into a live studio audience discussion programme. In this way, fan communities of each contestant could discuss the media performers directly, and interpret their acts and dialogues within the house instantly.

These fan communities could be also considered 'interpretive communities'. Supporters of different contestants come together in a shared/common realm and talk about interpersonal relations among the contestants, and then try to create their own preferred meanings, instead of the meaning attached by the production company. They also discover that they are not alone in their preference and constructions. The devoted participants of *Görmedikleriniz Duymadiklariniz* built fan networks in order to continue their activities outside the studio. Official online discussion forums are also significant in the construction of fan communities. Baym notes four communicative practices in computer-mediated fan culture: informing, speculating, criticising and reworking (Baym 1998: 114). We can apply the same patterns to the fan communities of *Biri Bizi Gözetliyor*. They circulate information about the contestants and events; they speculate about the relations among the contestants and about the show itself; they criticise mainstream media responses to the show, comment on the 'reality' (and sometimes on the 'verisimilitude' of the show), and evaluate social and cultural trends highlighted through the actions of the housemates. Other topics of conversation are mainly based on these interpretative practices that end up creating a group identity (Baym 2000). By using Internet forums and sharing the same watching activity, the members of fan communities establish virtual social relationships. For instance, some members of *Biri Bizi Gözetliyor* fan communities establish friendship ties, and carry this friendship to face-to-face communication. Thus, a viewing activity becomes incorporated into everyday life and is transformed into (cultural) consumption. The process of re-working means that the fan communities create their own new texts and sub-texts from the original texts. They create their own narratives but those are not dependent on the main narrative in circulation.

During the first season, the fans of Eray, who came second, organised special gatherings with his elder brother, and then with him after the end of the show. The fans of *Biri Bizi Gözetliyor 1* even carried a petition campaign against the voting system. The fans of some *Biri Bizi Gözetliyor* contestants remained exclusively committed to her/him, and linked his/her habitus (personality and ethical values) with their own lives, ambitions and standpoints. They exchanged information about their favourite contestants, made moral judgements about the events occurring in the house and actions of the contestants. They followed the contestants' personal lives after the show, and tried to keep in touch with them. Here, 'talk' is a key element both within reality TV and in the establishment of fan communities. Through the act of 'talk', both contestants and fans of contestants express their personalities, or what they think to be their personalities, and frame standpoints for themselves. For example, in the third season of *Biri Bizi Gözetliyor*, fans of the winner, Kaan, organised a birthday party upon his request for his best friend among the contestants. In the third season, the fans of Gaye identified with her 'philosophy' when she explained why she had decided to participate to the show. They adored her because of her open ambition to become a media personality and her aggressive and insulting attitudes towards other contestants. She became a symbol among some of the audience, as a powerful woman acting like a man ('*erkek gibi kadin*'), one that also implies a borrowed masculinity. Gaye refused to wear a swimming suit during *Orada Neler Oluyor 3*, staged in a holiday resort, not because of any religious belief but because she constantly refused to present herself as a woman and wore casual men's sportswear. She swore frequently and terrorised her fellow contestants. Her fans interpreted her attitudes as a strategy to fight male domination and lauded her bravery. Some fan groups visited her house to meet her family. To them, Gaye was the ideal Turkish woman, who refuses to be commodified by the media industry, consumption culture and patriarchy.

The most interesting feature of *Görmedikleriniz Duymadiklariniz* for the fan communities lay in the fact that it created an open space to discuss private issues concerning the lives of the contestants and their interpersonal relationships. For Turkish television audiences, accustomed to see 'specialists' talking about 'serious' matters in almost all discussion programmes, the gossipy nature of the discussion offered by *Görmedikleriniz Duymadiklariniz* was totally new. For the first time on television, ordinary people were talking enthusiastically about other ordinary people, as if they were in a hot political debate. These live discussions were an opportunity for the fan and anti-fan communities to produce their own meanings and contribute to the creation of the new star system. Jonathan Gray conceptualises anti-fans as fans 'who strongly dislike a given text or genre, considering it inane, stupid, morally bankrupt and/or aesthetic drivel' (Gray 2003: 70). Anti-fans generally express their dislike through 'hatesites'. *Biri Bizi Gözetliyor* anti-fans are more visible in *eksisözlük*,[7] a daily web dictionary, created by upper- and middle-class Turkish university students. Several entry writers of *eksisözlük* dislike the idea behind the emerging reality TV culture and severely criticise most of the contestants, openly expressing their antipathy for them. They write about contestants' backgrounds, comment on events and situations in the show. That means that they follow the programme very carefully. A non-fan, on the other hand, is a member of an audience who watches a programme, but not with deep devotion (Gray 2003: 74). Non-fans also watch reality TV, but their involvement to the narration is limited. They do not feel any embarrassment if they miss the show, nor acknowledge it as a daily event.

Fan reception does not exist in isolation, but is formed through the interaction with other fans within a social and cultural community (Jenkins 1992: 76). Intertextuality also plays an important role in the strengthening and the establishment of fan communities, as seen in the intertextual circulation of the *Biri Bizi Gözetliyor* text through several other television programmes where the audience is invited to participate. According to John Fiske (1992), fan culture shows the 'productive power of audience'. For example Radyo ODTÜ, one of the local radio stations in Ankara, organised a competition show among the listeners for the best imitator of season three's most aggressive female contestant, Gaye. Fans of *Biri Bizi Gözetliyor,* through their participation in online discussion forums and in *Görmedikleriniz Duymadiklariniz*, challenge the preferred meaning constructed by the production company. Some also take their involvement into the realm of slash fiction, participating in the writing of scenarios and the characterisation of the show's contestants. Their interpretative strategies are different from the general audience because they are emotionally attached to the performers of the show, and follow their everyday life routines in the house. They interpret their behaviours, actions and talks and support their acts in front of others. They compare the participants' behaviours and problems with their own socio-private experiences and make moral judgements (Hill 2000: 198). They attend audience discussion programmes as much as possible. As Estella Tincknell and Parvati Raghuram state, 'the audience always knew more about the events being enacted than any one of the "characters", just as they would if *Biri Bizi Gözetliyor* really was a fictional drama' (Tincknell & Raghuram 2002: 207).

As Henry Jenkins puts it, 'media fans take pleasure in making intertextual connections across a broad range of media texts' (Jenkins 1992: 36). To receive information they need about their favourite contestants, fans make use of other media and texts such as discussion programmes, talk shows or commercial publications. The tabloid press in Turkey feeds these needs and desires, and *Biri Bizi Gözetliyor* fans were recognised as a special target by the tabloid press. Therefore, the stories based on the House and the characterisation created by and for the contestants, were strategically circulated by the media industry in order to enlarge market share and increase audience ratings.

## Conclusion

In this chapter we have outlined several topics of discussion arising from the five seasons of *Biri Bizi Gözetliyor* and their intertextual circulation in the Turkish media. Surprisingly, we have observed that each season had its own theme such as political correctness, hegemonic masculinity, gender roles, being a dutiful citizen, being respectful of dominant moral codes and so on. All the contestants have shown a rather anti-political attitude, typically characterising the clichés concerning the stance of youth in contemporary Turkey. One of the biggest criticisms of the show was that it promoted a new state of mind among the youth who thought they could easily become rich and famous only by participating and being visible in a big game show like this. These new televisual identities are frequently referred to as 'media monkeys', both by critics and the contestants themselves. The term was first used in a talk show in Turkey while describing the participants of various entertainment shows said to 'sell their privacy in return for fame'. We borrowed this term to point to the manipulation mechanisms used by the media industry and the enthusiastic and voluntary engagement of 'ordinary' people so they might become media celebrities with their fans eagerly watching and following them for the duration of each season until they are displaced by a new cast in a new season and the old ones fall like autumn leaves.

The Turkish film industry used to be one of the largest in the world during the 1960s and 1970s and a very strong star system helped in the promotion and circulation of the films. After the demise of this system in the 1990s, no other system as bright as the one created by the reality TV had ever invaded the screen. The new star system and the new fandom brought by *Biri Bizi Gözetliyor* has now replaced the glamorous past.

*Notes*

1   The term was introduced in English, and no translation was provided by any production company, television channel or critic. This may be the result of the fact that producers wanted the audience to believe that the format was an 'import' rather than a local discovery.
2   *Digiturk* is a the first digital television broadcasting in Turkey and it comprises several channels, movie and sports salons and one channel only devoted to the live broadcasting of *Biri Bizi Gözetliyor*.
3   Just as in *102 Milyon*, in which the contestants were supposed to survive on far-below-poverty-level minimum wage, so in *Biri Bizi Gözetliyor* the winner should represent the lower classes, some viewers claimed.
4   As a result of incessant fights among the housemates, the production decided to disqualify a few and replace them with others.
5   Votes were automatically counted through a special telephone line provided by a private GSM company.
6   A popular discussion show hosted by a well-known journalist.

7   *Sour dictionary*. http://sozluk.sourtimes.org

*Bibliography*

Adakli-Aksop, G. (2001) 'Televizyon Türlerinde Dönüsüm', *Ankara Üniversitesi Iletisim Fakültesi Yıllık 1999*, 229–53.

_____ (1998) *'Türkiye'de Reality Show'lar'*, unpublished MA thesis, Ankara University.

Andrejevic, M. (2001) *'The Kinder, Gentler Gaze of "Big Brother": Reality Television in the Era of Digital Capitalism'*, unpublished PhD dissertation, University of Colorado, School of Journalism and Mass Communication.

Baym, N. (1998) 'Talking About Soaps: Communicative Practices in a Computer-Mediated Fan Culture', in C. Harris and A. Alexander (eds) *Theorizing Fandon: Fans, Subculture and Identity*. New Jersey: Hampton Press, 111–29.

_____ (2000) *Tune In, Log On: Soaps, Fandom, and Online Community*. London: Sage.

Bondebjerg, I. (1996) 'Public discourse/private fascination: hybridization in "true-life-story" genres', *Media, Culture and Society*, 18, 27–45.

_____ (2002) 'The Mediation of Everyday Life: Genre, Discourse and Spectacle in Reality TV', in A. Jerslev (ed.) *Realism and 'Reality' in Film and Media*. Northern Lights Film and Media Studies Yearbook, Copenhagen: Museum Tusculanum Press, University of Copenhagen, 159–93.

Bourdieu, P. (1984) *Distinction: A Social Critique of the Judgement of Taste*. Cambridge: Harvard University Press.

Dell, C. (1998) 'Looking That Hunk of Man!: Subversive Pleasures, Female Fandom, and Professional Wrestling', in C. Harris and A. Alexander (eds) *Theorizing Fandom: Fans, Subculture and Identity*. New Jersey: Hampton Press, 8–108.

Ferveit, A. (1999) 'Reality TV in the Digital Era: A Paradox in Visual Culture', *Media, Culture & Society*, 21, 6, 787–804.

Fiske, J. (1992) *Television Culture*. London: Routledge.

Gray, J. (2003) 'New Audiences, New Textualities: Anti-fans and Non-fans', *International Journal of Cultural Studies*, 6, 1, 64–81.

Hill, A. (2000) 'Fearful and Safe: Audience Response to British Reality Programming', *Television and New Media*, 1, 2, 193–213.

Jenkins, H. (1992) *Textual Poachers: Television Fans and Participatory Culture*. London: Routledge.

Langer, J. (1998) *Tabloid Television: Popular Journalism and the 'Other News'*. London: Routledge.

Lewis, L. (ed.) (1992) *The Adoring Audience: Fan Culture and Popular Media*. London: Routledge.

Roscoe, J. (2001) 'Big Brother Australia: Performing the "real" twenty-four-seven', *International Journal of Cultural Studies*, 4, 4, 473–88.

Tincknell, E. and P. Raghuram (2002) *'Big Brother*: Reconfiguring the "active" audience of cultural studies', *European Journal of Cultural Studies*, 5, 2, 199–215.

# CHAPTER 11

*Marco Centorrino*

# GRANDE FRATELLO
## Interactions between Tension and Obscenity in Big Brother Italy

This chapter intends to perform a textual analysis of the third Italian edition of *Big Brother* (*Grande Fratello* – running from 30 January to 8 May 2003), highlighting its structural components. It will focus on more than just a 'product', and will deal mainly with the daily interactions inside the house, viewable 24 hours a day on the satellite channel Stream. Subsequently, I will briefly look at the media coverage officially dedicated to the event: the daily highlights and the weekly show on Thursdays, broadcast by the channel Canale 5; a comedy programme dedicated to *Grande Fratello*, also broadcast on a weekly basis, by Italia 1, the magazine and the programme's website.[1] From a methodological point of view, I will start with the content, in other words what happened in the house during the 99 days the cameras were running, and then try and single out which elements were selected for media representation (highlights, articles, and so on) and how this representation took place. To achieve this, I shall apply interaction models, in particular those created by Erving Goffman, to analyse the contestants' strategies and the final product offered to the viewers.

We will see how certain peculiarities of the Italian edition reflect Italy's television culture and, in general, those culture industry models which have become increasingly pervasive in recent years,[2] for example the extra-textual debate surrounding obscenity and the soft-porn aspects integral to *Grande Fratello 3*. In wider terms, we will find a series of other features which play a major role in media entertainment, and which owe their origins to the reality show. All these aspects will be placed within a logical framework, allowing us to reflect on media trends and on the possibility of 'exporting' them for cross-cultural analysis.

## A comparative study of previous editions

The methodology adopted in the initial phase of the work, in which I focus on what happened inside the house, involved above all a task of classification. I chose to identify the main thematic areas distinguishing the various editions of Grande Fratello.[3] Such an approach, comparing Grande Fratello 1, 2 and 3, allowed me to establish a point of departure and see how the third series had evolved from the previous two.

### Daily routine

The housemates' daily routine was the fulcrum around which Grande Fratello 1, in particular, revolved. Day by day, the contestants and the public discovered together how the game worked, the implications of interaction constantly under the gaze of the cameras, and the consequences of forced isolation. The following year, such aspects were naturally less evident, since there was not the same element of surprise which had distinguished the first edition, despite the fact that the organisers had changed the rules, increased the number of contestants and, consequently, varied the frequency of the evictions.

In 2003, in Grande Fratello 3, the main innovations focused on the house, which now had a sauna, a gym and above all a luxury suite which the contestants were allowed to use as a reward on certain occasions. It represented an extra prize, linked to the weekly task, which the winner was usually allowed to share with another member of the household.

### Games

Games were a constant of the three editions. They encouraged the competitive and cooperative spirit of the competitors in order to achieve intermediate goals (together) or final victory (usually for themselves alone). The weekly tasks and especially the nominations,[4] which the contestants used to try and evict their rivals, characterised much of the life in the house over the three years, yet they took on different roles in each series. In Grande Fratello 1, for example, the financial award was expressly coveted. We witnessed a series of alliances between the male contestants, aimed at prolonging as much as possible their 'survival' in the house (thus increasing the possibility of winning the final prize money), while trying to fix the nominations so that the female contestants were evicted. The value of the prize money was also continuously stressed in the appeals that the contestants made to the viewers. In the last few days, the 'survivors', awaiting the final judgement, even tried to come to an agreement on sharing the prize money, regardless of how the viewers voted. In the second edition, the least successful in terms of viewing figures, this idea was reintroduced, but to a lesser degree.

By the third season this emphasis on winning the cash prize had been greatly marginalised and relegated to a minor role. So much so that the contestants themselves, during the game, spent some of the money to 'buy a nomination'[5] or to pay for the services offered in the suite. The prize money was only given prominence on the final evening when the winner said that she intended to use it to buy an apartment for her and her family.

*Tensions*

While almost absent from the first edition, moments of tension assumed a growing importance in the following two years. In *Grande Fratello 2*, in fact, less than a week into the game, one of the female contestants withdrew after spending two days in tears. But what really created a sensation was when one of the male contestants lost his temper because he had run out of cigarettes, and proceeded to go round the house brandishing a stick and threatening to smash everything up. He then went into the Diary Room and took out his rage on the programme organisers. Immediately afterwards he left the house, while his housemates watched on, terrified by the violent outburst they had just witnessed. In *Grande Fratello 1* one of the contestants had threatened to do something similar (albeit without such violent outbursts), but had been promptly dissuaded by his housemates.

In 2003, there were significantly more situations of tension. On at least two occasions a fight nearly broke out between two groups of housemates and there were daily arguments between the members of the couples or between other individuals.

*Obscenity*

At dawn on 19 September 2000 Italy discovered live television sex. Pietro and Cristina, contestants in the first edition, hid behind a sofa and, covered by a curtain, tried, at least in part, to conceal their movements, while leaving no doubt in the viewers' minds as to what they were doing. This sexual encounter instantly became a major news story in Italy, leading to a flood of debates, comments and expressions of moral condemnation in the ensuing hours. It was not the only encounter between the two contestants and, in the end, both profited in terms of popularity. Cristina won the game, and Pietro is one of the most popular personalities from the three editions.[6] Moreover, he was the subject of a successful nude calendar, as were other contestants.[7] This is not to be taken lightly, since in recent years calendars have become a symbol of the national star system in Italy. Every December there is tough competition, especially between the magazines, to see who can engage more or less famous personalities, and immortalise them nude for their new calendars.

From then on, the sexual theme seems to have escalated. In *Grande Fratello 2* there were sexual relations involving another couple, and one of the contestants revealed that she had been the lover of a former football player, a declaration which was to lead to criminal proceedings being initiated against her. The player involved did not welcome the intrusion into his private life, and decided to take legal action.

In *Grande Fratello 3*, lastly, there were thirty or so sexual acts involving four couples, one of which, for the first time in the three editions, was already together before the game began. Moreover, the contestants often talked about sex.

## Defining soft porn

The use of words such as 'erotic' or 'pornographic' may seem arbitrary. Above, I adopted the even more specific label of 'soft porn'. I should perhaps try and explain this choice. Firstly, we ought to remember that in Italy, unlike in many other countries, the definitions of pornography and obscenity are somewhat ambiguous. Even legislation is rather vague, and merely refers to 'public morals', leaving judges to decide whether the boundaries of such 'public morals' have been overstepped. Nor do the codes of practice regulating publications and television broadcasts help clarify the issue, which, moreover, has received little attention in Italian academic circles. Renato Stella (1991), for example, in his essay on the consumption of pornographic material in Italy, while making a careful distinction between the genres and discussing the differentiation between eroticism and pornography, does not examine the boundary between hard-core and soft-core, but merely proposes a kind of scale:

> Pornography ... denotes the sexual act; it surrogates or mimes it, and has the declared and specific aim of substituting it to induce it, which the consumer of pornography knows he/she cannot do without (graffiti ... postcards, calendars, jokes, all the way up to hard-core). (Stella 1991: 165–6)

This definition, however, introduces an important point in its identification of 'surrogate' or 'mimed' sexual relations (also see Alberoni 1986). In fact, Italians seem to be in line with other European consumers as far as the use of hard-core material is concerned (as the statistics quoted by Stella illustrate). Compared to other countries, however, they are targeted by soft-core material (in other words, where the sexual act is not explicit, but 'mimed' or alluded to) on a much larger scale, to the point that some see it as having apparently been metabolised by Italian mass culture, while it is also the target of fierce criticism to the foreign observer, as the following quote, relating to a debate on Italian television through British eyes, illustrates:

> On Italian TV, women are objects, continually shown in various states of undress. There's a new RAI programme, for example, where girls will have to compete to see who dances best. The problem is that since the 1980s Italians have focused on exaggerating women's qualities, while in Great Britain they have tried to do the exact opposite, with the aim of putting men and women on the same level so that they could adopt the same roles. (Rigillo 2003)[8]

And it was in the early 1980s in Italy, at the same time as private broadcasters (both local and national) began to grow in importance, that a film genre called 'commedia all'italiana' became popular, in which female nudity played a major role.[9] Precise guidelines were, however, followed: the genitals were rarely shown, and even then only for a few seconds, and sexual acts were – to use Stella's term – 'mimed', while the actors' bodies were almost always concealed by sheets or shrouded in darkness.

In my interpretation of the soft-porn genre, this type of film may serve as a point of reference, since the sexual act is not explicitly shown (hard), but imitated or 'mimed' (soft), while remaining a declared and specific aim within the plot. The viewer, then, does not see what is happening, but 'looks through the keyhole' and reconstructs the missing bits. The same kind of mechanism is behind *Grande Fratello*, where contestants having sex tended to conceal their bodies (as in the quoted example of Pietro and Cristina, hiding behind a sofa), but made no attempt to disguise what they were doing.

Still, it remains difficult to ascertain to what extent soft porn has really become a part of the national media culture, although it is perhaps telling that while the films mentioned above used to be broadcast late at night, they are now shown in the afternoon, without prompting any kind of outraged reaction.

## Structuring relationships in Grande Fratello

The four categories I have mentioned so far help to textually structure the Italian version of *Big Brother* for an international reader. The 'daily routine' category covers ritual behaviour in the house: everyday activities, related to the immediate environment and the interaction between the members of the household. The 'game' category includes activities related to the competitions. Examples include the weekly tasks set by 'Big Brother' and the game itself, which, through the evictions, leads to a final winner. It should be noted that these activities involve a ritual in which previously established rules are accepted and taken as a point of reference, and then supplemented with judgements and sanctions imposed by outside 'referees'.[10] The 'tension' category groups together those situations in which the interactions undergo a sudden change, leading to a verbal confrontation or episodes of physical violence. In such cases, the contestants themselves, without the help of outside 'referees', decide on rules, judgements and sanctions. Finally, and bearing in mind the work of Jean Baudrillard (1987), the 'obscenity' category defines 'that which no longer holds any secrets', in other words, all those events which in normal social interaction are usually hidden, yet in the house are laid bare, not only because of the presence of the cameras, but because of the way the housemates behave. As Baudrillard puts it: 'Everywhere, a loss of secrecy, of distance and of the control of illusion' (Baudrillard 1983: 45).

There are moments in which the television cameras not only show the 'scene', but also 'behind the scenes', thus removing, within the structure of the programme, any difference between the two dimensions and making even the unmentionable presentable 'on stage'. This is obscenity of a pornographic – or more precisely soft-porn – nature, which goes beyond even the concepts expressed by Baudrillard, given that, rather than simply watching a programme, the viewer is given the illusion of being a 'privileged voyeur', in a position to observe things which are normally considered 'unobservable' (as we shall see in more detail when we consider the research data), without running the risk of being discovered. Seeing the 'familiarity' of the personalities on the screen, it is also possible to trigger those mechanisms of identification which amplify the perception of obscenity (Giacchetti 1971).

Considering what happened in the three editions of the programme, we can bring the four elements together in a model which shows how, over the years, two of them (daily routine and games) have displayed a tendency to adopt a secondary role, while the other two (tension and obscenity), have become pre-eminent:

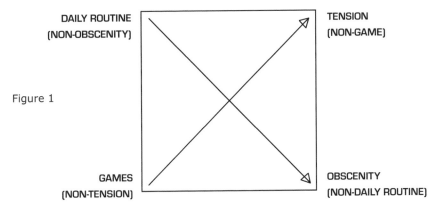

Figure 1

DAILY ROUTINE (NON-OBSCENITY)

TENSION (NON-GAME)

GAMES (NON-TENSION)

OBSCENITY (NON-DAILY ROUTINE)

In my interpretation, the four variables are interconnected in a relationship of mutual dichotomy. The *obscene* is that which departs from *daily routine*, from rituality. Meanwhile, the moments of *tension* should, I feel, be interpreted as *game* situations in which the rules of the ritual, pre-codified and applied by a 'referee', cease to apply and are overridden by strategic rules established by the contestants. Only the housemates have the power to direct the interaction, and put an end to the confrontation or fuel it. In this way, a logical framework is obtained, in which the positions of the combinations and the direction of the vectors are a function of time. This corresponds to the changing nature of the series over the three editions and lays the groundwork for the interactional analysis to come.

The prize money, for example, which played a vital role for the contestants in *Grande Fratello 1*, was hardly mentioned by the inhabitants of the house in 2003. By contrast, situations of tension multiplied. Moreover, the contestants had got used to the rituals of the house (after three years, they hardly noticed the cameras or the forced co-habitation), while sexual encounters and erotically-charged situations came increasingly to the fore.

## Grande Fratello 2003: interaction in the house

In order to consider how the contestants behaved with regard to the four thematic groups, I adopted an interactonist approach, based on the models drawn up by Erving Goffman. In recent years, Goffman's works have fuelled intense debate (Jameson 1976; Giddens 1987; Smith 1999; Fine & Smith 2000). Some see his work as overly preoccupied with secondary problems, and thus irrelevant as high-level sociology, while others cite him as one of the most important sociologists in the second half of the twentieth century. However one views his output, there is no doubt that he left an important mark on the study of everyday interaction, while refusing to adopt traditional methodological approaches which he considered an obstacle to analysis. In this way, Goffman managed to reduce social complexity to a limited number of mechanisms, and his microsociology has become a basis for obtaining a macroscopic view:

> While Weber and Durkheim provide no empirical phenomenology of these frag-
> ments of religion, of this ritual of minor encounters, it could however be said that
> the entire work of Goffman represents an attempt to provide as much material
> as possible for building such a phenomenology, and to describe this ritual where
> it is now manifested: in face-to-face encounters. (Maranini 2003: 9)

And, in a certain sense, the format of *Big Brother* seems to be a metaphor for some of Goffman's best-known theories. The theatrical model (Goffman 1959), for example, fully reflects the concept of person-actor on which the programme is centred, and also that of the *frame* (Goffman 1974), in other words the context in which the representation of everyday life is played out. This, I feel, is an apt label for the house-stage in which the contestants play out their rituals and strategies. Lastly, in the course of his research, Goffman also dealt with the theme of the game, and tried to identify its fundamental elements:

> It's true that games differ from each other, and it is true that they are adorned
> with fragments and trimmings from real life. But this is just the top-coat of

paint ... Nobody playing chess thinks the King is a real king, or the Queen a real queen; this would make the game unplayable. What attracts people to playing games ... are much more elementary fantasies, desires and needs. In Goffman's description ... these are represented by the need to face difficulties, to test one's strengths and to take risks, to challenge destiny, and to struggle with fellow beings for basic commodities. What counts in this struggle is aggression, intimidation, skill and strength; chasing and finding the prey ... all enveloped in fiction, camouflage, disguise and trickery; lastly there is the need to take risks, to gamble, and the fascination of danger. (Maranini 2003: 12–13)

Goffman, then, seems to be an appropriate point of reference for the analysis of a 'game of life' such as that proposed in *Big Brother*, and can help us identify the rules and roles which the contestants used to relate to the four themes under discussion (daily routine, games, tension and obscenity). I tried to identify these elements by performing a situational analysis of the 99 days that the cameras were running in the house of *Grande Fratello 3*. This involved viewing hours of footage recorded from the satellite channel that broadcast the programme around the clock, during which time the contestants were constantly filmed, except for when they were in the 'Diary Room'. I viewed the recordings day by day, and transcribed the most significant dialogues for the purposes of the structure outlined above. In this way, I produced a diary using Goffmanian methodology, which allowed me to subsequently classify the various elements.

Before moving on to the description of the data collected, below I have summarised the general picture of the contestants taking part in the 2003 edition (Table 1), the moment when they entered the house.[11] Notice, by the way, that their profiles display a sort of common denominator: before the game began, most of them had temporary jobs, and apparently no clear 'career plans'. Some of them had already tried to break into the world of show business, as extras in films or television commercials (as emerged during the game). For many of them, then, *Grande Fratello* may have represented more than just an experience, but a fundamental career move. This evidently influenced their attitude inside the house, where the real final prize, more than money, was probably fame. It should in fact be remembered that the 2003 contestants had greater experience than those in the previous editions, since they had already seen, as viewers, not only what happened in the house, but above all what happened to the contestants once they came out.

| NAME | SURNAME | NOTES | RESULT ACHIEVED |
|------|---------|-------|-----------------|
| Luca (Male) | Argentero | 24 years old, from Moncalieri (Turin). Single, university student. Disco barman. | Third place. |
| Manila (Female) | Barbati | 28 years old, from Milan. Single. Dance teacher. | Came into the house together with Franco on day 71, to replace Fedro. Evicted on day 78. |
| Marianella (Female) | Bargilli | 31 years old, born in Tuscany, lives in Rome. Single. Conference hostess. | Evicted on day 92. |

| | | | |
|---|---|---|---|
| Fedro (Male) | Francioni | 34 years old, lives in Rome. Single, formerly a fashion entrepreneur. | Withdrew on day 67 due to a death in the family. |
| Andrea (Male) | Francolino | 24 years old, grew up in Matera (Basilicata). Single. Calls himself a sculptor 'of shadows'. | Evicted on day 43 |
| Pasquale (Male) | Laricchia | 31 years old, born in Puglia, lives in Milan, where he works as a personal trainer. Going out with another of the contestants, Victoria. | Evicted on day 78. |
| Raffaello (Male) | Orselli | 35 years old, lives in Tuscany, where he works as a skipper. Single. | Came in on day 8, evicted on day 36. |
| Victoria (Female) | Pennington | 19 years old, born in Texas, lives in Milan with another contestant, Pasquale. Swimming instructor. | Second place. |
| Floriana (Female) | Secondi | 25 years old, from Rome. Single, works in a bar. | First place. |
| Angela (Female) | Sozio | 29 years old, lives in Puglia. University student. | Evicted on day 57. |
| Sergio (Male) | Squillacciotti | 32 years old, from Naples. Single, sales representative. | Evicted on day 29. |
| Marika (Female) | Suppa | 26 years old, born in Puglia, lives in Milan, where she works in a bar. Single. | Evicted on day 15. |
| Erika (Female) | Terzi | 26 years old, lives near Milan. Flight assistant. | Evicted on day 1, a few hours after the beginning of the programme, by the other contestants. |
| Massimo (Male) | Zino | 25 years old, lives in Rome. Single. | Never entered the house, since he was excluded in favour of Raffaello by the viewers' phone-in vote. |
| Franco (Male) | Bicicca | 28 years old, lives in Tuscany. Shop owner, single. | Came into the house on day 71. Fourth place. |
| Claudia (Female) | Bormioli | 26 years old, lives in Marche. University student, single. | Evicted on day 85. |

Table 1: The contestants of *Grande Fratello* 2003

*Daily routine*

After the first few weeks, the contestants acquired a fairly ritual rhythm. According to the rules, watches were not allowed, although Floriana hid one, which was found and confiscated on day 87. It seems, however, that she was the only one to use it.

Generally, the contestants got up around midday, and the first hours after rising were dedicated to everyday activities (personal hygiene, housework and so forth). They had lunch at around 4pm, and dinner after midnight. In this group of activities I also included hours spent in the sauna and gym (usually around 7.00pm), the time spent preparing for the weekly broadcast on Thursday, the times when one of the inhabitants had to leave the house after being evicted, and the organisation of the bedrooms. As the number of contestants changed, in fact, so did the arrangement of the beds. This was probably the most boring part of the programme, in which its 'documentary' aspects were most evident, with the contestants involved in a routine which often seemed to try and substitute the daily routine of life outside the house.

The innovations introduced by 'Big Brother', such as allowing pets into the house, did not significantly change the daily routine. At these times, the contestants basically performed what Goffman (1967) defines as ritual interaction. That is, they were careful to endanger neither their *self*, the 'mask' worn in that certain context (*frame*) or – from another angle – the image of themselves projected to the outside, nor that of the others. They adopted ceremonial behaviour, by participating in that cooperative game which the Canadian scholar considers as serving to advance the interaction itself, by adapting to the system of expectations developed by the other social actors. However, we perhaps need to make a brief digression on this subject. The frame of the house of *Big Brother*, in fact, seems to display the same 'anomaly' found by Pier Paolo Giglioli (1997) in his research on the legal proceedings involving a large number of leading Italian politicians in the 1990s.[12] Giglioli highlights that, in reality, the frame in which the politicians were placed – the courtroom – was subject to a double system of expectations and judgements. Judgement was passed on them both by the judges and the viewers as the trials were broadcast on television.

The contestants of *Big Brother* found themselves in the same situation: exposed to the judgement of the other inhabitants of the house and to that of the viewers. Hence we might conclude that the moments of daily routine in the house functioned primarily to maintain interpersonal relationships.

*Games*

Games also saw ritual behaviour on the part of the contestants, who adapted to the rules dictated by 'Big Brother', and 'acted out the script'. Due to the lack of interest generally shown by the contestants in the final prize, we should add that even the weekly nominations – through which candidates were selected for eviction, to be subsequently subjected to the viewers' votes – followed highly repetitive patterns. Some of the contestants, for example, were nominated every single time.

Instead, the contestants seemed to be more interested in the games related to the weekly tasks, where the spirit of cooperation and Goffmanian rituality were evident, than in the wider game and final victory. In the preparations for each task, mostly carried out in the afternoons, the contestants displayed new selves, ready to follow the advice of a leader, according to the skills required by the challenge. In the third week, for example, the contestants had to cycle 50km per day on an exercise bike. Pasquale, who was a personal trainer, immediately instructed the others on the importance of correct breathing and gave advice on the special diet they would need to follow. As the days passed, he followed their progress and, lastly, during the Thursday broadcast, he was the first to complete the distance within the time allowed.

Another task, which involved making carnival masks, brought the artist in the group to the fore. The mechanism was perpetuated over the 99 days, during which the various situations were characterised by a series of roles and rules – both those imposed by the programme authors, and those established by the contestants for purposes of group management. In the dynamics of the house, therefore, such periods saw the other housemates participate in a ritual of deference (Goffman 1956) in their relations with a temporary leader.

*Tensions*

However, when the rules within the group were not respected, there were moments of tension, which could be subdivided into three sub-groups. Firstly, there were arguments between the members of the couples formed before and during the game, above all sparked off by jealousy. Secondly, there were conflicts between other individuals, usually related to everyday situations (for example, when someone did not do their share of the housework). Lastly, and most striking, were the arguments between the subgroups which the housemates had formed. On two occasions in particular, there was nearly a fight. On the evening of day 13, an argument between two of the contestants over food consumption degenerated when a third housemate joined in. This prompted the involvement of all the other members of the household and led to the formation of two factions. In the early afternoon of day 31, we saw furniture kicked, fists banged down on tables, a salt cellar broken and a few shoves and pushes, all because Floriana was thought to have kissed Andrea (Claudia's boyfriend). By then, however, the factions had already been created, so when (as Goffman put it) we saw the 'throwing-down of the gauntlet' which characterises strategic interactions, each of the contestants already knew where they stood. In such moments, ritual was overridden by strategies: the social actors of the house challenged each other and this time the objective was to rip off their adversaries' 'masks', whilst keeping their own intact.

*Obscenity*

During the 99 days, the inhabitants of the house not only broke the game rules, but often failed to conform to that ceremonial behaviour which, according to Goffman, regulates daily routine. During the night, in particular, they practically removed all thresholds of demeanour (Goffman 1956), that is, that element of ritual behaviour through which one's emotions are 'contained' and filtered. It is this attitude that allows us to maintain adequate control of the interaction in which we find ourselves participating.

I have already highlighted how the scenes of sex were numerous, despite the cameras and the other inhabitants (even if the participants did use blankets and towards the end built a sort of hut, to conceal as much as possible). On the night of day 22, for example, two women had to wait for one of the couples in another room to finish having sex, before they could go to bed, and commented on the situation: 'When are they going to finish? My budgies are quicker than this: she lifts up her tail, he comes along and …

chirp, chirp, chirp … It's all over' (Floriana). On the dawn of day 38, to quote just one of the many examples, another couple had sex despite the fact that there were four other people in the room at the time.

The contestants seemed to want to play on erotic themes without showing any signs of embarrassment, and often talked about their exploits (on day 37, Andrea confided to his friends: 'Number 78 tonight'). Nor did they show any inhibitions in the stories they told. One of the girls (day 39) explained to the rest of the group how, covered with sugar and cocoa, she had had sex with her boyfriend while balancing on the window ledge of a hotel room. During the act, she had begun to vomit: 'And while I was being sick, I turned round and said to him: more, more, more!' (Angela). Nor was any embarrassment evident in her housemates' reaction: 'But were you at forty-five degrees or ninety degrees on the ledge?' (Andrea).

On day 55, meanwhile, another of the women, after being provoked by one of the couples, in what seemed a playful tone, announced: 'I don't go for women, but since she [Marianella] fancies me, I'll go in the middle and you two can do what you want with me… [Floriana]. She then told of how a former boyfriend had involved her in a threesome with another woman, after she had been blindfolded and tied up. She added: 'But I was young, very young. I didn't even realise the other person was a woman' (Floriana).

The subject of contraception was completely ignored, and, unsurprising, in week nine one of the women thought she might be pregnant. This showed the programme's producers in a very hypocritical light, given that earlier they wanted to give the impression that they were committed to dealing with social issues, by forbidding the contestants to smoke inside the house and stressing that this decision had been taken as part of an anti-smoking campaign.

The producers also appeared to have used the gaming and casting process to accommodate and even encourage the soft-porn activities. For example, they chose to include an existing couple among the contestants, but more strikingly in a task on 13 March 2003 contestants had to answer questions about the lives led by the others outside the house. It thus emerged that on Saturdays Angela liked to go out without underwear. Another example is the suite, with its spacious bath, where almost all the contestants were involved in erotic situations, stimulated by the surroundings.[13]

Behaving in an uninhibited manner did not apparently give the competitors an advantage or, at least, there was no direct correlation between final victory and un-inhibited attitudes inside the house, as happened in other countries. It appears evident, however, that such attitudes above all helped make things easier for the contestants when they left the house (ensuring them even more immediate visibility) and, secondly, created interest around the programme.

## Ritual and strategies

Completing the situational analysis, I found behaviours and rituals that followed a model and could be used to complete the scheme proposed previously (see Figure 2, overleaf).

While still acting inside the same frame the contestants changed their perception of it depending on the time of day and associated rituals. The rules and the rituals, basically divided the day into three parts (morning = daily routine; afternoon = games; evening = obscenity) during which moments of tension were strategically inserted.

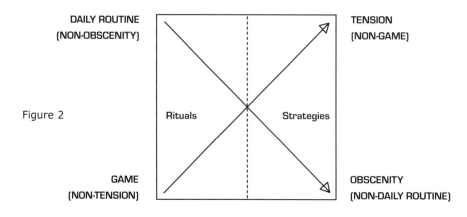

DAILY ROUTINE
(NON-OBSCENITY)

TENSION
(NON-GAME)

Figure 2

Rituals

Strategies

GAME
(NON-TENSION)

OBSCENITY
(NON-DAILY ROUTINE)

*The public selection*

Using this structure, I will now comment on which of the elements identified were selected and used for media representation and mass broadcast. A first thing to take into account is the weekly show and the highlights. The Thursday evening show was highly successful, and achieved a higher audience share than even current affairs programmes. It is telling that on the evening of 20 March 2003, at the same time as the attack on Iraq, 35.2 per cent of viewers were watching the show on Canale 5.[14]

The perspective adopted by the broadcasters, going back to the model drawn up previously, seems to have focused on the games/tension vector, with extensive coverage of the nominations and weekly tests, but also of the conflicts. On a couple of occasions, there were attempts to embarrass the evicted contestants. When Andrea left the house, for example, he received a surprise dinner invitation, which turned out to be from the mother of Claudia (the girl who had become his girlfriend inside the house). The scene was recorded and then broadcast the following week. Claudia herself, when it was her turn to go into the studio during the show,[15] was immediately shown a piece of film – false, as it turned out – where Andrea, in the period in which they had been apart (she inside the house, he outside), was shown kissing another girl. Another contestant had to watch an interview with a former boyfriend she had never mentioned and comment on it on live television.

The framework was strengthened by the presence of various additional figures, such as Claudia's mother. In the first programme, she warned her daughter ('Behave yourself'), and later expressed her disapproval between clenched teeth as her daughter and Andrea went into the *suite*, where they then proceeded to have sex for the first time. The daily highlights, meanwhile, summarised all four of the thematic groups. This led to an official reaction from the government body for the protection of minors, which cautioned those responsible for the daily clips, considered unsuitable for a non-adult public. The organisers consequently made a public apology.

*The magazine*

Daily routine and obscenity also seemed to be the heart and soul of the programme's official magazine. Every edition included a weekly diary and pages of erotic gossip, accompanied by eloquent photos. What emerged was a representation of the sexual element that was ambiguous and voyeuristic:

> The contestants in this third edition seem unable to control themselves. The allusions to sex are continuous; kisses, massages and fondling frequent. Right from day one, Marianella warmed up the atmosphere by kissing Claudia on the mouth and confessing she was bisexual … Once, visibly drunk, the girl from Marche [Claudia] went so far as to sprinkle salt over the stomach of the girl from Tuscany [Marianella] and then lick it up. Now that her beloved Andrea has left the house, who knows if Claudia will finally let her instincts run wild! (*Grande Fratello*, 10–12 April 2003, 32–3)

> Angela was the first to go topless without feeling any embarrassment whatsoever. One by one, the other girls followed her lead. Even the prudish Victoria delighted her fans with an erotic shower, during which she showed off her beautiful breasts. (*Grande Fratello*, 15–17 May 2003, 33)

Such portrayals by the Italian press have recently been the subject of much debate. Even the most respected and politically serious magazines have for years adorned their front covers with naked women and other images of an erotic nature. Moreover, the covers often advertise articles on sexual issues (albeit viewed from a scientific or social perspective). In other words, for the Italian culture industry, nudity seems to have become the ideal way of packaging almost any product.

*The website*

As elsewhere, in Italy the programme organisers set up an official website. Of specific importance here was the web diary, which highlighted the interactions between the contestants in minute detail, accompanied by photos and images. Naturally, considering the characteristics of the medium and the service offered, it covered all the thematic areas referred to here. The impression I gained, however, is that the site's function was essentially that of maintaining a high level of tension, while focusing yet again on obscenity:

> The long sexual abstinence of the Pasquale-Victoria couple was beginning to become worrying. But tonight's the night and, tired of talking, the two head off to the bedroom with knowing smiles. A few minutes later, wrapped up in a bundle of blankets, we see those unmistakable continuous rhythmic movements which leave little to the imagination. (www.grandefratello.com, day 22, 4.30am)

> Maybe it's the intense perfume of the bath foam that she poured into the jacuzzi, or it might be the sinuous and sexy curves of the lovely Texan [Victoria]. Whatever it is, Pasquale has come back to his senses and all at once has been transformed from a sheep into a wolf. The jacuzzi creates stimulating waves and currents and the passionate couple tenderly embrace in their $n^{th}$ sexual performance. Turning this way and that (they have better luck face on than from behind), the two lovers wallow in a bath of passion and hormones, wrapped round each other in

all sorts of improbable positions. But, when love is in the air … Once they have 'rearranged' themselves, the two lovebirds abandon themselves to Hollywood-style luxury. Pasquale gets out of the tub for a moment (but long enough for us to get a good look at his weaponry) to go and get a bottle of champagne and two glasses. (www.grandefratello.com, day 23, 7.34am and 7.48am)

*Parody*

Finally, the proposed scheme also echoed in media formats not officially part of the package. The programme *Mai dire Grande Fratello* (an unofficial parody broadcast on a separate channel) made much of the programme's obscenity. It did so, however, using irony, or rather, self-irony. The erotic scenes were often rebroadcast and subtitled, to help viewers understand what the contestants were saying, and were also accompanied by the off-screen commentary of a comedy trio (Gialappa's Band) whose ironic obser-vations highlighted their ridiculous aspects.

Alongside this, however, the programme also had another determining role, by creating a highly popular element in Italian television: the catchphrase. The continuous repetition of particularly original situations or phrases (the winner declaring, for instance: 'I'm a woman inside, outside, and all around') seems to have a strong impact, above all in youth culture. The impersonations of the contestants, while they were still inside the house, made it possible for them to construct a 'mask' of success, which they could 'put on' when they left the house, and then use for their first steps in the world of show business. For example, parody was often used to comment on Pasquale's proverbs, most of which were incomprehensible or nonsensical. Consequently, in the variety programmes in which Pasquale has been invited to participate since his eviction from the house, he has often been asked to provide comment with one of his popular sayings.

By interpreting each contestant in the house as a 'product' to be marketed within the system of the culture industry, we can see that parody helped both affirm a brand and identify the characteristics of the 'product' itself.

## Conclusion

Since 2000, the Italian media debate (rather than academic debate) has focused on the morality of broadcasting *Grande Fratello* (see also Mathijs 2002). Interest in this issue has, however, waned, and the media outside the official *Grande Fratello* circuits displayed general indifference towards the 2003 edition of the programme and its fans. The media seem to have metabolised the innovation (unlike the public, who continue to provide extremely high viewing figures) and, after a period of 'acclimatisation', to have accepted it as normative television:

> Yet, this series has not lost the status afforded to it from the beginning, summarised here by Barlozzetti, who supervised the first Italian edition of the programme: '*Grande Fratello* is above all a great and wholly television event: a space/time of TV squared, in which the medium is celebrated as the origin and final goal of life'. (Barlozetti 2002: 170)

The definition of 'TV squared', intended as television whose point of reference is no longer external reality, but television itself, should not, I feel, be interpreted exclusively in relation to the event's longitudinal aspect and cross-media saturation. Instead, *Big Brother* represents 'TV squared' because it encapsulates in a single container all the elements of Italian television entertainment, and is based on a point of strength mentioned by Liesbet van Zoonen:

> We rediscover on television what has become ever more invisible in the world around us, the private life of ordinary people; initially mostly in the enacted fantasies of sitcoms and soaps, but currently in a variety of formats in which real life is shown. (Van Zoonen 2001: 672; see also her chapter in this book)

As Paolo Taggi puts it, *Big Brother* thus becomes a hybrid of success, because:

> It is not just a programme, but an integrated entertainment project, which encapsulates all of television. It is not a container that assembles or juxtaposes different genres, but a place which makes them interact. (Taggi 2000: 216; quoted in Pezzini 2002: 62).

To which Pezzini adds: 'It is ... more of a "television philosophy" than a genre or macrogenre' (Pezzini 2002: 61).

The themes of daily routine, games and tension, for example, are principal features of most popular television programmes in Italy. The public and private television networks are full of afternoon talk shows in which, to cite one case, the guests tell of sexual betrayal or explain their dysfunctional relationships with their families. Unlike *Grande Fratello*, there is a presenter in the studio ready to mediate and direct the discussion. But clearly, the mechanism is even more effective when the only barriers between the arguers are the walls of a house. This is a form of television, in other words, that excels itself, a hyper television. We need merely consider the obscenity highlighted in *Grande Fratello*, whereby the viewer, as anticipated when illustrating the categories chosen for the analysis, is put in a position to go beyond that hyper-reality which for Baudrillard permeates traditional television pornography. The sexual relations in the house, despite being hardly visible, become 'more pornographic than porn itself'.

In conclusion, this analysis has shown how *Grande Fratello* represents the essence of mass entertainment in Italy. The contestants – directed by broadcasting choices, but also aware of the experiences and careers of their predecessors in the house – are ready to follow rules and adopt roles that will bring them success, in the name of false spontaneity. The important thing seems to be to elicit 'what has not yet been seen'. Once the threshold of interest is breached, there is a shift towards a new theme in a continuing race to boost viewing figures (on the part of the broadcasters) and to achieve fame (on the part of the contestants).

*Notes*

1   Both Canale 5 and Italia 1 are free-on-air broadcasters. Both are part of Silvio Berlusconi's Mediaset group.
2   On the theme of the Italian culture industry, see Morcellini & De Nardis 1998, and Morcellini 2000.
3   From a methodological point of view, I was influenced by a number of studies already published in Italy, on issues related to the media handling of judicial issues,

in particular Giglioli 1997 and Tomeo 1973.

4   Under the rules of the game, every 7 or 14 days, during the Thursday show, the contestants are called one at a time into an isolated room (the 'Diary Room'), where they are asked to nominate a certain number of housemates they want to evict. At the end of the evening, a list is drawn up, and the contestants who have received most nominations are subjected to the vote of the viewers, who phone in to say who they think should leave the house the following week. The contestant receiving the most votes, obviously, is evicted.

5   In *Big Brother 3*, the contestant judged the best in the weekly task was often offered the possibility of using a small part of the final prize money for buying immunity. If this contestant was nominated by his/her housemates, he/she could avoid being subjected to the judgement and was thus certain to remain in the house. The rules also allowed this immunity to be given to another contestant.

6   He has started a career as a film actor. In particular, he had a leading role in the film *Ricordati di me*, directed by Gabriele Muccino, which was a great hit in Italy in early 2003.

7   In particular, the calendar of one of the contestants in the first series, Marina La Rosa, published by a well-known magazine, was a great success. The organisers of *Big Brother* also produced a calendar, depicting the faces of all the contestants.

8   A case in point concerns the debate sparked off between Italian and English commentators by an article written by the British journalist Tobias Jones for the *Financial Times* (16 January 2003), with its emblematic headline: 'My Italian TV hell'.

9   This term had actually been coined a number of years earlier and originally referred to films by the leading Italian comic actors (such as Alberto Sordi and Nino Manfredi). In the 1980s, however, it was applied to comic films with soft-porn characteristics.

10  For a more detailed discussion, see, amongst others, Carzo & Centorrino 2002.

11  The information is taken from the cards prepared by the show's organisers, together with the contestants themselves.

12  The proceedings were triggered by the Tangentopoli ('Bribesville') investigation, linked to the corruption of certain politicians.

13  An unofficial *Grande Fratello* website published an interview with one of the potential contestants, who was excluded in the final round of auditions. The interview, which was published on 16 February 2003, can be seen at: http://pub133.ezboard.com/ fgrandefratellopointfrm188.showNextMessage?topicID=9.topic

14  Information from *Il Corriere della Sera* (1 May 2003, 33), according to which the 13 programmes of the show recorded an average of 8 million viewers (33.1 per cent, compared to 31.3 of the previous year and 35.4 of the first edition). The average viewing figures for all the airtime reserved for the programme was, however 23.2 per cent, while 84.4 per cent of Italians over the age of 4 watched at least one minute of the weekly show (*Il Sole 24 Ore*, 13 May 2003, 20). On the occasion of the final programme, a 30-second advertising slot was sold for 96,000 Euros.

15  During the Thursday show, the evicted contestants are led from the house immediately into the studio, where the live broadcast is on air.

*Bibliography*

Alberoni, F. (1986) *L'erotismo*. Milan: Garzanti.
Barlozzetti, G. (2002) *Eventi e Riti della Televisione. Dalla Guerra del Golfo alle Twin*

*Towers*. Milan: Franco Angeli.

Baudrillard J. (1983) *Les stratégies fatales*. Paris: Editions Grasset & Fasquelle.

_____ (1987) *L'autre par lui-même*. Paris: Editions Galilée.

Carzo D. and M. Centorrino (2002) *Tomb Raider o il destino delle passioni. Per una sociologia del videogioco*, Milan: Guerini e Associati.

Elias, N. (1982) *The History of Manners*. New York: Pantheon.

Fine, G. A. and G. W. H. Smith (eds) (2000) *Erving Goffman*. London: Sage.

Giacchetti, R. (1971) *Porno Power. Pornografia e società capitalista.* Bologna: Guaraldi Editore.

Giddens, A. (1987) 'Erving Goffman as a systematic social theorist', in A. Giddens, *Social Theory and Modern Sociology*. Cambridge: Polity Press.

Giglioli, P. P. (1997) 'Processi di delegittimazione e cerimonie di degradazione', in P. P. Giglioli, S. Cavicchioli and G. Fele, *Rituali di degradazione. Anatomia del processo Cusani.* Bologna: Il Mulino.

Goffman, E. (1956) 'The Nature of Deference and Demeanor', *American Anthropologist*, 58, 473–502.

_____ (1959) *The Presentation of Self in Everyday Life.* Harmondsworth: Penguin.

_____ (1967) *Interaction Ritual*. New York: Doubleday.

_____ (1969) *Strategic Interaction*. Philadelphia: University of Pennsylvania Press.

_____ (1974) *Frame Analysis*. New York: Harper & Colophon.

Jameson, F. (1976) 'On Goffman's Frame Analysis', *Theory and Society*, 3, 119–33.

Maranini, P. (2003) 'Introduzione', in E. Goffman (ed.) *Espressione e identità*. Bologna: Il Mulino (translation of *Encounters. Two Studies in the Sociology of Interaction*. Indianapolis: Bobbs-Merrill [1961]), 7–20.

Mathijs, E. (2002) '*Big Brother* and Critical Discourse: The Reception of *Big Brother* Belgium', *Television and New Media*, 3, 3, 311–22.

Menduni, E. (2002) *Televisione e società italiana.* Milan: Bompiani.

Morcellini, M. (ed.) (2000) *Il Mediaevo*. Rome: Carocci.

Morcellini, M. and P. de Nardis (1998) *Società e industria culturale in Italia*. Rome: Meltemi.

Pezzini, I. (2002) 'L'autunno della tv: i generi', in F. De Domenico, M. Gavrila and A. Preta (eds) *Quella deficiente della TV*. Milan: Franco Angeli, 52–66.

Rigillo, N. (2003) 'Non Esportate la TV Italiana' in *City_News M@g*, (Online Daily, School of Journalism, Università Cattolica in Milan, 25 March). Available at: www2.unicatt.it/unicatt/seed/mag_gestion_cattnews.vedi_notizia?id_cattnewsT=1692

Smith, G. W. H. (ed.) (1999) *Goffman and Social Organization: Studies in a Sociological Legacy*. London & New York: Routledge.

Stella, R. (1991) *L'osceno di massa. Sociologia della comunicazione pornografica*. Milan: Franco Angeli.

Taggi, P. (2000) *Vite da format*. Rome: Editori Riuniti.

Tomeo, V. (1973) *Il giudice sullo schermo*. Rome-Bari: Laterza.

Van Zoonen, L. (2001) 'Desire and resistance: *Big Brother* and the recognition of everyday life', *Media Culture & Society*, 23, 5, 679–88.

## CHAPTER 12

*Magriet Pitout*

# BIG BROTHER SOUTH AFRICA
A Popular Form of Cultural Expression

After its success in the Netherlands, the Endemol *Big Brother* format was sold to 18 countries, South Africa amongst them. Under the guidance of executive producer John de Mol, a broadcast agreement was reached with *M-Net* – a pay-television channel in South Africa – for the 2001 production of the first series of *Big Brother* South Africa.

In this chapter, I intend to focus on the significance of *Big Brother* as a symbolic form of popular culture and deconstruct its popularity with South African audiences. Why do audiences want to watch a show where others' behaviour, embarrassments and hardships seem to be entertainment? With this research question in mind, I will consider the theoretical framework of this study. I would like to argue that *Big Brother* South Africa requires an approach that sees this television show, and television in general, as a form of cultural expression, touching upon several key issues in contemporary South African media culture such as postmodernity, ethnicity and power struggles. As these key issues suggest, much of that approach is informed by postmarxist cultural studies, building upon work of Antonio Gramsci and Michel Foucault (see, for instance, Crehan 2002; Foucault 1980). In relation to *Big Brother* it means that the relationship between popular culture, the media and its audiences is investigated via conceptual tools derived from the vocabulary of cultural theory and cultural studies: hegemony, polysemy, intertextuality, synergy, representation and audience activity (Lull 2000; 2001). In addition there is also the need to deal with concepts such as modernity, post-modernity and voyeurism and the growing importance of interactive television in an attempt to critique the popularity and cultural significance of *Big Brother* in South Africa because as a pioneer in audience interactivity, this programme can be used as a case study to illustrate the possible implications of disruptions of the boundaries between producer, text and audience.

Reality programmes are now a focus of much media research and there is an ongoing debate about the 'realness' of these programmes. In fact, what can be more 'unreal' than being under surveillance for 24 hours? Although these debates need critical attention, it is beyond the scope of this study to investigate the concept 'reality' and/or 'realism'. The emphasis in this chapter is on *Big Brother* as a form of cultural expression, its popularity and the implications of its interactive nature for future media events. I would like to start by setting the scene for *Big Brother* South Africa by looking at its location, the composition of the group of contestants and major signifiers of South African lifestyle.

## Big Brother: the South African context

South African producers customised the location (the house and surroundings) to give the programme a South African flavour in order to 'speak' to local South African viewers. For example, the back yard where many of the recreation activities took place was equipped with *braai* facilities (a barbeque), a jacuzzi, a lawn where the participants could relax in the sun and gather around the fireplace for a traditional *braai* and *potjieskos* food cooked over an open fire (*potjieskos* is a kind of stew consisting of meat and vegetables). These are the major signifiers of the typical *white* lifestyle (see the discussion of hegemony).

In the first South African series twelve contestants consisting of a cross-section of South Africans – six whites, two blacks, three coloureds and one Indian – entered the *Big Brother* house. The division of gender was six males and six females. The contestant who remained longest in the house received one million rand. After initial nominations the fate of a nominee was in the hands of the voting public.

In common with most international versions, the contestants were restricted in their alcohol and food supplies. Although they received a weekly allowance, this was forfeited when the contestants were punished for transgressing rules such as discussing possible nominees for eviction or when they could not complete a task as a group successfully. Nominations for eviction were confidential and the contestants could only cast their votes by visiting the diary room where they spoke with an invisible *Big Brother*. As Estelle Tincknell and Parvati Raghuram (2002: 202) say, all these elements contribute to the sense of structure, imprisonment and the controlling role of the omnipotent, ever-watching and imaginary *Big Brother*. This of course heightens the programme's contradictory position between reality and television's representation of reality.

Despite being broadcast on the pay-television channels *M-Net* and *DStv*, which are in fact minority channels because of the small portion of the total population of South Africa who can afford subscription fees, more than a million viewers watched *Big Brother 1* and *2* respectively (Big Mama 2003). All television viewers could also see an evening highlights show on a free-access network every evening at 6.30pm. This version was censored by bleeping out swearing and steamy sex scenes. *DStv* subscribers, however, could watch the full uncensored 24-hour-a-day version on channel 37 while Internet users could also access the house any time they wished to do so. Furthermore *Big Brother 1* was nominated by the Press Club in Pretoria as 'the news event of year' because of its high profile in all the media. As a result of this and similar media coverage, contestants thus became instant celebrities and some of them were offered lucrative jobs as television and radio presenters, modelling contracts and guest speakers at a variety of functions.

## From modernity to postmodernity

*Big Brother* can be seen as a classic case whereby technical, economic, social and political changes in the media contribute to a large extent to the passage from modernity to postmodernity and contribute to the formation of a postmodern culture (Fourie 1997: 5). Pieter Fourie (1997) and Luc Van Poecke (1994) make a distinction between paleotelevision (modernity) and neotelevision (postmodernity) as they explain the formation of a postmodern culture. As far as programme content is concerned, in paleotelevision (modernity broadcasting) a clear distinction exists between education and entertainment. The main aim of entertainment programmes is to educate the public. Media users must be educated and emancipated from media content that provides vulgar, cheap thrills and instant gratification. Paleotelevision is also regarded as one-way communication – 'top-to-bottom' – and is to a great extent free from commercial influences. With a top-to-bottom approach audiences are effectively ignored as part of the communication process.

Postmodern broadcasting (neotelevision) on the other hand is characterised by the fading of the boundaries between the information, entertainment and educational functions of the media. In an infotainment programme such as *Soul City* in South Africa, the programme producers use the soap opera format to reflect on and portray the social realities of South Africa's diverse cultures such as poverty, basic health issues, AIDS and malnutrition. The question is, can this programme be regarded as a non-formal educational programme or as entertainment drama? The answer is both: although *Soul City* entertains it also contains strong educational messages. Other than the majority of soaps where promiscuity is romanticised, *Soul City* shows the consequences of promiscuity (for example AIDS and venereal diseases) and provides answers and solutions to these problems.

Neotelevision defines programmes where the distinction between the private and public sphere is becoming increasing blurred. This is especially evident when we look at the confession and talk-show genres (for example *Oprah Winfrey* and *Jerry Springer*). *Big Brother* is a combination of both, with the 'Diary Room' allowing audiences to witness the most serious episodes of deceit and backstabbing while openly confessing their deepest secrets. One example of this is the fact that one of the contestants, Margaret, publicly disclosed that her father committed suicide. She also openly claimed to be a virgin but she was the first one to take off her bikini top in the jacuzzi and then jump in the sack with Irwin. Viewers also learned of Ferdinand's disputes with his father, his attachment to his mother and sister, and his love life. In addition, Janine told the housemates how she was abused by her former husband. Janine also had no qualms to demonstrate oral sex using a cucumber and cottage cheese. After her eviction Janine justified her demonstration by saying that it gives her complete control over her partner.

Ronald Sennett (1977) regards the revelation of the deepest secrets in public as post-modernist narcissism – the emphasis is not only on the need to know oneself but also on the need to justify the deed and behaviour in all its intimacy (Fourie 1997: 272). Neotelevision emphasises the shift from the communicator to the recipient (media user). Although diversity is important, the target audience is a global market and the meaning of a 'national' character becomes less important.

According to Fourie (1997: 272–3) and Van Poecke (1994: 1–27) paleotelevision tries to present a transparent window on reality, attempting to hide all visible signs of the apparatus of television production. Neotelevision, however, forces the public to acknowledge the camera equipment. In this way viewers are made aware of television's reconstruction of reality or aspects thereof. The South African media promoted the voyeuristic aspects of the show, advertising the presence of 24 cameras and 60 microphones that would record every move the housemates made. Often, the contestants themselves were aware of the camera moving in their direction zooming in on one of them. With the exclamation 'the camera is on me' they would take a different persona.

Neotelevision suggests a format whereby television has a conversational and interactive appearance with the viewers at the centre. (Another example is the conversational style of television news presenters who directly address viewers or discuss news items with fellow journalists, further enhancing the direct involvement of viewers.) Mark Pelgrim, presenter of *Big Brother,* would psyche up the live eviction audience and the viewers at home employing an urgent direct address to camera edging viewers on to vote and warning them that time is running out.

Liesbet van Zoonen (2001: 670–1) contends that the public debate about *Big Brother* is symptomatic of the collective needs and desires awakened by this pro- gramme. As discussed above, many arguments start with the distinction between the public and private spheres. The trademark of Endemol products (such as *The Bus*, *Fear Factor*) is that they are based on our basic instincts – our primordial fears, experiences and emotions. The fact that these programmes create moral panic and that the debates are grounded in the distinction between public and private spheres, suggests that this division is deeply embedded in the subconscious mind of members of our society. According to van Zoonen, this intimate domesticity is a somewhat recent phenomenon. In pre-modern societies the private sphere did not yet exist as a separate terrain because public and private lives were intertwined. Even the private lives of the aristocracy did not have an independent character because they were part of a general display of status and power. The arrival of the industrial revolution, urbanisation and the bourgeois presented a modern private character to ordinary human experiences. As van Zoonen says:

> Private and public spheres gained momentum and impose their own codes of conduct: rationale and restraint belonged to the public realm, then populated by men; emotions and spontaneity belonged to the private sphere, the 'natural' domain of women. (van Zoonen 2001: 671, see also her chapter in this book)

With *Big Brother* this distinction fades away and our deep-seated primordial desires for knowledge about people's private lives are satisfied as we watch the contestants' most intimate moments.

## Hegemony and ethnicity

Alistair Leithead (2001) states that although all productions of *Big Brother* internationally have generated heated debates within the host countries, nowhere has the series generated the kind of reaction it had in South Africa. This was because of the country's history of apartheid. I think this issue can best be explained when it is framed through hegemony. Hegemony, broadly speaking, means the dominance of one social class over others. The dominant class (usually the bourgeoisie) is successful in projecting their ideological views as 'natural', 'taken for granted' and 'legitimate'. Their views become the consensus view. However, hegemony is potentially always under threat because the subordinates pose a challenge to hegemony and consensus (Crehan 2002). Society is therefore regarded as a constant struggle between competing ideologies for hegemony. In South Africa apartheid, and ethnicity as the cultural issue on which this ideology was based, has always been seen as hegemonic, yet under threat.

From 1950 to 1994 South Africa was racially segregated under the ideology of apartheid. Since the early 1950s, black South Africans were classified according to ethnicity and assigned to particular territories called black homelands (or Bantustans). In 1994 the homelands were terminated and incorporated into the new provinces of South Africa. In the apartheid years the mainstream media in South Africa portrayed and perpetuated the ideology of apartheid (and by implication the practice of racism), portraying the blacks as inferior and incapable of governance. In the post-apartheid era media had to come to terms with this legacy. In political terms, the current underlying dominant ideology is that the ruling class (the ANC) with its credo of the unification of all inhabitants of South Africa under the 'rainbow nation' umbrella. For *Big Brother*, this meant that casting created a particularly south African problem for Endemol. The producers were required to present a programme which was recogniseably a microcosm of South African society, which is 80 per cent black. The cable station that broadcast the series, however, had an 80 per cent white subscription base. This was a 'forced' composition of the housemates along racial lines to represent the rainbow nation ideology.

In the words of Neil McCarthy, Executive Producer of the first season, the host pay-television network (*M-Net*) were

> in a rather precarious position politically inside South Africa because it had strong associations with the previous (apartheid) regime. This legacy was still attached to them and they could not afford any radical incidents emerging from the house that might reflect badly on them. (Jones & Mathijs 2003)

To best reflect the political transformation that has taken place since the legalisation of the African National Congress (ANC) in 1990 and its coming to power in 1994, the composition of the housemates had to reflect the composition of the new South Africa. However, there was not much interest in black townships because the *Sowetan*, a newspaper mainly aimed at blacks in townships, did not give much publicity to the *Big Brother 1* competition. Furthermore, because *Big Brother* was broadcast on two pay channels *M-Net* and *Dstv*, the black majority could not watch because many could not afford to access these channels and were therefore automatically excluded. To get the demographics of the South African society somewhat representative, the selectors had to make do with the limited number of blacks that entered the competition. As McCarthy describes:

The black participants were very hard to identify and this was due to the fact that we had so few and also because of the very delicate racial politics that still exist within South Africa. Race is probably the single hugest informing factor in South African history and remains the most noted issue is South African politics. (Jones & Mathijs 2003)

With South Africa's history of apartheid, the blend of people belonging to different cultural, racial and religious groups contributed to the excitement and media hype. Having black and white people living in the same house in South Africa would have been illegal ten years ago and this is part of what made *Big Brother* such a compelling format.

Viewers were seeing blacks and whites living together side by side, sharing all facilities, swapping beds, engaging with issues of sexual tension, jumping into the jacuzzi, and this in itself was an electric concept for South African viewers. (Jones & Mathijs 2003)

Before the first broadcast, the most frequent questions asked were whether racial discrimination would raise its ugly head, and how the viewing public would react to the integration of different races and cultures in a television programme. It is the idea of establishing an example that has been at the heart of *Big Brother* South Africa and in a country still struggling to come to terms with the legacy of apartheid, entertainment can quickly become a social experiment, says Alastair Leithead (2001). In an interview with Leithead, Karl Fischer said that in South Africa everything has in one way or another a political resonance because of where we have been and where we are going. All the debates raging outside the house, from the public to intellectuals and academics, perhaps say more about our society than about the housemates themselves. Such ideological requirements problematised the selection of contestants because they are selected for their entertainment value and their ability to push up ratings and not because of the colour of their skin. Boring and placid people are not regarded as fun, no matter their race. As McCarthy notes:

We had to create a drama, but we had to make sure that that drama was within certain limits. It couldn't be drama of a destructive kind and something that might be seen as socially detrimental or destructive. And that might be seen to fuel racial tensions ... I can recall perhaps five times when they (the housemates) engaged with each other on the basis of race; when they spoke to each other as you as a black person or me as a white person. (Jones & Mathijs 2003)

So, ideology was at the centre of the set up of *Big Brother* South Africa. But the actual run and reception of it was also influenced by issues related to hegemony, as Ranjeni Munusamy's (2001) article '*Big Brother* cameras hide nasty story of race' shows, especially when she bemoaned the fact that the vulgar foul-mouth Ferdinand Rabie won the first series. Munusamy attributes this to the viewers' desire to see rowdy, drunk troublemakers. And therefore, a salt-of-the-earth person like Vuoy (black male contestant) who minds his own business, keeps his body parts sacred and most important, his emotions in check does not have a chance. The most biting criticism comes from Munusamy's reference to the ideology of apartheid: Nobesutho (black female contestant) and Vuoy survived because they were not exhibitionists, never licked chocolate from someone else's butt or jumped into the sack with anyone else. They both survived being voted out because they were invisible and they were invisible because they are black. The white audience out there are used to having blacks around – but firmly in the background. She continues by saying that Riaad (Indian) destroyed any chances of winning by daring to get involved in an argument with Ferdi about race who foul-mouthed him when he called Riaad a 'fucking curry-muncher' (Munusamy 2001). Although there might be truth in Munusamy's lashing-out at the underlying white bourgeois ideology in *Big Brother*, in all fairness neither Riaad nor Vuoy or Nobesutho ever showed popularity with the voting public (they never received more than 5 per cent of the votes). And what Munusamy neglects to say is that Vuoy and Riaad received lucrative job offers. Nobesutho on the other hand guarded her privacy fiercely and was adamant to continue her studies. What cannot be denied though, is that voting occurred along racial lines because the *Big Brother* voters are largely white. There were, however, viewers who liked the two black participants and even regarded them as role models, as is evident from the discussion of polysemy later on. Since the emphasis is on the recipients, texts are open which afford viewers the opportunity to interpret messages differently. Not only because they are individually different but because they are also informed by so many messages that can influence their interpretation.

## Intertextuality: contestants as marketing commodities?

*Big Brother* was big news when it hit South Africa for the first time and most of the time people did not even need a television to know what was going on in the *Big Brother* house. An intertextual relationship existed between media users, television and print media (see Tincknell & Raghuram 2002 for a detailed discussion of intertextuality and *Big Brother*). Much of this synergy between the media and secondary texts is created by the producers, as is evident from the marketing strategies that came into operation; for instance a *Big Brother South Africa* magazine was launched on 3 December 2001 and a CD made by the housemates was released later on.

But other forms of intertextuality appeared as well. Newspapers belonging to the Naspers stable and a host of other print media saw the opportunity to boost their circulation figures, and therefore zoomed in and reported in great detail on the private lives of the twelve contestants. Hungry for scandalous happenings in the house, the media magnified and sensationalised the housemates' activities. Examples they concentrated on included Ferdinand's attics in the jacuzzi, his defecation in the garden, the arguments between the housemates, emotional outbursts, and the continuous speculation whether Lara and Steven did or did not have sexual intercourse and whether the two would continue their affair after leaving the house.

Even the *Sunday Times* in South Africa, who in the beginning of the series kept a low profile regarding *Big Brother*, published on its front page the sordid details of Bradford Woods' 'criminal' past. He was the biggest troublemaker in the *Big Brother* house, but also one of the strongest contenders to win the million rand. Brad's petty fraud story would normally not even appear on the last gossip pages of *Sunday Times*. In real life he is a violent social oddball and was recruited to cause conflict in the house. Loved by sections of the public, they wanted to know more about him, therefore Brad had great news value. In an interview, Mandy de Waal (2001) asks Grant Shippey, Chief Executive Officer of Amorphous New Media if that takes *Sunday Times* into the realm of *Sun Magazine* and the rest of the United Kingdom's scandal rags, or if *Big Brother* is really big news? Shippey's answer was that in the context of Bradford's celebrity and his position as a market commodity, his behaviour in the house was relevant and in the public interest.

Another example of intertextuality is the continuous visual access to the house made possible via the Internet. By means of chat rooms, viewers could interact with one another and make decisions about voting based on their conversations. Furthermore, through the Internet, *Big Brother* fans were also able to register as members and received daily e-mails to keep them up to date with the happenings in the house, air their views and deconstruct the day-to-day events. In addition, the Internet allowed viewers to vote for the eviction of a contestant. According to Mike Cathie, Marketing Director at Microsoft South Africa, *Big Brother* was perhaps the biggest multi-media event ever staged in South Africa, including the involvement of television, the Internet, radio and print. This huge audience created a great opportunity for Microsoft to draw attention to its NET vision of 'empowering the wider population through smarter solutions and better software'.

Yet another important element of *Big Brother*'s intertextuality is its ability to allow active audience interaction. Interactive programmes such as *Big Brother*, have revived the interest in audience studies because audiences do not merely respond to interactive texts, they may in fact contribute to changing them. Researchers like Ien Ang (1985), Dorothy Hobson (1982) and David Morley (1981) set out to prove by means of ethnographic and reception research, that audiences are active agents in making sense of media messages, the text remained the primary determinant of meaning. That is, although audiences actively negotiate meaning while interacting with texts, they could *not* intervene in the formulation or creation of a text. The genre typified by *Big Brother* demonstrates a relationship which breaks down the division between audience and text in significant ways. This series raises interesting questions for cultural studies to reconfigure present-day conceptualisations of the relationship between the audience and the television text (Tincknell & Raghuram 2002: 199).

One of the basic assumptions of the cultural studies approach is that audiences are active agents in making sense of texts. Therefore texts cannot be imposed on audiences because during the process of meaning making, negotiation takes place where audiences internalise messages within their existing frames of reference and social and cultural circumstances. Where the activities of audiences are centred on negotiating meaning, a definitive methodological and conceptual problem arises because audiences are contingent and fleeting groupings create problems for the researcher (Tincknell & Raghuram 2002: 201–2). For example, many websites have been deployed where viewers can partake in the narrative development of interactive shows. By making audience participation central to the 'plot', *Big Brother* marked a new moment for interactive television. For media and cultural researchers this invention can be seen as the watershed of the ongoing debates about the precise relationship between text and audiences (ibid.).

Interactive audience participation is further enhanced by the fact that audiences, with the press of a button or click of the computer mouse, determine the fate of a housemate. And this is exactly what makes reality TV unique and popular – no other television genre affords viewers the opportunity to so actively exercise their choices and voice their opinions. Through electronic messages and voting poles on the Internet, magazines and letters to newspapers, viewers actively take part in and even rewriting the format and script.

## Eruption of trash television: Big Brother or Big Brothel?

Like in many other countries, *Big Brother* South Africa caused moral panic, especially from sections of conservative Afrikaans-speaking South Africans who condemned the programme in no uncertain terms. The heading of the article in *Beeld* says it all: 'Loerbroer fokus op die banale, teer op slegte instinkte' ('*Big Brother* focuses on banalities, and feeds on people's sordid instincts') (Jackson 2001: 22–3). This newspaper deplored the contestants' behaviour – their drunkenness, their continuous sex talks and the 'evil' happenings in the jacuzzi, all examples of moral decay.

Members of the organisation Christians for Truth (Christene vir die Waarheid) showed their aversion to 'pornographic big brother' by shouting slogans such as '*Big Brother* – Big Brothel'. One banner carried the following words, 'Peeping is a sin ... what you watch = what you are ... Jesus sets peepers free'. One member of the organisation said that the naked running about of housemates whilst drunk would arouse viewers sexually (Van Wyk 2001).

One of the most distinct differences between the housemates was that the two black contestants, Nobesuthu and Vuoyo, abstained from lying in the sun, heavy drinking and partying. In fact, they rarely (if ever) touched beverages containing alcohol. Apart from occasional sneering racial remarks such as 'naked white bums' when Ferdinand and Tim were running naked in the garden after heavy drinking, these two contestants mixed quite comfortably with the rest of the group and were rarely nominated for eviction – perhaps because they were 'invisible' and not a threat to the other contestants as Munusamy has said. Eventually both were amongst the five finalists. Because of the antics of the other housemates, white viewers phoned *Beeld* making it clear that they preferred the black guy (Vuoyo) as a role model for their children (Leithead 2001).

This issue of morality also led to discussions of the 'voyeuristic nature' of *Big Brother*. One reason given by intellectuals and media personalities for the widespread popularity of *Big Brother* is that its voyeuristic nature allows viewers to act as Peeping Toms for 24 hours a day. Grant Shippey, in the interview with Mandy de Waal, says that in South Africa, *Big Brother* affords viewers the opportunity to become participants in mass voyeurism by taking pleasure form previously forbidden fruits: 'what was previously a sin is now very much mainstream in South Africa'. Tincknell and Raghuram (2002: 201–3) maintain that *Big Brother* is an artful combination of the voyeuristic aspects of the reality programme with the competitive elements of the game show. This combination produces a text whose apparent banality is mediated by crucial moments of suspense such as the emotional outburst while intoxicated, or the nomination of a housemate for eviction.

Furthermore, the direct and unmediated emotions of real people contribute to the feeling of 'realness' – they are, after all, real people like the rest of us. They do the same things as us: sleeping, taking a shower, drink too much or too little, using the toilet, making food, getting bored, and show a deep-seated need to touch and to be touched. These were hitherto private spaces not open to viewing by the public. In addition, each intimate look and touch between contestants might suggest sexual innuendos and this is enhanced by a voiceover commentary fraught with possible sexual encounters. By agreeing to participate, the contestants give their implicit consent for viewers to 'gaze' at them, and this puts them in a powerful position.

However, Jane Roscoe (2001: 480) argues that explaining the popularity in terms of its voyeuristic nature is limited because it is not always the most appropriate way to describe the relation between housemates and their audiences. Roscoe contends that one should also consider exhibitionism and a satisfaction of scopophiliac tendencies. *Big Brother* may not necessarily or always be about sexual pleasures but about the pleasure of watching events unfold before our eyes and about gaining pleasure from watching people whom we can relate to because they are in many ways like us. They are not professional actors and, according to Roscoe, this enhances the possibility of identification. Ferdinand Rabie, winner of the first *Big Brother*, was especially renowned for his swearing but also for his 'Ferdi-isms'. Jenny (2001) compiled a list of the funny things Ferdi had said in his own innocent sweet way. Because he was Afrikaans-speaking he had a remarkable way of mutilating the English language. The following are a few of Jenny's Ferdi-isms:

- Ferdi was talking about a dream he had, where somebody cut him along his 'ribbers' (ribs – *ribbe* in Afrikaans).
- Do you want me to lawn the mower with this thing?'
- Ferdi was telling Irvan that he could make a woman so happy that she would be in her 'seventh element'! (seventh heaven)
- When asking Leigh for more croutons for his gazpacho: 'Please can I have some more bread crumbles?'
- He also decided that getting involved with any girls in the house would be unwise, stating: 'I would be cutting my own neck off if I got involved with anyone in this house.'
- 'I'm chilt baby, I'm chilt' (as in chilled).
- 'Sing loud right down from your anus through your aorta and out your friggin' mouth.'
- Talking to Big Brother on Friday evening, Ferdi said: 'I don't like men much, I actually don't get along with them that well – I like women. I'm actually the perfect lesbian.'
- 'If you want smoked salmon just walk through the smokers' section of a restaurant with salmon and you will have smoked salmon!'
- One of the housemates had the runs and he said: 'He is shitting his lungs out!'
- 'Come on people we're acting like children here, let us be adultery about this.'
- 'Hey folks, we've got to order some bumfloss' (toilet paper).

These expressions provided humour and entertainment and viewers were continuously retelling Ferdi-isms. This playful gossiping served as social cement for conversations between *Big Brother* fans. The viewers who voted for him loved him because they experienced him as honest and loyal (Burger 2001). This may explain the popularity of Ferdinand Rabie, the winner of *Big Brother*. Yet, on the other hand, he also showed his 'dark' side, and some viewers were up in arms because of his swearing and unruly behaviour especially when he was drunk. After such a bout he did, however, always apologise in the Diary Room for offending Big Brother, viewers and the housemates. The example of Ferdi seems to back up Roscoe's claim about mundane behaviour as pleasurable. Roscoe's explanation, however, does not always hold water – watching people sleeping, reading, sitting around doing nothing or exercise, can be very boring. That is perhaps why the highlights of the day concentrate more on gossip, conflict and sexual innuendos because this is the stuff people want to see and talk about. During the remaining weeks of *Big Brother* viewers complained bitterly about watching the 'nothingness' in the house (Burger 2001).

# Conclusion

There are limits to explaining the popularity and success of television programmes like *Big Brother* because of its complexity. There are many theoretical and methodological frameworks that can be applied to investigate the series and some may provide contradictory perspectives. *Big Brother* personifies how new technologies work in tandem to give people more freedom to become actively involved with media events when exercising their choices. The combination of the Internet, cellular (mobile) phones and television provides a platform for a collective experience characterised by the desire for everyday commonalities. According to van Zoonen (2001: 671) this desire does not stem from major international events such as a royal wedding (or the war in Iraq) but from a desire firmly rooted in ordinary humdrum everyday experiences. This lies at the heart of the popularity and success of *Big Brother*.

The analysis of hegemony reveals that race is still a big issue in South Africa and voting inevitably occurred along racial lines because the *Big Brother* fans are largely middle-upper-class white bourgeois and their culture has been foregrounded at the expense of the other race and cultural groups in South Africa. *Big Brother* Africa (produced in 2003), provides an interesting contrast. The aim was to mirror Africa's continent by bringing twelve contestants together from 10 countries in Africa: Ghana, Nigeria, Kenya, Tanzania, Angola, Botswana, Malawi, Namibia, South Africa, Zambia and Zimbabwe. Here, the casting problems were magnified as they tried to capture the ethnicity of an entire continent. There were complaints about the composition of the group. For example, Stefan from Namibia was blond and good looking; Alex from Kenya, Mwisho from Tanzinia and Zein from Malawi were clearly of 'mixed-blood' descent. The rest exhibited such 'un-African behaviour' that people did not want to associate with the programme (Kalyegira 2003).

*Big Brother* Africa and South Africa might be credited with an important positive social outcome. Many saw it as an education in cross-national tolerance. It effectively challenged the stereotypes held about certain ethnic groups such as South Africans as violent and Mozambicans as poor. Housemate Mda says that watching her fellow participant, the gentle Nigerian Bayo, waking up early to start cleaning the house, shattered her belief that Nigerians were all lazy and loud. In the end the viewers saw that their fellow Africans were also people, 'like you and me', who flirt, quarrel, cook, shower, get bored and go to sleep (Lopez 2003). And, in the end sex sells, whether you live in Europe, Canada, Australia or in a remote village in Africa.

*Bibliography*

Anon. (2001) 'Goeie Nuus – vir elke lidmaat', *Weeklikse nuusblad van die Ned Geref Gemeente Meyerspark*, 27, 9, 1–8.
_____ (2001) 'South Africa's reality TV race test'. Available at: http://news.bbc.co.uk/1/hi/entertainment/tv_and_radio/145386.stm (accessed 16 April 2003).
_____ (2002) 'Loerbroer is nuusmaker van die jaar', *Beeld*, 21 June, 3.
_____ (2003) 'SA se beroemdes en berugtes', *Rapport*, 5 January, 5.
Ang, I. (1985) *Watching Dallas: Soap Opera and the Melodramatic Imagination*. London: Methuen.
_____ (1991) *Desperately Seeking the Audience*. London: Methuen.
Big Mama (2001) 'Ninety percent Boesman'. Available at: http://www.entertainment.

iafrica.com (accessed 15 August 2002).

Burger, K (2001) 'Die mag van die loervink', *Naweek-Beeld,* 15 December, 3.

Cathie, M. (2001) '*Big Brother* SA and Microsoft create Internet magic'. Available at: http://www.microsoft.com/southafrica/casestudies/bigbrother/html (accessed 14 April 2003).

Crehan, K. (2002) *Gramsci, Culture, and Anthropology*. Berkeley: University of California Press.

De Waal, M. (2001) 'BB confirms our basic traits'. Available at: http://www.media toolbox.co.za/pebble.asp?relid=2814&p=40 (accessed 16 April 2003).

Fiske, J. (1987) *Television Culture*. London: Routledge.

Foucault, M. (1980) *Power/Knowledge*. London: Pantheon Books.

Fourie, P. J. (ed.) (1997) *Introduction to Communication: Film and Television Studies*. Cape Town: Juta.

___ (ed.) (2001) *Media studies. Volume One: Institutions, Theories and Issues.* Cape Town: Juta.

Heug, M. (2003) *BB: Swapping camp 'n continent*. Available at: www.entertainment.iaf rica.com/features/247499.htm (accessed 10 November 2003).

Hobson, D. (1982) *Crossroads: The Drama of a Soap Opera*. London: Methuen.

Idriess, I. (2003) '*M-Net* & *Big Brother* Africa – Selling Immorality to Nigerian Youths'. Available at: www.lagosforum.com/expressyourselfresponsibly (accessed 10 November 2003).

Jackson, J. (2001) 'Loerbroer fokus op die banale, teer op slegte instinkte', *Beeld*, 24–5.

Jenny's Ferdi-isms (2001) Available at: http:/www.702.co.za/features/832579.html (accessed 13 November 2001).

Jones, J. and E. Mathijs (2003) 'Interview with Neil McCarthy' (24 October 2003).

Kalyegira, T. (2003) *Is Big Brother African?* Available at: www.monitor.co.ug/bgafric/ bbjuly_aug_sept/index.php–41 (accessed 10 November 2003).

Leithead, A. (2001) 'SA Big brother reflects division'. Available at: http://news.bbc.co.uk/ 1/hi/world/africa/1701526.stm (accessed 16 April 2003).

Lull, J. (ed.) (2000) *Media, Communication, Culture*. Cambridge: Polity Press.

_____ (ed.) (2001) *Culture in the Communication Age*. London and New York: Routledge.

Marketingweb (2002) Marketing figures. Available at: http:/allafrica.com/stories/ printable/20021213009/html (accessed 17 April 2003).

Morley, D. (1980) *The Nationwide Audience*. London: British Film Institute.

Munusamy, R. (2001) 'Big Brother cameras hide nasty story of race'. Available at: (accessed 16 April 2003).

Nieuwoudt, S. (2001) 'Spektakel sonder maskers', *Naweek-Beeld*, 19 May, 3.

O'Sullivan, T., J. Hartley, D. Saunders, M. Montgomery and J. Fiske (1994) *Key Concepts in Communication and Cultural Studies*. London: Routledge.

Roscoe, J. (2001) '*Big Brother* Australia: performing the "real" twenty-four-seven', *International Journal of Cultural Studies*, 4, 4, 473–88.

Schiffman, B. (2000) 'Big brother bridges the gab between television and the Internet'. Available at: wysiwyg:25/http://www/forbes.com/2000/07.18/feat.html (accessed 14 January 2003).

Sennett, R. (1977) *The Fall of Public Man*. New York: Knopf.

Serugo, M. (2003) 'The show that kept Africa on the edge'. Available at: www.monitor. co.ug/bgafric/bbjuly_aug_sept/big57.php–19k–9Nov2003 (accessed 10 November

2003).

Steenveld, L. (2000) 'Defining the undefinable', *Rhodes Journalism Review*, 11 August.

Tincknell, E. and P. Raghuram (2002) '*Big Brother*: Reconfiguring the "active" audience of cultural studies?', *European Journal of Cultural Studies*, 5, 2, 199–215.

Van der Merwe, M. (2001) 'It was just one crisis after crisis', *You*, 13 December, 13–14.

Van Poecke, L. (1994) 'Mediacultuur en identiteitsconstitutie in het licht van postmoderne swakke classificatie en framing', *Communicatie. Tydscrift voor Massamedia en Cultuur*, 23, 3, 1–27.

Van Wyk, M. (2001) 'Mense in Bfn wys afkeer van "pornografiese Big Brother"'. Available at: www.news24.com/Die-Volksblad/Nuus/0,4166,5-83-1092757,00.html (accessed 11 October 2001).

Van Zoonen, L. (2001) 'Desire and resistance: *Big Brother* and the recognition of everyday life', *Media, Culture & Society*, 23, 5, 669–77.

Wong, J. (2001) 'Here's looking at you: Reality TV, *Big Brother*, and Foucault', *Canadian Journal of Communication*, 26, 489–501.

# CHAPTER 13

*Jane Roscoe*

# WATCHING BIG BROTHER AT WORK
## A Production Study of Big Brother Australia

This chapter details a production study of *Big Brother* Australia. In doing so, it provides a case study of an innovative multi-platform media event. It is an example of a format that delivers its content across television, the Internet, telephony, print media and radio, in addition to the live events on site at the theme park, *Dreamworld*, where the *Big Brother* house is situated. It also provides an opportunity to examine the indigenisation of an international 'reality TV' format. It also draws on interviews with many of the key creative personnel, textual analyses, as well as on an audience survey conducted on the *Big Brother 2* website. Key issues concerning the development of the format, interactivity and media convergence are analysed and explored. It is also an attempt to move beyond the very tired and simplistic readings of 'reality TV' that seek to position it as evidence of television's 'dumbing down' or as an example of the democratisation of media. Both positions fail to consider the more interesting questions of how these programmes have changed contemporary broadcasting practices, the complexity of the productions and the innovative relationships constructed between the producers, texts and audiences. This chapter thus takes as its starting point the notion that these programmes are not cheap and dumb, but rather they are complex productions that speak to a media-savvy audience who are sophisticated in their understanding and use of the various platforms. It provides an alternative analysis that seeks to move beyond such simplistic readings of the form.[1]

# The rise of popular factual entertainment

Somewhere along the way television changed.

Reality-based programming, often referred to as 'reality TV' now dominates schedules across the world. A brief look at the TV guide in any number of international locations will probably reveal a week packed with DIY shows, cookery programmes, docu-soap formats such as *Popstars*, and most recently 'reality game shows' such as *Survivor* and *Big Brother*. Certainly in Australia, these shows not only fill the schedules, but also top the highest ratings lists. These are shows that have been able to attract large audiences, thus appearing to satisfy viewers, networks and their advertisers. While initially they were globally cheap to make in comparison with home-produced dramas and documentary (for example, *Funniest Home Videos*, or various emergency style shows) today's programmes are far more sophisticated and expensive to produce. In Australia Network Ten paid $AUS 28 million to secure the second series of *Big Brother* and the first *Celebrity Big Brother*, and is rumoured to have paid about the same for series which aired in April 2003.

James Friedman has argued that 'the proliferation of reality-based programming in the year 2000 does not represent a fundamental shift in televisual programming' (Friedman 2002: 7). However, I would suggest that in fact there has been a very significant shift in the contemporary television landscape, and that popular factual entertainment is both a symptom and response to those shifts.

There has been a marked swing towards 'light entertainment' in factual programming, and a greater circulation of new television formats. Together this has changed the look of prime-time television. In place of the long-running dramas and current affairs shows are docu-soaps and reality game shows. There is nothing new about formats; soap operas and game shows have been circulating internationally for some time (Mapplebeck 1998). What is new is the configuration; these formats seem to be at the nexus of the local and the global. That is, they seem to be both reflective of local cultures and adhere to a desire for local content, yet do so within a framework that is clearly designed to be universal and easily sold around the globe much like any other franchise.

There has been considerable debate as to the reasons and consequences of this shift to light entertainment and this reliance on formats. Some critics have argued that popular factual entertainment programmes like *Popstars* and *Big Brother* have directly contributed to the decline in drama production in Australia. Others have argued that such programmes have undermined the documentary project. Both positions see the new television formats as the reason for less local production across factual and fictional programming. What both positions fail to acknowledge is that these new formats are both a consequence of, and a response to, the wider changes in production and policy that have resulted in less drama and documentary.

The contemporary broadcasting landscape has been changed by technological developments, changes in regulation practices and specific changes in production processes. Audiences are more fragmented, sophisticated, knowing, and as a consequence, more demanding. Our relationship to (and with) television has changed; media convergence means that content is now often delivered across a number of different platforms resulting in new relationships between texts and audiences. We might engage with this content simultaneously across different platforms, for example watching the television show while also accessing the website and sending an SMS (short message service delivered via cell or mobile phones) to the show. While this may not yet be the experience of the majority of viewers, recent studies have shown that it is the experience of certain groups of viewers, in particular young people (Lealand 2001).

Reality formats have changed the broadcasting landscape, but why are they so popular in so many different countries, across so many cultures? Like McDonalds, what they seem to do so well is translate the global product to the local context. Examining the process of 'indigenisation' provides some insight into why a programme like *Big Brother* seems to have done so well.

## Making it Aussie: indigenising an international format

One of the significant things about *Big Brother* is the way in which it has been translated from an international format into a local phenomenon. Formats are traded around the globe, with the expectation (or assumption) that the local buyer has merely to add the local talent into a pre-determined structure (Moran 1998). To a certain extent this is true. Each format comes with a 'Bible' that details every aspect of a show, from the opening graphics, to the number of scenes per episode, to the choice of host. *Big Brother* is no exception. Originally developed by Dutch company Endemol, the Bible lays down details such as how Big Brother should speak to housemates, provides challenges and tasks, and designs for the house. The Bible lays out a blueprint for an international brand. However, it is a misconception that the brand cannot be developed or changed. The Australian *Big Brother* provides a good example of this in that there are a number of ways in which the format has been 'indigenised' and made 'Aussie'.

### The house

One of the most obvious ways in which the format is made local is through the design of the actual house. In Australia the *Big Brother* house is set in the grounds of the *Dreamworld* theme park on Queensland's Gold Coast. When series one went to air in 2001, the house looked very different from the images Australian audiences had been offered of the UK and US houses. It was surrounded by bush in a theme park on one of Australia's busiest and most commercial holiday hotspots. A tourist mecca, the Gold Coast embodies the Australian lifestyle – surf, sand and sunshine. The house itself was designed to capture these very qualities and to reflect a sense of 'Australianness'. Tim Clucas (Network Ten executive, and network commissioner of *Big Brother*) remarked, 'we wanted this to be a real Aussie house, that means relaxed lifestyle, sunshine, backyard pool, backyard BBQ, a real Aussie *Big Brother*' (Clucas 2001).

The house was a far cry from the overseas versions, which looked to Australian audiences like prison compounds. In the second series the comfort was stepped up again, the furnishings supplied by Freedom Furniture (an aspirational furniture store), a spa had been added, and the whole house redecorated. Hanging around the pool and having a 'barbie' (barbeque) are all signifiers of the relaxed Australian lifestyle, something the show attempted to tap into and represent. It was important then that the house represented the 'local', yet it was also comfortable for other reasons, the house had to be a 'non-issue'. It was suggested by the producers that once you take the house out of the equation, the participants focus on themselves (rather than their surroundings) and the audience are also then able to focus on the participants and their relationships. It seemed to work and perhaps it is not surprising that around the globe *Big Brother* houses were spruced up for the second and third series.

*The cast*

It is not only the house that represented a certain version of Australian national identity, the housemates also embodied certain characteristics associated with a certain version of national identity. While the producers claim not to be casting particular characters, they acknowledge their desire to reflect Australia in their choices:

> In terms of the casting it was about trying to find, to some extent, Australian types. People who represented the types of people you would meet in the community, and it was useful to think about that without having a shopping list of any specific types. (Peter Abbott, executive producer, in Roscoe 2002)

There was much discussion about the choice of housemates and whether they were representative of Australia. The housemates in the first series seemed to embody the ideals of health, fitness and certain 'outdoorsiness', a central trope of Australianness. The winner, Ben, could be described as the archetypal Aussie male. He is a rugby fan, likes his beer, has a dry sense of humour, calls everyone 'mate' and inhabits what can be called 'good bloke country' (Sherborne 2000). In the second series, Peter (the winner), looked remarkably similar to Ben, and exhibited many of the same 'blokey' characteristics. Marty, the runner-up in series two, was also an archetypal character, a young naïve country boy who embodied 'rural Australia', a land full of drovers (someone who drives cattle, sheep, and so on, to markets, usually over long distances) and farmboys.

In the second series there was an attempt to update the representation of Australia that had been offered in series one. There had been some criticism that the participants in series one had not been a diverse enough group, and not really representative of 'Australia'. However, it should be noted that the producers never made any such claims to represent the nation. This was a discourse drawn on by critics and audiences. Certainly in series two there was, on the surface at least, a greater range of identities on offer, from the 'rural young male' (Marty), to the bisexual city girl (Sahra) to the older sporty woman (Shannon) to the mixed heritage social worker (Turkan). All of the participants seemed to be more sophisticated, media savvy, more 'aware' and certainly more 'knowing' about the actual format and so much more aware of being 'on show' at all times. In spite of these surface changes, the same discourses seemed to structure the experience of being in the house.

A key discourse is that of 'mateship'. Mateship is central to notions of national identity in Australia. Significantly, it is a discourse that is associated with a certain version of Australian masculinity (Turner 1994). It was noted by many people who worked on the show how 'mateship' seemed to be at the centre of the *Big Brother* experience. For example, Dave English, who worked as day-producer on the first series, noted how the housemates reacted to losing tasks. They did not seem to care whether they won or lost; it was more about being in it together: 'It's a cultural thing ... They don't seem to give a bugger whether they win or lose' (English 2001).

In the public discussions of the show, mateship often featured as a key indicator of what the show was about, and it's Australianness. The house activities often focused on activities that might bond the participants together (for example, painting the living room) as well as being a site in which individual housemates were able to exhibit the qualities of mateship (for example, supporting someone through an emotional crises).

Perhaps the most obvious expression of this was a moment from series two when housemates got up at dawn to celebrate ANZAC Day.[2] These activities mobilise discourses of national identity that draw on representations of masculinity and mateship.

*Challenges*

While also reflecting the 'Australianess' of the show, the indigenisation of the challenges also illustrates the ways in which formats develop and ideas get traded amongst the producers of the other national versions. This unofficial trade in ideas parallels the official international trade in the actual format:

> In the second series most of the challenges were new and developed by the Australian team. Half-way through the series the Endemol 'Bible' had not even been opened according to the Tasks Producer Jonathan Summerhayes. 'We haven't even had to open [the Endemol Bible] this year ... we have come up with our own'. (Summerhayes 2002)

As the format developed in Australia, these ideas about what works and what does not are shared amongst the producers in other countries:

> We are sharing my stuff with the UK at the moment. I got theirs last year, and I also got some stuff from Greece. It is a bit hard to colloquialise those tasks. You look at some of those tasks on paper and think, how the hell did some of this work? [A challenge] may be big in Norway and Sweden, but it just wouldn't work here. I remember the English looking at our 'Fire Task' at the beginning of last year thinking that it would never work, but once they saw what we got out of it they went ahead and did it too ... The Army Task was quite good ... I think our version was one of the best. The English did take that one as well and they did it beautifully. I saw that and was speaking to the English producer about their ideas. We like to use each other as guinea pigs. We had a look at what they did and tried it out. But what works somewhere doesn't necessarily work in other countries. (Summerhayes 2002)

It is easy to think that formats are unchanging, that they are examples of static television, and certainly earlier formats such as *Wheel of Fortune*, do look as though they have remained unchanged since their inception, hardly touched by the local. But the new television formats such as *Big Brother* are clearly 'alive' in the sense that they are constantly being reworked, with national versions responding to the successes and failures of each national version.

## Producing Big Brother

The style of the Australian *Big Brother* was also to a certain extent indigenised, with producers responding to the context in which the show was shown. In Australia, the daily show was broadcast at 7pm each night, with a G-rated audience (suitable for all viewers) in mind. It also followed the very successful long-running soap opera,

*Neighbours*. It ran on Channel Ten, a commercial broadcaster who has most recently reinvented itself as the 'youth channel' with their target audience being 16 to 39 years old (Green 2001).

Peter Abbott talks about the broader social and cultural factors that impacted on how the show was made, and the relationship between himself and the housemates:

> In terms of how we ultimately made the show, I think it [cultural differences] had most effect upon our structural style and our editing style because classic *Big Brother* has four scenes a show ... my sense was – or the sense of a lot of us was – that we should be making something that more closely followed an Australian soap opera model which involved more scenes. (Abbott, in Roscoe 2002)

> I think the audience is ready for it because they have a literacy in the grammar of soap operas, which means you can come into the scene two-thirds of the way as long as you know what the plot line is. The classic format is not for this time-slot. (Abbott 2001)

The (mostly) non-authoritative relationship between Big Brother (Peter Abbott) and the housemates also owes something to cultural differences:

> It's a very Australian thing. Only in Australia would the housemates, when I come over the loud speaker saying, 'This is Big Brother', say 'Hello Pete'. I said 'stop it' but it's that Australian attitude to authority that goes back to our culture ... there is no culture of authoritarianism in Australia and there is no culture of inherited respect. (Abbott, in Roscoe 2002)

The relationship also changed between the first and second series. The housemates had seen the first series and, like the audience, knew how the game was played. Generally more media savvy, the second set of housemates already had a different relationship with Big Brother. This was not just the case in Australia, but in other versions around the globe, as Abbott notes:

> I think from my discussions with other Big Brothers, inevitably one has to become tougher because the housemates become more knowing. They play a tougher game with you and you have to become much tougher with them within limits ... in the second season where everyone understands a bit better what's going on you can start tightening the screws without getting rebellion. (Ibid.)

Clearly the format has changed and developed over the first and second series. The producers have responded to both the experiences of overseas *Big Brothers* and also the specificities of the Australian context. It is also clear that the production has to respond to both the expectations of the audiences (who by now know the game) and the housemates (who have learnt the rules from series one).

## Making live TV

> Although live transmissions form but a tiny proportion of programming, that tiny portion sets the tone for all TV. (Stam 1983: 24–5)

Television trades on itself as a live medium, and its potential to be unmediated, but this assumption is ideological rather than ontological. Very little on television is strictly 'live'. In fact the very notion of 'live' is problematic. Live often refers to 'live to tape' or describes broadcasts that actually have a delay.

Two of the *Big Brother* shows are 'live', the *Monday Live Nominations*, and the *Sunday Live Eviction* show. There are also other 'specials' that are live, including the Mastercard Challenge, and in series two, the unplanned live coverage of Turkan's threat to leave the house (7 May 2002). All have a 30-second delay required by the network censors, but for intent and purposes, this is as 'live' as television gets. Occasionally things do go wrong, but this is in effect what gives live television its edge; audiences are aware that technology sometimes fails and it is part of the experience.

> We've had some minor technical issues, and I never see that as a problem, it's actually a good thing. We had some satellite problems last week that everyone thought was a conspiracy because it conveniently went down as the evictee was announced! We didn't even know it had happened until the network executive came in ... the viewing audience is aware of the medium, and you don't say things are live when they are not. (Scott 2002)

Although television trades on its liveness, apart from sportscasts and the live reporting of political events or disasters (for example, September 11) there is little that is live on TV. Those working in the Australian TV industry do not have a lot of opportunities to work 'live' (and it is not surprising that those working on the live shows have backgrounds in event television such as sportscasts). Many of those working on *Big Brother* talked about the excitement of working on the live shows, especially as the above quite suggests, because of the unpredictability of it all.

Richard Stomps, the Supervising Producer on the Monday night *Live Nominations* show notes:

> You can't just stop and re-record. It's not live to tape which is a completely different thing. You are responding to what is happening and the best example of that was Tuesday night [May 7] with Turkan where suddenly the whole show, which was the intruders coming in, became a totally different show. It was exciting, more exciting when you suddenly have someone wanting to leave the house. And no one could have predicted it. (Stomps 2002)

Liveness is also important for audiences. It is another way in which viewers are drawn into the *Big Brother* experience, but also acts as a signifier of the 'realness' of the participants and the show itself. When we watch the programme live, we are more convinced that we are watching non-actors in an unscripted drama, as this quote suggests:

> Live television ... bridges the gap instantly and unites the individual at home with the event afar. The viewer has a chance to be in two places at once. Physically, he may be at his own hearthside but intellectually and, above all emotionally, he is at the cameraman's side. (Jack Gould 1956, cited in Corner 1999: 26)

## The multi-platform experience: the real experiment

Much has been made of the idea of *Big Brother* as a social experiment, and yet the real experiment is in terms of the format itself. *Big Brother* is an innovative multi-platform media event delivered across television, the Internet, telephony, print media and radio, and as such can be seen as a precursor to fully interactive television (Roscoe 2001). In a recent paper, Stuart Cunningham has argued that *Big Brother* is innovative in a number of ways:

- It is an international system that achieves technology-transfer and format style up-grades around the world very rapidly.
- It assists in problem-solving for major services industries like advertising and mar-keting which benefit from innovative marketing strategies.
- Technological innovations in the successful trialing of such large-scale multi-platform delivery systems.
- Regional innovations due to successful trialing of regional capacity for large-scale production. (Cunningham 2002: 10–11)

Comments made above confirm the first point. There is much that can be drawn from a study of the production of *Big Brother* in terms of the latter points. Although not discussed in-depth here, it is worth noting that the show has provided an opportunity for new advertising strategies that allow advertisers to promote their products across various platforms thus extending their relationships with their consumers. They have also been given the opportunity to attach their product to certain types of content in exclusive relationships. For example, Energiser Batteries linked their product to the audition tapes in series two. After buying a pack of batteries, consumers were given a code number that would allow them access to audition tapes through the website. Such strategies have been innovative and successful.

Likewise, the show can be seen as a testing ground for future multi-platform media events as well providing training for local crew and emerging talent. It is the biggest television production ever to come to Queensland and as such has provided a rich environment for younger members of the crew and for regional post-production services.

## Developing a fan base

One of the most significant things about *Big Brother* is the way in which it has been able to mobilise and engage audiences across a number of delivery platforms. *Big Brother* has created an active fan base as well as an audience for the show. The show has rated well with Channel Ten's target audience; in the first and second series they have managed to secure (and retain) over 50 per cent of the 19–39-year-olds. However, it is not just that people are watching but they are participating in a number of ways across the various media platforms.

There are three important ways in which *Big Brother* has allowed for participation on behalf of the audience: through the siting of the House at *Dreamworld* theme park, through *Big Brother Online*, and through telephone voting. These activities and sites are central to the creation of a fan base. Here I am drawing on the work of those who see fans as active in their appropriation of texts, critical in their understandings of them and, importantly, also see the fan as a producer rather than a consumer of texts (Abercrombie & Longhurst 1998; Jenkins 1992).

The location of the house, production facilities and the studio set at *Dreamworld* allow for a number of different spin-off events and experiences. It brings together entertainment and education – the location set with the theme park – and is certainly unique in terms of the worldwide *Big Brother* productions. For the fan of the show there are opportunities to go behind the scenes and find out more about how the show is put together. Visitors to the *Big Brother* exhibit are able to view the control room, although they cannot visit the actual house while the series is running. At the end of the series, the house is open to visitors; here they can visit the mock-up Diary Room and have their photograph taken, and share a confession or two. For the fan visitor it is a chance to engage in what Nick Couldry calls a 'shared fiction', that is, the shared experience of being there. He suggests that this experience is not always about memories or nostalgia, but is an 'anticipated act of commemoration', an experience to be remembered in the future when watching the show (Couldry 2000:69).

Being on site can enhance the viewing experience and enjoyment of the show because it allows access to the processes of production that are so often hidden. Seeing the banks of TV screens in the control room gives a sense of how much material there is, and how little makes the 7pm show. It erodes the usual distinction between the viewer and the producer by allowing the visitor access to knowledges that are specialised and usually reserved for those working in the industry.

In every *Big Brother* there is always a crowd to greet the week's evictees, but, in Australia, the crowd is managed and regulated in quite a specific way. One of the reasons locating the house at *Dreamworld* was so attractive was the possibility of using the large auditorium to turn the eviction show into a live event. The eviction show has evolved into a forum in which a whole range of fan activities can be performed. The live audience are there to be seen, both by the evictee on arrival in the auditorium, but also by the audience at home. They are encouraged to dress-up as their favourite housemate, and conscious that prizes await the best-dressed fan of the series. Sarah-Marie's fans dressed in her trademark pyjamas with bunny ears (and often false breasts!) and performed the bum-dance on request from the host, Gretel. In series two, farmboy Marty look-a-likes littered the auditorium. By the time the evictee has reached the auditorium at the end of the eviction show, the crowd has been primed to roar with excitement. For the evictee, it's the first time they will experience 'fame', and their arrival on stage is not unlike the appearance of a pop star at a concert. The fans cheer, the evictee waves and thanks them for being there! What the show does very successfully is turn the experience of being an audience into an active participation in which the viewer is as much a producer of the text as a consumer of it.

## Big Brother online

The website is a central component of the event that is *Big Brother* and it provides the audience with a range of activities that allow it to construct different relationships with the text and other viewers.

> We never intended to be just a support site for the TV show. It's actually about something extra … More depth is what we like to think. Also, it's a direct interface to viewers and users. (O'Donnell 2001)

The *Big Brother* website is extensive; in the first series users could access live streams, a diary section, chat and forums, photo and housemate profiles. These services were all provided free of charge. In the second series (2002) a new component of the website was introduced, Dsuite, which was a premier paid service. Live 24/7 streams were only available through Dsuite, as was on-line voting. There were other changes to the site too. For example, the Diary section was updated every thirty minutes, and that gave a real incentive to fans to return several times a day. There were also more competitions and polls, as well as various promotions that linked advertisers directly to the content and to audiences. The live chats were expanded giving viewers greater opportunities to directly engage with the producers of the show and evicted housemates.

The importance of the website in the development of the format was highlighted in the results of a survey conducted on users of the site at the end of series two in 2002. A questionnaire comprising of 27 questions was posted on the official site for ten days at the end of the series. The survey generated 40,000 responses 23,000 of which were fully completed questionnaires. Overall the survey suggests that the opportunities for interaction are a key drawcard to audiences, and that the site provides a forum to extend their relationship with the television show.

Over 90 per cent of the respondents said that the website had enhanced their *Big Brother* experience; 45 per cent of the respondents were visiting the site at least once a day with over 90 per cent saying they visited at least once a week. Significantly, 60 per cent said that the website actually made them watch the television show more. In a format such as *Big Brother* the delivery of content over the different platforms is an important way in which the format itself is developed, and the relationship between the producers, text and audiences. The survey also suggested that not only do audiences engage in different ways with the content on different platforms, but that there may also be different types of audiences associated with those platforms.

For example, according to audience figures collected by Southern Star Endemol and Network Ten during series one, in the target audience group (18–39-year-olds) the gender split was relatively even. In both series one and two the gender split of website registered users was also evenly split, yet the respondents were 80 per cent female and only 20 per cent male. While one must be cautious about making claims on the basis of self-selecting samples, it is of interest that so many females responded to the survey. The fact that the sample is so biased towards females goes against most of the research and commonly held views about Internet usage. Most research tends to argue that the Internet is a male-dominated cultural space (Seiter 1999), although recent studies have shown the popularity of TV show sites with young females (Livingstone 2001). With regard to the *Big Brother* site, content is a key issue and this is the most likely reason for the bias in the sample. The younger girls especially are attracted to the site because of how the content is pitched. The website reflects the sort of language and discourse found in teenage magazines and related media. It mimics patterns of communication – gossip, celebrity chat, emotional issues found in what is culturally regarded as 'feminine' texts. Males are clearly visiting the site, but are perhaps using the site in a different way. It is likely that females are spending longer on-line engaging across the different parts of the site, while males are accessing specific areas possibly for shorter periods. This corresponds also to the greater emphasis on 'psychological discourses' in series two. Whereas in series one, these discourses seemed to attract the slightly older professional women to the daily TV shows (Clucas 2001), in series two, the focus on emotional issues and relationships seem to be mostly engaging a younger female audience.

The relationship with audience members is potentially extended through the multi-platform experience in a number of ways. Updating the diary section every half-hour was a particularly successful strategy which gave 'fans' of *Big Brother* access to the most up-to-date information/inside gossip (which is the fans' 'currency') and provided a reason to check the website at regular intervals during the day. It also allows a relationship to be built with audience members that is of a different quality. This is where the development of the format is also of keen interest to advertisers. Through a multi-platform delivery, advertisers and broadcasters now have the opportunity to talk to a member of the audience for an extended time each week rather than for the 26 minutes of a specific television show. As noted earlier, the development of new advertising strategies that integrate brands and services across the platforms is a key way in which *Big Brother* has been a leader with continuous innovation over the two series.

The experience of *Big Brother* shows that websites can do more than merely replicate what is represented on a particular television programme. They provide a site for audiences to interact (with the show and each other) and can be used to build loyalty to the product/brand. Far from turning people away from television, the survey results suggest that the website actually drives audiences to the show and to the other platforms. It clearly 'adds value'. It is worth noting that recent studies (in the UK and NZ) looking at young people's use of media shows that many have both TV and computers in their bedrooms, and that they use both media concurrently (Lealand 2001). Young people will watch TV shows while at the same time have the associated website open (and are probably sending out multiple SMS). Such patterns of usage are not unusual, and are likely to become more commonplace. Attention spans are not shorter, rather attention is spread over a larger number of media. Producers no longer have the undivided attention of an audience member for a specific time, instead they have the opportunity to engage with them across platforms for extended periods. *Big Brother* is successful partly because it mimics contemporary patterns of media use.

## Reality format futures

This chapter probably raises more questions about the development of formatted Reality TV than it answers. Even so, examining the production of *Big Brother* in Australia has provided rich data to explore the changing nature of contemporary popular factual entertainment, particularly the development of reality 'event television'. In particular, greater media convergence, both in terms of technological developments and audience uptake, has meant that there are greater possibilities for the delivery of content. This has been capitalised on by the producers of *Big Brother* who have made good use of the online environment and telephony to allow audiences greater opportunities for interaction, and qualitative advantages for advertisers and brands.

While *Big Brother* is an international format, a brand in itself, it is not an unchanging product. Rather as this case study shows, it has been indigenised and developed for and by the specific cultural and social context of Australia. Here we see the intersection of the local and the global and the negotiation of this terrain. There are indications that the relationship between producers and participants, producers and audiences, and between audiences and texts is constantly changing, which is why the format seems to be able to continue to intrigue audiences and scholars alike. For those who work on the show it also provides an opportunity to make a different type of television.

Event television is not the norm, and so provides training and opportunities to both experienced practitioners and emerging producers in Australia.

While many critics (across the world) have been quick to dismiss the format, taking *Big Brother* seriously, as a cultural product and an experiment in multi-platform delivery, allows a different view of the show. Far from being cheap and dumb, it is in fact expensive, complicated and geared to a sophisticated viewer. As digitalisation provides greater access to more channels, as format trade increases and media convergence becomes the mainstream, it will be formats such as *Big Brother* that lead the way. Reality TV is not going away, but it will never be the same.

*Notes*

1   Acknowledgments: This research was supported by a grant from Griffith University. I would like to thank members of the *Big Brother* production team who gave up their time to talk to me.
2   ANZAC (Australian and New Zealand Army Corps WW1). ANZAC Day is 25 April and commerates the anniversary of the ANZAC landing in Gallipoli in 1915.

*Bibliography*

Abercrombie, N. and B. Longhurst (1998) *Audiences*. London: Sage.
Abbott, P. (2001) Interview with Peter Abbott, Executive Producer of *Big Brother* (series one and two), 9 June, Brisbane.
Clucas, T. (2001) Interview with Tim Clucas, Head of Factual Programming, Network Ten, 22 May, Gold Coast.
Corner, J. (1999) *Critical Ideas in Television*. Oxford: Oxford University Press.
Couldry, N. (2000) *The Place of Media Power*. London: Routledge.
Cunningham, S. (2002) 'Culture, Services, Knowledge, or is Content King or are we just drama Queens?' Unpublished paper, *Communications Research Forum*. Canberra, 10–11 October.
English, D. (2001) Interview with Dave English, Day Producer of *Big Brother* (series one), 22 May, Gold Coast.
Friedman, J. (2002) 'Introduction', in J. Friedman (ed.) *Reality Squared: Televisual Discourse on the Real*. New Jersey and London: Rutgers University Press, 1–24.
Green, J. (2001) 'More than TV: Channel Ten and diversity in free-to-air broadcasting', *Media International Australia*, 100, 49–64.
Jenkins, H. (1992) *Textual Poachers: Television Fans and Participatory Culture*. London: Routledge.
Lealand, G. (2001) 'Some things change, some things remain the same: New Zealand children and media use', *SIMILE*, 1, 1. Available at: http://www.utpjournals.com/jour.ihtml?lp=simile/issue1/lealand.htm
Livingstone, S. (2001) 'Children on-line: emerging uses of the Internet at home', *Journal of the Institution of British Telecommunications Engineers*, 2, 1, 1–7.
Mapplebeck, V. (1998) 'The Mad, the Bad and the Sad', *DOX*, 31, 10–12.
Moran, A. (1998) *Copycat TV*. Luton: University of Luton Press.
O'Donnell, L. (2001) Interview with Louise O'Donnell, Executive Producer of *Big Brother Online* (series one), 22 May, Gold Coast.
Roscoe, J. (2001) '*Big Brother* Australia: Performing the "real" twenty-four-seven', *The*

International Journal of Cultural Studies, 14, 4, 473–86.

_____ (2002) 'Interview with Peter Abbott', Continuum, 16, 2, 225–34.

Scott, C. (2002) Interview with Cathie Scott, Supervising Producer, Live Eviction Show (series two), 10 May 2002, Gold Coast.

Seiter, E. (1999) Television and New Media Audiences. Oxford: Oxford University Press.

Sherborne, C. (2000) 'Eddie McGuire Inc', The Eye, 20 April–1 May, 31–5.

Stam, R. (1983) 'Television News and its Spectator', in E. Ann Kaplan (ed.) Regarding Television. Los Angeles: American Film Institute, 23–43.

Stomps, R. (2002) Interview with Richard Stomps, Supervising Producer, Monday Live Nominations show, 10 May 2002, Gold Coast.

Summerhayes, J. (2002) Interview with Jonathan Summerhayes, Task Producer of Big Brother (series one and two), 10 May 2002, Gold Coast.

Turner, G. (1994) Making it National. Sydney: Allen & Unwin.

## CHAPTER 14

*Pamela Wilson*

# JAMMING BIG BROTHER USA
Webcasting, Audience Intervention and Narrative Activism

This is the story of the first season of the American *Big Brother* and how its 'reality' narrative was almost hijacked by a motley assortment of activist online fans and media/ culture jammers. It was a spectacularly singular conjunctural moment in media history, right at the cusp of the new millennium. A window of opportunity emerged for only a brief time, by television standards. Located in this moment of flux – technological, programmatic and narrative – was the soft, open vulnerability that allowed for the invasion of this slickly-produced corporate television game show by an assortment of amateur narrative terrorists whose weapons were clever words rather than bombs. Such intervention, which caught the producers unaware, could perhaps only have happened once, in this first season of the American version of the highly-touted *Big Brother*. The form was new, the formula was flexible, the unscripted narrative was emergent from the psyches of the not-yet-jaded improvisational players, the events were being closely followed around the clock by avid online viewers, and the Hollywood set was relatively unprotected. Prior to this time, no one at CBS or Endemol Productions would have suspected that chaos could or would come from the skies. After this extended moment of vulnerability, future participants were selected less for their down-home 'aw shucks' naïveté and more for their ratings-drawing glamour, the formula became more fixed, and the chances for narrative disruption became increasingly curtailed.

The North American introduction of *Big Brother* – a hybrid concept inspired by Orwell's classic treatise on political oppression in a futuristic police state that held control over the minds of its subjects – inspired a new form of media activism that reflected the intersection of a countercultural anti-capitalist social movement ('culture jamming') with the shifting technological sands of the show's dual webcasting/broadcasting. The show's narrative was multilayered: it emerged minute-by-minute on the streaming web feeds, but was controlled, produced and structured through the selective editing of the producers for the nightly television recap. The 'characters' were real people living in a fishbowl, surrounded by cameras and creating an emerging narrative shaped only partially by the producers' constraints but open enough to allow for improvisation. Enter the culture jammers, seeking to disrupt and subvert the intentions of the corporate producers and to influence the outcome of the 'story'. A new form of media intervention into television was born: *narrative activism*.

The narrative activism found in the *Big Brother* case can be seen as a form of media/culture jamming and part of a larger social movement. Media/culture jamming, a purposefully playful and/or subversive activity reflecting the condition of postmodernism closely allied politically with the growing anti-corporate and anti-globalisation movement, might be defined as the appropriation of new media technologies and information systems to invade, subvert, intercept and disrupt corporate systems and their products. The early concept of culture jamming is attributed to the writings of William S. Burroughs, who in a seminal 1969 piece stated, 'Our aim is total chaos'. The theory and practice of culture jamming have been elaborated most fully by cultural critic Mark Dery in his 1993 essay 'Culture Jamming: Hacking, Slashing and Sniping in the Empire of Signs'. According to Dery,

> 'Culture jamming' ... might best be defined as media hacking, information warfare, terror-art, and guerrilla semiotics, all in one. Billboard bandits, pirate TV and radio broadcasters, media hoaxers, and other vernacular media wrenchers who intrude on the intruders, investing ads, newscasts, and other media artifacts with subversive meanings are all culture jammers. (Dery 1993)

Similarly, Naomi Klein calls culture jamming 'semiotic Robin Hoodism' or 'counter-messages that hack into a corporation's own method of communication to send a message starkly at odds with the one that was intended' (Klein 1999: 280–1).

There are many forms of culture jamming, but those that focus on media consider it to be semiological guerrilla information warfare, using words as weapons (a concept attributed to Umberto Eco), turning the tools of mass media against the corporate forces themselves. This has been a movement especially enabled by the rise and rapid growth of online media culture and the radical possibilities of the Internet; it is part of what Kevin Michael DeLuca and Jennifer Peeples (2002) describe as the transformation of the public sphere into the 'public screen'. For cultural critics like Dery, culture jamming is also an intensely political act, even as it grows out of a postmodern impulse. As he says of his own politics:

> I'm deeply committed to a progressive politics whose calls for social justice, economic equality, and environmental action are founded on an economic critique of the catastrophic effects of multinational capitalism. At the same time, I'm profoundly influenced by the postmodern emphasis on cultural politics (as

opposed to the old New Left emphasis on political economy). The intertwined histories of feminism, the civil rights movement, multiculturalism, and gay and transgender activism remind us that hacking the philosophical code that runs the hardware of political and economic power is crucially important, too. In that light, I'm naïve enough to believe that ideas matter and that intellectual activism can, in its own small way, be an engine of social change. (Dery 1993)

The question as to whether social change – or at the very least a public cultural critique – might be produced by attempts to affect, subvert, or disrupt the well-oiled mechanisms of commercial television is one that begs to be asked in light of the narrative activism surrounding the multimedia corporate production *Big Brother*.

## Big Brother and an innovative system of programme delivery

The premise was simple: ten people; no privacy; three months; no outside contact. In the summer of 2000, the Dutch company Endemol Productions, working with CBS television, selected ten contestants to participate in the first US version of *Big Brother*: part game show, part documentary, and part soap opera. This group would live together for more than 12 weeks, isolated in a house on a Hollywood studio lot, surrounded by corridors of surveillance cameras. Every two weeks, one contestant would be voted off the show, with the last remaining contestant winning the $500,000 grand prize.

The CBS television version of *Big Brother*, with concurrent live streaming online feeds in partnership with America Online (AOL), received public regard as a moderately successful-but-mediocre television event. It gained even more acclaim as an unprecedented, momentous hit on the Internet with its remarkable crossover Internet presence and the strong and loyal online audience it created and maintained. In fact, this became the most noteworthy aspect of the entire US *Big Brother* venture: journalist David Kronke reported that *Big Brother* 'has changed the way television and new media can interact'.[1] AOL's publicity articles touted the 'unprecedented convergence between television and the Internet' achieved by the CBS-AOL *Big Brother* alliance as the 'largest ongoing webcast in history', and claimed a 'tenfold increase in participants [of] the streaming webcast during peak usage time in the first week' (AOL website). The official AOL website, however, was only the tip of the iceberg in terms of online audience involvement in the *Big Brother* series. Online fans created and contributed to dozens of private websites and portals devoted to *Big Brother*.[2] AOL itself sponsored more than 14,000 unofficial fan pages about the *Big Brother* programme.

The 'action' that took place in the *Big Brother* house was supposed to be naturally occurring, although the producers structured the daily activities of the houseguests around a series of programmed 'challenges'. A high degree of self-consciousness also curtailed the spontaneity of the contestants' behavior. As Endemol Producer John Kalish later remarked of the American contestants,

They were always talking about how they were being edited, story lines, looking into cameras, being aware of it. They never let go of what the other houseguests in other countries did, which was finally to let go of the idea of being observed. These guys never did. They always referred to themselves as 'characters' as opposed to people. (*Big Brother* official website)

The only site in the house from which events were not transmitted over the live web feeds was the Red Room, a room to which the houseguests could go as individuals for private interviews with the producers (who often used these interviews as a way to elicit plot information or to otherwise manipulate the developing narrative) and where they revealed their choices for banishment.

Although the premise of *Big Brother* only required audience participation in the narrative in very limited and ritualised ways (the call-in votes every two weeks to oust the one member of the household), audience involvement, to the point of intervention and disruption, proved to be a hallmark of the American version of the *Big Brother* phenomenon. Neither the producers nor the network anticipated the level of public involvement that the *Big Brother* TV/online programming innovation would incite. The opportunity to invade or disrupt, or, seen in a more positive light, to contribute to, the narrative of a live television series was an opportunity that appealed both to fans and critics of the show, and intersected with a number of personal and organisational agendas unknown to the producers.

The dramatic highlight of the American show was the escalating narrative tension in the tenth week, an intersection of increasing interventions from the outside world with a 'groupthink' mentality among the six remaining sequestered houseguests, that culminated with the houseguests planning a mass walkout from the show, ostensibly to embrace an idealistic collective solidarity. Seeking their 'chance to make history' and make a profoundly anti-capitalist statement as they chose friendship over prize money, they also gravely threatened the very premise and foundation of the show's competitive commercialism, as well as the ability of the network to continue its run. The planned walkout was ultimately defused and contained by the producers, and the show ended successfully by commercial standards, despite the seemingly tenuous hold the producers seemed to have over the narrative outcome for a few days as chaos from outside intervention and internal rebellion threatened to radically alter the programme's planned plotline.

*Big Brother* broke new ground in establishing a multiplicity of ways that a television programme could use to reach its audience. In fact, one might argue that *Big Brother* consisted of several different programmes, several distinct audiences and multiple versions of its narrative. In addition to television, press accounts and the web feeds, the other official mode of disseminating the narrative of the programme was the CBS/AOL *Big Brother* website,[3] which posted daily summaries of narrative highlights and contained the official commentary from the producers. Other, unofficial versions of the narrative were posted by online audience members as updates on message boards, chatrooms and portals with links to a variety of connected sites.[4] Based upon these distinctions, we might theorise that the perception of the narrative events (that is, the actions and happenings in the lives of the *Big Brother* houseguests/contestants) would be complex, and that these perceptions would vary depending upon the exposure of an audience member to selected media forms (the TV show, the online feeds, the message boards, the official *Big Brother* website, press commentary). In fact, Endemol producer Douglas Ross remarked on the privileging of the online viewer:

> I think that the Internet viewer really does understand the show better than the average TV viewer. People who aren't involved in the Web, and just watching it on TV, except for the dedicated viewer who just watches it as a soap opera, I don't think the average viewer really gets it. (*Big Brother* official website)

*Big Brother* was highly unusual in that the circumstances of its production provided for a shared role in shaping such meanings. How did amateur culture jammers 'invade' the narrative world and irreparably effect the 'plot' of the series? Who produced *Big Brother*, in the end?

## Invasions from the skies and other interventions

The first outside invasion of *Big Brother* occurred when someone tossed several tennis balls containing faked newspaper articles over the fence into the *Big Brother* compound. In spite of the producers' efforts to try to prevent the contestants from seeing the balls' contents, the contestants managed to read two of these faked 'articles' containing negative comments about the show and its participants. These had an immediate effect on the contestants' morale. This, the first incursion of the outside world into the seemingly secured diegetic world of the houseguests, created enough alarm both inside the house and among the producers that the CBS/AOL website ran the following disclaimer entitled 'A Statement from the Executive Producer':

> The minute we saw what was going on, we told the houseguests over the PA system to bring the tennis balls and the papers into the Red Room. We quickly discovered that the photocopied newspaper articles were fake. We then told all the houseguests that this was a hoax and that the articles were bogus. We acted quickly to set the record straight because our number one concern, of course, is for the houseguests' safety and psychological well-being. (*Big Brother* official website)

Shortly thereafter, a web page (ZAP Design) claimed responsibility for the intrusive tennis balls.[5]

The producers' reaction to this first invasion was strong. Concerned that one particular contestant might request a voluntary exit as a reaction to this prank, Endemol broke its own rules about no outside contact and provided him with a packet of reassuring letters they had hastily requested from his family. This contestant, George, was a roofer from Rockford, Illinois who had quickly become a popular favorite based upon his sympathetic embodiment of an American archetype of the simple, beleaguered working man. As an added bonus, the reading of the letters from his young daughters to the other houseguests provided Endemol with some tear-filled, poignant moments for the television viewers (*Big Brother* official website). Thus, Endemol appropriated the events and used them to their own advantage.

Day 50 marked the beginning of the intensified external campaign to shape the narrative events. That afternoon, the contestants were in their enclosed outdoor courtyard. The producers, having apparently received a phone tip about a low-flying plane with a banner, came over the loudspeaker and asked them to sequester themselves immediately in the men's bedroom. A few hours later, however, the banner-bearing plane returned. According to the CBS/AOL website, 'The airborne prankster returned and passed the house at low altitude, proudly and clearly displaying the streaming message, 'BIG BROTHER IS WORSE THAN YOU THINK – GET OUT NOW'. The online activist group Media Jammers later claimed responsibility for this first banner. The 'media jamming' plans were hatched in an online *Big Brother* forum on the website Salon.com. 'That's where the revolution was born,' explained Media Jammers founder Jeff Oswald:

We were just goofing around trying to think of ways to get messages in. We talked about catapults, compressed air cannons like the ones they use to shoot t-shirts into the crowd at sports events, etc. We had a guy scout out the location and tell us how difficult it would be to get in range. So ... I figured our best shot was the banners. (*Big Brother* official website)[6]

There would be more to come from Media Jammers.

A campaign by George's fans to 'Save George' soon emerged as well. The website OurBigBrotherGeorge.com was set up by corporate supporters to raise money for George's family in his absence. It was rumoured on the message boards that the site was either illegal or unethical, and it was eventually shut down. However, George's hometown of Rockford, Illinois rallied behind their local television hero with spaghetti dinners and other fundraising campaigns to help support George's family. Some George-supporting fan groups used their website to sell t-shirts to benefit George, while others mobilised massive phone campaigns to get viewers to cast their telephone votes for another contestant so that George could maintain his chances of winning the $500,000. For most of the online fan community, however, the attempt by George's fans, and particularly corporate interests to help a particular contestant win, was scorned as an unethical and unfair intervention.[7]

While the message boards heated up with irate fans who felt cheated by, and protested, the 'Save George' campaign, tensions grew inside the house as well. The houseguests were bonding with each other and feeling a growing distrust against Big Brother (the producers), perceived as their captors and programmers. A strong collective ethos had developed among the houseguests. The conditions of the shared lived experience had become antithetical to the competitive spirit of the game show mentality. The tension between competitive individualism and collaborative collectivism informed the group dynamics for several weeks to come and, ultimately, led to their most dramatic moments.

In the wake of the airplane banner chartered by Media Jammers, the activist online organisation began to receive a great deal of attention. On 27 August, Media Jammers' Oswald posted an update on their website describing the group's philosophy and intent for future involvement in the *Big Brother* operation:

As our belief is that this is a universal, grass roots operation, we fully advocate and encourage anybody with a desire to engage in interloping on *Big Brother* to do so of their own accord on their own terms the best way they see fit ... Our ultimate goal is to make actions stick, that will generate ongoing dialogue about the destructive force of this CBS debacle ... A unanimous [contestant] walk-out, although it would be a thing of poetic beauty, is highly unlikely right now. However, if we maintain our efforts, we're confident they will eventually see that we ... were honest about our motives, and sincere in our belief that losers talk, heroes walk. We maintain that the message is, has been and always will be that by walking out together, they will be respected for it, salvage their dignity, and have more of a chance to accomplish their individual goals. If they stay and participate to the end, they will only be ridiculed and forgotten: *Nine losers, one wealthy loser* ... More planes will fly, more banners will be seen. Count on it. Have fun with it. Keep watching the skies... (Media Jammers website)

On 30 August, three more suggestive and subversive banners flew simultaneously, also reportedly commissioned by Media Jammers: '9 LOSERS AND 1 WEALTHY LOSER? OR 10 WINNERS?' accompanied by 'LOSERS TALK – HEROES WALK – TOGETHER' and 'THERE IS DIGNITY IN LEAVING'. That day, Media Jammers reiterated their goal; to tell the contestants to 'walk out on this turkey of a production … We state clearly that our ONLY target is CBS/Endemol Entertainment and the production *Big Brother*' (Media Jammers website).

That same evening, the viewing audience voted contestant Brittany off the show. The online fans, especially those who did not like George, attributed Brittany's loss to the 'Save George' corporate and community campaigns and vowed to get retribution. The houseguests, however, were unaware of the campaign by George's supporters to vote Brittany out of the house. The dramatic tension now was the irony of what the viewers on the outside knew that the houseguests on the inside did not know. Would Big Brother tell them? Would the Media Jammers banners tell them? Would they find out? And what would they do if they found out?

## The Megaphone Lady, Brittany's secret and more banners

On 2 September a new character known as The Megaphone Lady unofficially entered the world of *Big Brother*. Kaye Mallory, a Los Angeles school teacher and an active member of the online 'Big Brother Watchers' fan group, had been participating as usual in the discussions and updates on the fan email list when she announced that she was 'getting a bullhorn and going down there to yell messages to them!' Early that evening, Mallory drove as close to the *Big Brother* house as she could get, began shouting through a megaphone: 'Fight *Big Brother*, the editing sucks! We love you guys!'[8] Mallory's cohorts on the *Big Brother* Watchers fan list were ecstatic. A half-hour later Mallory went back to the *Big Brother* house, and shouted: 'You're worth more as a group against Big Brother. If you walk out together, you will be famous!' The *Big Brother* producers promptly called all the houseguests into the house. When Mallory returned home to her computer, she rejoined the discussion on the fan email list about her actions. Although some fans criticised Mallory for interfering where she did not belong, other members of the fan community gave her suggestions for future drive-by shoutings, and many applauded Mallory's initiative in allowing the voice of the fans to penetrate into the world of the *Big Brother* house.

Two days later, Mallory returned to the house to reveal to the houseguests CBS' new plan to revive the flagging audience interest in the show by bribing one of the boring houseguests to leave and then replacing that person with a provocative alternate: 'On Wednesday, Big Brother will offer you money to leave. Don't take the money! It's a trick! Don't take the money! We hate Big Brother! We love you guys! Don't take the money! Fight Big Brother!' Mallory shouted. On her website, Mallory reports on what followed:

As a delightful surprise, Ms. Megaphone was featured as the opening of the Monday night BB show on TV. They even had subtitles so everyone would know what was said. Subsequently, on the live Wednesday show, BB offered them the money, but they'd upped the initial offer to $20,000 and when that was refused, they upped it to $50,000. Nobody took the offer. We're very proud of them for not selling out! … I'm glad the HGs had two days to think about their options. (Mallory's website)

That Wednesday night brought a new twist, a producer-sponsored intervention. Endemol decided to bring banished Brittany, who had been well-liked by everyone in the house, in to the studio and allow her to speak to one of the remaining contestants by phone for two minutes. Josh, her erstwhile love interest on the show, was sent to the Red Room for a private conversation with her. In the days that she had been out of the *Big Brother* house, Brittany had gained a better understanding of the dynamics of the household and the motives of the players. She revealed cryptic pieces of information about the orchestrated campaign to 'Save George', and she told Josh which contestants he should trust. When later questioned by the other houseguests, Josh refused to divulge what he had learned, but he seemed troubled.

The next day, Mallory returned with her megaphone to find security guards patrolling the *Big Brother* lot. When she got the chance, she shouted more information to the houseguests. The following description of her visit on the CBS website reflects a growing corporate attempt to discredit the narrative intrusions by the fans:

> At 9pm PDT, 'Crazy Megaphone Girl' began screaming muddled messages to the houseguests. Each guest listened intently, with the hope of garnering some information from the outside world. Big Brother swiftly sequestered the group. (*Big Brother* official website)

> When Mallory returned to the *Big Brother* house, she was harassed by the security guards, who engaged her in a car chase to try to intimidate her to leave the area and not to return. (Kaye Mallory's website)

In the meantime, new banners had been flying to try to discredit George. The information from the outside world was making all of the houseguests uncomfortable, especially George, who was feeling attacked, and Josh, who had secret knowledge he was afraid to reveal. While tensions rose, the houseguests tried to decipher the fragmented messages from the Megaphone Lady and the banners.

## The climax: the aborted walkout

> Our first project 'Jamming Big Brother' is almost complete. We have interfered with the creative direction of this CBS 'reality' show to the point of altering the outcome and raising awareness of the abuses the producers have committed against the contestants, their families and the viewers of the show. We have done so by introducing outside messages to the contestants who are supposedly cut off from any contact from the outside world. Our most successful tactic has been to fly aerial banners over the 'house' on the CBS studio lot in Los Angeles, with messages encouraging the contestants to walk out or otherwise rebel against the manipulative producers. We have also worked with other groups who have tried to communicate with the contestants through various means including bullhorns and delivery of written messages into the compound. (Media Jammers website)

On Saturday morning, Josh revealed Brittany's 'secret' to George and George called a meeting of all the houseguests. When the houseguests gathered in the kitchen to hear George's plan, the streaming web feeds blacked out for about 10 minutes. CBS/Endemol censored this crucial discussion from the online audience.[9] When the web feeds returned, it was apparent that an empassioned George was trying to convince the others that they should walk out and split the money between them. Influenced by Media Jammers and Mallory, George explained that, 'That thing with the Megaphone Lady, I put it together. Think back to the beginning, and it's obvious ... I'm positive, we all could have been winners long before this. The thing was there all along. We are bigger than the show and they need us ... We are all winners.' Despite some skepticism among the houseguests, many saw the opportunity to make television history by undermining the rules of the game and showing that, as one stated, 'We are more than money' (*Big Brother* official website).

Within forty minutes, all the players agreed that they would walk out together on the following Wednesday, realising that their action would sabotage the show. They also correctly anticipated that the producers would try to talk them out of it. Having made a pact, however, they were proud and self-congratulatory: 'We have decided to make all decisions as a group ... It's about sticking together', said one player. According to George, the information from the Megaphone Lady and the banners helped make the outcome clear.

Endemol Producer John Kalish later remarked that he and the other executive producers, Douglas Ross and Paul Römer, also gathered to watch the 'riveting' actions of George and the other houseguests:

> It was startling. It was engaging, but looking at the reactions of the rest of them is what alerted me to the fact that this was something completely different. This was something that needed to be dealt with. Ultimately, it was a combination of fascination, excitement, and a little bit of concern ... This was the greatest thing that could happen to the show, and yet potentially the most devastating. [We were] living at the edge here. (*Big Brother* official website)

After their decision, the houseguests were riding high on their ebullience. They felt defiant and independent of the control of Big Brother, the producers. They also realised that the world already knew their plans through the programme's web viewers. As they headed outside to toast their decision, Big Brother commanded them to go inside because the Megaphone Lady was back. Defying Big Brother, they stayed in the yard, and Mallory told them to walk tonight, to stick together, not to wait until Wednesday. The producers blasted loud music over the intercom to drown out her words, making it difficult to hear the houseguests as they discussed their walkout. At the same time, all the web feeds switched to empty rooms inside the house, so the online audience could not hear or see what was happening in the courtyard. Once again, the producers successfully implemented an information blackout strategy during a moment of high narrative tension.

After the walkout decision has been made, another batch of airplane banners arrived. Some banners supported the rebellion, while others told the contestants to stay in the house. The houseguests began to realise the magnitude of their decision to leave, and some exhibited misgivings. In the Red Room, the producers explained to individual contestants that if everyone voluntarily walked, they would forfeit the grand prize as well as their weekly stipends. The dialogue between the contestants revealed the clash of value systems that had come into play, between the 'noble' act of defying Big Brother in favour of group solidarity and, on the other hand, the competitive, materialistic desire to stay, play the game, and win the grand prize. When discussing leaving, one contestant commented, 'They will ask us why we came in the first place', to which others replied, 'I think the money is why we all came in the first place, but the game taught us ... that you should not give up control of your integrity or image to someone else.' One added,

> It's an amazing sign of America that the six of us are so different and so cohesive ... If I'm gonna walk, we're showing our integrity, that even though we all need money very bad we are gonna make something bigger than that. To put a message like this to society is worth much more than money.

On Saturday evening, when the houseguests prepared to enter the Red Room as a group to confront the producers, Big Brother made them wait. About 10 minutes later, they were told to come to the living room. At this point, the web feeds were switched to the chicken coops, affecting another blackout of information. Apparently, a group meeting took place during this period when the cameras were not on the houseguests. Soon thereafter, in the Red Room, contestant Jamie had a long but unrecorded discussion with producer John Kalish. When she emerged, she told the others that he said they had 'made a commitment to the people outside who are watching this show to be in the house, and that they are breaking that commitment if they leave'.

About this pivotal conversation, producer Kalish later remarked:

> I thought, this is the moment of truth ... We couldn't let them think they were going to undermine the show or undo us by making this decision. We had to be very strategic in how we were going to respond to it.

So the producers 'called their bluff' and told the houseguests that they were making preparations for them to leave the house. Just as a parent might react to a young child who packs his suitcase and threatens to run away from home, Kalish reportedly told the most gullible contestant Jamie, 'I'm not going to try and change your mind,' just as he planted many doubts in her mind about the wisdom of the decision (*Big Brother* official website).

After the Red Room meeting, Jamie's and Eddie's support for the walkout began to waver. Fellow contestant Curtis encouraged them to stay, astutely explaining that 'I can see John's point of view ... [but] John, however, DOES work for Big Brother.' Similarly, houseguest Cassandra suggested that the 'guy in the Red Room' might not have everyone's best interests at heart.

The following morning, the negotiations continued, as Kalish returned to the control room to continue targeting Jamie. Interestingly, many fans at this time still believed that Endemol and CBS had engineered the whole walkout scenario as a publicity ploy or to trick the contestants, or to play 'mind games' on the viewers. Fans were also divided as to whether the group should stay or leave. Early that afternoon, the houseguests gathered for a final decision. After some negotiation they realised that they were no longer unified. A fan post on the Updates Board summed up the situation exquisitely:

> *Eddie says he came to his senses.*
> *The rest now have changed their minds.*
> *Back to routine.*

The 'revolution' was effectively squelched. Big Brother had maintained control.

## Narrative activism and the exposure of 'reality's' constructedness

The thwarted rebellion by the *Big Brother* contestants was the most dramatically compelling aspect of the series in its first American incarnation. The moment-by-moment suspense of the walkout weekend was especially riveting to the online viewers, who watched the webcast and heard the houseguests wax lyrical about leaving *en masse*, even as they waffled about trading in the chance to win the game (and the prize money) for a moment in television history. The audience that watched only the television programme and not the Internet feeds missed this dramatic arc. Internet viewers were shocked to find that CBS did not feature the planning of the walkout on its Saturday show at all. Only on Monday, when the *Big Brother* household was safely 'back to routine', did CBS air a half-hour recap of the plans for the walkout and its demise.[10]

*Big Brother* spawned a remarkable exhibition of narrative activism, in spite of the producers' attempts to limit contact between the show's participants and the outside world. The emergence of disruptive and narratively subversive elements, both within and beyond the confines of the *Big Brother* house, provides a new model for conceptualising the interactive potential of the new hybrid television/Internet documentary game show genre. *Narrative involvement* by an audience might be considered to be the contribution of audience members to reshaping the narrative in complicity with the programme's producers. This might range from suggestions about plot developments to more activist campaigns to save a programme or protest a particular storyline. In the case *Big Brother*, narrative involvement would include the invitation for viewers to call in to vote on which contestant should be banished from the show. In contrast, *narrative activism* involves audience interventions that contradict the plans or desires of the corporate producers, and change the narrative outcome of a programme. In the case of contrived documentary game shows such as *Big Brother*, both types of narrative intervention are potentially subversive, since producers shape the so-called 'naturally-occurring' actions that produce the narratives even if the programmes are seemingly unscripted. However, it is the documentary aspect of the narrative intervention into *Big Brother* that is the most notable in this situation.

There has been a history of well-documented audience activism regarding dramatic and comedy television series. Letter-writing campaigns and campaigns to boycott advertisers have been used in attempts to save programmes with low ratings but loyal audiences, to attack programmes with values contradicting those of the viewers, and to show other types of support for the quality or nature of certain types of programming. No doubt the responses from such viewers of ongoing series (almost all dramatic, fictional narrative series) have affected the way that producers and writers subsequently shaped the characters and story arcs of the shows to cater to public likes and dislikes (see Brower 1992; D'Acci 1994; Jenkins 1992; Montgomery 1989; Ryan 1991; Seiter *et al*. 1989; Swanson 2000; Hendershot 1999).

However, *Big Brother* is perhaps the first time that viewer activism has intersected with documentary programming in such a way in the history of American television. The nature of reality TV in the past (*Cops*, *Real World*, and so forth), as well as on the concurrent *Survivor*, had been to air episodes of edited documentary action (and I use the term 'documentary' in the loosest sense here) into a completed narrative that had taken place in a more distant past than that of the edited *Big Brother* footage, which was at most 2–3 days old when it aired, and often on the same day. Most importantly, web viewers could watch and hear the events as they were unfolding in the daily lives of the houseguests; viewers could also compare and contrast what they had observed via the web feed to the edited narrative that Endemol/CBS constructed for the nightly broadcasts.

The discrepancies between these two versions of narrative reality created a major source of disgruntlement and discontent for the online fans and other viewers, since they exposed the constructedness of this (as any) documentary narrative in a way never before revealed in an American 'reality' television show. Rarely, if ever, does a documentarian provide an audience with a parallel version with the full, unedited footage, allowing them to see what has been selected and what has been omitted to create the final 'documentary'. We are socialised to believe that documentary and other nonfiction (reality) forms are 'truth'; however, the dual modes of sharing the *Big Brother* happenings created a disjunctive and troubling awareness for many viewers that the two audiences were receiving two different versions of the 'reality' of the lives of the houseguests. *Big Brother*, the multifaceted programme phenomenon, and particularly the existence of both its television version and its online version, had provided opportunities never before seen on television for viewers to see the mechanisms of constructedness behind the editing of so-called documentary and reality shows. The ability of fans to use the Internet not only to follow the moment-by-moment action, but also to organise and mobilise as activists and interventionists, provided a crack in the surface of the network or producer's total control over the television product. In so doing, it inadvertently provided a space through which viewers or fans could actively participate in the very production of the programme and affect its narrative outcome, even (especially) having the opportunity to work towards goals directly at odds with those of the official network and programme producers. In effect, the audience and fans caught the network and its production company off-guard as they appropriated an opportunity to become, to a significant extent, co-producers of the programme's narrative. Ultimately, however, Big Brother (the corporate producers) regained control of the wheel and steered the show back onto its original course.

Narrative activism and media/culture jamming takes the much-discussed concept of interactivity to a new level. Following Mark Dery's theory of culture jamming, we might consider narrative activism an act of social protest in its potential desire not only to subvert the narrative outcome of a television programme, but also to make statements about the media and capitalist globalisation at a larger level. The activist organisation Media Jammers exemplifies this intervention:

> Media Jammers is a grass roots 'culture jamming' organisation created to raise awareness of irresponsibility in the news and entertainment media through high profile stunts, hoaxes and general media mayhem ... We practice and advocate safe, legal means of interfering with media events, taking control of the message and exposing the incompetence, lack of integrity, distortions and abuses of the media, holding them accountable for the consequences. (Media Jammers website)

Oswald remarked in retrospect:

> Our 15 minutes of fame was a lot of fun, and I did enjoy the notoriety. I really liked knowing that we were making network executives sweat. I never thought it would be seen as such an impact on future 'audience interactivity'. I was amazed

at how people were inspired to influence the show after we did our thing. We had control of the direction of the show for a few days, and then others stole our thunder and inspired complete anarchy. (Oswald 2001)

When asked about how the idea for 'jamming' *Big Brother* originated, Oswald replied:

The *Big Brother* project happened because it was just too easy. CBS provided us with all the tools we used to mock them. The live video feeds were crucial to our success. And every time we forced the producers to make a choice, they accommodated us by making the wrong one. It all played to our favour. (Oswald 2001)

The culture jamming of *Big Brother* came from various sources with diverse agendas, some political activists, some fans, some pranksters. The long-term effects of such culture jamming may arguably have been minimal due to the appropriation of the interceptions by the producers and their subsequent integration into the programme's structure, yet the short-term effects were noticeable jolts to the corporate producers and had a profound effect on the behaviours and beliefs of the *Big Brother* participants, effecting the outcome of the programme in numerous ways. In their decentralised efforts to disrupt and subvert the corporate control of the outcome of 'reality' television, even for a short time, the culture jammers provided new insights into the more radical possibilities of challenging the hegemonic control of the media giants by throwing small rocks with their slingshots.

*Notes*

1   See articles by Kronke and Jesdaunun, as well as the related article by Charski. News reports indicated that the AOL-sponsored site was the most highly-visited new Internet site in July of 2000, the month the programme premiered, with more than 4.2 million visitors. Some of the most notable of the reviews and cultural commentaries on the reality TV game show trend in the popular and academic press included articles by Carter, Sheppard, Boal, Poniewozik *et al.*, Rosenbaum, Miller, Rothstein, Wolcott, Sheffield, August *et al.*, Sardar, Podhoretz, Johnson, and Knight. An issue of *Variety* on 25 September 2000 (vol. 380, no. 6) had a number of articles devoted to the spread of 'reality TV' programming in various countries, including the UK, Hungary, Switzerland, South Africa, Argentina, Brazil, the Philippines, Australia, Korea and the US. Also, there was an interesting BBC News-sponsored opinion forum entitled 'Are we turning into Peeping Toms' on 23 July 2000, just after the premiere of both the US and UK versions of *Big Brother*, to which viewers on both sides of the Atlantic (as well as some from Asia) posted their insights (see http://news.bbc.co.uk/hi/english/talking_point/newsid_834000/834731.stm).

2   Many fan sites were internationally based and served as sites for fans of the *Big Brother* series in various countries, such the UK-based Orwell Project (http://www.orwellproject.com) or the Netherlands-based Big Brother Central (http://www.BigBrother2000.org). Others were specifically devoted to serving the audience of the US show.

3   http://bigbrother2000.com or http://webcenter.bigbrother2000.aol.com.

4   For the best literary commentary on the *Big Brother* phenomenon, in a tone

alternately fond, fascinated and scathing, see the series of *Salon* articles at http://www.salon.com/ent/tv/bb/index.html.

5  Graphic designer at ZAP Design in LA. http://www.zapdesign.net/articles/

6  Jeff Oswald, personal correspondence; Big Brother 2000 official website. For information on the grassroots activist Media Jammers organisation, see http://www.mediajammers.org.

7  Letter entitled 'CBS/BB Improprieties' dated 1 September 2000 from 'D I N Only' and posted on an AOL message board, then reposted 3 September 2000 on Joker's Commentary Board by 'Kerry'. The letter writer urged fans to take action against the perceived ethical improprieties.

8  From 'An Interview with Ms. Megaphone', on Kaye Mallory's Ms. Megaphone web page, http://bennyhills.fortunecity.com/billmurray/532/bb/meg-run1.html. The remarks from the Big Brother Watchers fan group can be found in the archives of the Big Brother Watcher egroup, now at http://groups.yahoo.com/group/bigbrotherwatchers.

9  There was a running joke among the online fans that CBS/Endemol would place one or more cameras on the chicken coop in the courtyard, with close-ups on the chickens, whenever the producers did not want the online audience to see or hear some action happening in the house. This move was affectionately dubbed the 'chicken cams' by the fans and recognised as a strategy by the producers to engineer an information blackout. In an interview on the official website, long-time Endemol producer Paul Römer discussed his use of the 'panic button' by which the producers could blackout the online feed. In his earlier European shows, he remarked, he had tried to keep the breaking news off the Internet to 'save' it for the TV show. However, after a while, he realised the advantage of showing most of the action on the web feeds: 'People saw things happening live and they wanted to see what we did with it on television. The moment I would show it on television the Internet side went sky-high because people wanted to see what happens now. I learned there was a mutual benefit. We are not competitors. We were really helping each other – but that's a big change of mindset for a television producer.'

10 For some popular press accounts of the aborted walkout, see articles by Elber, Braxton, Moore, Armstrong and Bianco. Some post-mortems of the US *Big Brother* phenomena included articles by Wyman, Shister, McDaniel and Zerbisias. During the run of the programme, the CBS/AOL website published extensive interviews with several of the Big Brother executive producers, including Paul Römer (24 August 2000), Douglas Ross  (21 September 2000) and John Kalish (13 October 2000), all available at: http://webcenter.bigbrother2000.aol.com/entertainment/NON/.

*Bibliography*

Anon. (2000) 'AOL's Big Brother Website Setting Records in Unprecedented Convergence Between Television and the Internet: Ambitious Alliance Between Popular CBS Television Series and World's Largest Interactive Services Company Sets Webcasting Records as Largest Ongoing Webcast in History', *The Hollywood Reporter*, 18 July. Available at: http://news.excite.com/news/bw/000718/va-america-online

Armstrong, M. (2000) 'Squashing Another 'Big Brother' Revolt', *E! Online*, 11 September. Available at: http://www.eonline.com/News/Items/0.1.7074.00.html?ibd

August, M., J. Chu, R. Dry and K. Earley (2000) 'Reality Bites Back', *Time*, 156, 10, 14

September, 20.

Bianco, R. (2000) 'Brother' Walkout?', *USA Today Online*, 13 September. Available at: http://www.usatoday.com

'Big Brother Strikes Fan Pages!' (2000) *The Orwell Project*, 29 July. Available at: http://www.orwellproject.com/beware.htm

Boal, M. (2000) 'Summer of Surveillance', *Brill's Content*, 3, 5, 66–71, 122–5.

Braxton, G. (2000) '*Big Brother* Guests Threaten Walkout', *Los Angeles Times*, 11 September. Available at: http://www.calendarlive.com/calendarlive/calendar/20000911/t000085524.html

Brower, S. (1992) 'Fans as Tastemakers: Viewers for Quality Television', in L. Lewis (ed.) *The Adoring Audience: Fan Culture and Popular Media*. London: Routledge, 163–84.

Burroughs, W. S. (1998 [1969]) 'My Mother and I Would Like to Know', in B. Rosset (ed.) *The Evergreen Review Reader: 1967–1973*. New York: Four Walls Eight Windows, 234–6.

Carter, B. (2000) 'Television's New Voyeurism Pictures Real-Life Intimacy', *New York Times*, 149 (51283), 30 January, 1.

Charski, M. (2000) 'TV Companion Site Creates Buzz', *Inter@ctive Week*, 7, 28, 17 July, 48.

Cox, D. (2000) 'Notes on Culture Jamming: Spectres of the Spectrum: A Culture Jammer's Cinematic Call to Action'. Available at: http://www.sniggle.net/Manifesti/notes.php

D'Acci, D. (1994) *Defining Women: Television and the Case of Cagney and Lacey*. Chapel Hill: University of North Carolina Press.

DeLuca, K. D. and J. Peeples (2002) 'From Public Sphere to Public Screen: Democracy, Activism, and the "Violence" of Seattle', *Critical Studies in Media Communication*, 19, 2, 125–51.

Dery, M. (1993) 'Culture Jamming: Hacking, Slashing and Sniping in the Empire of Signs', *Open Magazine Pamphlet Series*. Westfield, USA & Amsterdam, Holland.

Downes, S. (2000) 'Hacking Memes'. Available at: http://www.firstmonday.dk/issues/issue4_10/downes/index.html

Elber, L. (2000) 'Big Brother' Members Mull Walkout', Associated Press, 9 September. Available at: http://news.excite.com/news/000909/19/big-brother

Hendershot, H. (1999) *Saturday Morning Censors* ,Durham: Duke University Press.

Jenkins, H. (1992) *Textual Poachers: Television Fans and Participatory Culture,* New York: Routledge.

Jesdaunun, A. (2000) '*Big Brother* Finds Fans Online', Associated Press/Internet (28 September). Available at: http://dailynews.yahoo.com/h/ap/200000928/en/big_brother_Internet_1.html

Johnson, B. D. (2001) 'We Like to Watch', *Maclean's*, 114, 5, 29 January, 56–8.

Klein, N. (1999) *No Logo*. New York: Picador.

Knight, B. A. (2000) 'Watch Me! Webcams and the Public Exposure of Private Lives', *Art Journal*, 59, 4, 21–6.

Kronke, D. (2000) 'Web Interaction on "Big Brother" Could Alter Reality TV', *Miami Herald*, 5 October. Available at: http://www.herald.com/content/tue/entertainment/tv/digdocs/077750.ht

Lasn, K. (1999) *Culture Jam*. New York: Quill.

McDaniel, M. (2000) 'O, Brother; At Last, the End is Near', *Houston* Chronicle, 27

September. Available at: http://www.chron.com/cs/CDA/story.hts/headline/enter-tainment/683555

Media Jammers Website (2000) http://www.mediajammers.org/faq.htm

Miller, E. D. (2000) 'Fantasies of Reality: Surviving Reality-Based Programming', *Social Policy*, 312, 1, 6–16.

Montgomery, K. C. (1989) *Target: Prime Time: Advocacy Groups and the Struggle Over Entertainment Television.* Oxford: Oxford University Press.

Moore, F. (2000) '*Big Brother* Walkout Flops', Associated Press, 13 September. Available at: http://news.excite.com/news/ap/000913/22/ent-big-brother

Munford, P. (2000) 'How Nasty Nick united two worlds', *Guardian* Unlimited, 21 August. Available at: http://www.guardian.co.uk/Archive/Article/0,4273,4053643.html

Nielsen/NetRatings (2000) 'Media, Reality Sites Favored', *Lycos News* (18 July). Available at: http://news.lycos.com/headlines/Technology/Internet/article.asp?docid=RTNET-WEB-AUDIENCE-DC&date=20000718

Oswald, J. (2001) 'Personal correspondence', 28 February 2001.

Pinsker, B. (2000). 'Big Brother Surfaces as Fan Site is Chased Off the Web', *Inside.com News*, 17 July. Available at: http://www.inside.com/story/Story_Cached/0,2770,6909_11,00.html

Podhoretz, J. (2000) '*Survivor* and the End of Television', *Commentary* 110, 4, November, 50–2.

Poniewozik, J. *et al*. (2000) 'We Like to Watch', *Time*, 155, 26, 26 June, 56–63.

Rosenbaum, S. (2000) 'Peeping Tom TV: The beginning of the end or the birth of meaningful media?', *Television Quarterly*, 31, 2–3, 53–6.

Rothstein, E. (2000) 'TV Shows in Which the Real is Fake and the Fake is Real', *New York Times* (5 August), B11.

Ryan, C. (1991) *Prime Time Activism: Media Strategies for Grassroots Organizing.* Boston: South End Press.

Sardar, Z. (2000) 'The Rise of the Voyeur', *New Statesman*, 13, 630, 6 November, 25–8.

Seiter, E. *et al*. (eds) (1989) *Remote Control: Television, Audiences and Cultural Power.* London: Routledge.

Sheffield, R. (2000) 'Reality', *Rolling Stone*, 849, 14 September, 138.

Sheppard, R. (2000) 'Peeping Tom Television', *Maclean's*, 113, 15, 10 April, 58–62.

Shister, G. (2000) 'Lack of Sexual Chemistry Hurt "Big Brother", Producer Says', *Kansas City Star Online* (28 September). Available at: http://www.kcstar.com/item/pages/fyi.pat?file=fyi/3774cb5a.928

Soukup, M. (2000) '*Big Brother* Mutiny Brewing! (And that's just one of the many developments CBS is censoring from its much-hyped "Reality TV" Series)', *Salon*, 22 August. Available at: http://www.salon.com/ent/tv/feature/2000/08/22/bb_web/index.html

Swanson, D. C. (2000) *The Story of Viewers for Quality Television: From Grassroots to Prime Time.* Syracuse: Syracuse University Press.

Wolcott, J. (2000) 'Now Voyeur', *Vanity Fair*, 481, September, 128–32.

Wyman, B. (2000) 'Who Screwed Up "Big Brother"? Everyone', Salon, 29 September. Available at: http://www.salon.com/ent/tv/feature/2000/09/29/bb_final/print.html

Zerbisias, A. (2000) '*Big Brother* Made Reality TV Real', *Toronto Star*, 29 September. Available at: http://www.thestar.com/editorial/entertainment/20000929ENT11b_EN-ZERBTV.html

# CHAPTER 15

*Janet Jones*

# EMERGING PLATFORM IDENTITIES
## Big Brother UK and Interactive Multi-platform Usage

> Just as inclusivity of the electric age is shown in its destruction of old power arrangements, so it is displayed in the new character of knowledge required to grasp what is happening. (McLuhan 1969: 34)

### 'Power' to the audience

The broadcasting industry in the UK is moving into a world of digital plenty leaving behind a far more comfortable and predictable world of analogue scarcity. Simultaneously it is attempting to reshape its relationship with audiences with integrated interactive content. As the computer and television consoles in our homes merge and become exponentially more powerful, television executives are increasingly looking to interactivity to woo promiscuous audiences.

This longitudinal study of *Big Brother* audiences is part of a larger and dominant critical concern to understand the impact of a developing multi-media culture and the interplay between interactivity, media convergence and hybridity. Changes in the technical landscape bring a new complexity of production processes constructing innovative relationships between producers, texts and audiences. As these new relationships are being forged then it becomes necessary for media scholars to investigate the emerging psychology of audience interaction. The study of *Big Brother*, an interactive reality media event stripped across a multitude of platforms, allows us to delve into the detail of how these new media products are being received by audiences.

Some futurists glamorise the potential of iTV (interactive television) suggesting that technology has the power to transform individual viewer's preferences and behaviour to such an extent that television as a social and cultural force that we know today will disappear. John Hartley (1996, 2002) talks of the new DIY media consumer where audiences not just use up the product, but work on it and add value to it. Henry Jenkins (1992) has investigated this area in terms of fans reworking, rewriting and transforming the text, but he also stresses the importance of interactivity across platforms:

> Reality television has become the testing ground by which the media companies experiment with new approaches to marketing and consumer relations. Reality TV is also the space where consumers get the chance to test new ways of interacting with media content. In fact, the media 'convergence' that has been so long predicted for the better part of the last decade is here right now – and reality television shows us what it looks like. (Jenkins 2003: 2)

Research on the way audiences use iTV is still in its infancy and the purpose of this study is to contribute to a growing body of work that is committed to developing a new analytical framework underpinning these new communication products and their users.

I designed this audience research to probe into how important the interactivity created through converging media was to the success of *Big Brother* UK. As Jenkins suggests, reality TV is a format that has proven its ability to mobilise and engage audiences interactively across a number of different delivery platforms. This internationally franchised series has shown that is can successfully engage the audience with a combination of liveness, interactivity and immersion (or event management). When different media (Broadcast, Internet, Interactive TV, mobile SMS and MMS, tabloid narratives, landline phone, and so on) are used congruently, they combine in interesting ways. *Big Brother* has been successful because it has effectively mimicked contemporary patterns of media use especially amongst 15–30-year-olds. *Big Brother* is a prototype acknowledging the teleology of youth consumers with their techno-embracing patterns of media use and this study attempts to quantify just how meaning is constructed across these different platforms by exploring some of the implications of user control over content and the emerging identities of the new interactive media platforms. It uses quantitative and qualitative data from a web-based questionnaire linked to *Big Brother*'s web site in 2000, 2001 and 2002 to map the emerging use culture associated with multi-platform interactivity. This newly created audience mobility, I argue, is particularly attractive in reality TV formats allowing audiences to customise their viewing behaviour and to develop strategies for watching that cater to a sense of authorship and control over the content.

## Interactive commercial potential

Finding the interactive audience in the UK is not only a commercial proposition but a political one too. Digital penetration in British households is rising steadily and it is possible that a large majority of households will receive their media digitally through broadband, satellite or cable by the 2010. The UK government hopes that the impending analogue switch-off (freeing up valuable frequencies for mobile phone networks) will force UK residents to divest themselves of the coat hangers and soggy bits of string commonly used to receive analogue signals from local transmitters and invest *en masse* in digital consoles. As of June 2003, ten million homes (40 per cent of the population) had digital television:

> The commercial question centres on just how quickly, if at all, consumers are likely to move from a more *single track* viewing environment to one in which there is an expectation of interactivity and control over the medium. The future of iTV depends in part on today's 15–24-year-olds, the leading edge of the interactive consumer market. Young audiences spend more time gaming than watching television and are learning to habituate themselves towards media interactivity. The industry hopes that they might provide a catalyst for a dramatic shift in consumption. (ITC 2003)

The aim of packaging and cataloguing an audience for interactive television is not just to deliver advertising revenue, the key to making money in the multi-platform media age is to encourage us all to participate in what is now called the 'return path' economy. Revenue is collected by convincing audiences – or more appropriately, *interactive consumers* – to respond to a variety of stimuli. Every phone call made, text message sent and television remote control vote cast, nets the producer a small income. Media events that harness the power of all media such as *Big Brother* and more recently *Pop Idol* have shown that they can attract up to eight million return path interactions (votes) in one evening.[1]

## Research methodology

A self-reporting questionnaire (linked to the *Big Brother* website for 24 hours each year) was central to the research process. To generate both quantitative and qualitative data both open questions encouraging one sentence or short paragraph answers and closed (tick box) questions were used. Over 30,000 responses were received over the three years and this had the advantage of a large data pool that could then be easily interrogated providing a statistically meaningful quantitative tool for analysis. We also had thousands of short written statements from the respondents, varying in length from 20 words to 300 words that provided the core of our qualitative data.

Self-reporting questionnaires alone are a blunt tool and perhaps not an entirely satisfactory method of detailed audience interrogation (only those who had access to the web could complete this questionnaire). However, in support of the data I found that the web-based demographic profile was largely consistent with Channel 4's broadcast audience profile although the skew that a web based questionnaire would normally generate was quite evident with fewer older respondents and a greater concentration of younger viewers. Also, the fact that this audience questionnaire reached only those interested enough in the programme to surf the Channel 4 website and spend 20 minutes answering a questionnaire, allowed us to study specific fan attitudes towards the multi-platform viewing experience. At the very least it enabled a clear focus on *regular* and *repeated* viewing attitudes, thus making it possible to get data on how viewers actually *dealt with* (rather than glanced at) the show.

## iTV – an oxymoron?

The industry definition of iTV is 'a mechanism for allowing viewers to influence and control programmes or content in a natural or intuitive way making them feel they are part of the television experience' (Good 2001). In fact Peter Bazalgette, the executive producer of *BigBrother* UK, suggested that *Big Brother* was the first genuinely democratic media product because it privileged its audience with the power of interactivity and control in a way that no other programme had ever done in the past (Bazalgette 2000). The houseguests were allowed the free run of the cage, but the cage was (ostensibly) under the audience's control. Certainly there was a real move towards putting viewers in the driving seat by allowing them unprecedented access to the broadcast rushes through the web and interactive television and giving them a say as to how the saga might end. The intention was to enhance the viewing experience through an expectation of ownership over the narrative.

At a human level interactive communication is personified by face-to-face communication but this organic process is complicated when applied to media technologies. No matter how many interactive features are incorporated into a specific technology it cannot hope to capture the richness and spontaneity of face-to-face communication (Kim & Sawhney 2003: 219). Thus, one might argue that machine interactivity can be seen as a mirage or a delusion.

Heinz Pegels asserts that an ideal interactive network should have no top or bottom but a plurality of connections that increase the possible interactions between components of the network leaving the user free to choose his or her own centre of investigation and experience. It is important, in his view, that there should be no particular organisation or hierarchy embedded within the network (Pegels, cited in Landow 1992: 13–25).

Pyungho Kim and Harmeet Sawhney believe that there is an irreconcilable contradiction between the economic models of television and interactive media because true interactivity involves empowerment of its users (Kim & Sawhney 2003: 223). They argue that interactivity is inevitably artificially grafted onto television without taking into consideration that any commercial system is inherently a hierarchical, centralised and closed network system (Kim & Sawhney 2003: 226). Pamela Wilson concurs with this view concluding that *Big Brother*'s format only allows for a very limited and ritualised degree of audience participation in the narrative (Wilson 2004). Her article in this volume describes what happened when there was a real threat to the power of the producer, personified in this instance by *Big Brother*. Wilson's story lends credence to Kim and Sawhney's assertion that iTV, in its commercial form, is essentially an oxymoron whereby the producer cannot secede the locus of control and thus, the balance of power cannot strictly shift from the centre to the periphery and we must disagree with Bazalgette's definition of this phenomenon as a 'truly democratic media product'. If so, then almost any form of interactivity within the television environment might be construed as inherently subversive. It may be true, to an extent, that interactivity is simply channelled for the commercial benefit of the producer leaving little room for anarchic responses on behalf of the users, however I feel we need to undertake a deeper analysis and broaden our definition of interactivity and audience agency to begin to understand the way that audiences make meaning in their engagement with iTV.

If meaning is centred on reception, content has to be modified on reception. This inevitably involves a degree of anarchy, but the question is how much disruption can be introduced into the system before it weakens the centre unacceptably. Users may need to be allowed to bypass the intermediaries on occasions. Industry's biggest fear is the emergence of an uncontrollable, fragmented, open and unlimited diversity of interactive messages. For this reason producers may need to control and limit the scope and nature of interactivity (ITC 2003).

## The Big Brother interactive game board

Within the *Big Brother* game/documentary framing, the game board is consciously set up with the viewer at the centre of the activity. There are many opportunities built into the format that allow viewers to engage in some way in the narrative. For example, they can vote to exclude houseguests, suggest tasks for them to do and control the webcams through their PCs. Access to the house is possible 24 hours a day, seven days a week and this allows the audience to experience a sense of control over its viewing. The audience-gaming conditions are not always explicit but there does appear to be prevailing patterns in understanding and meaning-making on behalf of the audience.

The most significant of these implicit game rules can be demonstrated through the following data. One important rule can be evidenced by the viewers' response to the question, 'I think the winner should be the person who is true to themselves'.

Figure 1
I think the winner should be the person who is true to themselves
(N=8177: 2001 survey)

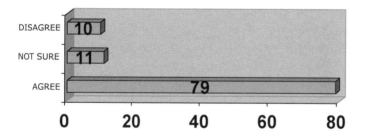

The large number of people who believed this statement to be true suggests that this audience values highly the person who appears to be the most genuine and does not put on a performance. This would suggest that the vast majority of these respondents needed to be given the confidence to gauge the apparent authenticity of each contributor. The viewers must feel that they are positioned as judge and juror to successfully referee the actions of the houseguests in order to spot what they regard as 'false' behaviour. Thus, the game board has to provide access to the houseguests in a way that reassures the viewer that this is possible. If the gaming conditions are right, viewers should be confident that houseguests cannot elude the reality net. The data in Figure 2 supports this.

Despite the obvious 'game setting', it is also interesting to note that respondents were not happy with the idea of the *houseguests* 'playing the game' as evidenced in Figure 3.

Figure 2
I think it is impossible for the housemates to fake it all the time for the cameras
(N=8177: 2001 survey)

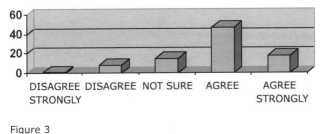

DISAGREE DISAGREE NOT SURE  AGREE   AGREE
STRONGLY                            STRONGLY

Figure 3
I think the winner should be the person who ...
(N=8177: 2001 survey)

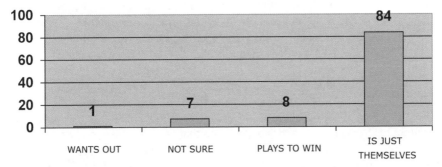

It appears that in order for the viewers to get 'pore close' to these subjects then they must believe, despite the artificial environment, that they are witnessing the 'real' person and are largely intolerant of any sign of 'game-playing' on behalf of the houseguests as this would make it more of a charade and less of a reality TV experience. Certainly, the UK winners so far have been those characters scoring the highest on the personality indexes 'honest' and 'sincere'. The following table indicates which descriptive characteristics came up most frequently in relation to houseguests' personalities (2000 survey).

| 8 most common reasons for liking a character | 8 most common reasons for disliking a character |
|---|---|
| level-headed | has ulterior motives/two-faced |
| straight forward | manipulative/scheming |
| normal-seeming | dull and boring |
| observer rather than a player | fake personality |
| honest and down to earth | unattractive |
| genuine | fawning |
| seems real | plays game too well |

Table 1

Given that the format allows the audience to sit in judgement of the actuality, it is important to assess how essential the multi-platform, interactive, live and immersive elements were to this perception of witnessing reality. The study of genre hybridity also features strongly in the way audiences negotiate their relationship with the footage (see Jones 2003).

## The caché of 'liveness'

Television trades on its 'liveness', with implied associations between 'liveness' and 'realness'. Yet television is temporally messy and often deceptive. Many formats such as news, current affairs and game shows all encourage a high degree of temporal fudging, attempting to foster the illusion of 'liveness' and immediacy – the caché of instantaneity. There is often quite a deliberate attempt at deception. For example, *Who Wants to be a Millionaire* employs script devices that encourage the viewer to believe that they are watching the show live even though it is usually pre-recorded. I call this façade 'live-ish' presentation, where the script deliberately fakes the time of recording to synchronise with the time of transmission. It also changes its tenses to accommodate this impression.[2] *Big Brother*'s E4 and web output is also 'live-ish'. There is a fifteen-minute delay built into the 'live' feeds on E4 and the web with a team of people employed to edit out anything that is legally or morally unacceptable. In a 21-hour period, Channel 4 reported that over 1300 edits had been made to the supposedly 'live' output.[3] John Corner calls this type of viewer deception 'cognitive and emotional fraud' (Corner 2002) and it contributes to the hermeneutics of suspicion that have recently grown around the reality TV formats. Despite the live-ish quality of its E4 and web output, the perception of witnessing a live event had a noticeable impact on the reception of *Big Brother* UK.

Figure 4
How important is it that you can see events live in the Big Brother house?
(N=12,340: 2002 Survey)

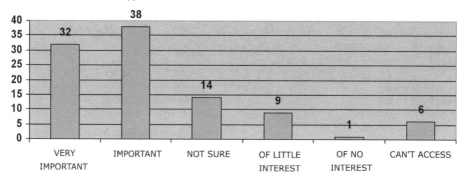

This quantitative data strongly confirms the expectation that access to live actuality contributes to the fan's appreciation of this format. The quantitative data below suggests exactly why this might be. The following comments are reflective of the majority of respondents who valued the ability to see events in the house live.

- I would feel badly cheated if it wasn't live.
- It has become part of life to see what they are up to in between TV shows.
- It would not seem real if I couldn't view it 24/7. I like to view as events happen.

- I like to see things happen as they happen not being edited to portray someone in a bad way.
- It's important that they [the houseguests] never think they are off the hook.
- Watching pre-recorded stuff wouldn't be the same.
- Well seeing as I get a totally different picture from the highlights programmes as I do the live programmes, it would seem unreal without the live feeds.
- It wouldn't seem real without the live show because it would be like a normal television show not a reality show.
- Live footage really lets the viewers see the houseguests' true personalities.
- It wouldn't work without the live stuff because who knows what's happening when the cameras are off.
- At least with continuous live footage you are left to draw your own opinions. Editing can be very manipulative – particularly if a whole day's footage is reduced to one thirty-minute show.
- When they show the highlights on Channel 4 they don't show you what really happened. They sometimes make things look different than what it was.
- It would feel more like a soap if the live stuff wasn't available.

In summary, the primary reasons given to highlight the importance of 'liveness' relate to:

i) user control and empowerment
ii) a distrust of the producer's version
iii) a feeling of deprivation if anything should happen in the house 'behind closed doors'
iv) breaking the implicit 'reality contract' or gaming rules if live access were to be denied (see the following section for a detailed analysis)
v) an enhanced viewing pleasure from the perceived sharing of temporality with the houseguests

There is also a minority view expressed by those who feel that the sense of 'reality' does not depend on 'liveness' (reflective of approximately 10 per cent of the population of respondents who disagreed or strongly disagreed with the question posed in figure four).

- I didn't watch any of the live feeds during season one and it still felt real. If anything, knowing that a live feed isn't actually live (there's a delay of 20 minutes or so) makes it feel like it's being censored.
- Seeing it live doesn't make it more believable. The recorded show is just as believable.
- I do not have access to E4 and it does seem real to me.
- I have no interest in sitting watching people doing nothing and would rather have the highlights which makes for more interesting viewing.

The reasons used to minimalise the importance of 'liveness' can thus be summarised under the following general categories:

- I have no access and still enjoy the show so 'liveness' couldn't be important.

- I enjoy the 'producer's cut' or 'edited highlights' and I don't want to waste time with the raw event.
- It's not live anyway so, why bother?

## That chicken's dead

*Shipwrecked* (2001), a pre-shot survival-based reality TV programme filmed on a remote island, featured a famous moment where one of the characters was seen strangling a chicken. Later it transpired that the scene had to be 'set-up' for the cameras, because, although the incident really did happen, the cameras had not been pointing in the right direction and had failed to capture the original event. The producers chose to re-stage the death of the chicken because it was a valuable photo-opportunity. When this story was leaked, it tarnished the reputation of the show's 'reality' status. The participant involved was later interviewed and revealed her reaction to the decision to recreate the death of the chicken: 'I had to get into the bikini I was in that day. I had to try and act out the positions I was in, act surprised, act disgusted, and I remember watching the show back later and thinking, that chicken's alive!'[4] She also admitted that, 'there was a director and a lot of the times we had to be told what to talk about'. When confronted with these challenges to the authenticity of the footage, the executive producer remarked:

> I'm not sure that these programmes can ever show participants as they really are. The rules and situations that they have to deal with ensure that they give us, and the producers, a performance but not reality. What we do is give people a situation to perform in an unscripted way. I think that this is what disting-uishes reality TV from documentary. I think audiences realise that this is a totally fabricated situation we put them in and we ask them to perform in a way that is entertaining television and they do that knowingly. (Think TV, 21 June 2002)

The corollary with an improvised stage production is interesting. There are also times in *Big Brother* when the fans are totally immersed in the narrative unfolding and participate in it like a Greek chorus. This is most obvious when houseguests are expelled from the house at weekly interviews and a live audience is primed to greet them with posters, banners, cheers and boos. Lisa, a housemate voted out during the fourth UK *Big Brother* season, commented on how it felt to be on the receiving end of the crowd's hostility: 'It was an incredible feeling coming out of the house to a chorus of boos. They booed me but they tried to shake my hand and said they loved me, they loved my character.' Here, the audience is performing a role written for them. It is an interactive, live ritual, acted-out on the film set. The tabloids framed Lisa as a villain: cast her in that mould, and the audience performed the part that was expected of them. They became a conscious part of the spectacle. This aspect of the narrative was artificially synthesised, constructed by a hostile press and some exaggerated editing, but this hounding of houseguests (common to all territories in which *Big Brother* has aired) is an important part of the live audience ritual or gaming technique. The distancing from the original factual premise in favour of a degree of 'fabrication' now requires audiences to interact with a very different set of expectations.

So what makes it all right for *Big Brother* to ask its audiences to knowingly play a synthetic role scripted for them by the tabloid press while it is not appropriate for the producers of *Shipwrecked* to shoot fabricated situations for broadcast? I believe that in the latter an implicit reality contract with the audience was broken, and in the former gaming rules were established and accepted. The dead chicken fiasco forced audiences to adopt a frame that privileged the 'performative'. This had an alienating effect for viewers whose primary satisfaction comes from experiencing 'the real' in this form of reality TV. *Big Brother*'s appeal, however, is multi-dimensional. It appears to be able to simultaneously exploit the caché of 'liveness' and the premise of artificiality which I explore in the following section.

## Hypermediacy and the aesthetics of Big Brother

Jay David Bolter and Richard Grusin's definitions of *immediacy* and *hyper-mediacy* are useful when analysing the relationship between *Big Brother* and its audience. Immediacy is where the medium is downplayed in order to achieve the effect of transparency and realism, and hyper-mediacy is where the medium is fore-grounded and draws attention to its own artificiality (Bolter & Grusin 1999: 42). Docu-soaps partially maintained their link to the traditional documentary construct, relying on conventional single camera, field-directing techniques. *Big Brother,* however, pushed the factual envelope consciously into the domain of constructedness (Corner 2002). In the wake of false claims on reality, what better antidote than a programme that makes the set up so transparent that it features the cameras as icons in the introductory credits. Its very constructedness is part of the attraction (see Jones 2003).

*Big Brother* oscillates successfully between immediacy and hyper-mediacy. The realism, so necessary for a successful relationship between viewer and housemate, is achieved in a hyper-mediated environment with the format deliberately drawing attention to its artificial premise by foregrounding the camera's presence. This effectively alerts viewers to how the illusion of reality is created. The introduction of a sporting element combined with the intimacy of vicarious living and highly sophisticated casting in the *Big Brother* house provided an appealing combination of documentary, game show and soap opera. Hence the text deals with genre in a playful fashion, drawing attention to itself in the process and forcing the viewer into a postmodern interpretation by characterising relationships between viewer, contributor and producer in a reflexive mode of inter-textuality. Traditional interpretative frames are missing and new ones imposed. I argue that the hyper-mediated environment is aided by access to alternative platforms or viewing modes that promote different forms of interaction and audience engagement. Bolter and Grusin suggest that two styles can comfortably co-exist within one story-world. The representation can effectively oscillate between immediacy and hyper-mediacy, between transparency and opacity. I believe that, for *Big Brother*, these styles not only sit comfortably side-by-side but they are essential to the success of the format and feed off each other with the hyper-mediated style being associated more with the 'new' and interactive media. Hyper-mediation is particularly connected to the aesthetics of the world wide web (Bolter & Grusin 1999: 19), but is also increasingly connected with the aesthetics of iTV.

## The fear of mediation

Video streams (delivered live through the web and iTV) are apparently unmediated with no obvious producer intervention. Yet they are surrounded by a very sophisticated layer of textual packaging in a magazine format that can be accessed in harmony with the live video streams. Findings from this research indicated that overall the web's attractiveness was its timeliness, its absence of mediation and its strong association with reality or indexicality. It provided a window on the world, a photo-realistic representation suggesting transparency and immediacy. Historically, webcam-based media products have been associated with surveillance imagery and low-grade images denoting a direct relationship between what is in front of the camera's lens and its transmitted representation. This new popular visual demotic came to signify essential truthfulness in the 1980s and 1990s. A significant test of the importance of this unique platform came in the 2000 series of *Big Brother* UK when the houseguest Nicholas Bateman was found to be cheating, playing one member of the house off against another, and was asked to leave in disgrace through the back door. This was well-timed to the midway point of the run and generated the highest audience figures for Channel 4 in its twelve-year history. Interest was galvanised through the web and mobile phone network and for the first time viewers were treated to the drama unfolding live, watching it wherever they could find the nearest computer screen. Viewers' mobile phones had alerted them to events taking place in house. Mark Lawson, writing in the *Guardian*, reflected on the drama of Nick's eviction, 'People were huddled excitedly together around a tiny unreliable image. In a quite unexpected way, the future of television has turned out be a mirror of its distant past.'

During the first season of *Big Brother* UK (2000) my research showed that while relatively few people actually spent time viewing webcams, the fact that they could was more important. It acted as a safety net, a way of checking the veracity of the producer's cut. In subsequent seasons iTV via satellite became available with high picture resolution and perfect sound quality. This study tracked the subsequent viewer shift from web-streams to E4 making iTV the new medium of choice through which to view 'liveness'. At this point, 'liveness' broke free from its association with low-quality images and became synonymous with the 'feeling' that comes with material that is 'live to air'. Viewers experience this through an implicit understanding of 'liveness' as distinct from pre-recorded and pre-edited material or 'the producer's cut' as described below.

The grammar of traditional televised narratives is connected to what is commonly known as 'time compression'. Television viewers are accustomed to stories being formulated for them and these stories are almost always the product of single-camera direction. This means that there is one camera (usually out in the field) that is required to capture the dynamic of the moment. Inevitably this leads to fudging the time line in the pursuit of a clear and watchable narrative, and the edit suite is the place where the filmmaker is able to condense and package that moment. The illusion of a continuous real-time event is built up through an acceptable abbreviated form encompassing well-established industry directing techniques. For these *Big Brother* respondents, however, temporality, or the need/desire to share the same temporal space, is critical to the user's sense of 'the real' and the indexical value of the image is in inverse proportion to the degree that the medium *obviously* takes over. For example, one respondent summed his feelings up like this:

> BB seems easier to live with. It's on all the time, there's no escaping it. Because of this you get to 'know' the people better in an 'everyday' (as far as possible) situation such as sunbathing, eating, rather than being 'on camera'.

The following comments are typical of a majority of respondents who valued access to live feeds (see figure four). There is a notable desire expressed to experience the real through 'liveness' *and* a shared time zone:

- It wouldn't seem as real without the E4 coverage as it lets you watch in real time, for example when you wake up in the morning, they're waking up and when you have lunch they have lunch.
- It's almost more ordinary being able to see the boring bits, more realistic and it seems less directed. Watching the highlights is just the most exciting bits of the day.
- They do nothing on a Sunday morning too! Watching the live feeds gives you the feeling that it really is a challenge to stay in the house for as long as they do.
- It's far better for the viewer to be able to see things going on as they are happening.
- I like BB more because it's happening at the time you watch not like *Survivor* where it is pre-recorded.

*Big Brother* is broadcast 24 hours a day, seven days a week for the entire run in 'real time'. Its temporality signifies an authenticity that implicitly denotes accuracy. Twenty-six static and mobile cameras ensure the best seat in the house for the web and iTV audience. The ability that E4 and the Internet provides to select what room and character to follow provides an important sense of audience agency in this regard. The perception is that of uncontrolled action, no time compression and a lack of obvious mediation. As Jonathan Steur suggests, 'telepresence' and 'vividness' are crucial ingredients of interactivity; real-time interaction and the immediacy of response are vital for creating vivid interactive media environments.

## That live chicken 'feels real'

In the UK, the 1990s saw a preponderance of personalised narratives on television. Audiences worldwide became transfixed with watching the daily lives of their countrymen on televised in a dizzying array of docu-soaps.[5] This form of populist documentary established many of the conventions later integrated into *Big Brother* (Dovey 2000). These were typified by foregrounding the personal, emphasising performance with a reliance on a soap-style narrative. Yet, the docu-soap's popularity waned in the UK in the late 1990s as the production techniques were exposed as synthetic with viewers losing faith in the format's ability to present more than just the illusion of intimacy between contributor and viewer (Jones 2000; 2003). Thus *Big Brother* was well-poised to capture the *zeitgeist* rendering the search for authenticity and personalised narratives more apparently accessible.

One main advantage of this format is evidenced in data collected on the audience's relationship with the live production elements. The data show that the option of viewing the rushes live is an important condition in satisfying the audience's need to 'judge' the authenticity of the contestants on *Big Brother*. I have also been able to establish that the medium of choice for 'liveness' switched from web-streams to iTV as the series went into its third season. This is evident in the data provided in figures five, six and seven overleaf.

In 2001 (Season 2) iTV penetration was still relatively low, yet there was a relatively high dependence on live web-streaming.

Figure 5

Do you think Big Brother would have seemd real without access to the house on the web? (N=12,340: 2002 survey)

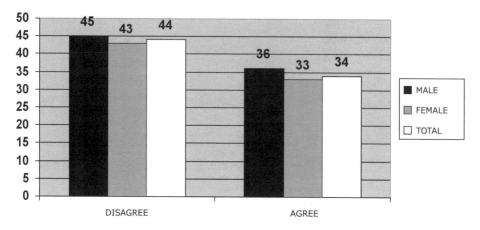

Here 44 per cent of the respondents said they depended on the web to verify the television version's claim on reality. The fact that they could watch the rushes, albeit on a small and low-grade screen, gave them confidence in their own ability to negotiate their relationship with the houseguests. However, 34 per cent did not feel that access to the live webcast was required to give the actuality a degree of authenticity. The following table shows responses to a question about how our informants differentiate between the benefits of the web compared to the broadcast cut.

| Top 5 Reasons for Watching on the Web (in ascending order) | Top 5 Reasons For Watching on terrestrial television (in ascending order) |
| --- | --- |
| Keeps me up-to-date | Addictive |
| Because it's live | Entertaining |
| Sneak preview | Diary Room |
| Because it's uncut/unedited | More real than soaps |
| Seems more real | I'm nosey |

Table 2

A year later, in 2002, the live web feeds were subscription-only and relatively expensive and the web platform had taken on a new profile. Our repondents reported that they were using the web in the following ways:

ii) to interact with text elements/magazine summaries like a print source or almanac
ii) to utilise it as a type of archive news resource. Searching for information about certain characters in typographic detail. Effectively answering the question – 'I know the story so far but how did we get here?'

iii) for those who could afford the subscription charge they were using the interactive video enhancements such as the fancam (follow your favourite houseguest around for the day) or the pancam (control the camera with your keyboard to place your gaze in the direction of your choice)

This view was confirmed by the trends apparent in this longitudinal survey. For example, when my respondents were questioned in 2002 about their motivations for web-viewing, the profile had changed considerably from 2001.

Figure 6
I enjoy viewing the webcams to double check that the edited highlights (broadcast each evening) are a true reflection of the events in the house (N=12,340: 2002 Survey)

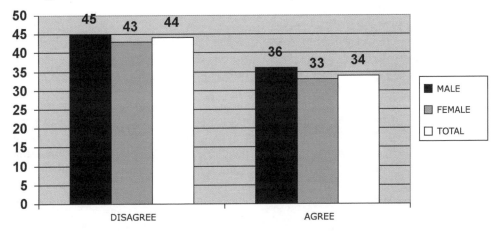

Here we see a reversal of the pattern of usage from the previous year. In a single year, the web platform had changed its profile. This was no longer the medium that fans went to first to experience 'liveness' and immediacy. This role had been usurped by iTV (E4) as shown in the following chart.

Figure 7
I enjoy watching E4 interactive to see the real events unfold live (N=12,340: 2002 Survey)

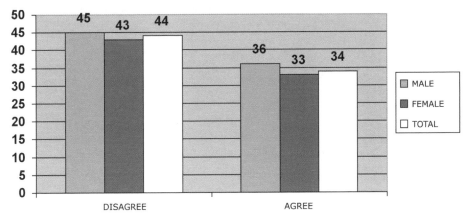

Here we see that the indexicality associated with web-cam viewing had been partially displaced by the iTV platform. It should be noticed that this was also a convenient commercial strategy employed by the producers to improve the ratings for E4 where advertising revenue could be maximised.

I would conclude that there is still a high degree of fluctuation in the process of new media platforms acquiring meaning, but, viewers are assigning qualities to the platforms that allow them to begin the process of mapping expectations associated with these new media products. In 2002 my *Big Brother* respondents were using E4 to police the broadcaster's cut and the web was performing a newly distinctive function as archive, magazine, specialist interactive tool (customised and expensive) and official chat room.

## Multi-platform reality

Because viewers can choose how they consume this programme, this naturally invites them to make comparisons between platforms. This section investigates how viewers' expectations of the real are constructed to accommodate each discrete platform. The act of making platform comparisons encourages the audience to analyse its own viewing behaviour and motivations. The reality factor, as we have noted previously, is crucial to the success of this media product. Yet many viewers were quick to point out that the broadcast programmes were far from real when compared to the live feeds. In fact a reality hierarchy developed as the relative veracity of different platforms was compared.

Responding to questions, viewers typically stated that access to the raw footage gave them a feeling of control over the programme that was unique to *Big Brother*. They took pleasure in policing not only the activities of the houseguests but also the way the producers edited the material.

I argued earlier that the docu-soap format had lost some of its claim on the real after the audience lost faith in its essential truth claims and began viewing it as largely artificial (see Hill 2002). In relation to *Big Brother,* docu-soaps and 'broadcast-only' reality TV programmes are arguably one-dimensional with only a single broadcast window available, no access to 'liveness' and no opportunity for interaction with the characters or control over the narrative. Given that the *Big Brother* format offers a variety of windows on actuality, it is interesting to see how important these were to the programme's fans. In theory, the web viewer, or interactive television viewer, was watching genuine, unedited events unfolding and the following data shows that this fan audience depended quite heavily on the alternative platforms.[6]

As this was a web-based survey, one might expect a higher proportion than average would choose the internet option. It is interesting, however, to see such relatively high percentage for E4 digital, given that the penetration of Digital television was approximately 30 per cent when this data was gathered. Once E4 came on stream in 2001 the lure of a broadcast-quality signal pulled many away from the Internet in favour of a cleaner picture with 12 per cent claiming to have abandoned watching *Big Brother* on the web in favour of E4, although 24 per cent told me that they continued watching both. The number of video streams on the web went down in 2002 as the E4 interactive option gained popular exposure.

The attractiveness of the E-4 transmission from those who chose it as their first choice platform:

| First Choice Platform | Percentage Response First Choice Platform | Reasons Given |
|---|---|---|
| Channel 4 terrestrial edited highlights and live eviction shows | 41 per cent (still the first choice, but only 4 per cent higher than the Internet) | Very high mediation (packaging of event included voice over, highlight editing with graphics and music) High entertainment value. Low temporality (usually displaced by at least 24 hours). Visual input (a great deal of variety in imagery and clear framing of the event through contextualisation and storytelling) |
| The web subscription-based live feeds surrounded by archive text, news flashes and chat rooms | 37 per cent (the magazine format, chat rooms and hypertext were useful elements of this platform aiding in the immersion process. The web had acquired a 'catch-up' quality that iTV could not rival) | Low perceived mediation for the video element. Very high shared temporality. Ability to interact with text elements/magazine summaries like a print source or almanac or archive. Ability to interact with video enhancements such as the fancam (follow your favourite houseguest around for the day) or the pancam (control the camera with your keyboard to place your gaze in the direction of your choice) |
| E4 digital-edited streams. Choice of live or pre-recorded as-live plus text news flashes and interactive voting | 19 per cent (63 per cent of respondents said that they had watched E4 at some point). This has increased with each year as many more subscribers to digital services had access to the channel | Relatively low mediation (some editing for taste, decency and legality). Very high temporality (15-minute delay but the caption 'live' appears on the screen). Visual input of broadcast quality. Ability to interact through selection of video stream. Ability to vote and access supplementary text information |
| Mobile phones text news flashes | 3 per cent | Relatively high mediation (headlines and limited descriptive accounts). High value in connectedness while on the move High perceived temporality (messages sent within 20 minutes of the action). Textual input only |
| Friends and family | 1 per cent | Social connectivity (value of engaging in 'water cooler conversations') |
| Press | 0.5 per cent | Background detail. Unofficial gossip |

Table 3: How do you stay up to date with what's happening in the *Big Brother* house? (N=12,340: 2002 Survey)

- Much more intense and naturalistic, enclosed. You get to see far more of BB. Because you can watch it live you don't have to rely on good/bad editing and it makes it easier to get closer to the core of people.
- To get information about how the show is being handled, interest in the public's reading of character and their reaction to the participants (keeping in mind how the footage is being edited.).
- Nothing is edited. You can see related conversations and hear what everyone has to say.
- See what's going on during the day/night, as in to catch whole conversations rather than being shown which ones they want me to see. It's a real-life soap opera, it has all the intensity of *Friends*, but these are real people and real relationships.
- We watch everything live. Nothing is cut, you get to see the bad things about people and know it's not scripted.
- It's real fly-on-the-wall stuff.
- I am fascinated by how the producers edit the footage to manipulate the audience into thinking certain characters are nasty.
- I like to see the bits that would be censored/taken off the TV by producers for certain reasons.
- I like comparing the net with the broadcast programme to see what the personalities of the individuals are like normally, and not what's just suited to TV, for example the quieter moments.
- Fraudulent editing detracted from the [broadcast] shows. Certain contestants, particularly Melanie, were betrayed as negative characters purely due to the agendas of the producers. Unlike Craig, 'The Saint', whose arse-wiping was never shown and any mention suppressed.

A distrust of the broadcast edited highlights was almost universal amongst those who chose E4 or the web as their favourite platform. These viewers were effectively claiming the rushes as their own property and reinforcing the audience's right to have a non-mediated, undisturbed version of events.

The grammar of normal television allows for the editing and condensing of material. This is what the viewer expects and has become used to over a lifetime of viewing. The terrestrial broadcast offers an officially-doctored version that is spun like a political story and the word 'official' was often used as viewers tried to clarify their impressions of the broadcast platform:

> I liked E4 because you can watch *Big Brother* when it is not *officially* on and I can move from screen to screen at the touch of a button to see what is most interesting but I hate the gaps in the sound, it makes me want to hurl my remote control at the screen. (My italics)

The obvious 'flaw' in the E4 output comes from the broadcaster's obligation to mute the sound fairly frequently to prevent profanity and problems with taste and decency and also to edit footage to prevent any breach of copyright. These respondents were very intolerant of the obvious and frequent sound interruptions that were a feature of this viewing platform and many criticised the explicit and heavy-handed censorship. They saw it as an unjustified interference and a breach of an implicit promise (that of shared temporality and low mediation). It was clear from these responses that viewers believed that the producers were breaking one of the new grammatical rules established for this platform. A common sentiment is typified by the following quote:

> Although the pictures are clearer on E4 the sound interruptions on E4 are too annoying, they are always censoring something, I feel they must be keeping the best bits for the evening programme.

One viewer noted in frustration that the sound cuts on E4 'act like a slap in the face'.

## Sharing a temporal space

The potential of the love affair between television and mobile phones is well recognised within the industry:

> T&M [television and mobile] strategies enable us to break free of the restrictions of the current platforms and allow us to take our favourite brands and programmes on the move. We send around 1.6 billion text messages a month and this creates a whole new generation of people with strong opposable thumb muscles. Content consumed on the move has a high temporal and personal convenience value and the future of mobiles is 'My TV' where the television is a permanent 'always carry' accessory in people's lives. (David Docherty, quoted in ITC 2003: 9)

*Big Brother* viewers were able to purchase a special mobile phone card that linked them with the programme's producers. Not only do their mobile phones ring with the *Big Brother* theme tune they can also receive text messages about their favourite characters at any time of the day and night. Two fans commented:

> The mobile-phone is my favourite format because it keeps me up to date with whatever's going on *wherever I am*, especially when you miss highlights you can still find out what's happening. (My italics)

> The mobile-phone and E4 are my favourite formats because by the time Channel 4 transmits the show it is *already out of date*. (My italics)

That *Big Brother* could be considered 'out of date' if not viewed as it is happening is more in keeping with the transmission of a live sports fixture and reinforces the importance of the 'event' in the minds of the audience. I would predict that as this form of reality TV becomes more interlinked with live media then its shelf life will be more of a factor in managing its success.

## Do we still need the producer's cut?

The audience's relationship with the *Big Brother* output is characterised by instantaneity. Traditional contextualisation through the producer's cut is only one way the fan works to build meaning through immersion with this franchise. As discussed previously, many respondents quite naturally positioned themselves as editors, privileging their access to the 'unauthorised' cut.

We can see this positioning in the following responses to a question asking for viewers to relate their 'most memorable moments'.

I don't have just one particular moment. *I enjoy watching it when others think a particular time was boring*. I find it really interesting to see how these people interact. (My italics)

The party after Sandy admitted he was leaving and the houseguests were passing goods across the divide with impunity (*not shown on Channel 4*). (My italics) Spencer and PJ showing their true colours. They became the dregs of society with their homophobic comments. *I feel strongly this should have been broadcast on Channel 4*. (My italics)

There was great sensitivity on the part of the viewer to the power of the producer; yet, this sensitivity was not enough to put them off the broadcast highlights. There is strong evidence that the producer's cut was necessary despite the fact that the broadcast programmes scored low on the veracity, timeliness and reality scales (with the exception of the eviction shows). The evening broadcast output did score well on the entertainment scale. Although surprisingly, 14 per cent of respondents said they thought that *Big Brother* would work well without the conventional Channel 4 broadcast versions. 67 per cent thought that the transmission highlights were essential. Viewers commented:

It needs to be edited so people can just see the best bits.

Without the Channel 4 show I wouldn't have a clue what was going on. Web news flashes don't give you the full picture and while Channel 4 coverage is highly edited it gives you more body language. The whole point is that it's real.

It wouldn't work without the Channel 4 version because it wouldn't give you the *feeling* of it being at TV show. (My italics)

The grammar or *feeling* of a television show has many associations. By selecting and condensing events the viewer can relate much more easily to a programme. This is how we are trained to watch television and because of this, the packaging of houseguests is not just acceptable but often desirable. The producer's cut is less real but not unattractive in the media mix. The comments indicated that viewers were reassured by the presence of the webcams and E4 live feeds. They needed the power to accept or question the dominant frame. The act of choosing may indirectly contribute to the overall sophistication and media literacy of viewers; making comparisons between formats allows for a customisation of viewing, maximising the entertainment potential of this series.

## Conclusion

Readings of conventional single-platform television have been built up over fifty years, yet today audiences are just starting to develop an understanding of multiple-platform, interactive television. This study has shown how *Big Brother*'s predominantly young techno-confident viewers have been able to navigate a new grammar of reception emerging from multi-platform interactivity. The evidence presented here suggests that the 'feels real' aspect of *Big Brother* is enhanced by offering a panoply of platform choices allowing the viewer freedom to move between them. The codes of realism associated with levels of mediation, timeliness and interactivity all combine to enable viewers to interpret and control the viewing experience.

*Big Brother* appears to have appropriated what is attractive in the docu-soap genre and created a media event, exploiting the embryonic stage of convergence. The format, although a derivative of the docu-soap, has evolved and mutated to keep up with the greediness of the audience for unmediated actuality. *Big Brother* privileges its viewers with a primary and unmediated access to 'the real' so that they are able to successfully develop strategies that allow them to sit in judgement of the actuality, despite the format's obvious constructedness. The range of platforms and modes of viewing enhance the necessary perception of witnessing reality. Each platform effectively opens up a new window on the actuality allowing the 'platform-surfer' to acknowledge the real and the surreal whilst having some 'interpretative fun' with the mediation. Essentially, a 'reality net' has been created through the convergence of media providing a measure of confidence and control so viewers feel able to catch out the producers and the houseguests should they attempt to bear false witness. This power is dependent on fostering a special intimacy between houseguest and viewer through three elements: 'liveness', 'interactivity' and 'immersion'. These have not been so successfully emulated in other RTV formats.

As the battle for console supremacy continues it becomes more evident that the technological apparatus in our homes and jacket pockets each represents a gateway to information for audiences that can be exploited by entrepreneurial media bus-inesses. For example, the industry now regards the web as a uniquely-placed primer to galvanise interest and support pre-broadcast. There are increasingly more examples in the contemporary media landscape where the web leads the transmission such as the popular youth entertainment series *Celebdaq* and *Tribe* and the internationally syndicated *Robot Wars* that begin each new series with web-based interactive versions. Essentially, the broadcast version is becoming the second window.

Yet television's ideological influence remains with the producer firmly at the centre. Users/viewers are still configured as a reactive, homogenised consumer mass within the interactive television system and it continues to appear as an asymmetrical structure. Karen Scott and Anne White also suggest, in their study of the BBC's *Walking With Dinosaurs*, that 'interactive TV does not unleash the new liberties of actions offered by new technologies. The medium is unexploited. Socio-economic forces rather then technical opportunism shape the new technology' (Scott & White 2003: 328).

Given that the industry definition of interactivity is that of people consuming directly through their television sets, then it must be seen as a commercial imperative to exploit this new technology. Yet finding a sustainable and financially lucrative formula may become a precarious job for these interactive industry pioneers. They need to embrace notions of creativity and audience agency that allow users the ability to create their own messages or content and at the same time maximise their 'return path' revenue. The ITC report posits an interesting but dangerous future for the UK media industries should anarchy be allowed to reign in connection with a potential interactive television revolution. They predict a 'Goodbye TV' option where P2P (person to person) activity grows in importance and prevalence with the industry finding it hard to adapt commercially (ITC 2003: 25).

Inevitably there are interesting problems on the horizon. The success of iTV will depend in part on how much control the producer can retain and also on how much interaction with their consoles consumers actually want. The implicit promise is that interaction and 'virtual conversation' could make television a more individualised experience. Liesbet van Zoonen and Chris Aalberts' research into iTV in the everyday lives of young couples suggests that attachment to our televisions is based on constructing a sense of togetherness and shared experience and shared history. They call this 'gezellig', the dutch term for a sense of togetherness or shared experience and everyday conversation (Van Zoonen & Aalberts 2002). For example, a second television set in the home is considered not to be gezellig. Can iTV be gezellig? Can we collectivise iTV and turn it into a medium of shared meaning? Indications are that for now its use culture is predominantly individualised.

*Notes*

1  It is also interesting to note that more viewers voted during the combined *Big Brother* and *Pop Idol* ballots than voted in the last UK general election, prompting a review of balloting procedures for the 2005 general election.
2  The UK producers of *Who Wants to be a Millionaire* have experimented with a genuinely live version of the programme (Christmas ratings sweep, 2002) in order to attract extra revenue through return path telephone voting. Thus, for this one show only, one of the lifelines available to the contestants 'ask the audience', became 'ask the nation'. Interestingly, in this genuinely live version, the script never once drew attention to the fact that this was a uniquely live event. It heavily promoted the exclusive opportunity given to the home viewer to phone in answers to the questions, but refused to highlight the concept of a one-off live programme. This was part of the show's philosophy of presentation. Flagging-up a unique live show would potentially damage the 'live-ish' reputation of the whole series.
3  Tim Gardam, Head of Programmes. Transcribed from Think TV, Channel 4, 2 June 2002.
4  Think TV Broadcast on Channel 4, 21 June 2002.
5  A word search using the *Guardian/Observer* CDROM reveals that the term docu-soap only significantly entered our lexicon in 1998 with 110 references by headline writers and columnists to this form of broadcast television. In 1999 there were 121 references. A survey conducted by Collins English Dictionary polled the UK population to find the top buzz words of 1998 and 'Docu-soap' made it to the top ten surrounded by 'Girl Power' and 'Furby'.
6  Line producers, of which there were four, were charged with editing and mixing the output of all 26 cameras down to four final streams of video.

*Bibliography*

Bazalgette, P. (2000) 'Royal Television Society speech by Peter Bazalgette'.
Bolter, J. D. and R. Grusin (1999) *Remediation: Understanding New Media*. Cambridge, London: MIT Press.
Corner, J. (2002) 'Performing the Real: Television in a Post-Documentary Culture', *Television and New Media*, 3, 3, 255–69.
Dovey, J. (2000) *Freakshow*. London: Pluto Press.

Duffy, D. (1969) *Marshall McLuhan*. Toronto: McClelland and Stewart.

Good, P. (2001) 'Royal Television Society speech by Peter Good, Head Interactive Content, Channel 4'.

Hartley, J. (2002) *Communication, Cultural and Media Studies: The Key Concepts*. London: Routledge.

Hartley, J. (1996) *Popular Reality: Journalism, Modernity, Popular Culture*. London: Arnold.

Hill, A. (1997) *Shocking Entertainment: Viewer Response to Violent Movies*. Luton: John Libby Media.

_____ (2002) '*Big Brother*: The Real Audience', *Television and New Media*, 3, 3, 323–40.

ITC (2003) *Future Reflections: Four scenarios for television in 2012*. Bournemouth Media School. On-line. Available at: www.itc.org.uk (14 June 2003).

Jenkins, H. (1992) *Textual Poachers: Television Fans and Participatory Culture*. New York: Routledge.

_____ (2003) 'Convergence is Reality', *Technology Review*. Available at: http://www. technology review.com/articles/wo-jenkins (20 August 2003).

Jones, J. (2000) 'The Postmodern Guessing Game', *Journal of Media Practice*, 1, 2, 75–84.

_____ (2003) 'Show Your Real Face: investigating the boundaries between the notions of consumers and producers of factual television', *New Media and Society*, 5, 3, 401–22.

Kim, P. and H. Sawhney (2002) 'A Machine-like new medium: theoretical examination of interactive TV', *Media Culture and Society,* 24, 2, 217–33.

Landow, G. P. (1992) *Hypertext: The Convergence of Contemporary Critical Theory and Technology*. Baltimore, MD: John Hopkins University Press.

Nichols, B. (1991) *Representing Reality: Issues and Concepts in Documentary*. Bloomington: Indiana University Press.

Scott, K. and A. White (2003) 'Unnatural History? Deconstructing the *Walking With Dinosaurs* Phenomenon', *Media Culture and Society*, 25, 3, 315–22.

Steur, J. (1995) 'Defining Virtual Reality: Dimensions Determining Telepresence', in M. Levy (ed.) *Communication in the Age of Virtual Reality*. Hillsdale, NJ: LEA, 33–56.

Winston, B. (2000) *Lies, Damn Lies and Documentaries*. London: British Film Institute.

Van Zoonen, L. (2001) 'Desire and Resistance: *Big Brother* and the Recognition of Everyday Life', *Media Culture and Society*, 23, 5, 679–88.

Van Zoonen, L. and C. Aalberts (2002) 'Interactive television in the everyday lives of young couples', in M. Consalvo and S. Paasonen (eds) *Women and Everyday Uses of the Internet: Agency and Identity*. New York: Peter Lang.

## CHAPTER 16

*Jon Dovey*

# IT'S ONLY A GAME SHOW
## Big Brother and the Theatre of Spontaneity

### Orientations

It is clear from the history of documentary film and television that each age produces its own form of realism, its own 'regime of truth' (Foucault 1977: 13). These forms of representing social reality change through time, subject to multiple determinations of technology, economics and epistemology. In this chapter I want to argue that formatted reality TV game shows like *Big Brother* might be best understood as simulations, that in reality TV games we see the dominant mimetic traditions of representation being redeployed as part of a different system of representation which is that of simulation.

The reality TV game is one aspect of the cultural logic of an 'order of simulation' which has a profound, symbiotic relationship with reflexive modernity and networked culture, just as the tradition of documentary observation had a symbiotic relationship with modernity through its basis in empiricism. The understanding of simulation as a system of representation which emerges from my analysis of reality formatted game shows also has some useful analytical purchase when considering a wide range of factual television practices in which the impulse to record social reality has been completely swallowed by the impulse to simulate social reality in performative models. Factual television practices have by and large abandoned empirical observation that rested upon the *lack* of relationship between observer and observed and replaced it with the observation of simulated situations that *only* exist because of the intervention of the TV production. Factual TV has moved from direct empirical observation to the observation of simulated social situations. This move has occurred for a number of reasons which this chapter will elaborate below. In brief, empiricism itself, as a way of producing knowledge about the world, has undergone numerous shifts as a result of scientific and philosophical experience. Today knowledge is just as likely to be produced through a process of the simulation of unobservable processes as from their direct empirical observation. The 'facts' of 'Factual TV' are subject to the same processes of production as the 'facts' of sociology, science or military planning, all of which rely upon simulation systems. Secondly, this diffusion of simulation overlaps with a generalised sense that public culture has lost any claims to seriousness that it may once have made and instead become the domain of playfulness, games and pleasure. Reality itself is now produced through ludological processes – we have reality TV game shows and 'Alternate Reality Games' online.

Traditionally game activities have been defined as those activities that stand in opposition to productive labour – activities that in some way are marked out from day-to-day reality. The reality TV game show, however, combines these previously discreet areas in a hybrid that suggests that perhaps the ludic has become a dominant aspect of our cultural life – even reality is a game now! Here the activities of the psychic day-to-day, forming and breaking relationships and alliances, performing the self in a range of interpersonal contexts, responding to challenges set according to system rules, all represented in a surveillance mode that signifies 'reality' – all these real activities of everyday life are here structured as game.

Before I attempt the work of defining precisely what I mean by simulation, I need at the outset to dissociate my use of the term from either of its dominant constructions as (a) computer graphic images made without any pro-filmic object, as in movies like *Shrek*, or (b) the use derived from Baudrillard in which a theory of the simulacrum places final emphasis upon the 'disappearance of reality'. I do not mean either of these. By using simulation I want to refer to a representational mode based on making models of complex structures and behaviours, models that consist of *dynamic rule-based systems*. This model-based way of generating knowledge about the world might be deployed in role plays using social actors as well as by the mathematically-based models that are computer simulations. Moreover the simulation, in my understanding, is not about unreal states, any more than documentary or fiction occupy the realm of the 'unreal' – the simulation as a material practice produces real knowledge about real things in the real world and has real effects upon real lives.

In this chapter I want to apply some of the work that I have been doing in thinking about what a 'New Media Studies' might be – that is to say a discipline that looks at 'New Media' but which also therefore represents a methodological renewal of 'Media Studies'. This renewal does seem to me to involve interdisciplinary cross pollination with various aspects of computer science and 'cyberculture studies', such as the study of Human Computer Interaction, Artificial Intelligence, software theory and study of networked systems (see Lister *et al.* 2003). In this context I argue that *Big Brother*, although disseminated primarily through good old steam television, is in many respects a typical New Media object in so far as it is an international brand that exists as a multi-platform hybrid of traditional and new media. A programme like *Big Brother* not only delivers audiences to advertisers but also to phone lines, cable subscription and Internet use as the viewer is drawn into a simulated game-world in which the distinction between old and new media ceases to be meaningful.

Most scholarship to date on reality TV, my own included, has been conducted within the traditions of television and documentary studies. These researches have by and large taken their lead from the popular debates occasioned by reality TV with particular reference to ethical anxieties and to the questions such programmes pose to traditional formulations of the public sphere. Without entirely losing touch with these questions I want to approach the topic from a different angle. I want to think about *Big Brother* as a system, in which the system software might be just as important to a textual analysis as the semiotic content of the text itself. Here I am applying some of the ideas of Espen Aarseth (1997) in which he argues that textual analysis of new media must emphasise the machine-based text production system as much as the content produced by that system. For Aarseth the text is a machine, not metaphorically but literally, 'a mechanical device for the production and consumption of verbal signs':

> Cybertext ... is the wide range (or perspective) of possible textualities seen as a typology of machines, as various kinds of literary communications systems where the functional differences among the mechanical parts play a defining role in determining the aesthetic process ... As a theoretical perspective, cybertext shifts the focus from the traditional threesome of author/sender, text/message and reader/receiver to the cybernetic intercourse between the various part(icipant)s in the textual machine. (Aarseth 1997: 21–2)

## Points of origin

The line I want to develop is largely derived and inspired by a paper by Bernadette Flynn, published as 'Factual Hybridity: Games, Documentary and Simulated Spaces' (2002). In this research Flynn made a series of analytical links and connections between *Big Brother* and *The Sims* computer game. (*The Sims* is a computer simulation game in which the player has the opportunity to build houses and create animated families to inhabit them – a computer simulated doll's house in which the emotional and physical well-being of the sims – the characters – is the players' responsibility.) Flynn's study brought together in a single frame two of my main areas of research, games and documentary, and allowed me to start to think about how a New Media Studies perspective might help us to understand reality TV. In her paper Flynn states:

> In the *Big Brother* and *The Sims* households, documentary techniques and AI modelling are deployed in an attempt to create a place of authenticity or emotional purchase through the vehicle of simulated 'real' experience. *Big Brother* quite deliberately exploits the space between aspects of dramatic realism (the personal, subjective) and those of the artificial and the performative. It is in this marginal space between the real and the simulated that one of the fascinations of the *Big Brother* and *The Sims* projects resides. (Flynn 2002: 50)

Flynn's article recounts many striking similarities, cross-fertilisations and mutual echoes between *The Sims* computer game and *Big Brother* – it draws our attention to the commonly ludic qualities of both and to their shared media histories. What I have been interested to try and do here is to ask some more questions about *why* this might be and then try to apply some of answers to the way we think about a whole range of simulation-based television programmes with *Big Brother* as the main focus.

My other point of origin, also cited by Flynn and co-incidentally an outcome of the 'Visible Evidence' conference series, is Mark J. P. Wolf's essay, 'Subjunctive Documentary: Computer Imaging and Simulation' (1999). Wolf argues that documentary shifts into the subjunctive mode when it deploys simulations that use computer imaging in order to represent phenomena which cannot be empirically observed, for example outer space, radio waves, sub atomic particles, brain activity and so forth:

> In this era of computer simulation there is a greater willingness to trade close indexical linkage for a new knowledge that would otherwise be unattainable within the stricter requirements of indexical linkage that were once needed to validate knowledge empirically. (Wolf 1999: 274)

Though sharing my interest in the ways that simulation replaces empirical observation as a method for the production of knowledge Wolf is solely concerned with the simulation that uses an animated computer graphic interface to represent the maths that has been used to model the natural phenomenon in question. Wolf's subjunctive documentary occurs where computer simulations are used to represent 'what could be, would be or might have been', in the case where these objects are not available for empirical/optical observation – whereas the formatted reality game shows and simulated documentaries that concern me continue to use optical empirical observation as a method. However, the similarity lies in the principle of using a 'model' to represent social processes that might not be susceptible to direct empirical observation. My interest here lies in TV texts that use social actors in a systematised model rather than in computer simulation of images that lie beyond optics.

## Simulation as model

The definition of simulation I want to use is derived from computer applications within the social sciences. Nigel Gilbert and Jim Doran (1994) argue that first of all simulation is a process of modeling:

> We wish to acquire knowledge about a target entity T. But T is not easy to study directly. So we proceed indirectly. Instead of T we study another entity M, the 'model', which is sufficiently similar to T that we are confident that some of what we learn about M will also be true of T. (Gilbert & Doran 1994: 4)

Typically the phenonema under consideration are dynamic, a model therefore consists of 'structure plus behaviour'. Simulation happens when we observe the behaviour of the model, when it is 'set running':

> Computer simulation is an appropriate methodology whenever a social phenomenon is not directly accessible, either because it no longer exists … or *because its structure or the effects of its structure, i.e. its behaviour, are so complex that the observer cannot directly attain a clear picture of what is going on*. (Gilbert & Conte 1995: 2; my italics)

This justification for the use of simulation is interesting because again, like Wolf above, it lays emphasis on complex structures and behaviours which are not directly observable – an important part of the argument to which we will return below when we discuss how identity and sociality – the content of the reality TV game – are complex and *dynamic* processes subject to multiple networked determinations rather than linear cause and effect.

Nigel Gilbert and Rosaria Conte (1995) then go on to present case studies which use computer simulation to produce conclusions on a range of topics from the emergence of political leaders, business organisation, kinship structures, urban settlement patterns, and the development of social structures in Paleolithic cultures. In one fascinating example of this work, Robert Reynolds gives an account of a simulation process used to try and explain why a particular ritual gift of livestock occurred in an isolated indigenous Peruvian community. The problem for anthropologists was to understand what advantage was conferred upon the donor of the fertile female livestock to a herder who did not belong to his kinship group. By designing a simulation that factored in kinship networks, herder behaviour patterns and regional distribution researchers were able to show that the cooperation represented by the livestock gift actually promoted maximum outputs from the livestock over a number of generations. In other words they 'proved' the economic value of a culturally-evolved ritual process using simulation. They were able to do this through the use of what the authors describe as 'cultural algorithms ... which allow us to model explicitly the way in which our beliefs affect our actions' (Reynolds 1994: 244). The 'cultural algorithm' is a programme that allowed researchers to interconnect micro-level individual agents' behaviours with wider belief systems.

Thus simulation is used here to address a fundamental problem of social science described by Susan Strum and Bruno Latour in the introduction to their essay 'Redefining the Social Link: From Baboons to Humans' (1999), in which they argue that there has been a disjunction in the social sciences between, on the one hand, those researchers who propose a model of society which is 'ostensive', 'something which is "there", that can be pointed at so to speak', which is made up from interactions between micro- and macro-level agents and, on the other, with ethno-methodology which argues that society *only* exists as a fluid process of interactions between agents:

> In the light of these studies, the conventional distinctions between micro- and macro-levels become less clear-cut and it is more difficult to accept a traditional definition of society. Instead society is more compellingly seen as continually constructed or 'performed' by active social beings. (Strum & Latour 1999: 116)

Simulations using computer programmes are being used to address fundamental problems of societal organisation and evolution in ways that are explicitly designed to take account of highly complex interactive systems whose characteristics are always permanently emergent rather than fixed or predictable by any linear cause and effect mechanical method.

## Sites of simulation

In a less arcane field, simulation is also of course widely used by the military; this has been growing for many years. In 1996 the US Department of Defense Modeling and Simulation asked the National Research Council to convene a conference in which military trainers and members of the entertainment industries could share information. It was attended by game developers, film studio representatives, theme park industries, military trainers and universities (Prensky 2001: 315). Marc Prensky, in his book *Digital Game Based Learning* (2001), claims that the US military are the biggest spenders in the world on simulation games for training:

> The military uses games to train soldiers, sailors, pilots, and tank drivers to master their expensive and sensitive equipment. It uses games to train command teams to communicate effectively in battle. It uses games to teach mid-level officers how to employ joint-force military doctrine in battle. It uses games to teach senior officers the art of strategy. It uses games for team work and team training of squads, fire teams, crews, and other units; games for simulating responses to weapons of mass destruction, terrorist incidents, and threats; games for mastering the complex process of military logistics and even games for teaching how *not* to fight when helping maintain peace. (Prensky 2001: 296)

It is clear that warfare is now conducted on the basis of knowledge produced through simulation. This highly rule-based mediated version of war of course produces its own counter image in the form of terror – a viral resistance to the systemic totality of the computerised war machine.

Real world uses of simulation to produce knowledge are not confined to social science or military planning. There are numerous other examples. Currency markets use simulations everyday in order to calculate the best market advantage for speculation. In science simulations are used increasingly in recognition of the fact that understanding emergent behaviour is an important aspect of understanding many natural processes, for example in immunology to predict micro-biological behaviours.

Finally we can see this growth of simulation as a method reflected in entertainment from computer games to staged factual television programmes. In his seminal work on computer games and simulation Ted Friedman (2002) has made the connection between simulation as a way of producing knowledge and postmodernism, using the work of David Harvey and Fredric Jameson. Harvey observed in *The Condition of Postmodernity* (1989) that mapping the world is an inadequate response to our experience of space in the contemporary era:

> How adequate are such modes of thought and such conceptions in the face of the flow of human experience and strong processes of social change? On the other side of the coin how can spatialisations in general ... represent flux and change? (Harvey 1989: 206)

'Simulation', argues Friedman, may be the best opportunity to create what Fredric Jameson calls 'an aesthetic of cognitive mapping which seeks to endow the individual subject with some new heightened sense of its place in the global system'. (Jameson 1991: 54, quoted by Friedman 2002: 14)

> Representing flux and change is exactly what a simulation can do, by replacing the stasis of two- or three-dimensional spatial models with a map that shifts over time to reflect change. And this change is not simply a one-way communication

of a series of still images but a continually interactive process. Computer simulations bring the tools of narrative to mapmaking, allowing the individual not simply to observe structures, but to become experientially immersed in their logic. (Friedman 2002: 14)

Simulation is used then to represent complex processes with multiple agents and causalities at work – in this way it seems to answer a theoretical need for ways of producing knowledge that take account of the levels of interaction between micro-level agents and macro-level forces as well as to address a need articulated by postmodern theorists for a method of representation that takes account of rapid change. In all the cases cited above, real-world knowledges are being produced that have real-world effects – embodied, direct and material. The simulation has become a significant way of producing knowledge, modifying behaviour and entertaining ourselves.

## Simulation and mimesis

A potentially confusing aspect of this argument is the apparent contradiction between the 'zero degree' realism of the surveillance style of a show like *Big Brother* and the idea of simulation that I have argued is about representing what is often unobservable. Mimesis and simulation are different, though clearly simulation may deploy mimetic representation as part of its interface with the algorithmic engines that constitute the dynamic system. In other words the images of the 'real' to which viewers are so attached (see Hill 2002; Jones 2003) are the interface that creates access to the underlying software system of meaning production.

Mimetic representation can be seen as part of the age of mechanical reproduction. The mechanical age has a philosophical basis, not only in empiricism, but in understanding phenomenon and behaviours as having a cause and effect logic – what is known as mechanical causality. Extended to representation we might observe that mimesis has a similar mechanical causality in so far as it asks us to understand that *this* signifier equals *this* signified in *this* real world – a chain of signification. Of course the inadequacies of such a model of explaining meaning have been pointed out ever since the system itself was formulated – this attack reaches its *reductio ad absurdum* in Baudrillard's theory of the simulacrum.

Simulation, on the other hand, may help us to understand a world that no longer seems susceptible to cause and effect logic, but more and more to non-linear causality and network logics. By network logics I mean the understanding that all events or behaviours may have multiple determinants and variable outcomes, that any given node in a network has numerous in and out points. Planning or predicting outcomes in a network therefore becomes a cybernetic problem, a matter of feedback estimation, of probability management and of risk calculation. Such processes have strong correlations with the experience of living under conditions of reflexive modernity in which daily life is chaotic and complex, fraught with management difficulties that are a consequence of our increased mobility and by the daily dilemmas of 'life politics':

Individuals are now expected to master these 'risky opportunities' without being able, owing to the complexity of modern society, to make the necessary decisions on a well-founded and responsible basis, that is to say considering the possible consequences. (Beck 1994: 8)

## Big Brother as gameplay

In the case of *Big Brother* the mimetic content produced by the system is centred upon another and different kind of simulation, that of the game in which the players are called upon to perform certain roles in accordance with a set of rules. Here the simulation in question is not a computer programme (though as we shall see computing is a central feature of the generation of the *Big Brother* effect) but of a kind of play more akin to 'let's pretend'. There are two levels of play in operation here. First, to use Roger Caillois' (1979) definitions of play, the whole event is staged within a space characterised by mimicry in which participants are called upon to play a part in an imaginative construct, here the houseguests are playing a version of themselves which engages audiences in endless speculation around whether or not this performance of self is a true 'authentic' self or calculated performance. At the second level the day-to-day action in the house is structured by games of 'agon', competition in which houseguests compete against one another or against *Big Brother* to win food supplies and treats, and so on.

Moreover, this game play takes place within the overarching context of a social psychology experiment that uses 'role play' and observation as its method (see Palmer 2002). The entire apparatus of *Big Brother* resembles a social psychology experiment designed for mass entertainment consumption. The isolation, surveillance, comments from psychologists who explain behaviour and the confessional 'Diary Room' all mark the programme as psychology laboratory. As such it is a deliberately designed 'model' of human interaction in exactly the same way that a computer simulation is a model designed to investigate other natural and social processes. The experimental or behaviour modification techniques of psychology are here adapted to entertainment TV.

I want to establish that these forms of 'play' are also simulations that are con-comitant with computer simulations in the way that they are models of 'behaviour plus structure' which exist outside of the day-to-day but which are designed to model it. Many of us are familiar with this process through the experience of role play – how many of us have been on any sort of training in the last ten years when we were not at some point asked to go into role to simulate professional conditions? Here we encounter simulation as an embedded form of social learning. Although the object of role play was originally behaviour modification and training it has some similarities with simulation in so far as it also sets up a model situation outside everyday perimeters in which the participants are encouraged 'to see what happens if...'. This social role play also has much in common with play theories, deriving in psychology from the work of Joseph Moreno who invented psychodrama as a therapeutic technique which effected personal change through direct embodiment of improvised role play. Moreno's development of the technique encompasses children's play and storytelling as well as the use of theatre, founding the 'Theatre of Spontaneity' in Vienna in 1923.

For the purposes of this argument I want to think of performative role play as a kind of human simulation. This move, from computer simulation to play as simulation, is a potentially disorienting move in my argument. It relies on argument by homology or similarity. As such I want to explain it by returning to Raymond Williams' discussion of 'base' and 'superstructure' which is an attempt to relate the work of culture (superstructure) to the work of the economic base of society. Here *Big Brother* is the work of culture and our experiences of identity and belonging in a complex society that is economically and technologically determined are the 'base'. Williams writes:

> In the later twentieth century there is the notion of 'homologous structures', where there may be no direct or easily apparent similarity, and certainly nothing like reflection or reproduction, between the superstructural process and the reality of the base, but in which there is an essential homology or correspondence of structures which can be discovered by analysis. (Williams 2001: 153)

I am suggesting that there is an 'essential homology' between forms of knowledge production developed by the economic base – simulation – and forms of factual television represented by the reality formatted game shows that simulate the conditions of everyday life in a laboratory designed to entertain rather than enlighten its observers. What unites the computer simulation and the reality game show, and thus lies 'behind' the homology, is the idea of the ludic, a playful, experimental pursuit played out according to a set of rules that nevertheless allow considerable scope for improvisation, performance and the emergence of unexpected behaviours.

## Factual Television as playtime

Factual Television, once the spine of Public Service Broadcasting, the inheritor of, in the UK at least, a Reithian tradition to inform and educate the public, has taken a remarkable turn over the last ten years. From being the worthy but low-ratings part of the TV schedule, factual TV entertainment formats are now brand leaders in the ratings war between channels. This transformation from seriousness to popularity has occasioned much cultural hand-wringing. We will return to some of the productive issues arising from these debates below. For now I want to establish the common ludic framework that lies behind computer simulation, role play and reality game shows.

Simulation is now the driving force of a great deal of factual TV programming – the impulse here is – What if? 'What would happen if we got a burger cook to pretend to be a cordon bleu chef?' (*Faking It*, Channel 4, 1999–2003); 'What would happen if we persuaded wives to swap families for two weeks?' (*Wife Swap*, Channel 4, 2002); 'What would it be like to live in a Victorian House?' (*The 1900 House*, Channel 4, 1999). The latter example fits precisely the impulse toward simulation described above – that is to say we use simulation to explore processes that we cannot observe either because they are too complex or because they are no longer available to us, that is, historical. The biggest majority of factual programmes are now based in events that have been set up and constructed by the producers themselves – 'Factual' TV has, more or less, abandoned any notion it ever had of observational documentary practice in which the attempt was made to capture reality as it actually happened without intervening in any way. Instead there is only intervention – only recording and editing of simulated conditions. Stella Bruzzi has already established this development in documentary studies in what she describes as the performative mode of documentary filmmaking:

> The traditional notion of documentary as striving to represent reality as faithfully as possible is predicated upon the realist assumption that the production process must be disguised, as was the case with direct cinema. Conversely, the new performative documentaries herald a different notion of documentary 'truth' that acknowledges the construction and artificiality of even non-fiction film. (Bruzzi 2000: 154)

In factual TV this turn toward constructed simulation rather than observation has been even more marked. On television the constructed documentary form has become dominant, its factual quality guaranteed only by the casting of non-actors into the producers' scenarios. The camera only captures events that are happening *because* the camera is there. In the docu-soap – the forerunner of the reality game show – dramatic narrative structure and casting techniques together with a self-conscious performance of subjects for camera all ensure that we are looking at experiences constructed and modified for the series itself. Without the camera's fame-conferring gaze there is no event worth filming, there is no reality. With evacuation of power or embodied politics from the domain of factual television the techniques of observation (including surveillance) are adapted for the simulated environment and the *mise-en-scène* is given over to the narrative structure of the game show. The significance of the outcome of these narratives is intensified by their role in regimes of celebritisation. Far from being a key site for the maintainance of public communication, these factual diversions are a key site in the production of celebrity through their commodity links with the press, magazines and web articulations of these new 'celebrities of the everyday':

> Celebrity is a world in which organised and professional conflicts resolve in simulation, performance, mimicry and blurring; a world in which authenticity is deferred and superficial fragments circulate. (Gamson 1994: 156)

## Vérité to simulation

Rather than seeing these developments as part of the spread of the mode of simulation, in some way it is also possible to see them as a revival of and triumph of Jean Rouch's original notion of *cinéma vérité* in which the camera is only ever seen as a catalyst that provokes performative events that become the content of the film (see Winston 1995: 148–69). This is a persuasive argument but I would want to put it into a wider cultural context. First of all it is necessary to point out that the differences between a Jean Rouch film like *Chronique d'un Eté* (1961) and *Big Brother* are vast. Rouch's work exists within the very limited forum of cinematic documentary exhibition and a subsequent life in the academy; *Big Brother* is a mass form within popular culture – so differences of intention, economics and distribution are obvious. However, it is true that they do share the fundamental assumption that the production itself provokes and creates the action, as well as a certain fascination with questions of identity and experience within the realm of the banal and the everyday. Given these important similarities it does seem worth asking the question as to why the more sophisticated reflexive mode argued for by Rouch and others remained marginal until now?

Both observational (Direct Cinema) and reflexive (Cinéma Vérité) modes of factual representation were achieved during the exact same period (late 1950s/early 1960s) as the first realisations of the meanings of an image saturated, stage-managed society – the period in fact of the publication of Daniel Boorstin's *The Image* (1963) which offered one of the first analyses of image-based public life and the mass effects of the PR industry. I would argue that the direct observational mode of documentary practice emerged in response to this moment as a way of seeming to 'get behind the scenes' of a foregrounded stage-managed reality. Hence films like *Primary* (Richard Leacock, 1960), *Meet Marlon Brando* (Maysles Brothers, 1965), observational rock performance films, such as *Don't Look Back* (Richard Leacock and D. A. Pennebaker, 1966), all attempt to show reality by direct observational techniques of the backstage process of stage-managed performative events. The observational mode clearly emerged as the dominant TV documentary tradition in response to and as part of these cultural circumstances.

However, by the end of the century this kind of observationalism can be seen to be played out for a number of reasons. Firstly, and most significantly for the purposes of my argument, observational documentary operated as part of the philosophical belief system of empiricism. Observable and repeatable natural phenomena, perceived by bourgeois gentlemen ('scientists') who agreed upon one another's integrity, were the foundation of knowledge. However, this foundation has clearly suffered multiple philosophical and pragmatic shocks over the last hundred years. Philosophically, for instance, relativity, and new ideas about the ways in which observers effect what they observe; pragmatically, in so far as science now more often that not concerns itself with processes that are in fact not observable, sub-atomic processes or astronomical cosmology, for instance. Here empiricism can be seen to have outstripped its own project, to have as it were reached the edge of the observable world before moving on into ways of representation that depend upon simulating natural phenomena.

These broad philosophical shocks are reflected within documentary practices where they took the form of challenges to empirical observation by the politics and problems of representation. I have argued elsewhere that the career of the British documentarist Nick Broomfield is paradigmatic of this 'loss of faith' in observational documentary in favour of a reflexive mode (Dovey 2000: 27–35).

However in thinking about how 'reflexivity' became mass-entertainment simulated reality game shows we also need recourse to political economy, first of all, within the sphere of regulation. By the end of the 1990s, documentary practice was assailed on all sides by a huge crisis of credibility as result of a number of 'faking scandals'. Starting in 1996 when German TV producer Michael Born was prosecuted and jailed for four years as a result of selling more than twenty faked documentaries and culminating in the UK in 1998–99 when the press 'exposed' a number of documentaries as 'fake', these campaigns led to the regional commercial franchise Carlton TV being fined £2 million by the commercial regulator the ITC for 'faking' the documentary *The Connection*, transmitted in October 1996 (see Winston 2000: 9–39). Factual television and documentary practice was under severe ontological pressure. What emerges from this feverish bout of self-questioning and doubt? *Big Brother* was conceived during precisely the same period that these scandals were circulating amongst the 'mediocracy' of Europe. The perfect beauty of the reality game show in this context is that because everything is set up no one can be held accountable for fakery. Since the whole event is a game any quasi-legal obligations that producers may previously have had to meet are displaced. Of course accuracy and truth remain at the core of viewer's engagements (See Jones in this volume). However, the whole terrain of debate has been shifted from the legalistic to the ludic. Problem solved.

The second aspect of political economy which helps us understand the shift from the empirical to the simulated are the market conditions for programme supply. The growth in numbers of TV channels leaves broadcasters competing with one another (and with other forms of leisure such as games, DVD, Internet, and so on) more fiercely than ever. In addition the numbers of suppliers willing to supply programmes has never been greater. There is therefore a tendency within these markets not to produce diversity but homoegeneity. In other words a successful formula is either immediately imitated or else actually copyrighted and distributed globally as a format. By 2000 the TV markets of the world were dominated by format sales:

> Wherever one turned in the Cannes Palais, one was confronted by the format frenzy. Not only were soap and game show specialists like Holland's Endemol and Britain's Pearson pushing shows like *The Big Diet* and *Greed* respectively but even once proper purveyors of highbrow drama like Britain's Granada unleashed an entire catalogue of concepts ranging from *Heartbreak Hotel* to *Ha Ha Bar*.
> (Guider 2000: 12)

The formatted programme is itself a rule-bound construct – hence the fact that the history of formats in TV has mostly been for selling game shows. Now that most factual programmes are also game shows then we should not be surprised that factual representation is also subject to the same kind of commodification. Formats work on the basis of the production of an all-inclusive document – referred to in the trade as the Bible – that documents every aspect of the production. This then becomes the commodity upon which intellectual property is founded and which is then sold on to the purchasers of the format in other territories. The deal may also involve varying degrees of consultancy from the vendor – often to ensure that quality control of their original product is maintained when it transfers to other territories.

It is clear therefore that although there are connections between the reflexive documentary mode and popular factual television of the late 1990s and early twenty-first century there are also big differences. Empirical observation appears now to be of only limited utility – it needs to be augmented by simulation in order to have anything very useful to say about our shared world. In addition the structural situation of programme-makers themselves, in terms of regulation and competition, has inclined them toward the reality game show format. The net result of these developments is that factual television has become a very playful ludic zone, where performance, challenges, rule sets and games of all kinds dominate the structure of programmes. Like a simulation a game might also be defined as a dynamic rule-based system.

## Reality TV game shows as identity simulation machines

I now want to bring together the previous two sections to bear upon thinking about *Big Brother* as a text machine, in Aarseth's sense, a simulation system that exists across multiple platforms. This multiplicity of distribution marks out *Big Brother* as a quintessentially new media form. Just as cinema is no longer experienced only in a darkened auditorium but through video, DVD, toys, comics, TV spin-offs and press coverage so access to the *Big Brother* story world is available via network TV, cable subscription, online subscription, text messaging and of course the press. At the heart of this story-producing mechanism is a simulation, a rule-based game system that changes over time allowing viewers limited interactive potential to determine the outcome.

The reality game show is a closed system like the experimental simulation or psychology lab. The *Big Brother* house, the *Fame Academy* building, the *Survivor* jungle location or *Temptation Island*, are all closed environments, fiercely policed by security guards and surveillance. Into this closed system with its own perimeters the system managers – the producers – introduce characters cast on the basis of what we might call their character algorithms. In *The Sims* computer game characters are developed according to a set of algorithmically controlled possibilities, for example 'Neat', 'Outgoing', 'Active', 'Playful' or 'Nice'. Writing about narrative and simulation Barry Atkins has observed:

> That popular fiction is essentially formulaic is a common enough negative observation – and 'Sim City' is almost nothing but a collection of formulae given graphical expression on screen. Even so, this kind of formula fiction is full of contradictions: formulaic, but unpredictable: open ended, but always nudged in particular directions; visually unrealistic, but grounded in our understanding of the observed world. (Atkins 2003: 114)

This 'formula fiction' is in some way re-created in the casting process by the producers when they choose houseguests according to sets of characteristics which they hope will create drama and narrative – the belligerent character, the flirt, the mother figure, the quiet but deep one, the eccentric and so on. For the producers these characteristics constitute the algorithms that they hope will make the simulation run in an interesting way – that is, stimulus from X applied to character Y might well have outcome Z. Of course, the real fun is when the unexpected happens, just as in computer games based on Sims part of the pleasure occurs when the AI (Artificial Intelligence) does something you had not predicted as a result of its interactions with other AI's. Jane Roscoe (2001) has described these moments as 'flickers of authenticity' – the moment where the simulation appears to break down and the viewer effect of the 'authentic' is created. Part of this effect is due to the possibilities for unpredictable emergent behaviour to arise from the simulation. Another way of putting this would be to talk about the process of improvisation in music or drama, set keys or rhythms might be established at the start of a jazz piece but no one quite knows where it will go nor will one performance repeat the music of the last.

The 'character algorithms' are then set in to dynamic motion through the experimental framework of the many challenges and tasks that constitute the daily life in the identity simulator. As we have observed above this daily diet of 'challenges' and games is consistent with many other types of factual entertainment that have a commonly ludic content. This game-playing is also reminiscent of role play situations, especially those associated with team-building efforts in the contemporary workplace where we are encouraged to bond through play.

The meanings produced by this process are also technologically mediated in more than the obvious representational ways of surveillance camera technologies. Apart from the apparatus of surveillance and mimetic representation there is also the influence of the computer networks and databases upon the viewing experience. Most obviously this involves our ability to have a participatory relationship with the simulation by interacting through voting to change the conditions of the experiment by removing particular characters, or in the summer 2003 run of the series in the UK by voting to put characters back into the house. There are of course numerous other opportunities to participate in the programme, from chatting about the show face to face on our daily round, participating in online chat forums, receiving text messages, limited forms of gaming based on knowledge of the participants or predictions of their behaviour and so on.

However, more interesting for my metaphor of the machine of narrative in the reality game show is one of the first examples of what Lev Manovich has called 'database filmmaking' (Manovich 2001). As footage is being shot in *Big Brother* or the *Fame Academy* it is digitised and logged by a team of researchers who have to name sequences, give them tags, that give sequences an identity in the database, for instance B picks his nose, or C cries, D is asleep, and so on. Every day packages and stories are put together by producer/editor teams working with another researcher who calls the clips back off the database by using a search engine and putting in searches for particular tags – so the whole process of narrativisation of character – the core of the meanings produced in these shows – is being mediated by database processes in which the tagging and the search engine play a very significant role. At one level this is not so very different from labelling one's rushes and then selecting, however here the search engine *itself* has been programmed to do some of the clip finding that previously would have been dependent upon the memory networks (and notes) of an assistant editor. In other words the system software itself will be playing a role in the selection of materials, however invisible that role might appear to be.

*Big Brother* is a simulation in so far as it is a closed system, bound by rules, into which characters are introduced who are set up in dynamic role play. The *Big Brother* environment is a model just as a computer simulation or a psychology experiment is a model. The simulation is mediated by digital technology systems particularly the search engines which help to 'automate' the process of narrativisation.

The question that remains is: if *Big Brother* is a simulation – what is it a simulation of?

## Reality TV and reflexive modernity

In *Freakshow* (2000) I argued that some elements of contemporary factual media, especially its emphasis on First Person Media and intimacy should be attributed not merely to greater commercialisation and marketisation of television but also to attempts to represent identity and sociality after the end of tradition. I used one of Anthony Giddens' formulations of the consequences of reflexive modernity:

> Life politics is about how we live after the end of tradition and nature – more and more political decisions will belong to the sphere of life politics in the future. (Giddens and Pierson 1998: 149)

The reflexive modernity argument is that in contemporary social life identity and ethics are under constant re-evaluation for all kinds of reasons. Essentially the description of contemporary society in the West as a condition of 'reflexive modernity' argues that the project or trajectory of modernity has been radically transformed by its own success (this is rather like the argument about empiricism above – itself constitutive of modernity – that it has through its own success reached the limits of its own aims). The social structures of modernity have been transformed by their own fulfillment. Formations of class, labour, gender and technology that underpinned the formation of modernism have all been radically challenged. Neo-liberal employment practices in which short term and freelance employment in the context of a highly aspirational culture deny the subject the possibility of long-term security or personal development (Sennett 1999). Increasingly flexible family structures that break out of nuclear family models as a result of changes in sexual and gender politics leave many of us with neither ethical map nor moral compass. Changes in gender roles also cut across our experiences of work, parenting and identity. Similarly our relationship with nature, which as Giddens explains was previously a 'given' is now under scrutiny, reproductive politics are now opened to a degree of choice, genetics opens up whole new areas of ambiguity which we are trying to learn to deal with. Moreover these scientific developments occur within a context of widespread mistrust of scientific technical systems, described by Ulrich Beck as part of 'risk culture'. This instability of identity and social structure is all experienced within the context of a consumerism marked by aspiration to a high degree of social mobility – where lifestyle choice replaces class, education or gender as determining social identity.

It is hardly surprising then that these questions of 'life politics' are reflected in the mediated discourses of everyday life that have become the staple fare of factual TV. We observe and participate in *Big Brother* as participants try out identities, experimenting, playing with different ways to relate to one another. We overhear them discussing the ways in which the issues above impact upon their own lives. We watch as they try and form intimate relationships in an impossibly paradoxical situation. This focus on identity work should not be misinterpreted as a merely individualistic concern, for identity in this context is deeply wedded to belonging, to group consciousness. The narrative action of *Big Brother* is constituted as on ongoing improvised drama of affiliation and exclusion, driven by the weekly eviction process that is deliberately designed to undermine group identity whilst at the same time the daily action of challenges and tests is designed to reinforce it.

Subsequently other commentators have made the same set of connections, notably Ib Bondebjerg in his article 'The Mediation of Everyday Life: Genre Discourse and Spectacle in Reality TV':

> This reflexive modernity and the new awareness of the self in public and private life as well as of the mediation of the self in a network society moving from a nation state to global frames … is the fuel of the new reality genres … It is also a reflection of the deep mediation of everyday life in a network society which creates a strong need for audiences to mirror and play with identities and the uncertainties of everyday life, thus intensifying our innate social curiosity. (Bondebjerg 2002: 162)

In the context of this pervasive 'make over culture' it should therefore come as no surprise that factual programming looks increasingly like part-identity lab, part-intimacy simulator in programmes like *Wife Swap* (C4, 2002) in which husbands and wives swap for two weeks, *Trading Races* (BBC2, 2001) in which participants swapped skin colour and lifestyle, or the very successful *Faking It* on Channel 4 in which subjects are asked to try to learn a new professional identity in just four weeks. *Wife Swap* is a particularly interesting text in this regard. The title is of course designed to suggest some kind of salacious content but in fact the programme turns out to be exactly the blend of sociology and voyeurism that a producer might dream up thinking about the questions of reflexive modernity. Each programme brings up questions about who does what kind of domestic work, how work outside the home is gendered, how this new status of women in the workforce effects parenting and attitudes to parenting. Equally the men, the husbands who do not swap, are also called into question, the traditional man, the new man, and everything in between, has been portrayed and more often than not found wanting in yet another example of the contemporary 'crisis of masculinity'. These fundamental questions of life politics around who does what work – emotional, domestic and paid – are exactly the issues thrown up by Giddens' analysis of reflexive modernity.

The reality game show can also be seen as having a productive role in this processing of the themes of reflexive modernity. At a primary level its clear that the talk we talk about *Big Brother* or *Survivor* or *Fame Academy* is as much about ourselves as it is about the participants – our water cooler conversations are the site for viewers to do our own identity work; when I express a preference for an Irish, lesbian ex-nun as *Big Brother* contestant I am saying more about myself and what kind of man I am than about anything else. Whilst the primary goal of the reality game show is profit through entertainment and participation these programmes also actively produce the conflicts and problems of reflexive modernity as a by-product of their discursive effects. When *Big Brother* in the United States gets tangled up in debates and arguments about race it is reflecting something significant about America; when the Portuguese *Big Brother* sparks a national debate about domestic violence after an incident on the show we are seeing a culture in the process of modernisation coming to terms with a conflict between traditional gender roles and contemporary European culture; when the Danish *Big Brother* generates a public conversation about child abuse and incest after a participant confession we are seeing one aspect of the crisis of the family which is at the heart of reflexive modernity. Although the reality game show does not set out to do public service work – far from it – it nevertheless can be seen to reflect and produce debates that raise questions about the way we live now, in terms of identity, relationships, gender and ethics.

## The liminal and the ludic

The original UK participants of *Big Brother* made up a little song which they performed whenever the unpleasant act of nomination threatened to destroy their collective identity, their '*cri de coeur*' had only one lyric: 'Its only a game show'. I have tried to argue that a Factual TV that bases itself upon simulated processes is inevitably ludic. The simulation and the game have a great deal in common and overlap in ways that have something significant to tell us about this particular conjunction in cultural history. Analysis of factual TV to date has taken place within traditions of TV news or Documentary Studies methods framed, by and large, by questions of the public sphere. The new protean hybrids of factual TV call for a shift in our methodological frameworks. We are called upon to find a way of understanding new forms that eschew the possibility of offering us direct access to the world we all share but can only ever simulate it. Forms which make our shared world – social reality itself – subject to the rules of a game, produced through processes of play. I have argued that the use of a specific kind of simulation theory allied with play theory offer us useful ways of understanding how the reality TV Game text works. These two theoretical frames together point us at the direction of thinking about the functions of popular culture, the carnivalesque, the game – parts of our shared culture that lie outside of the ostensible discourses of power and sobriety but which are nevertheless intimately related to them.

In 'Playing For Real', Nick Couldry (2002) has already touched upon the usefulness of the anthropological work of Victor Turner (1982) in understanding *Big Brother* as media event. I would extend this to thinking about *Big Brother* as ritual process. Turner's work explores the importance of play and ritual in human culture arguing for the central importance of ludic activities in what he describes as the liminoid zone of cultural life.

Computer Games theorists (see, for example, Wright 2002) have also pointed out that the simulation and the game have a common provenance in Turner's liminoid zone, which is demarcated through ritual as outside of quotidian normal life but is related to it through play. This idea of the liminoid zone of culture locates games of many kinds – sport, carnival, gambling – and argues that they have always served important social functions in modern societies, functions which whilst not ritualised in the classical anthropological sense may nevertheless take on some of the significance of ritual. The game clearly belongs to the liminoid zone of activity that is outside of work yet related to social structure – the simulation might also be thought of as occupying the same liminal relationship to social reality. Using these concepts it is possible to argue that *Big Brother* represents the emergence of a simulated form of factual TV that takes its place alongside many other forms of emergent practices of representation and knowledge production in which the simulation/game is the central paradigm.

Previous methods for thinking about moving-image factual representation of social reality have occurred on what Brian Winston (1995) called the 'Battlefields of Epistemology'. That is to say the documentary made an argument about the world, more often than not its critics also participated in this argument about what the world is or should be. Through the process of factual representation a correspondence was assumed between the debates of the TV text, the responses of audiences or critics and social reality itself. More than any other text *Big Brother* shows us that this framework has only residual value. In its stead we find ourselves having to work with methods derived from theatre, performance, ritual, play and simulation to begin to locate the meaning of the reality game show. Like other forms of liminal culture the reality game show is not without social meaning – however this social utility is a-by product of the game itself, rather than being its *raison d'être*. *Big Brother* is a game show – it is concerned centrally with play and playfulness. Yet is a game that, like certain kinds of cultural ritual, demands to be taken with a degree of seriousness.

*Bibliography*

Aarseth, E. (1997) *Cybertext*. Baltimore: Johns Hopkins University Press.

Atkins, B. (2003) *More Than a Game: The Computer Game as Fictional Form*. Manchester: Manchester University Press.

Beck, U., A. Giddens and S. Lash (1994) *Reflexive Modernisation*. Cambridge: Polity Press.

Bondebjerg, I. (2002) 'The Mediation of Everyday Life: Genre Discourse and Spectacle in Reality TV', in *Realism and Reality in Film and Media*. Northern Lights Year Book, Copenhagen: University of Copenhagen, 159–93.

Boorstin, D. (1963) *The Image*. Harmondsworth: Penguin.

Bruzzi, S. (2000) *New Documentary: A Critical Introduction*. London and New York: Routledge.

Caillois, R. (1979) *Man Play and Games*. New York: Shocken Books.

Couldry, N. (2002) 'Playing for Celebrity', *Television and New Media*, 3, 3, 283–393.

Dovey, J. (2000) *Freakshow: First Person Media and Factual TV*. London: Pluto Press.

Flynn, B. (2002) 'Factual Hybridity: Games Documentary and Simulated Spaces', *Media International Australia*, 104, 42–54.

Friedman, T. (1999) 'Civilisation and its Discontents: Simulation, Subjectivity, and Space', in G. Smith (ed.) *On a Silver Platter: CD-ROMs and the Promises of a*

*New Technology*. New York: New York University Press, 132–50. Available at: www.gsu.edu/~jouejf/computergames.htm.

Gamson, J. (1994) *Claims to Fame*. Berkeley: University of California Press.

Giddens, A. and C. Pierson (1998) *Conversations with Anthony Giddens: Making Sense of Modernity*. Cambridge: Polity Press.

Gilbert, N. and R. Conte (eds) (1995) *Artificial Societies: The Computer Simulation of Social Life*. London: UCL Press.

Gilbert, N. and J. Doran (eds) (1994) *Simulating Societies: The Computer Simulation of Social Phenomen*. London: UCL Press.

Guider, E. (2000) *Variety*, 9 October, 12.

Harvey, D. (1989) *The Condition of Postmodernity*. Cambridge, MA: Basil Blackwell.

Hill, A. (2002) 'Big Brother: The Real Audience', *Television and New Media*, 3, 3, 323–40.

Jameson, F. (1991) *Postmodernism, or, the Cultural Logic of Late Capitalism*. Durham: Duke University Press.

Jones, J. (2003) 'Show Your Real Face: A fan study of the UK *Big Brother* transmissions (2000, 2001, 2002)', *New Media and Society*, 5, 3, 400–21.

Lister, M., J. Dovey, S. Giddings, I. Grant and K. Kelly (2003) *New Media: A Critical Introduction*. London and New York: Routledge.

Manovich, L. (2001) *The Language of New Media*. Boston: MIT.

Moreno, J. (1969) *Psychodrama*. New York: Beacon Press.

Palmer, G. (2002) 'Big Brother: An Experiment in Governance', *Television and New Media*, 3, 3, 295–310.

Prensky, M. (2001) *Digital Game Based Learning*. New York: McGraw Hill.

Reynolds, R. (1994) 'Learning to co-operate using cultural algorithms', in N. Gilbert and J. Doran (eds) *Simulating Societies: The Computer Simulation of Social Phenomena.* London: UCL Press, 223–44.

Roscoe, J. (2001) 'Real Entertainment: New Factual Hybrid Television', *Media International Australia*, 100.

Sennett, R. (1999) *The Corrosion of Character.* New York: W. W. Norton.

Strum, S. and B. Latour (1999) 'Redefining the Social Link: From Baboons to Humans', in D. Mackenzie and J. Wajcman (eds) *The Social Shaping of Technology*. Buckingham: Open University Press, 116–44.

Turner, V. (1982) *From Ritual to Theatre: The Human Seriousness of Play.* Baltimore: Johns Hopkins University Press.

Williams, R. (2001) 'Base and Superstucture in Marxist Cultural Theory', in M. Durham and D. Kellner (eds) *Media and Cultural Studies Keyworks*. Oxford: Blackwell.

Winston, B. (1995) *Claiming the Real*. London: British Film Institute.

_____ (2000) *Lies, Damn Lies and Documentaries*. London: British Film Institute.

Wolf, M. J. P. (1999) 'Subjunctive Documentary: Computer Imaging and Simulation', in J. Gaines and M. Renov (eds) *Collecting Visible Evidence*. Minneapolis: University of Minnesota Press, 274–91.

Wright, T., E. Boria and P. Breidenbach (2003) 'Creative Player Actions in FPS Online Video Games: Playing *Counter-Strike*', *Game Studies*, 2, 2. Available at: www.gamestudies.org/archive.html.

# Epilogue

*Gary Carter*

# IN FRONT OF OUR EYES
## Notes on Big Brother

Reality Entertainment (also, Reality Television): a term referring to **durational**, non-scripted, **multi-media** event **entertainment formats** in which **members of the public** take part in **representational contests**, in which the audience has **control** over (part of) the outcome. For example, *Big Brother* (Endemol).

## Entertainment formats

Three entertainment programmes from the last 10 years – *Survivor, Who Wants to be a Millionaire* and *Big Brother*[1] – have acted as agents of change, and embodied change, in the contemporary media landscape. These changes continue to be visible onscreen to audiences, and felt off-screen by producers, broadcasters and advertisers, around the world. The *off-screen* changes include a dramatic escalation in the speed of trade in intellectual property (specifically, the licensing of formats for entertainment programmes), and significant changes in the business model behind such transactions, largely as a result of a dramatic increase in the perceived value of formats. The on-screen changes were construed as the emergence of a new form of electronic entertainment.

It is possible to see these three programmes and their journeys round the world as defining the point at which the entertainment industry – or at least the television format sector of that industry – moved closer to two intersecting futures: a digital one, in which the volume of imagery is magnified (the area of intersection) and intellectual property ownership is highly contested; and a globalised one, in which the volume of imagery is magnified, and intellectual property is moved around the connected world faster and faster, while presenting a uniform face, or brand, to the consumer.

The global success of *Millionaire*, the British game show licensed to more territories in less time than any of its predecessors, indicated the new direction the production of entertainment on television was to take in the immediate future. Through a rigorous insistence on standardisation of image, content and production methodology by Celador, the production company which owns the format, *Millionaire* became arguably the first non-scripted entertainment programme to become a global brand, and the first to earn significant revenue through exploiting another medium, the telephone, which interacted with the programme and was conceptually consistent with the central idea.[2]

There had been previous attempts by producers to build global brands out of formats in this way. The migration of audience brand identification from broadcasters to specific programmes, a migration which producers had long predicted, depends on the creation of the programme as brand. This was something producers had claimed to be about to achieve and it was desirable because it would increase their power in the face of the broadcaster/advertiser relationship. But in the case of *Millionaire* the programme was so monumentally and strikingly successful in audience terms that Celador was able to use this success as leverage for consistency. Nor was this the first programme to utilise developing (mass calling) telephone technology: it was that here the use of the telephone was integral to the concept, and it coincided with the boom in global telephony of the late 1990s. The succession of global hits that followed, particularly *Big Brother*, all learnt lessons from the way *Millionaire* had been dealt with and controlled as a property.

The *on-screen* changes visible to audiences marked the emergence of what is often called a 'hybrid genre', reality TV. The first audiences to see the outlines of this new form with any clarity were Swedish, and they gathered in unprecedented numbers on 13 September 1997 to watch *Expedition: Robinson*, the first series based on the format *Survivor* (at the time, owned by Planet 24, now *Castaway*).[3]

## Multi-media

Reality TV is something of a misnomer, and not because it has nothing to do with reality, but because it will in time come to have less and less to do with television. It is already a partial misnomer because television is not the only distribution medium involved. The multi-media aspect of reality (let's leave television out of it for a moment) is integral to this form, and not only, as sometimes seems to be the case, because a spread over such technology is financially rewarding. Rather, the multi-media applications are integral to the form, as I hope to demonstrate.

*Big Brother*, of course, is probably the best example of this argument, primarily because the conceptual world that the format inhabits, inherited from Orwell and inverted (the many watching the few, rather than the few watching the many), has to do with issues of control through all-pervasive surveillance and monitoring. But that notwithstanding, it seems evident that it is only a matter of time before television is no longer the dominant entertainment medium, and that the central battle of convergence (computer vs. television) is inappropriately framed, suggesting that either will 'win', rather both will disappear on the way to becoming something new. However, it seems that Reality Entertainment – to use a rather more precise term – is here to stay, even though it will undoubtedly continue to change in front of our eyes. You would be hard pressed to find a broadcaster who would acknowledge that *Big Brother* signals the beginning of the end of television as we know it, but you only have to look at their websites to realise that it is true, and that even they know it.

It is my contention, then, that Reality Entertainment is a more accurate term than reality TV. Because of the present dominance of television as the distribution medium of entertainment, television currently defines the form, and so it is difficult to avoid describing the outlines of that form without appearing to refer to television exclusively. However, this is a result of position, and the position is only one of several potential positions in a journey. We have not arrived, we are only beginning.

## Durational

Time is measured to the nn:nn:nnth degree in television. Television is obsessed with time. Time costs money in production. Time earns money, when sold to an advertiser. A programme is time made available to a programme maker. Time is manipulated, folded, edited, repositioned, inside a programme. Broadcasters fight for time (*Big Brother* 'wins its day part', as my American counterparts might say), and schedules are battles for dominance of time.

The format of *Big Brother* was originally pitched inside the industry and later to the public with variations of the line '10 contestants – 100 days – 1 winner'. Such pitch lines, elevated to something approaching the status of *haiku* in Hollywood, are compact summaries which remain, meme-like, in the consciousness of the individual, and which unfold to reveal all the salient features of the central idea. The temporal aspect of *Big Brother* was revealed at an early stage as being one of its dominant features, but its influence went further, representing and adding to the forces that changed the perception of time in contemporary media.

In *Big Brother*, the 'series proper' that is, the central television series carrying the narrative of competition is composed of daily episodes which depict the events of the previous 24 hours in the *Big Brother* house; the cycle of (weekly) nominations and evictions, and the weekly omnibus which edits down the events of the preceding week. The whole arc of the format is mathematically constructed around the hundred days the contestants spend in the house.

*Big Brother* signaled a changed conception of the duration of a narrative arc in (unscripted) entertainment. It was common enough for soap operas to run for years; it was common enough for telenovelas to have a narrative arc spanning 100 episodes or more. It was common enough for game shows to run in seemingly endless series: but at the time *Big Brother* was launched it was an innovation for an entertainment (game) format to shape a story that would take three months of daily prime-time episodes to tell: its dominance of schedule time was built into this format from the beginning (in fact, when *Big Brother* was originally developed, it was intended to span a year).

Reality Entertainment stresses duration, but it also stresses 'nowness', 'liveness', the 'round-the-clock' aspect of the content. This is probably because 'now', in media, is a signifier of the real: 'going live' is usually taken as the greatest proof of the reality of the occurrence that that medium depicts. *Big Brother*, like others in this form, brings 'now' as close as possible to the viewer through the 24-hour turnaround from house to screen, and then blurs the edges of this 'now' in order to stress it. Even though the regular episodes of the series are edited summaries of what happened in the 24 hours or so before transmission, the convention is that of the present. Temporal markers reinforce this: day indications, time indications are prominently displayed and referred to, and echo the durational aspect of the format. The three months which make up the narrative arc of the series, and the presence of the garden as part of the environment mean that the wider, seasonal 'now' becomes part of the narrative: in the Netherlands, for example, the contestants enter the house in the sunlight of late summer, and emerge into the dark cold of New Year.

Because television production is expensive, producers seek to record as little as possible. In that sense, the skilled producer records only as much as she needs to tell the story she is telling, in the time available. In Reality Entertainment, given the conventions of enclosed space as setting which have emerged within the form, and the observational nature of the form, far more material is recorded than is necessary to meet this formula.

This fact, and the technology used in production (including our habituation to it, particularly our habituation to relatively degraded visual signals as in home videos and public surveillance), has enabled the clustering of 'para-series' around the central narrative, which I have called the series proper. These para-series include, for example, live unedited 24-hour streams from the house (streams which have threatened to eclipse the series proper in popularity in some territories, like South Africa); live interventions into other programmes on the same broadcaster of the '… and now let's go live to the *Big Brother* house' variety and late-night 'uncut' specials, not to mention the fanzine status of other programmes on the *Big Brother* broadcaster (for example, in the coverage of *Big Brother* UK on Channel 4's breakfast show, *RI:SE*). This reversioning and repurposing of material, this disclosure of the previously unseen, this ability to spread and contract means that a series like *Big Brother* represents a new kind of weapon in the time war waged in all media, and particularly in television: the schedule. Reality Entertainment series in some ways represent a digital dream for producer and broadcaster: hours and hours of material, from different vantage points, endlessly exploitable, and cheaper and cheaper per minute, at every turn.

## Members of the public

In television, it is common to talk of 'real people', or 'ordinary people', the implication being, I suppose, that the more usual voice heard is that of 'unreal' people, or 'special' people. Enough has been written of the development of celebrity culture in the last decade, perhaps, but in this context I am using the word 'celebrity' to mean someone who is famous primarily because of the marketing constructions of what they represent, rather than their ability or achievement in the public domain. The reward of fame has come to be something of an end in itself, certainly in developed media markets.

Brands are significant not only because of their values, and the way this can be transformed into monetary value, but because they indicate the attachment of a brand name to goods produced by a third party: big brands are no longer manufacturers, they are producers of image, and as such, brand names 'float'. Celebrities are brands: they don't do anything, except associate with things, and their value derives from their associations in the public consciousness and the way these associations can be attached to consumer objects. It is possible to earn significant revenue from who you are without worrying about what you do. But perhaps even more than that, the construction of the self as a public brand is a desirable end in itself, because it is the logical extension of the ways in which brands have been created as signs of individual identity in consumer culture. It is the extension of the principles of capitalist marketing and licensing to a logical conclusion: a personal one.

Reality Entertainment series like *Big Brother* are platforms for the creation of celebrities out of 'real people' by association with the brand of the programme itself. Even after the many series of *Big Brother* round the world, the number of individuals who have had that on-screen exposure and association is relatively small, globally, and the amount of media exposure afforded to them is enormous. Contestants become identified with aspects of their physical and/or emotional identity, or with actual events, and become objectified, a process heightened by layers and layers of mediation.

This is by way of clarifying why people might wish to take part in such series, and how media and audiences use them, but it does not explain what they are *doing*. What they are doing gets to the heart of what I believe Reality Entertainment is about.

## Representational contests

The function of play ... can largely be derived from two basic aspects under which we meet it: as a contest *for* something or as a representation *of* something. These two functions can unite in such a way that the game 'represents' a contest, or else becomes a contest for the best representation of something. (Huizinga 1970: 13)

In these terms, formulated by the Dutch historian and game theorist Johan Huizinga, *Millionaire* is the representation of a contest, while *Survivor* and *Big Brother* are 'contests for the best representation of something'. That representation is framed by the constructed, fictional or semi-fictional environment which provides the setting (in *Big Brother*, the house and garden, the show itself). The contest element is clear. The question is, then, if Reality Entertainment is a contest for the best representation of something, what is that something? The answer lies, it seems to me, in this question of what the contestants are doing, beyond the level of competing: they are performing themselves.

*Big Brother* is, of course, a popularity contest, but it is perhaps no accident that it came from a culture in which the popular injunction *'Doe maar gewoon'* (literally 'Just behave normally', or perhaps 'act naturally') is completed by the observation, *'Dan doe je gek genoeg'* – 'And it's crazy enough'. In some ways, the winner of a series of *Big Brother* represents the embodiment of a national standard of performance.

Within the television production industry, it is common to hear that television is 'all about telling stories'. Within the entertainment sector, it is common to hear that Reality Entertainment is 'all about casting'. More than one *Big Brother* producer of my acquaintance has remarked on the fact that however much planning goes into a series, however much the producers feel they understand the contestants before they enter the house, the contestants always surprise them – and the series becomes in some way a creative dialogue between the contestants and the editorial team. In addition, the suggestions which are made by the performances of the inhabitants are further mediated (and refined, in performance terms) by the editorial team.

Reality Entertainment is a form of entertainment which takes as its subject, per-formance, which is to say that what the audience is interested in is the authenticity or otherwise of the individual performance, the degree to which it is coherent, 'real' and continuous. This would explain why the continuum of performance (from identity to the performing arts) is often the overt subject and always the subtext of Reality Entertainment – from the performance of the self in *Big Brother*, to the performance of masculinity by men in *Boy Meets Boy*[4] (Evolution Film and Tape Inc. for Bravo, USA) to singing in *Pop Idol*.

There is a relationship between this representational competition (or the audiences' judgements on the authenticity of the contestants) and the stressing of simultaneity and 'liveness' in Reality Entertainment. As a producer once explained to me, when transmitting 'live' events it is important to have a few mistakes, a few cracks in the surface of the transmission, because this is what the audience is waiting for. This is true, of course, in the sense that if 'live' television is exciting it is because it is 'live' – real, authentic – and as technology develops the audience only knows that, paradoxically, when it goes wrong. This explains the success of 'blooper' programmes, and is a good argument for those Americans who include hidden camera programmes in the category of Reality.

Audiences watching Reality Entertainment series make judgements about the authenticity of the contestants: in order to do that, they wait for the 'crack' in the performance (that moment when unguarded authenticity shatters or fails to shatter the performance); audiences make judgements about the authenticity of the depiction of the contestants by waiting for the 'crack' in the surface of the programme. And this is why my mother, despite herself, watches the *Big Brother* contestants sleeping. Reality Entertainment is about reality and unreality – of the self.

## Control

Contemporary media is in search of interactivity. You can see this demonstrated in all media, not just television. What is really meant, though, is interactivity as a means of control. We – producers, broadcasters, advertisers – seek to give audiences control, as a way of controlling them, or at least as part of the ongoing battle to control their attention. When I refer to audiences here, of course I am referring to younger audiences, under 40, since these are the most commercially attractive. Audiences thus defined are media literate, technologically experienced, and they seek control because they are now relatively well-versed in the production of media, its history and its grammar. They are also – problematically for entertainment producers – skeptical.

Reality Entertainment hands over elements of control – or the semblance of control – from the editorial team, preferably to the audience. In the case of *Survivor*, control is handed to the other contestants, in the final 'council' meeting. In the case of *Big Brother*, control is handed to the public in audience-led nomination and eviction, depending on the variation of the format produced. The eviction of contestants from such series represents an extension of the remote control – if I don't like you, I won't watch you, as it were.

There is another way in which control is a feature of Reality Entertainment, and it brings together issues of performance and control. If Reality Entertainment is about performance, it places a degree of control over content in the hands of the contestants. The producers who report that *Big Brother* is a dialogue with the contestants sense this – there is a shift in the power relationship. Producers (particularly entertainment producers) are trained to produce events – to make them happen, to arrange them

– and I suspect that many of them find it hard to abandon this kind of authority when producing Reality. The failure of subsequent Dutch series of *Big Brother* to have anything near the success of the first has to do, I suspect, with the fact that the original production company, John de Mol Productions, now part of Endemol Nederland, was historically a studio entertainment company. If you compare that to the sustained success across three series of the UK version, for example, even though some of the same twists were added to the UK series as were in the Dutch, it is hard to avoid the conclusion that Endemol UK's experience with producing formatted lifestyle programmes like *Changing Rooms*, which share questions of performance, authenticity and representation, paid off in this regard.

## Conclusion

Is it paradoxical to attempt a definition of a form at the end of a book whose subject is an example of that form? Reality TV is difficult to talk about with any clarity or depth, particularly if like me, you work in the industry. Inside the industry, there is no clear, consensual definition – you can see this in the way that *Big Brother* is treated in industry competitions and awards ceremonies, where it moves from 'factual' categories, to 'feature' categories, to 'entertainment' categories. There are also regional variations in the way in which the term is used – in the US, I have heard it used to include everything from *Millionaire* through *Survivor*, *Big Brother* and *The Osbournes*, whereas in the UK it arguably excludes the former, includes the latter and throws in *Wife Swap* and *How Clean is Your House* for good measure.

Entertainment producers are wary of intellectual analysis, partly because it leads to discussions about responsibility, and partly because inside the industry such terms are usually marketing terms. These are intended, finally, to sell rather than to clarify. As marketing terms, they can be – and are – applied to almost any form. From inside the industry, then, it is difficult to see to which programmes the term refers, and it is difficult to think in any theoretical way about what distinguishes them. Therefore it is difficult to understand what such series might tell us about ourselves, our relationship to entertainment, and where we might be headed.

I am attempting a personal definition because I believe this emerging form is significant for the future. This definition is provisional, and positional. It is provisional because the form is developing, and positional because I am attempting a definition from a very particular place, from inside the television industry. More precisely, I am attempting a definition from within a very important sector of that industry, that sector which produces entertainment. Entertainment is important in television because it is where the money is earned. Entertainment – and perhaps particularly electronic entertainment – is important in cultural terms because it tells us more about ourselves, and how we see ourselves, than perhaps we want to know.

*Notes*

1   Although, in terms of first transmission dates, the chronology of these three programmes is *Survivor*, *Who Wants to be a Millionaire*, *Big Brother*, I am treating the order as if it were *Who Wants to be a Millionaire*, *Survivor*, *Big Brother*. This is because although *Survivor* was first on air in 1997 (as *Expedition: Robinson* produced by Strix for SVT, the Swedish public broadcaster), it was not until after the

Dutch launch of *Big Brother* that *Survivor* reached the wider international market through its transmission in a US version on CBS.

2   I am referring to two aspects of the programme. Firstly, 'Phone a Friend', the format feature which allowed contestants to phone out from inside the programme to reach a friend, seemingly in real time. Secondly, the feature which allowed potential contestants to phone 'in' to the programme's number, answer questions and find themselves in the contestant's chair in the next episode.

3   1,020,000 viewers.

4   *Boy Meets Boy*, an American reality series first broadcast on Bravo in 2003, follows a gay man (or, 'the Leading Man' as he is described in the series) and his female, straight, best friend, as they decide on a romantic partner for him out of 15 candidates. Half of the candidates are straight – pretending to be gay – while the others are gay. The Leading Man and his best friend are unaware of this division, believing them all to be gay. Through a series of eliminations, he has to choose a (gay) partner – in the final rounds it is revealed to him that some of the candidates are straight, and that if he chooses a straight man, the straight man wins a cash prize. I use the words 'gay' and 'straight' rather than homosexual or heterosexual to indicate the format's relationship to performed gender identity rather than sexual orientation.

*Bibliography*

Huizinga, J. (1970) *Homo Ludens*. New York: Harper.

# INDEX

# REALITY TV
## Realism and Revelation

### Anita Biressi and Heather Nunn

November 2004
£15.99 pbk
1–903364–04–5
£45.00 hbk
1–903364–05–3

Reality television has little to do with reality and everything to do with television form and content. *Reality TV: Realism and Revelation* takes the reality television phenomenon to be a significant movement within documentary and factual programming. This book analyses new and hybrid genres including observational documentaries, talk shows, game shows, docu-soaps, dramatic reconstructions, law and order programming and 24/7 formats such as *Big Brother* and *Survivor*. These programmes are both popular with audiences and heavily debated in the media; they are at the centre of heated discussions about tabloidisation, media ethics, voyeurism and the representation of the real. Through detailed case studies this book breaks new ground by linking together two major themes: the production of realism and its relationship to revelation. It addresses 'truth telling', confession and the production of knowledges about the self and its place in the world.

Anita Biressi is Senior Lecturer in Cultural and Media Studies at the University of Surrey, Roehampton. She is the author of *Crime, Fear and the Law in True Crime Stories* (2001).

Heather Nunn is Senior Lecturer in Cultural Studies at the University of Surrey, Roehampton. She is the author of *Thatcher, Politics and Fantasy: The Political Culture of Gender and Nation* (2002).

# THIS THING OF OURS
Investigating *The Sopranos*

Edited by David Lavery

2002

£14.99 pbk

1–903364–44–2

£42.50 hbk

1–903364–45–0

As a work of popular culture, an innovative television series and a media phenomenon, *The Sopranos* has made an enormous impact throughout the world. Audiences within the United States, Great Britain, Canada, Australia and Italy have come under its influence and contributed to the intense cultural conversation that this series has generated. Some critics have condemned it for racial and sexist stereotypes, excessive violence and profanity, others, such as Ellen Willis (whose seminal essay in *The Nation* is reprinted in this volume), have called it "the richest and most compelling piece of television ... in the last twenty years".

This timely collection investigates both the wide appeal and controversial reception of this highly-debated television text. With its mix of lighthearted commentary, biting satire and serious academic inquiry "including explorations of morality and redemption, representations of organised crime and the family, and characterisations of the psychoanalytic relationship" the contributors to this ground-breaking study present an exhaustive account of this landmark series in contemporary television.

David Lavery is Professor of English at Middle Tennessee State University. He is the editor of *Full of Secrets: Critical Approaches to Twin Peaks* (1994) and co-editor of *Deny All Knowledge: Reading The X-Files* (1996), *Fighting the Forces: What's at Stake in Buffy the Vampire Slayer* (2001) and *Teleparody: Predicting/Preventing the TV Discourse of Tomorrow* (2002).

'Unique collection of essays ... It mixes serious issues with light-hearted comment and explores the wider appeal of the series, discussing its themes while questioning the show's morality and asks whether it really represents families within organised crime. For media students and Sopranos affectionados alike.'
*What's On*

'It is a fascinating collection of essays that tackles ... reactions to the show in Britain and Canada, issues of masculinity and feminism, and, most intriguingly, the meaning of food.'
*The List*

# KEEPING IT REAL
## Irish Film and Television

### Edited by Ruth Barton and Harvey O'Brien

2004

£15.99 pbk

1–903364–94–9

£45.00 hbk

1–903364–95–7

This collection of essays considers the nature and direction of Irish film and television, including coverage of the first Irish-language soap opera, the New Irish Gangsters, Irish identity post-9/11, images of Belfast in contemporary Irish cinema, female punishment in Irish history and culture, and the 'Roy Keane' affair. *Keeping it Real* reflects a new popular and academic desire to extend the notion of Irishness to include not just the inhabitants of the State but also the wider diaspora – particularly of Great Britain and North America, questioning issues of national identity and ethnicity. The book will thus appeal to those interested in Irish film, media and cultural studies. Films discussed include *Odd Man Out*, *The Boxer*, *Nothing Personal*, *I Went Down*, *Ryan's Daughter* and *Resurrection Man*. Also featured is an exclusive interview with actor Stephen Rea.

Ruth Barton and Harvey O'Brien are Irish Council for Humanities and Social Sciences Postdoctoral Research Fellows at the Centre for Film Studies, University College Dublin. Barton is the author of *Jim Sheridan: Framing the Nation* (2002) and O'Brien is the author of *The Real Ireland: The Evolution of Ireland in Documentary Film* (2004).

# TELEPARODY
## Predicting/ Preventing the TV Discourse of Tomorrow

Edited by Angela Hague and
David Lavery

2002

£15.99 pbk

1–903364–39–6

£42.50 hbk

1–903364–40–X

'This is parody's mission: it must never be afraid of going too far. If its aim is true, it simply heralds what others will later produce, unblushing, with impassive and assertive gravity.'
Umberto Eco, *Misreadings*

In a cautionary attempt to dissuade those who may be tempted, *Teleparody: Predicting/ Preventing the TV Discourse of Tomorrow* fearlessly does go too far in its compilation of reviews of not-yet-existing, but all-too-possible, contributions to Television Studies. In the tradition of *Mad Magazine* and the online humour magazine *the Onion*, the contributors bring their critical skills to bear, examining the hypothetical scholarship surrounding such texts as *Baywatch*, *The Beverley Hillbillies*, *Bewitched*, *The Howdy Doody Show*, *Max Headroom*, *Mister Ed*, *Mister Roger's Neighborhood*, *Simon and Simon*, *South Park*, *Star Trek*, *The Teletubbies*, *Temptation Island*, *The Young Indiana Jones Chronicles*, and many more.

Both editors are Professors of English at Middle Tennessee State University. Angela Hague is the author of *Iris Murdoch's Comic Vision* and co-editor of *Deny All Knowledge: Reading the X-Files*. David Lavery is the author/ editor/ co-editor of numerous Television Studies titles, including *Fighting the Forces: What's at Stake in Buffy the Vampire Slayer* and *This Thing of Ours: Investigating the Sopranos*.

'The idea of reviewing imaginary books might be the best thing to happen to clarity, conciseness, and economy of expression in academic writing since *The Elements of Style*.'
From the Afterword by Robert J. Thompson, Director of the Center for the Study of Popular Television Syracuse University

'A bold and highly amusing book, often as outright hilarious as it can be insightful *Teleparody* collects numerous parodic reviews of non-existent books on television ... The book represents considerably more than excuse for academics to narcissistically chortle amongst ourselves or to scorn certain traditions of practice ... It is important that with a book such as *Teleparody* we do not discount its as a mere play ... As a discipline, we must find new ways to re-integrate talk of quality, but until more traditional academic languages have worked out ways to do this, several of these reviews do so parodically ... With ever-growing student numbers, ever-increasing numbers of courses worldwide, and with more and more academics from other disciplines 'dipping into' media studies, television studies is growing in power. More than just attesting to television studies' 'arrival' as a discipline, the *Teleparody* importantly reminds us that the field is already held back by certain traditions ... It is an encouraging collection, carving out a space for itself that is totally unique within television studies. The book is amusing, at times trenchant and acutely accurate in its criticism of television studies and of the review form itself, and, as parody should, neatly mixes critique with fun.'
*www.film-philosophy.com*